Diary
of a
Lost Girl

The <u>Autobiography</u> of *Kola Boof*

~~

DOOR OF KUSH

ISBN: 0971201986
Door of Kush Books and Music
Supervised by Cornel Chesney and Robert Wright.
Action: staff@doorofkushbooks.com
Kola Boof: kolaboof_email@yahoo.com
Book Cover Design: Marilyn Morse--Graphics, Too
*Copywritten butterfly used <u>by permission</u> of Gary Lohr
Gary Lohr © 2006 **Web site:** www.garylohr.com

<u>**Distributed in the U.S. by Baker and Taylor Books**</u>
Orders at Baker and Taylor: 908-541-7453

<u>**Door of Kush**</u>
324 S. Diamond Bar Blvd. #504
Diamond Bar, Ca. 91765
Tel.: 909-595-6273
Fax Orders: 909-595-5868
Email: staff@doorofkushbooks.com

<u>**Photos of Kola Boof:**</u>
Back Cover Photo by Kofi Suelo
Sudanese Embassy Photos by Gerald DeCosta
Kola Boof on the Radio Photo by WPFW
Kola cooking photo by Aquaman

———

How could I

not

dedicate this book

to the

Atlantic Ocean?

———

I do.

CONTENTS

The Diary of Kola Boof:

Inheritance (womanist prose):

" I am not a woman of color
...I am a _Black_ woman!"
                    --My Nana Glodine

                    (North Carolina)

Diary
of
a Lost Girl

# ACKNOWLEDGEMENTS

KOLA BOOF:

There are so many people who, in "good faith", have supported my work, my struggle to be heard...*and*...even when they did not completely understand my strange journey or agree with my verbose opinions, they offered empathy, kindness and encouragement, mainly because they believe in the sacredness of artistic expression and in freedom of speech. I love them and thank God for putting them in my life.

Alicia Banks, **Stefanie Horton** and **Ajowa Ifateyo**, thanks for being like sisters to me, always there with guidance and faith, you kept me alive. **Cornel Chesney**, **Robert Wright**, **Carl Nelson** at KJLH and **Nkenge Toure** at WPFW, thanks for rescuing my career. **Troy Johnson**, thanks for letting me get drunk on <u>aalbc.com</u> and for being the first to put my books on the map in America. **Derrick Bell**, **Chinweizu** and **Julius Stephens**, thanks for being my Hero Men, my father figures, whatever you want to call it--every lost black girl needs one and the three of you, through your integrity, wisdom and clarity, give me hope for my own sons. **Egyirba High-Anew**, thanks for my web site. **Stephen Elliott** and **Oliver Broudy** at Paris Review, thanks for believing in my writing and encouraging me to become better. **Joke Florizoone** in Belgium, you are a one of a kind human being, *I love you* and I'm thankful to have in you the one thing I thought I'd never have--a white sister. **Chris Stevenson** in Buffalo, I cherish you. **Gerald DeCosta**, there simply aren't words (*remember those ugly*

ass pictures I took in D.C.!), I love you for protecting me, Gerald. You're everything a big brother should be. King of Radio, **Joe Madison**, you know how much I love you. **Deng Ajak**, you are a hero to our people, I love you. **Kwaku Lynn Person,** I am so grateful for your wisdom, devotion to our people and your brotherly kindness towards me. You're another role model for my sons. **Boxer Mike Tyson**, thanks for the unexpected financial rescue when my little boy needed it. You saved my child and I'm both shocked and forever grateful. Hello to **Ashley Alexis McFarlane** and my new brother, the poet and "literary masturbator", **JAIR. Keith Boykin**, I am so inspired by your bravery and I just love you to death. Everyone in **THE KOOL ROOM** (Tonya, Roxie, Renata, Cynique, Yukio, Chris Hayden, Steve_s, Crystal, Yvette, Moonsigns, Nyibol Biol)...I love you! **Obadiah Holder** (keeping it real in Tennessee), I love you, King. **Gran Gran** (a.k.a. poet and radio queen M. Bennett Cooper), I love you dearly and I miss you. My love goes to not only you, Gran Gran, but to **Bubba**, also known as **Percy**, and to **Ladonna**, my sister whose voice I'd like to steal. She is "*so smooth*", both talking and thinking. I love you, Ladonna. Please say hello to **Mama Toni** at Java Juice for me and to all the **POETS**, I love them, fiercely. **Gaylon Alcaraz** and **Deidre Sanders**, my goddess flowers in Chicago, you know how much I love you. You're the best. **Kendra Moyer Williams** and **Khalindi Iyi, Ebony Roberts** and **Malik** at Black Star Books in Detroit-- you blessed me that day. Thanks. **Goddess Hayadia Isis** (*hey sis!*) and **Mark Fogarty**, I love you and thank you for being angels of wisdom and love in my life. **Jennifer Williams** in Texas, thank you, sister. **ABM**, I love and miss you. **Tee Royal** and all the ladies at **RAWSISTAZ.COM**, thank you so much. **Tracy Price Thompson**, I love you, sister. **Marilyn Morse**, my book cover fairy, *I love you* (and **Hi** *Bill!*). **Lily, the poet aka Mama Incense,** hello! **Nicholas Roman Lewis**--thank U for blessing my life! **Malcolm X** (known as "Red Rooster" in Sudan)--for **John Garang, Malcolm X** and **Marcus Garvey...ALWAYS**.

Ousmane Sembene (legendary director of the films *Moolade, Black Girl* and *Guelwaar*)--we have never met, yet you are the Hero of my life. There are no words to express what your films mean to me as an African woman.

GOD, there are so many people responsible for my good days--I pray the ones that I've forgotten to mention will forgive me--and I pray the ones that I did mention will still like me *after reading this book*.

NAIMA

The *Nile*...is a river in Sudan.

That is where this writer was born, in the hot metropolis of a city called Omdurman (which along with Khartoum and North Khartoum, in size and density, could be considered the New York City of North Africa). Unfortunately, my novels and poems have always pissed people off and made them contentious towards me--so as I begin now to sketch a portrait of myself and my life, as truly no one else could, I do so with the knowledge that the contents of this book could get me killed, and I ask that you, the reader, not come into this book expecting to "*like me*"--I'm not that kind of artist--I'm a very damaged and altogether unusual woman from a very different culture than yours, so it's important that you be prepared to expect the unexpected.

My ex-lover, Osama Bin Laden, once threatened my life because of a poetry collection I wrote; he felt I was prostituting myself for America (instead of for him)--my Ethiopian publisher was firebombed in 2002 for printing a collection of short stories I wrote, and on April 9th, 2003, an investigative Human Rights report presented on the floor of the UNITED NATIONS confirmed the "fatwa" and death threats that I had received from Sudan due to the books I write.

Read UN REPORT on page 427

My real name is Naima Bint Harith--but I call myself Kola Boof. I've learned that many Americans (especially whites and media types), think that's a comical name--but it's very special to me, because it's actually the greatest poem that I ever wrote. The name (as a poem) signifies four things--(1) the Kola nut, which is the favorite snack of African children as well as the symbol of prosperity, moral goodness and well being to Africans as a people. (2) The sound of the African drum (*"boof!"* comes the drums). And then finally, because as a teenager, I so loved silent screen star Clara Bow and cartoon sex kitten Betty Boop, and was (and am) a silent movie buff to the point that I wanted to create a sexy movie star type name that would still encompass everything that I cherish and sought to represent as an artist from Africa--aaand--as a womanist and a wombbearer. So in the poem "Kola Boof", I achieved all of that with two words and made it my name, and in fact, took it further by naming several of my books after the silent films that I loved so much as a teen (*"Flesh and the Devil"..."Long Train to the Redeeming Sin"..."Diary of a Lost Girl"*).

I don't want to jump too far ahead of the story, but I didn't learn to speak English until I was fourteen, and because of that, I didn't have a lot of friends in America and was a politely cheerful but introverted, emotionally unhinged young girl who took refuge in the books of Richard Wright, Alice Walker, Sherwood Anderson and Sylvia Plath while also being enamoured of the ghost misery (and magic) that can transform you in silent films. I had a very hideous childhood and spent most of my pre-adult years in Psychiatric care, something that many people have enjoyed making fun of and have tried to use to discredit my voice and my opinions--but all of this is why, as an African, I came to create the poem *"Kola Boof"* and to love it so much.

I am further blessed, because I'm also an American citizen, and not too many people can boast that they are the daughter of the land of the blue blacks (Sudan), the daughter of the River of Blood (the Nile), and also, the daughter of the mightiest nation on earth, America--and yet still--*both!* my countries (America and Sudan) are mainly infamous for their institutions of slavery, and moreover, it was slavery in modern day Sudan that caused me to come to the United States and be adopted and raised by the strangest Africans I've ever met..."*the Black Americans*". So you see, this is going to be a very interesting book.

Yet before we get to the heart of my experience, there's a few questions that I'd like to clear away up front, the main one being--"*why did it take so many years for this book to come out, when it was announced four years ago?*" And the answer to that is simple. Because of Osama Bin Laden--there was enormous interest in the book (and I was offered huge sums of money by two of the top publishers in the United States)--but we could never agree on how the book was to be presented. They demanded that his picture be on the cover of the book! (because after all, who in the hell had ever heard of Kola Boof? *Nobody*). And secondly, they wanted to remove all of my life story from the book and focus only on the chapters that featured my experiences with Osama Bin Laden. Nobody cared that I had been a feminist political activist, a secret agent for the SPLA and a published author--not just a bimbo, and because of that, and because I was hung up in contracts with various agents who were in agreement with the big advances being offered by these publishing conglomerates--I had to refuse the deals and just sit the contracts out.

I thought it would be tacky to come out with a book about Osama, with his picture on the cover, when the fact is--I only knew him for six months (against my will)--and I was basically being asked to trash him in a way that would be palpable to angry patriotric post 9-11 readers who wanted to hear about this evil satanic demon-man and his "pornographic" rape and sexing of a sinful African jezebel movie starlet...you get the picture. And unfortunately--that *really is* the picture, but I still have to represent Kola Boof.

I'm already a bizarre enough figure to those Americans who know about me (*"topless on the back of her books--like a savage!"*), and because of the complexities of my beliefs and my type of art, I couldn't just take the money and run (although, I wanted and needed to--because my two small sons and I were living under protection of the United States government, almost like house arrest at that time, with no income, no freedom and were in very real danger, and I couldn't very well go out and work a 9 to 5 job, and while I tried, as a mother, to get help by appealing to the media regarding the death threats and the situation of my children--I was accused of *making up fantastic stories to get media attention* and trying to *"make money"* off my books).

So this book, a literary memoir, is my chance to prove my story by telling it truthfully. This is my *"soul book"*, --it's going to be *my truth* through my art. There are plenty of photographs from my modeling days, my childhood and my life all over the internet--there's plenty of news footage and a documentary about my life (which includes footage of me with my sons) that can be watched online for free (the internet), and there are radio interviews with my adoptive Black American parents that you can listen to online for free. There's even footage online of me singing *"My Breasts Are Filled With Milk and Honey"*, a traditional African Nilotic mothering song, that you can watch online during Black History Month. That's really the best I can do in the way of images--is direct you to the internet--and in the case of Osama Bin Laden, who almost never allowed himself to be photographed with his wives--it's even more ridiculuous to expect that he would have posed for photos with a *Black* infidel mistress, and just as there are no photos of me with other important people in my life, for instance--the slain Dutch filmmaker Theo Van Gogh (who befriended me in 2002) or my late leader John Garang (my poem about him, "Choll Apieth", was read at his funeral) or Derrick Bell (my idol and good friend at New York University) or Stephen Elliott (the author of *"Happy Baby"* and *"Looking Forward to It"*) who rescued my career as a literary fiction writer by publishing my work at a crucial moment, the two of us chatting over the phone for months yet never taking a photo--likewise, there are no photos of me with Osama, other than the ones his brother took in Morocco (and by accident, as I wasn't supposed to be in the picture), which I don't have access to.

Naturally--the run-ins I've had with *The New York Times*, Connie Chung and others who, initially, because I was in hiding and couldn't give interviews, said I didn't exist and was a character made up by white college boys as a prank on the internet have made me bitterly agressive in talking about my experiences with Somi (Osama)--mainly because they accused me of lying about it and trying to "cash in" on it. And because I was _forced_ to reveal that I was with Osama, and initially tried to deny it (see the London Guardian Newspaper), because I didn't want to lose my American citizenship (categorized as a "suspected terrorist" under the PATRIOT ACT)--and because, for the life of me, I don't know why anyone on American soil would want to willingly admit to being "Hitler's girlfriend", which is what it's like to say you were "Osama's mistress"--I just never understood why people in the media attacked me as unfairly as they did in the beginning (or at least once they realized that "Arab Mistress" Naima Bint Harith was *black* and not white). Hopefully, by the end of this book, every question that anyone has about Kola Boof will be answered, that's my intention. I know things about Somi that not even his four wives (or sister-in-law Carmin) could tell--so regardless of what people believe or don't believe--I'm going to tell my story with as much naked truth as possible.

It's true enough that I've had unbelievable tragedy in my life, but even more so--God has been there for me in very big ways. I was adopted by Black Americans at the age of eight (I returned to North Africa via Israel in 1994 as a young adult). I don't know when I was actually born--my Auntie Ramah says March 3rd, 1969, the government of Sudan says March 3rd, 1972, and one of my Egyptian uncles says that I was born in 1970 or 1971--and it is not uncommon for displaced Sudanese people to not know their age--so for the duration of this book, I am just going to pick "7" as the age I was when my birth parents (Arab Egyptian archeologist Harith Bin Farouk and his only wife...MommySweet Jiddi...a *blue black* Gisi-Waaq Oromo) were murdered for speaking out against slavery in our country--and age "8" as when I was let for adoption by Black Americans.

My parents, Marvin and Claudine Prell Johnson, were a generous and loving couple in South East Washington, D.C., raising seven other children when they took me in. I couldn't speak a word of English and they couldn't speak Arabic, but they wanted me--so it didn't matter, you see. And although they fully support me in my career (and as I've said, there are radio interviews with my parents online), they have paid dearly for having Kola Boof as a daughter. In 2002, when death threats were being made against me from Arab Muslim extremists--I could not be found--so it was my Black American parents and my seven siblings who were terrorized and forced to move from their homes, and back in Egypt and Sudan, several of my Arab Muslim uncles were arrested, jailed and beaten just for being related to Kola Boof. This book, of course, is going to go into much greater detail about my origins and my families--*everything* is in this book--but the point I'm making is that through all the horrendous events you'll soon be reading about--I never was and am not now a *"victim"*.

As a very young child, I had to witness my birth parents being murdered in front of me. The *murhaleen* (part of Sudan's gestapo) burst into our home one night and escorted my Madhi Pappuh and Mommysweet out to the backyard to be executed. Mommysweet had already tucked me into bed, but my bedroom overlooked the backyard. I could have gotten up and went to the window and looked, but I thank God that I did not. For in quick Arabic fashion, my parents were put out of this world. I heard it and I still hear it, and there are no words to describe the obscene sound of what I not only heard...but opened up to receive. I am still mentally, emotionally and spiritually sick from it--I am truly a damaged person--but I am *not* a victim.

When I was born, my Pappuh decreed: *"This is Naima...the one who is victorious...the one who is praying."*

And that, I believe, is why I'm an artist. That feeling of not having enough room to live in ones own body--so that you must engage the world around you. This is why I don't ever back down from life-- because I am still that child, carrying that sound. I am still an orphan, alone in this world, and there is no time for any of us, I assure you, to back down...from our lives.

As a teenager, my American parents sent me to psychiatrists. They wondered why it was that I could remember so much of my life in Sudan, but could not remember the tools necessary to command the English language? As I told you earlier, I didn't really master English until I was about fourteen. And the psychiatrist explained to mother and father that because I had witnessed the murder of my birth parents and become "possessed" by it--I was holding on to every single moment that I had ever shared with them; every single memory. And that is true. I have never forgotten what it was that created me. That infused me with a ballad-like fearlessness. I call it...*blue sky.*

BINT IL NIL

My creation began as the result of an arranged *"blue sky love"* between two extraordinary people, neither of whom were from Sudan, but both of whom found themselves settled there, circa 1961, in a love nest right on the banks of Omdurman's Nile River.

Mahdi Pappuh (*my father, my God*), Harith Bin Farouk was an extremely tall, butterscotch-colored White Arab Egyptian with coily "mixed" hair--more nappy like Hebrew hair than slick like an Arab's hair. He was an archeologist and was studying religious coffees in Somalia when he first laid eyes on my mother (Mommysweet), whom he told me he fell in love with the very tender moment he first saw her. She was a fourteen year old charcoal-colored Gisi-Waaq Oromo girl-- Gisi (her family name), Waaq (her lineage, The Crow), Oromo (her tribe, Nomadic coffee worshippers). Her name was Jiddi and her father was her tribe's Chief, which is why she was called Princess Jiddi.

In our world, men pay a dowry to the girl's father for marriage rights, and in Sudan (where Pappuh owned a large house), the Northern men generally have only one wife.

Pappuh Mahdi immediately attempted to purchase Mommysweet for marriage, but because her father was the Chief and because they considered Pappuh a *"white man"* (as non-black Arabs are categorized as *white* in Africa), the dowry price was extremely high...and the most Pappuh was able to do was deposit a down payment. He told me that it took him until Mommysweet was seventeen to pay it off (in cattle), but that it was well worth it. Pappuh married her twice. First in a ceremony with her clanspeople and then at his family's mosque in Egypt. He was thirty-five to her seventeen, which is normally considered an ideal match, but the fact that she was so incredibly dark skinned--what we call *"Biblical Days Black"* (charcoal people, the originals)--didn't sit well with Pappuh's White identified Egyptian family. And please note, that although there have recently been colleagues of my father's in London who claim that he was Kushaf (a type of mixed race Nubian-Turkish tribe who live in North Egypt), that is not true--my father was Arab Egyptian, yes with Turkish blood, but no immediate Nubian blood. Regardless that these men in London worked with and knew my father, they are mistaken about his ethnicity.

Pappuh's family, the Kolbookeks, had spent decades trying to breed any signs of Africa out of their bloodline. My grandmother, Najet, in fact, never forgave Pappuh for bringing the *root* back into the family tree. She cursed him and complained bitterly about his lifelong obsession with the "Hemetic blood" (the blood of the original authentic ancient Egyptians), which was now considered a defect of the Cushite, Ethiopian, Somali, Nuba and Nubian peoples--as well as the dark Egyptian ghetto people of the Upper Nile (<u>Southern</u> Egypt is called "The Upper Nile", with many blacks living in the Kom Ombo region)--but this blood is *"not a stain"*, you understand, when it's in the veins of the Beja and Arab ruling class in Egypt (of which our family was still not accepted by, because of grandmother Najet's own great grandmother--a pureblooded Falasha--*a Black Jew*).

Najet would weep openly and complain about Mahdi Pappuh's tenure at the University in France years earlier where all he ever wrote about was his fascination with the *"abeed"* (Arab word for "slave stock" but used as *"nigger"*) and their grand history in Egypt. He had not returned home with a lovely, blond French wife--but instead with a high yellow, big-lipped nappyheaded Black American girl from Georgetown, D.C. (1956). Grandmother Najet had nearly had a heart attack! (to Egyptians before the civil rights movement, Black Americans were considered to be *"the lowest of all niggerstock"*)--and when he married Princess Jiddi in 1961, Grandmother Najet all but disowned him. She commanded him, "Leave Egypt and take Sheba with you! What will my friends think of me with mud on my foot!?"

And not only Grandmother Najet, but the entire family worried tremendously about the way they (as a clan) would be perceived by having a charcoal black wife in the stead. It was too radical.

So, you see, this was why my birth parents settled in Sudan instead of Egypt. Mahdi Pappuh wanted very desperately to be considered "a black man", and in fact, he spent his entire life depressed about it, to the point of becoming a heroin addict, because of course, in Africa--you have to be *black* to be black, and even more importantly, you have to possess the Crown (the nappy African hair) to truly be an African and a black person. There is no one drop rule--anywhere on the continent. You're either black or you're half-caste (mulatto) or Berber-Beja (mixed race). Arab is white. Black Arabs (like me) are "abeed" (niggers). It is not how Black Americans claim (*"Africans come in many colors"*)--that is not how we live in Africa; there are terrible caste systems, and most mulattos and mixed people would rather die than be called black or be grouped with blacks. The Dinkas, Nubians, Nuers, Shilluks, Lothu, Oromo, Masai, all of whom befriended and studied by my father, all of whom greatly respected and loved my father, all of whom accepted him as one of their tribe--would never--accept him as a *"black man"*. To his face, they told him: "you de white man, be proud." And this used to kill him inside. He often told me that this was why he married charcoal Mommysweet. He said that it was

25

his life's dream to have black sons.

Unfortunately, Mommysweet gave birth to six boys in a row--all born dead with their umbilical cords wrapped around their necks. I was her seventh pregnancy (and it's my understanding that I'm not the only seventh born-first girl after six stillborn sons in the literary world--the American author Gayl Jones, I've been told, is also the seventh born first girl in her family--so yes, it obviously does happen, and I refuse to believe that it's witchcraft). My Auntie Ramah (Mommysweet's best friend and dressmaker) told me that when I was born (which took place around noontime right on the banks of the Nile as Mommysweet was washing clothes) and they washed off and presented me to Pappuh, announcing that I was a healthy baby girl, he took one look at me and cried out, indignantly, *"Bitch!"*

Auntie Ramah and I would get such a bellylaugh whenever she told me this story, because it was the way that Auntie Ramah could tell a thing. She was one of those plump, down-by-the-riverside African women who can take anything hurting inside a person and transform it into ferris wheels of laughter. Metaphor was her gift.

Anyway, after I was born, Mommysweet never became pregnant again. It was amazing. People all over Omdurman declared her to be a jinn (a powerfully evil spirit) and avoided her whenever possible. They declared Pappuh a wimp for not killing her (as _some_ Muslim men are known to do in our world if a wife bore no sons), and they truly believed--with good reason--that Mommysweet was a *mute*. In fact, Mommysweet made sure that people thought she was a mute. I can honestly say that in my entire seven years as her daughter, I think she only spoke (using her mouth) maybe eight or nine times tops. This is not an exaggeration. Only Auntie Ramah could speak Mommysweet's Oromo language (Ramah being a red skinned Oromo from a clan in Tanzania that had bright orange-brown complexions), and although Pappuh had taught Mommysweet how to speak flawless Arabic, her religion of silence hurt me very deeply growing up. I was, after all, the only child in Omdurman whose mother never spoke to her.

She would come to the doorway of my bedroom every morning, just before the sun came up, and stand there with a basin of water until I woke up. Her presence, of course, woke me. Then she would smile and come to bed, roughly washing my face and hands with a hot rag, which was followed by brushing my teeth and having me spit and chew guddaim rinds. After that, she would give my hair 150 brushstrokes exactly--all the while studying my facial features intently, as though her stare could magically transform them. I looked more like my father and I think she had been waiting for me to look more like her, but sadly, I never did inherit Mommysweet's beauty, and yet I was just as spellbound by it as Pappuh and the men in town were.

I remember her face to be the black perfection of moon-lit nightwater on an African lake. Her body was firm but waif-looking, very thin as most East African women are thin, with a long swan's neck and delicate little hands and feet (which I did inherit). Her hair swung down her back like thick flowing robes of rough, knotted dark foliage and her nose was more slender and "upper class" than Pappuh's bulbous Arab one. She had full lips and high cheekbones, a large forehead (which I also inherited) and knife-like eyes, black and shiny as a crow's(Mommysweet and Ramah's tribes both worshipped the Crow as their God). She moved about the streets of Omdurman like an S-shaped cobra defiantly floating over lava coals--always with a basket atop her head, always dressed in flowing white. The Nubian women would call her "Baby Sister" to her face, but behind her back they would make fun of her name, Jiddi, because it means *bearer of sons.*

After washing me up and brushing out my nappy, shoulder-length hair, Mommysweet would kiss me three times--once on the forehead and once over both eyes, very gently and with a linger. Then I would be draped in one of the white cotton dresses she made for me by hand and a burka placed over my hair. Pappuh would usually be waiting downstairs for me, so as to share the first of his five prayers for the day (which is not normal).

In our culture, the men are served their meals first, before women and children, and must eat separately from the women and children. Boys, once about twelve, can start eating with men...but in our home, there were no boys, no live-in uncles, so Mahdi Pappuh broke the rules and had me eat all my meals with him. He taught me to keep this a secret and to never speak of it outside our home, because the mosque could have him imprisoned or even stoned to death for such a transgression.

Mommysweet would let me help her prepare the meals (to learn cooking, of course) and breakfast time, because of Pappuh being home in the mornings and telling us jokes from the newspaper, became my favorite time of day. Mommysweet would fix Pappuh's breakfast of Aseeda (a sweet porridge like cream of wheat) with panfried perch or tiger fish crumbled up in it, and with that she would serve him a stack of Kisra with honey poured over it (Kisra is a flat bread made from corn that everyone in Sudan eats every day, several times a day). To wash it all down, Pappuh would have a tall glass of fruit juice--usually tabaldi juice, orange juice or aradaib juice.

Mommysweet and I would have Jbna (coffee), but we'd make it Oromo style--*fried* first--and then add hot water and ginger to the caramel from the beans and pour it into tiny porcelain cups with two lumps of sugar, and occasionally, a little goat's milk.

For our breakfast, we'd have the same Aseeda porridge, but with a side of crunchy deep fried locusts (which tastes like a combination of shrimp and french fries)...and then Pappuh would be reading his newspaper, and all of a sudden, he'd look up as though startled and proclaim, "*Why Naima!*...they've written about you in the newspaper this morning!"

And each morning I would look to Mommysweet with a panicked expression of shock on my face, wondering what the story of the day would be, and Mommysweet would give a hearty giggle (but never say a word), and then Mahdi Pappuh would go on to read some silly imaginary story, "Why it says right here...blah, blah, blah."

In our mosque..."music" was considered evil. It wasn't allowed. But every morning, Pappuh would take Mommysweet's hand and sing to her after breakfast. He would grab her and kiss her and make her laugh. He would sing: "O...*blue sky love*."

And those were days of heaven for me, my little life...before the evil angels descended upon Sudan. Or rather--before I was old enough to recognize that even in blue skies, they do flutter about.

Pappuh Mahdi began to shoot heroin when I was around six years old. I'm taking my Egyptian Uncle Kar's word that that's when it began, anyway--and I think he's right. I honestly did not know about it in the sense that he was "*on drugs*". Of course, no one explained anything to me and I had just assumed that he was suffering from some Muslim men's disease (they had so many mysteries to them) that couldn't be discussed with females and was being treated for it. In retrospect, now that I've grown up and seen much of the world, I can recall that he had mild hallucinations and that he did look possessed, as though he wasn't Pappuh Mahdi anymore but rather someone imitating Mahdi Pappuh...and yet because he and Mommysweet would be murdered by the time I was seven...I never did get to really witness the destructive and dramatic effects of heroin abuse. I thank God, in fact, that I didn't have to watch my father reduced to such a state, although, as I said, evil angels began to flutter about.

In writing this autobiography, I have tried very hard to piece together everything from our lives in Sudan as accurately as I can (with the help of my Uncle Kar and several people), but I still don't have definite command of some of the intricate details of Pappuh's problems with varied officials in Sudan. But I do think (from memory) that our trouble started when the mayor's office wrote a note to Pappuh threatening to take our house away if he didn't shut up about something, but exactly what that first matter was all about, I don't know. Pappuh began to complain that he needed to earn more money to *"finance his opinions."*

Our home in Omdurman was *very large* and comfortable. Our financial status came in cycles; we would be dirt poor for six months straight and then very wealthy for perhaps an entire year in alternating cycles. Six months poor, one year rich--over and over again. I believe that Mahdi Pappuh was involved in adventures that were not clean, although, I have no idea what they could have been. I only know that he took trips out of the country to "hustle", as he put it, and always returned with lots of money, gold bracelets, fine silks and fresh lion's meat from Ethiopia; chunks of raw diamonds for Mommysweet (she collected diamonds as a hobby). For me, he would bring beautiful pairs of shoes that little Greek and Turkish girls had been privileaged enough to throw away. Our home was a happy one and our lives felt secure.

But then, Arab soldiers (white ones) came to our house one afternoon while Pappuh was away on a dig. I myself was at *kwalwa* (school for Muslim girls), but Auntie Ramah told me all about how she and Mommysweet had handled the situation.

The soldiers banged on the kitchen door while Mommysweet and Auntie were snapping peas and shouted that they had been given a "tip" that Mahdi Pappuh owned a collection of devil music (although it's widely spoken in Sudan, Pappuh was the only one in our home who could understand English, and he did indeed own albums by John Coltrane (whose song "Naima" I am named for), Frank Sinatra, Thelonious Monk, Miles Davis, Nina Simone, Aretha Franklin, Dionne Warwick...and his favorite...Mulatu Astatque, the jazz great of Ethiopia). The soldiers insisted that Mommysweet open the kitchen door, but without her husband in the house, she shouted back (as any Sudanese wife would) that she did not have the husband's permission and could not comply with their orders. So naturally, being men and bullies, they kicked in the door and came bursting in--only to find themselves instantly blinded and screaming like women because of the scalding pot of hot Asedi (grits) Mommysweet had thrown in their faces.

By the time they got their wits about them, Auntie Ramah stood before them barefoot with her shirt off so they could see the henna symbols on her loose titties. Muslims on the Nile believe in witches, I promise you that, and when the first one of them could make out her glowing redskinned face and orange nappy hair and the pearl-sparkle in her black raven's eyes--*they knew* who she was. This was "Oromo-Ramah", the most feared fire witch on the Blue Nile. She said: "Khaferi uhn khatiatak" (*pay for your sins, motherfuckers!*). Then she stuck her finger in her pussy hole and fished out a live Sourih-hayyal (a tiny snake that drinks milk from a bowl and is walked on a leash). Of course, to westerners this sounds outlandish, but it's very real. Countryside wild women who can keep pet snakes in their pussies.

You must understand that there had been a famous incident in our Zarpunni (the governing body of the women's neighborhood) only a year and a half earlier. Auntie Ramah had envoked *rem* (a curse) against a Black American meat vendor. He had become a regular with his cart at the Souq market, but he had the terrible distinction of selling fresh meat to the Noor-byd mdr (White Arab mothers) while selling *rotten meat* to the poor, desperate Black African mothers. His cart was the only one that African mothers could afford in the first place, but at least two little ones had become sick from the meat. It was a very peculiar and mysterious thing for our community to understand, his hate for only Black Africans and *Black* Arabs--not the white ones (of whom there are a great, *great* number in the Sudan, despite what western television shows you), but the situation eventually became so undeniable that two of the mixed-race Beja mothers began donning long, silky Italian wigs thinking this would make a difference, but he still sneered at all African women, refusing to make eye contact, and would offer them only the worst pieces of meat. So one day, Auntie Ramah appeared at his cart and spat a mouthful of goat's milk in his face. That got his attention and everyone else's at the market. She declared that he was actually an evil white woman's spirit inhabiting the body of a black man and that he would be dead in three days.

Three days later...they found him chopped up and packed on ice in his own meat cart.

So now the soldiers were terribly afraid to bother with Auntie Ramah (unless her back was turned--that being the only safe way to kill a witch). She held up the snake and chanted some Oromo words, but the soldiers ran off, she said. And of course, they would not tell their commander that they'd been deterred by two women. No, they would say that they had searched the house and found no devil music. So that it all came out flawless.

But I never will forget coming home that afternoon. Mommysweet, of course, would not *talk* but had fetched me from school early. Auntie Ramah was there when we walked in. She instantly noticed the look on my face and told me not to be afraid and began explaining to me what had happened. She was fully dressed in Muslim garb by then and had one of Pappuh's shirts spread out on the livingroom floor and was "reading" it (the sweat stains, neck dirt) like others might read a palm or look into a crystal ball. I had very little faith, actually, in Auntie's powers, because her own beloved husband, a blue black Mandari, had been kicked to death by Palestinians, because he had been promoted to a coveted post as foreman at a British company in Port Sudan. Ramah's magic had not saved him from the special racism and colorism that the ruling Arab groups (such as Palestinians) reserve for Sudan's nilotic and southern black Africans, so I asked her, "Does that work? What do you see?"

"I see that it's not music that frightens the city officials about your Pappuh." She had soaked his shirt in saved rainwater and was configuring pieces of gum arabic, eucalyptus and sheep's hoofs around it. She said, "Half the Muslims in Sudan listen to music in private or in the secular clubs, the Nubian Muslims even sing and dance to Allah, so it makes no sense they would care about Harith's music. More than half our countrymen drink Aragi and Merissa (alcoholic beverages). Your Pappuh is doing something else to anger them. I see he writes letters that they don't like and he's talking too much...in public."

"It's about the trees!", I said and looked to Mommysweet for agreement.

Mahdi Pappuh had written papers complaining about the forestland up in the Sahel region and how the Nimeiri government was allowing the denigration of vast timber so that the wood could be turned to charcoal, which was our country's primary source of cooking and heating fuel. But then a pall came over Auntie's face and she looked up at Mommysweet and she said, "Jiddi--Harith is putting poison in his body."

Mommysweet didn't look surprised or alarmed. Her eyes told Ramah that she already knew and then they didn't speak about it, but unfortunately, I had heard that Mahdi Pappuh was putting "poison" inside his body and I became very worried. I cried and told them that I worried he might die and Ramah assured me that he would not die. She made up some story about it being "medicine to heal heartbreak". But it was in the course of that week that I began to notice a cryptic panic in Mommysweet. I felt that the devil was about to show up barefoot, with all ten dicks exposed, any day.

It was the first time that Mommysweet ever kept me out of school for an entire week. Auntie Ramah came over every day with her children (Ian and Liv) and we would all have picnics or wash clothes or sit by the river and tell stories. I could tell that Mommysweet was worried terribly about Pappuh, on the edge of her seat every second, but she knitted, cooked, sewed and kept her wits for me.

My faqih (teacher) eventually showed up to enquire about me, but Mommysweet did what she always did--stared blankly at the person, saying nothing as the person talked and talked, and then rather suddenly, in the middle of their sentence--she just walked off without even motioning goodbye. This was always embarrassing for me, because I was usually the one left to apologize and soothe the other party, especially at the Souq. I started saying what Pappuh told me to say: "My father forbids my mother to speak in public." This wasn't the least bit true, but Pappuh felt it better to just blame Mommysweet's notorious rudeness on him.

One night during that week, however, Mommysweet did speak. She came and woke me from my sleep, saying softly: *"Daughter...you must come and help mother to pray."* And I cried all the way outside-- because my mother had actually spoken to me! I remember feeling so overwhelmed and honored, so incredibly shocked and exhilerated. I just couldn't wait for her to say something else, but of course, I knew by that age that it would be another year or so before she spoke again. Thus my tears were not only for having heard her beautiful, loving voice--but also for the agony of being made to long for it again. I thought it was very cruel.

Once outside the house, a tranquil Nile River night was upon us and Mommysweet took my hand firmly. I realized that we were going someplace, and this is what sobered me from my tears, because it was very unusual for women to travel at night, and without a man--unheard of. I also looked up and saw that Mommysweet was *topless*! Her little black breasts bare and pointy. My mouth hung open in a panicky fear, because although I had seen the southern and Nubian women of our country singing in the river and forests with their titties out, it wasn't something that Muslim wives did and certainly not northern women of Omdurman. We were neither southerners nor Nuba people, so I was terrified to see my mother topless outdoors, but Mommysweet pulled me along, my tiny feet padding just a little behind her as she floated serenely down the banks of the Nile river, an ivory headdress flowing down the satiny naked charcoal of her bare back.

Her sugary lyric replayed in my mind as much as I could play it and for as long as I could hold onto it: *"Daughter...you must come and help mother to pray."*

Up ahead in the dark, we suddenly saw a crescent flock of candlelight.

As we got closer, I was stunned, because here were all the women of our Zarpunni (women's neighborhood), gathered together at the riverside...each of them *barechested* (!), their black shoulders high and proud. I tremble now remembering the sight of it--black women gathered in a secret otherness from Arab women and applying spiritual fellowship in a way that was naturally soulful and uniquely African as opposed to the confines and spiritual limitations of a Muslim or Christian prayer meeting. I must name the faces so that it is written: Auntie Ramah, Alek, Amina, Mariama, Naima (the dark wife of Said), Naima (the lightskinned one with honey-colored eyes, Waleed's wife), Auntie Eyoun, Auntie Assis, Naima (Fahid's wife), Rahel Om, Ingrid (who looked Palestinian but whose mother was a pure charcoal Nubian), Auntie Arek, Agom, Ponis, Karel, Ursula (from Ghana), Ajok, Opal, and my mother Jiddi.

Many children were there as well, all of us patiently still, respectfully quiet and in awe of the black river fire goddess our mothers had summoned simply by bearing breasts and congregating in sickle fire and song.

"*Daughters will carry the heads of their mothers*", sang Auntie Eyoun, the eldest Zarpunni, her muddy voice hurtling over the Nile river in broken, aching soul-bites. To which the other women replied in song, "*...mothers will color the eyes of the daughters.*"

I remember being astonished by the movement of Auntie Eyoun's buttocks. Truly, there is nothing in nature more connected, simutaneously, to the spirit world and to the sensual world...than the *Ass* on a black woman. That's just the truth. Everything about it--the shape, rythm, the cushy-jello gravity of it guarantees that there will always be an us. And when I, as a six year old, saw those black women hike up their long skirts so as to walk into the Nile, and when I saw the seats of those skirts wrap around their buttocks lifting them high and tight--and when wet moonlight anointed their bare breasts and their womanly congregation of booty power shook the earth harder than cannons could--it was as if I were witnessing the actual birth of God and Man; of all humanity. I could not contain my joy at feeling...*free*! And I dashed into the river right behind Mommysweet and Auntie Ramah. I began dancing and singing and imitating the motherseeds, and although I had been told about the ancient Cushite women who bled their monthlies in the Nile for a thousand years, this had been the first time in my life that I could actually feel that the blood running in my veins was also the living dead (my ancestors) that run ever still in what Nilotic people call "*the river of blood.*"

Auntie Ramah led the Arab-Muslim prayer for my Madhi Pappuh to be returned safely to us. She threw rice as an offering. My Mommysweet led the prayer in ancient Nilotic Hebrew (the Cushitic language of the Nile river's original Black Jews)...and Auntie Eyoun led the prayer in the language of the Nubians--Nobbin.

Opal banged the tambourine against her wrist and ululated to the moon as Auntie Ramah prayed God speed: "...*dearest one, creator of time* (خردس خز سزسحخسحخرز سسخسحخخج)...your sweet daughter, Jiddi, O Allah, who has been a good servant and a good wife, she is worried about the evil angels aligned against her husband. O Allah (زحذذح) --bring him home. Let him set foot on peaceful ground; let the quiet moon and tranquil river entrance his mind the way home...(The women: *say it/say it*)...and let him be as a King at his noble table, sweet Jiddi at his feet, until a ripe good age. enchalla (حذذحخخحرخ)."

In the creed of the ancient Nubians, Auntie Eyoun said, "So let it be written...so let it be done." And in the song of the Nilotic Hebrews, Mommysweet sang, "Khu Sahu Sekem...buim mezuzah-shema".

I know that this night that I speak of is a big part of my becoming who I am today. For it was the first time ever that I felt a strong sense of myself as being whole...*in the world* (but powerfully so)...a part of something more tangible and deeply rooted than merely my family or the community. In Africa, it's really true that the people aren't always able to notice themselves by skin color, because it seems that almost everyone; everywhere you go for your entire life--is black--Black is normal/everyone is black--*so you don't realize you're black* (being submerged in an all-black world is the equivalent of living in a race-less society). But on that night, I actually felt what being black IS, what being *African* is--and once I experienced the power of knowing the makings of me...moving in me...I felt indestructible...and could never be ambiguous again.

I remember taking Mommysweet's free hand and whispering to the moon, "Please bring my Pappuh home, Allah. I promise to be good forever."

A week later, when Pappuh came home--he was mad at the

government and high on drugs, but as always, he treated Mommysweet and I like dolls. He grabbed us, kissed us and twirled Mommysweet around in a soft dance. She cried. He unloaded a carload of fantastic gifts, and in fact, for Mommysweet--he brought an automobile! (she never would learn to drive it and truly believed, according to Auntie Ramah, that automobiles, airplanes, radios, televisions, alarm clocks-- even the Cobra/arh Theatre just blocks from our house--were possessed by demons). But just the same, Pappuh insisted that Mommysweet must learn how to drive in case something happened to him.

"Pappuh, where were you!?"

"In jail, Naima. This whole country is a joke, and yet they don't want anyone laughing out loud. I don't know why Africans don't rise up and slit the throats of the Arabs!" Of course, he himself was an Arab.

Anyway, he was home safely, and as African women, we began to spoil the King. Auntie Ramah cooked a Khosaf (raisins, figs and bananas in a thick syrup with cream on top) and made a batch of Pappuh's favorite sweet--coconut cookies. His favorite meal, however, was baby lion's meat, pepper-brined and cooked over coals and served with a stack of Kisra dripping in honey and a stew we call Miris (sheep's fat, onions and dried okra). Unfortunately, it was tradition in our house that only Pappuh could prepare the lion's meat that we ate only on special occasions, maybe two or three times a year, so while Pappuh made the lion, Mommysweet and I made his next favorite dish-- Sudanese Spicy Cherry Soup (an African gumbo). I write about it here, because of all the dishes we ever made for Pappuh, this was the one that would make cooking a permanent and extremely important part of Kola Boof's adult life. For it was Pappuh's praise and genuine regaining of strength after eating this particular meal that inspired me to always cook and to love doing it.

First Mommysweet made the base, which was water, sheeps hoofs garlic, onion, Khubz crumbs (a rich Arabian bread) and milk. Then she added Aseeda porridge and sugar. After that all blended, she put in crab legs, chicken, sheep's fat, a cup of Hilumur, potatoes, peanut butter sauce and a big bowl of ripe cherries with the pits still inside. On top of that came the spicy part--"*bom*"--red hot scorpion peppers from the Kababish tribe in Kordofan. Once that was cooking, she slit open an egg plant and seasoned it and baked it. She then had me serve Pappuh the Spicy Cherry Soup poured over the baked eggplant with thick wedges of Hopu (cornbread) and watermelon pickled in shata (hot sauce). He nearly died praising us! He talked about that meal for two weeks, it was so good!

As was our way, we prayed five times a day to the east--and above our house and the river--the sky was clear and white as the baby blue skies in Mommysweet's shoe box full of diamond chunks.

We were blessed.

About a month later, I went to Mahdi Pappuh and asked, "Pappuh, can you please order Mommysweet to talk to me? She never talks."

"Oh, Naima. I cannot make your mother do anything. This is her house. Isn't it bad enough that I purchased her like a slave and took her away from her people, without her having any say in the matter? Isn't it bad enough that I forced her to learn Arabic and become a Muslim wife?"

"Then why did you do bad stuff to her, Pappuh?"

"Because I needed the right mud for planting sons. Your mother is a Waaq Oromo, the ancient tribe from Punt (Somalia) who gave birth to the Nilotics, the Nubians and the original Egyptians. Jiddi is the perfect woman, but she took revenge on me, you see. She killed all six of my sons but allowed you to live. If I am good to her, though, I have faith...she will let one boy slip through. I just know it."

"I feel so sad...that she won't talk to me. She and Auntie Ramah go for long walks and they talk in their language, but they won't teach me. They say that I will have a better life as an Arab Muslim. But I want to speak to Mommysweet."

~~

[*NOTE: White Editors complained that a 6 year old would not speak as well as I write that I did in this autobiography. I submit that they're wrong and that I did speak, at five and six, just as articulately as I'm describing in this book.]

~~

"Come, Naima. You will go away again with Pappuh. We will have excavations in Napata and Meroe next month. My comrades in Islam will not know. We shall bring Aunt Kem (his helper from the Dinka tribe) and pretend that Aunt Kem is my maid and that you are her granddaughter. Of course, you'll have to take off from school, but what does a female need with education anyway? Is that good?"

"Yes, Pappuh!" I was ecstatic!

But who would have known that Mommysweet would have such a fit? Or as we say in America: She just went straight...*the fuck off.*

Pappuh begged: "Jiddi, it's only for three months!"

First, she removed her top so that her breasts were bare. Then her silence erupted into action.

She busted all the windows in the livingroom, flipped over the dining room table, smashed the ebrig into the wall and turned over the hutch! She kicked the back door out. She took a mallet and bashed dents into the car that Pappuh had purchased for her, which had sat next to the house collecting dust. She busted out the windows and threw rocks at the sun and the river.

She screamed high pitched "sounds", but no words. Sort of like those dog notes that American singer Mariah Carey used to make at the end of her songs, or like Minnie Ripperton--that's what Mommysweet screamed out, only higher. You truly had to cover your ears, because I think that only dolphins can tolerate it.

I am certain that Pappuh would have given in and let Mommysweet have her way, but unfortunately, she did the thing that Nile river black women are known for--she bit him. In fact, she bit him so hard in the left shoulder and neck that he had to be hospitalized for two days. It was the first time I had ever seen a grown man cry. So for that viciousness, he insisted on taking me away to show Mommysweet who was boss.

I remember that Auntie Ramah came over after Pappuh drove off for the hospital, and I had been sitting on the porch crying while Mommysweet was gone topless, running down our river front screaming at the sun and cursing the river. Ramah slapped her across the face and hollered out, "*Jiddi!*"

Later, when Mommysweet was tucked in bed and given tea with sleeping roots in it, Auntie Ramah came to me and explained why my mother didn't want me to go. She said, "Your father's on drugs, Naima. He's also in trouble with the government and with Islamic gangs in the North. He's complaining about the Arab financing of a gang war between the Baggara people and the southerners (Dinka,Nuer,Shilluck). Your mother fears that he will get you caught up in this trouble. As well as that--your father is a man and he's Arab. Your mother is a black woman, so she is *deeply* distrustful of Arab men, Naima. She believes that they have sex with their own daughters and sometimes kill them to keep it a secret."

Of course, Mahdi Pappuh would never do something like that and most of the Arab Muslim men that I grew up around were very loving, wonderful fathers to their children, but still, there were a lot of Arab Muslims who carried out honor killings against their own daughters. There were homes in which fathers and sons routinely had sexual intercourse with daughters and then stoned them afterwards. There were numerous incidents in which Arab men would take the little homeless Dinka, Nuer and Shilluk boys who begged in the streets for pennies and would sodomize those six and seven year olds as a kind of "sport" much like frequenting prostitutes. You have to understand that in our culture, the "*virginity*" of females (for the wedding night) is the highest protected and honored thing that there is--so sodomy of both wives and of children was a rampant occurence as the lack of respect for women and lack of women's rights mixed with male supremacy and religious premium on the hymen--caused one of many "dirty little secrets" in our world. To Mommysweet (who hated Arab Muslim people, I was starting to realize), it just seemed like these incidents were more representative of Arab Muslim Sudanese culture than they actually were.

"Your mother loves your father", Auntie Ramah told me, "But she doesn't know him, Naima. She doesn't talk, because she lives in terrible fear of the Muslims and their ability to hear through walls. She believes Islam is evil, because the women are considered unclean and covered up as though they have a plague...which in our Oromo culture...is an abomination against God". The Oromo believed in *Gadaa*--the body of the woman and the circle of woman's self-determination and the woman's right to equal rule within the village of men. This, after all, was the reason why our ancient Oromo mothers had given up their own villages and agreed to live in the men's villages with men, they were the *Gadaa-Kwilxxu* (womanists).

"But the Muslims", Auntie Ramah told me, "do not respect free women. We are separated into a Zarpunni (woman's place, women's neighborhood) that is ruled and dictated to by the men of the mosque.

For more than a thousand years, niece, the Arab people have enslaved and raped and mutilated African women. They loathe blacks and have treated our children as the lower bowels of rats. The Arab, the Jew, the Caucasoid, the Spaniards and Latins, the people of India, the Foon (Asians)--they are *all* the bastard children of African slave women. This is why every race hates the African--it's because they come from us and cannot *get away*. They remain suspended in permanent niggerstock, but they want you to believe that we pure black ones are the niggers and not them. All of them are dirty piss-blooded trash. Lost eternally. Pollution--the Caucasoids, the Arabs, the Jews, the Foon, the Indians, the Spaniards and Latins--all of them are nothing less than world pollution. *God...is a black man.* Do you understand me?" It was scary the way she whispered in hushed tones when she said "God is a black man"--but I nodded that I did understand, and then my auntie said, "God is a black man. You, Naima--are an African. Your mother's blood was pure enough to dominate the Arab blood. *tatu*, little one. Jiddi made you out of clay and baptized you in the Nile. You must not misunderstand your mother's rage. She is a Queen, Naima. A queen alone...in a foreign land that is against her."

Auntie Ramah told me of "Caabudwaaq"--the great holy religious city of she and Mommysweet's race--the Oromo--the descendents of the Crow, the keepers of the coffee.

Then Auntie Ramah took me out to the river and we faced the setting sun as she carefully bared her breasts. I marveled noticing that her dusky pumpkin flesh was nearly identical to the dark orange of the fading sun. And then we prayed as ancient Africans would do...to the sun. "Our mother, the goddess Sudan", she taught me. "Our mother, the goddess Sudan--for she *IS* the Sun. O kiss of God's wife, the lioness. Blacker than all black put together. Mah-mah."

On the still-dark morning that Madhi Pappuh, Aunt Kem (the Dinka woman) and I set out for what would be his final archeological expedition, and the beginning, too, of our family's slow dissolve into the belly of evil angels, I fell asleep on the back seat of the jeep.

Mommysweet came to me in a dream--only it wasn't a dream. What I saw were more like memories of moments that had actually occured in our lives. Like the time Mommysweet had stood in the doorway of our home--too beautiful for words in a flowing curve-hugging cream lace goddessa gown, a single strand of bone white pearls clutching her pencil neck and her wild nappy hair loose. It seemed in the dream that I could actually taste the raspberry honey that she wore instead of lipstick on her lips (and most Africans don't need lipstick, they are born with separately colored or matted lips). I could smell the fragrance of her shoulders, Jovan Musk Oil, I believe from America. And on her cheekbones were painted intricate henna designs, a white tapestry against charcoal that highlighted the almond curve of her perilous eyes and covered her forehead like a veil. I could see her smiling at me again, just as she had on that day in real life. I could hear the song that was playing inside our house (and although I sung the words as a child, I had no idea what they meant). It was Nina Simone singing:

"I put a spell on you!...'Cause you mines!...a doop-doop dee!"

Images carried me sleeping as the raspberry honey on Mommysweet's lips became a sweet juice in Pappuh's mouth and I could see his juicy dark heart beating like a glowing bunch of red tomatoes beneath shallow waters. Then I saw Mommysweet planted in the center of our livingroom floor, sobbing horribly--and this was another actual event from our real lives that I was re-dreaming.

She had spilled her box of diamonds all around her and sat looking inside them as though glimpsing some nostalgic photographs or polaroids, but they were just uncut blue stones. Jagged, chunky, sliverous...iceburg white and sparkling clear. There was nothing inside them. I had been almost five and remember Mahdi Pappuh trying to get her to use speech to explain why she was so upset, but she wouldn't talk and kept crying, uncontrollably, so Mahdi Pappuh held her and rocked her and caressed the roughness of her hair for hours and hours until she finally fell asleep in the cave of his chest. Seemingly insane and pathetic--and then totally normal again the following morning.

In the dream, I next saw a beautiful boy behind the bushes. Calling me.

His face was that *"Biblical Days Black"* color and his beckoning arm looked too skinny and too familiar. Of course, I went into the bushes withhim--and there I saw Mommysweet in her flowing white goddessa gown, her face smeared by crying as she stood at the edge of the river just outside our house. There were these boys with her, each one reed thin and tall with a large oval head and satiny pretty charcoal skin. They waded into the Nile, their cold eyes dead as fish eyes. Six, beautiful, beautiful boys.

I jumped out of my sleep! Panting awake so as Pappuh looked down with conern. He said, "Just in time. We're almost at Atmu's house."

I had not been able to stare down the sorrow that tormented Mommysweet in my dream. I had not been able to bear it when she walked into the river behind them, her feet losing track of sanity and her beautiful raven's face submerged beneath the water's surface. Her lungs lonesome with the dead echo of the boys.

Arriving in Khartoum, we dropped in to visit a good friend of my father's, a Turkish-Nubian archeologist named Atmu Bahri. I always knew him as Uncle Atmu and was well aware, even at that young age, that Uncle Atmu and my father had reached an agreement that I was to grow up and become the wife of Atmu's then newly born son, Micah. In fact, many times when we visited with Uncle Atmu, his pale white Arab wife would sadly and grudgingly hand baby Micah to my father, and then Mahdi Pappuh would hand the baby to me, admonishing, "Be careful now...hold his head just right...this is to be your future husband after all."

Nothing disgusted Atmu's wife more, but because the mother has no say, there was nothing she could do about her son being married to a black Arab girl with nappy hair.

Anyway, I'll never forget that morning when we arrived at Uncle Atmu's house, because the whole block had been descended upon by an army of shiny black crows (I kid you not). Dark as velvet and braver than the sun. Beautiful velvety black birds everywhere!

"What the hell!" Pappuh had cursed in wonder.

But I knew by the dream that it was Mommysweet.

For there is no way to escape an African mother's love, and those who are African or truly Black reading this book--KNOW what I'm talking about. This is why I kissed baby Micah extra gently on his soft beige forehead that day and did not resist when his tiny infants hand wrapped around my fingers and gripped on to them for dear life. I had felt so loved, so cherished and adored when I saw the prestigous blackness of the crows Mommysweet sent to greet me. Holding the precious baby, I wanted to be a mother, too.

It was 1978.

The defining year of our lives.

That year...when the skies of Sudan were never bluer.

The beginning of knowing for me.

The beginning of that bittersweet march to my parent's bloody end.

I remember being a pretty little black girl, holding my arranged future husband, baby Micah, in my stick-bony arms and asking him in Arabic, "...*my baby hungry?*"

NIGHT OF THE LIVING DEAD

Our babies shall starve to bones--too weak to cry.
Our men will be lost inside the endless echo
of the wilderness they seek.
Our breasts will shrivel into drought--abandoned
and scorned.
And the whole world will not just witness it, but abide it:
    we--"the night"
    the living dead
for whom all Gods visit as a grave

        because without our own God, no prayer
        had a right
        had a right

(Comb YOU Nappy Head...the crown...the PROOF
cada-doot, Egypt/cada-doot Nubian
Comb you Nappy Head/come back to life)

<u>tima</u> <u>usrah</u> means "through fire comes the family". The "tima" represents the African race...it means, literally--"the result of great fire". The "usrah" is the bloodberry of the ancestors; the wombs of the mothers; the crowns of the scalps. The unification of the Nilotic flesh in all its black perfection. We call our hair--the one true hair--the *proof*. It is the nappy, wooly royal crown of our fathers and mothers. The unique mark that separates the African from all who came about to destroy him. This is the crown that validates him...and yet...my father

did not have that crown, but still felt very strongly that he was a black man and wanted to rescue...the black people of Sudan.

It is very hard to explain to an American--exactly what and who is black in an Arab ruled African country like Sudan. We do have a very, very large number of ruling White Arab Muslims in Sudan, despite what you see on television or hear reported--they live in Khartoum, Omdurman, the North of the country, and they are the ruling elite, and during news coverage of the war and the genocide in Darfur, the Sudanese government did an excellent job of keeping our nation's White Arabs out of public view...but just as well...there are hundreds of thousands of black people in Sudan, who look as deep dark brown as Kola Boof or who look as brownskinned and ethnic as Black Americans, and most of them would slap your face and declare war against your house if you called them *"black"*. They consider themselves to be Arabs. Their dream is to transcend their African origins and someday become fully recognized as upstanding, fully golden-skinned (gold skin is white in Africa) Arab Muslims. Most of these are mixed-race Nubians of the northern Sudan who have suffered so much racism and religious persecution over hundreds of years of British Colonialism, followed by Arab Minority rule (which included massive rapes and racial profiling-type lynching) that they (the Nubians) have bought into the Arabism that teaches that Africans are inferior savages left over from prehistoric times.

I remember as a small child being taught this in school. Being told that black people are inferior to Whites (Arabs being classified as white in Sudan, not Caucasoids). We were taught that the whitest Arab was the highest and most beloved "son" in the eyes of Allah...and that the darkest, most charcoal colored "son" was the last remnant of Asli-Nalla's evil impurity as a woman (she, charcoal black Asli-Nalla, being the Cushitic-Ethiopian mother fo the entire human race). Nubian men, the Arab Muslims taught us, could be tolerated if they submitted to

49

Islam and married lighter women (which are nearly impossible to come by in Sudan) to produce less African babies, "lighter babies"...but the Dinka men, Nuer and Shilluks and other extremely charcoal colored men were seen mostly as hopeless (and yes, for Nubians who are reading this book--I do realize that the Nubians are also charcoal black in color, but there's only 100,000 Nubians left, and therefore, since they live in closer proximity to the Arabs, they were seen as easier to breed lighter, as they've been doing it for much longer than the South). The Dinka, Nuer, Shilluk, Azande and other Southern tribes were hated and considered "human stains" against the northern Muslim people's longstanding goal of transforming Sudan into an Arab country as lightskinned as Egypt. One that their Arab neighbors could look at with pride and reverence. Of course, it didn't help matters that the Nubians, Nuers and Shilluk were also predominately Naturalists or were Christian (from British Colonialism) and refused to submit to Islam or to Arabism. They insisted on clinging to their African heritage and worshipping in their own God and their own trinity--God's goodness (the cattle) God's House (the Sun and the River are "churches" to Africans) and God's Wife, the Lioness (woman's bare breast and menstral cycle), and because the ancient blue black Cushitic people's and Nubians were once Nilotic *Hebrews* who had believed in the sanctity of the women's menstral cycle and women being topless (totally at odds with the Koran)--the Arab Muslims (who started out as invaders, not indigenous people) despised the true Africans even more.

From day one, the children of Sudan are conditioned from birth to abide by the differentials of hair texture, gradations of skin color, shape of lips and foreheads and tonality of the way one speaks Arabic. Only *good women* can produce *good people*, so that on the television and magazine covers of Sudan, a country where the overwhelming majority of people are ebony black to charcoal, there were never any black African women allowed on t.v. or in magazines--unless they were

50

as old as elephants, big as a rhino and played, ever briefly, the maid, or were cast as bit-part prostitutes. Only the White Arab woman of the north or a Palestinian woman or Middle Eastern women were *good women* and only from them could goodness come:

> *night of the living dead*
> *--coming dead from dark wombs*

It was during our visit with Uncle Atmu in Khartoum that I saw slaves for the first time in my life. Little charcoal Dinka children tied to the back doors of Arab Muslim houses just the way Americans keep pet dogs. In fact, this was why Mahdi Pappuh had stopped in. He wanted to see with his own eyes if it were true.

And it was true--even as early as 1978.

A man named Abu Fayid Ali, an official of Sadiq al Mahdi's "Umma Pary" kept three Dinka child slaves. I was with Pappuh Mahdi when he and Uncle Atmu and about twelve of their other "human rights" colleagues (all Arab Muslim men), went to the man's house to confront him about it and got cursed and called *abeed-shafa* (basically nigger lovers) before the city police officials arrived to threaten Mahdi Pappuh and the group with arrest if they didn't leave this good, clean upper class Arab neighborhood in peace. We saw the slaves though-- two boys, around ten or eleven and blacker than crude oil (the Dinka being the blackest people on earth, as well as some of the most beautiful), were chained on either side of the back door of Abu Fayid Ali's house and a little girl of about six (who looked to be their sister) stood inside the house, staring at us through the windows as though her greatest prayer was that either death would take her or that we would. Her tightly closed mouth spoke of unspeakable horrors, and yet the sky above us that morning was the most brilliant robin's egg blue that nature could produce.

"I pay my taxes, I go to mosque", cried Abu Fayid to his neighbors, as though he were being unfairly picked on. He was draped in something like a toga and his bone-faced Arab wife stood behind him screaming expletives from beneath her burkah. Her own caramel creamy children watched from a balcony at the top of the house--they didn't look to be skeletal or malnourished as the black Dinka children did.

The police said, "No one's breaking any law here. The man has servants." In Sudan--the law is religious, it's by Shariah, but very often--Islamic Scholars are not involved and the stupidest men rule via their personal prejudices and ignorance. There is no separation between church and state.

But anyway, this confrontation was particularly painful for Mahdi Pappuh, because he and Uncle Atmu had grown up with Abu Fayid Ali and once counted him as a close personal friend. I remember as we drove away from the house, Pappuh kept complaining to the other Arab Muslim men with us, "How can this be our same brother? How could he be doing something like this?"

I asked Pappuh, "Where are the parents of the Dinka children?"

"Probably at the bottom of a ditch", he said off the top of his head.

"No", said Kabir, one of the men in the back of the van. He told us, indignantly, "Only the father was killed. The mother was sold to a doctor in Egypt. They've had to cut out her tongue and chop off one of her feet to keep her from running away."

"This is a lie!", Pappuh cried out, furiously. "This is all a lie! I just do not believe it!" I stared at my father, noticing him so intensely that I thought I could hear the blood traveling in his head.

Uncle Atmu, who was driving, snorted and said something, which altogether was to the effect of: "Believe it my brother. I have not been lying to you all this time. Garang is not lying, either, with the stories he tells. There is a movement under foot. The government is paying people to get a war started. Didn't you read about the government complaining in the newspaper the other day about all the refugees pouring into Sudan from Kenya? Too many blacks, Harith. Gangs on horseback are being sent south to agitate the Dinkas. And in Darfur, the same thing. When they come back, they bring the wives and children. They sell them to politicians and businessmen right here in Khartoum. A lot of Palestinians buy slaves, it's so cheap to purchase one. Saudi Arabians, Jordanians, Syrians, Iraqis, Iranians, Libyans, Yemenese--you'll find Sudanese women and children with their tongues cut out working in homes all over the Arab world."

"Is this what we've come to?"

"*Come to!*" shouted Uncle Atmu. "Islamic gangs have been murdering southerners every since the British left the Arabs and the Egyptians in control of this country. Look at the 1955 massacre in Torit. Look at the hundreds of Blacks who were decapitated by Arab gangs in Juba in 1965. Look at Wau in 1965...Arab Muslims poured gasoline over the heads of pregnant black women and set them on fire."

Later that night, as Uncle Atmu's wife and Aunt Kem (the Dinka maid who traveled with us) served up dinner, there was a sudden sound from outside. Rocks pelting the house? Everyone was alarmed and everyone scrambled. I jumped up from the table and ran to protect my future husband--baby Micah. Gently, as I heard a rock crash through one of the livingroom windows, I raised baby Micah out of his crib and held him close to my tiny body, my smallish hands tucking the blanket over his head and my reed thin voice humming a lullaby. Arab teens outside were shouting epithets and daring Pappuh or Uncle Atmu (the Arab Muslim "*nigger lovers*") to come outside.

Uncle Atmu's wife, being a mixed race Arabian looking Sudanese woman married to a white Turk (Atma was whiter than my father), did not appreciate her marriage welfare or baby Micah being threatened all for the sake of some worthless black *abeed* stock (her own black blood was something she conveniently never spoke of). She hissed like a snake, "See what you've done! All for your precious niggers!" And with that she rushed upstairs in a complete rage.

Only moments before, she and Aunt Kem--whose skin was pure charcoal--had been trading recipes and tending the place setting, and in that moment, I think it clicked in my mind what racism really is and how suttle and natural it can be inside a person. To look at Atmu's wife, one would perceive a slender, angelic-faced Muslim woman in a stunning Burkah, but in reality, she was the typical selfish, skin-bleaching racist mosque princess who wanted to be white.

Aunt Kem, of course, being such a proud Dinka woman of true class didn't pay the Arab wife any mind. She grabbed a sharp butcher knife from the kitchen and stood ready to fight with the men if it came to it. You can't imagine how black she was.

In my head as an adult, I see Aunt Kem retrieve that knife over and over again--the placid look of acceptance on her unbelievably black face. I always think of how delicate and pretty she was, and more than that, how she couldn't have cared less about being pretty.

Uncle Atmu turned the porch light on...and the Arab teenagers dropped their rocks and haul assed down the street hollering like a pack of hyenas.

To which Auntie Kem remarked, "Oh, good then, let's eat."

We became nomads. Pappuh, Auntie Kem and I. Traveling from one archeological dig to the next.

As I was compiling my memories for this book and getting information from relatives who still live in Sudan and Egypt, my Uncle Kar (not his real name) asked me, "But don't you how skinny your Pappuh had gotten those last months before the murder? Don't you remember how his face had shrunken and his hands were like skeleton's hands? Don't you remember how the drugs made foam about the mouth?

No, I don't. I suppose that being so young, I only saw him as what he presented to me--my hero and protector. My truth.

"Don't you remember how Harith couldn't stand injustice? He was ashamed to be around it. He hated being a white skin!'

Yes, that I remember. Pappuh cursing the government and most Arabs.

Pappuh digging up fossils and pieces of pottery from the ruins in Napata (the ancient capital of Cush near the fourth cataract). Pappu taking my hands and making me read the hieroglyphics at Nuri and El Kuru--and the way he yelled at me when he was digging at the ruins of the ancient Kingdom of Meroe. I had nearly peed on myself as he yelled, "There are more pyramids in Sudan than in Egypt, Naima! You must stop being a little girl and understand what I'm teaching you! Everything came from here--it came from the blacks! It came from your little black pussy!"

He was obsessed. Angry. Impatient with God.

It was during these few weeks that I really got to know who my father was. He was *"me"*...as I've become today (sans the drug use.)

Uncle Kar: *"Let me tell you, Naima...it was when the British and the Egyptians succeeded in covering up the Nubian Valley that your father started losing it. They put a lake over the heart of Nubia and drowned a virtual universe of undiscovered archeological data, history and ancient artifacts...artifacts that your father saw as "the black roots" of Egyptian and Greek history. Harith fought an entire decade to stop the damn from being built! His whole life was one desperate attempt to save the black people of Sudan and to preserve their history--their greatness."*

In the 1960's, Mahdi Pappuh had campaigned mightily against the Sudanese government's creation of Lake Nasser/Lake Nuba--the largest man-made lake on planet earth. It conveniently covers the Nubian Valley on the Sudanese side and was responsible for the exodus of some 100,000 displaced Nubians who found their towns and villages submerged under water--all so the Arab Egyptians and the British could disconnect, as Pappuh claimed, the truth about the contributions of the Black Africans to the birth and glory of both Egypt and ancient Greece. Mahdi Pappuh believed that Nubia and Cush were the mother's of Egypt and Greece. It had been his life's dream to prove it.

Uncle Kar told me about verbal threats in the mid-sixties that had turned into actual beatings and death threats by the seventies: *"When they put in the lake...*your father attempted suicide. To him, it meant the end of authentic Nubian culture, and now that we're in the new century, Naima, I can tell you--he was right. The Nubian people have been dying off since the seventies. You can hardly find one who isn't breaking his neck to become an Arab Muslim by marrying out. The government still sterilizes some of their clanswomen."

"Still?"

Slavery, civil war, genocide. Mahdi Pappuh and other colleagues of his like Joseph Lagu, Lam Akol and Dr. John Garang (who was actually part of the Arab government when we knew him in 1978) saw it coming. Many of Pappuh's closest Arab Muslim friends (who have asked not to be named for good reason) say that my father predicted as early as the late sixties that the powerful Arab North would never accept total equality and brotherhood with the poverty stricken heavily Christian African South. He used to say, "The Muslims won't feel Muslim until they kill off the Christians. That's just the nature of all religions."

"But we're Muslims, Pappuh."

"Only because it's safer."

By the year 2002, the United States Secretary of State Colin Powell would call Sudan, "The single worst human rights nightmare on the planet."

In retrospect, I truly believe that we northerners knew about what what was in store for the southerners long before they did. This is the only way that I can explain the blank stare that I get from many Sudanese expatriots whenever I mention the fact that the slave raids and "false jailings" of certain liberal-minded Arab Muslims were already taking place when I was a little girl in Omdurman during the late seventies.

I tell them about being with my Pappuh Mahdi on his archeological tour in 1978 and witnessing the rounding up of the Nuer people by Arabs on horseback and they say--"no, that started around the mid-eighties". But they're wrong. The divergent Arab Muslim political parties who would do battle to become Sudan's present day terrorist regime were already enacting their campaigns of racial hate (we should say *colorist* hate since so many of the Arabs are black themselves) against the Black African southerners in 1978. Not only did I witness this rounding up, but I also overheard many Arab Muslim liberals come to Pappuh and complain about the similar incidents. Their Nubian maids and houseboys were suddenly being refused service at supermarkets or denied driving privileages for no legal reason or just plain beaten up in the streets by Arab soldiers.

Unrelated to race, but certainly a sign of the coming anarchy, was the day that Uncle Kar joined Pappuh on a dig near the fourth cataract. He and I decided to walk to the open market to get something for lunch...and on the way back, we came across one of the most horrid and unshakeable memories that I have in life--the sight of a group of Arab Muslim brothers (black ones) kicking and berating one of the men's wives for bearing only daughters and no sons. Uncle Kar being the man he is, he couldn't just pass and do nothing. He had me stay behind as he went over and argued with the men. He tried to talk to them about the will and word of Allah. He used stories of the Koran to plead for fair treatment of the woman (she looked mixed race and extremely light, my father's color)--but his plaintiff good works only brought out more evil in the men. They doused the wife and mother with gasoline and set her on fire!

Right in front of us, in broad daylight.

I cried for two days straight and Madhi Pappuh yelled at the police officials until he was blue in the face, asking them, *"What is Sudan coming to?"*--but nobody cared. She was just a woman, and worse than that--an Arab woman who had failed to give birth to sons, which in any Muslim society automatically makes a woman *nothing*.

Pappuh was next.

A few soldiers (police or whatever they were) showed up at our dig site one morning and kicked sand in Pappuh's face as he slept. They warned him that *"the evil eye"* was going to be turned on him. In our culture, the evil eye is a very serious thing. It means almost literally..."death is upon you."

Pappuh being an Egyptian, should have taken it more seriously.

Several co-workers at the dig told Pappuh, "Move your family to Kenya. Go to Europe. Move to Ethiopia."

"I am a warrior like Mohammed", was Pappuh's reply. "Allah will protect me."

But Auntie Kem told him many times, "The only people who like you, Harith, are the goodhearted ones. Those are terrible odds."

We went home and Uncle Kar returned to Egypt.

I imagined Mommysweet as a black crow presiding over the porch and couldn't wait to see her beautiful face again and to be wrapped up in her bosom of love. She was the best mother in the world and that's all I truly thought about as we drove the roads back to Omdurman.

Just like in Napata and Meroe and in the road where the gasoline-soaked woman burned to death...and on the city street where black children lived their childhoods as slaves tied to the back doors of rich men's houses--*the blue sky followed us.*

I am an orphan--a lost girl. It was the blue sky that created me. *night of silence/silent night...night of the livng*
Even on that night when my parents became a part of the next world and could no longer abide me. It was the insanity of the blue sky that kept me calm. I was calm because...I knew it would come back again...Sudan's blue sky. The insanity. Others who come from third world countries, like I do, will know exactly what I am talking about. And they will admit that there's no way...not to know.

We went home and the soldiers were waiting for us.
Mommysweet, just as I imagined, was there presiding over the porch of our house. Her black velvety crow-like flesh rising up into the shape of a menacing hooded cobra. Her mahoghany eyes, braver than the sun, summoning us home.
Auntie Ramah was in jail--accused by some local Arab women of being a lesbian. One of them, Nasiiba, claimed that Auntie Ramah had put a spell on her that made her dream every night of she and Ramah cuddled and licking--"like snakes".
The authorities at the jail wanted to question...*me.*
I knew, from staring into Mommysweet's eyes, that they wanted

to take me into a back room and terrify me into saying something horrible and untrue about my relationship with Mommysweet's dearest friend. And then they would have the blood of a child as an excuse to publicly stone my aunt in the streets.

Pappuh forbid it. He said, "You're not asking my daughter shit! She doesn't know anything about Ramah's grown woman's life. She's a little girl. And you get the hell away from my wife!"

I think we all knew that Auntie Ramah was a lesbian. Surely, we did. Even as young as I was, I knew without being told--her children knew it. It's just that we didn't have a particular word for it (as children), there was no reality or idiom for such a state of being--to Africans who were not Muslim or Christian, it was "natural flux"--a natural part of nature like catepillars turning to butterflies or crocodiles building nests, and hence, all around us, there were certain men and women that the old high priests of the rivers and swamps would have called *"Flower Children"*--people whose ancient root spirit was neither male nor female, but one half of each, so that they were special angels from the world of the Cushite Sky Gods. Or at least this was how Africa's non-conquered spiritual folks saw things (it's much like that in India, too, where they hold Eunuchs and hermaphrodites as "saints")--the fear and hatred of these gay people is not African in the least, but comes from outside invaders (the Europeans, the Arabs, the Christians and Muslims)--and this is really true, because the indigenous religions of Africa, the river and sun people, the ancient Nubians and Egyptians, they all saw it this way--*Some People are just gay.* I guess you call it "Pagan".

And I, Kola Boof, am not gay or bisexual, but I'm just telling you that before Islam and Christianity, Nilotic African people did not fear, hate or persecute homosexuals.

In my childhood, Many times, if we should happen upon two women bathing in a loving way at the river or see boys playing the secret "size" game that boys play (boys will be boys), or if we happened

61

upon the Muslim clerics and their well known penchant for sodomy--
then we were to pretend that we had not seen what we had seen and
erase it from our minds. And let me just say that if you think the
Catholic Priests are something with regard to molestation and sodomy,
then your minds would be blown by the rampant sexual acts among
Muslim religious hierarchy in the name of "purity" and "chastity" over
in Egypt-Sudan. Somehow...very unfortunately, these religions such
as Christianity and Islam have made sex and sexuality into something
dirty, something sinister and evil--and in turning sex into amputating
God's genitals--they have created a world of perversity.

And in Sudan, if you told someone that you had seen a sexual
act at the creek or in the forest or anywhere--they would only act as if
you were stone and warn you about the public ostracism that
acommpanies people who hallucinate things. Black African river/sun
people didn't want to discuss sex, and frankly found the subject boring-
-they had a *been there, done that* attitude and would look at you like:
"don't you know human nature?" They also felt that sex was "personal"
between two consenting adults and felt dirty just talking about someone
else's sexual habits. The Arabs, Christians and Muslims, however, took
a different view. They saw sex as evil, and furthermore, they saw
homosexual sex as unnatural and sought to eradicate it from human
nature.

My auntie Ramah, the person who raised me more than
Mommysweet did, was a lesbian and a good mother. She was a loyal,
committed friend to my parents (Pappuh adored her!), and she was a
truthful, nurturing, healing influence on my childhood. Before her
husband was killed she had been a caring, attentive wife (although
even back then, Pappuh and Uncle Kar said she should never have been
with a man--but women are forced to in our culture, you don't have a
choice). Auntie Ramah was a wonderful cook, a talented seamstress.
And now that her husband was gone, she and her accuser, Nasiiba, had

become like two moons rotating around some intoxicating forbidden world. Two women in full bloom.

"I won't have my daughter set foot in any man's jail!"

"We have orders to see the Mullah at once!"

Pappuh was livid. "Then you tell him to come to my home! But I will not have my child interrogated in some jail. And not out of my presence. You go back and tell your Mullah who I am...I'm an Arab man--an Egyptian! A Muslim father! I am *Harith Bin Farouk!* You make sure he knows who he's dealing with. Now get the fuck off my land and stay away from my wife!"

Within the hour, the tiny squat investigator from the jail was pulling up in front of our house. Name of Ali (I shall write this as best as I can remember it).

Pappuh jumped up from the kitchen table and literally flung himself outdoors.

Mommysweet, who was at the stove, looked at me with worry. I followed her as she hurried out to the porch.

"You're aware of the *murahaleen* are you?", the tiny fat man asked Madhi Pappuh threateningly. He had four soldiers with him.

We had heard of this swarm--*murahleen*--a title used by the Dinkas and other southern blacks to describe renegade Arab Muslim horsemen (usually far from our area)--killing parties who went to the homes of black southern religious and political leaders and put them out of the world.

"How do you know that I'm not one?", Pappuh shot back.

"Oh, you're not a real Muslim brother", said the investigator with disgust. "You're a traitor to Sudan, Harith. A traitor to Allah and an ape worshipper--just look at your wife."

Pappuh rushed at him--but the soldiers caught him in a net of arms and chests.

As they held Mahdi Pappuh and kept him from swinging a

punch, the investigator said something to my father that people have said to me all my life--"You talk too much". He said to Pappuh, "You use the fact that you're an Arab Egyptian, a white man...a Muslim. You use all these cards to do your crooked bidding against jihad and the true brothers. But your days are short, Harith--the evil eye is upon you."

That was all...that needed to be said. The little man turned around and went back to his jeep. He was gone as quick as he had come.

If I had known back then what the full weight of those words were--I wouldn't have been able to keep food on my stomach. I would have worried about it every waking moment. But I did not, at that time, really understand the seriousness.

Or that my parents would be killed that very night.

We ate dinner (what it was, I don't remember).

I overheard Pappuh telling Mommysweet that we should pack up in the morning and *"take a vacation"* to Ethiopia or Kenya. He seemed to think that we had plenty of time. He kept talking about *in the morning.*

Mommysweet, as usual, said nothing. But she doted on me every ten minutes. I remember that she was so glad to have me home and that she looked so...pretty. Her slender wand of a hand would pass me sugar cubes or pat my shoulder or run over the jungle thickness of my bushy African hair. I was given actual chalk (like they use on blackboards) to draw things with, which back then, was my favorite thing in the world.

I think I drew animals all over the stones in the backyard.

And then...just as darkness fell...*Auntie Ramah showed up*!

I felt her coming before I saw her.

Her heavy feet were ambling up the river's edge, her mouth moaning just a little and her body badly bruised from where the jailors had beaten her. I jumped up, saw her coming, and then ran yelling for

Mommysweet and Pappuh to come--Auntie was home! She had her children, Ian and Liv, with her. I just knew that Mommysweet would finally be moved to speak, say something to Auntie Ramah. That's really what my excitement was about.

It hurt me...to my heart...to see Auntie Ramah standing before us that night.

Her right eye blackened and swollen shut, her lip busted, her pretty orange skin covered in purple puffy blotches. She told us that she had been blamed by religious officials (both Muslim and Christian) for the birth of two sets of twins--both born on the same night and both born in Ramah's section of Omdurman (in our world, amongst many different ethnic groups, the birth of twins is seen as a curse or a warning from God that the community as a whole is not worthy of "grace"). Since Auntie Ramah was both a witch and a lesbian, many people thought that it must have been her who brought bad luck and caused two sets of twins to be born, but when the soldiers fetched the four newborns from the hospital and brought them to the jail and had Ramah hold each one--not one of them cried. So they released Auntie promptly and a different neighborhood witch was picked up.

"I just wanted you to know that I'm alright", she told us, as Ian and Liv held her hands tightly, their dark faces petrified with terror and their cheeks wet from crying. They had already lost their father, so the thought of losing Ramah was more than they could bear. They loved and needed their mama as tremendously as I did my parents. And I have come to know that this it the thing that really makes us children...needing and being protected by adults who love us is what makes us children, not youth. For without parents, there is no foundation, no ettiquette. Humans can be grown at any age. People in Africa know this, because thousands of "children" wander autonomously throughout the poor countries (I'm not saying that this is right--I'm saying that it's true), learning survival techniques, having sex with adults and earning a living...as young as nine and ten, running households and protecting other children. So, truly, it was a blessing for Ian, Liv and myself to even have parents who loved us, protected us and looked after our childhood innocence. We were given the opportunity to be *children*, which...I would like to stress to the western world...is a luxury and not a privileage.

Mahdi Pappuh and Mommysweet gave Auntie Ramah warm hugs.

"Goodnight", said Auntie Ramah.

But, to my disappointment, Mommysweet didn't speak a single word and Auntie and her children walked off into the night, the children literally holding their mother up.

There are some people who, throughout my life, have been brave enough to ask me the one question that I always hate to be asked.

"What was it like to hear the murder of your own parents--how did it feel?"

Well.

It was so overwhelming and so traumatic...that I can only describe it as being like a kind of birth. The world was confronting me with the reality that I was powerless to save that which I loved above all else. The reality that love, even the purest love of a child, can be placed in a box and marked nothingness. *No power.* I felt the most...unbearable horror. I hated my heart for continuing to beat. I couldn't believe in anything. I call it the "living dead", because in that morning--it was like a birth. I went downstairs and walked into the backyard where the bodies lay, and heard the sound of their blood seeping into the soil as if that were where it had come from...there was nothing else left in life for me to be afraid of. The very worst that could happen had happened. Like you can feel when your feet are going numb--I felt myself becoming fearless. The fearless ballad I told you about. I literally thought I was going to fly away. And more than anything else, I wanted to go with them wherever they were, I wanted to die, too. In fact, for many, many years after that moment (until I'd had my children), I don't think I'd wanted anything else.

That's what fearlessness is--being *ready* to leave this life behind. And that was how it felt.

Mommysweet tucked me into bed. I couldn't make out her features in the dark, because her velvet face was so black beside the moonlight spilling through my window as she leaned in and kissed my cheek and forehead. She said nothing, of course. Nothing at all. She was just glad to have me back with her...where I belonged.

Goodbye Africa

All night and into morning and up until noon I sat on the front porch of our house, not knowing what to do. Pappuh and Mommysweet's bodies lay in the backyard like crash dummies resting in blood that had long dried to black and now glued them to the ground.

All through the night, I had stayed near them to feel their warmth, to listen to their blood as it gathered to touch beneath the earth, and most of all, to feel for them in the silence--*to listen for them*. But come morning, I could not bear the sight of them. I don't like daytime anymore. In daylight, they seemed like dead bodies, whereas during the night, they had been almost alive, their blood hot and fluid like thoughts. They looked in the moonlight to be asleep--in a sleep so

deep that not even dreams could find them.

I was seven years old. I sat there crying...waiting for my parents to wake up.

I replayed the last lesson that Mahdi Pappuh had been teaching me over and over in my head--*that jihad would not stop until establishing* Khilifah (the worldwide domination of Islamic rule) *and that the evil eye was trained on Dar al-Harib* (the place of war; the South)....and that the five nations of ancient Nubia had been Wawat and Iretjet at the 1st Cataract, and then Yam, Kush and Medijay at the 3rd-5th Cataracts.

My parents were dead.

I knew that I should run and get help, but I was afraid to leave their bodies. I feared that someone would steal them.

It wasn't until noon that someone finally came by the house. It was the little cinnamon brown Arab boy who sold us the grain that Mommysweet used for making bread. He himself was no more than ten or twelve.

He came up to me, I told him what happened, and then he dropped his sack of grain and ran off quick to get Auntie Ramah.

When Auntie Ramah came back with the boy, she was out running him. Her shrieks and screams pierced the day like bolts of lightning. She ran right up to the porch, scooped me up in her arms, and then kept right on going until we were out back where the bodies were. She cried, holding me close to her, her sight impaired by the one eye being swollen shut from the police. She cried and screamed and cursed the universe and shook her fist crying.

~~

The authorities were called. Then they got in touch with Uncle

Kar in Cairo. He volunteered to drive down from Egypt and fetch me so that I could live with my father's mother--Grandmother Najet. Auntie Ramah and I both tried to persuade the authorities and my Uncle Kar that it would be better if I stayed with Ramah and was raised up with her children in Sudan, but Uncle Kar and some of my other uncles insisted that I should be raised in my father's religion (Auntie Ramah was not a Muslim, was a witch--and a lesbian, and everybody knew it) and that I should be brought to Egypt where my flesh and blood relatives could keep an eye on me. Grandmother Najet, who I really didn't know very well at all, had already made arrangements for the bodies to be wrapped and transported to the family mosque in Egypt. Uncle Atmu of Khartoum also had a say in my fate, suggesting strongly that I be raised Muslim in Egypt so that I would turn out a proper wife and mother for his son, my future husband, baby Micah.

It was too much, because Auntie Ramah was already like a second mother to me. She had been one of the women who helped deliver me from Mommysweet's womb. It was she who had often times oiled my scalp and braided my hair so that Mommysweet could catch up on laundry or prepare some complicated recipe. And I knew what Mommysweet would have wanted--she would have wanted Ramah to raise me, because she couldn't stand Grandmother Najet.

On the morning of the day that Uncle Kar was to pick me up from Auntie Ramah's house, I got up before dawn and snuck back home---(notice the word "snuck", a word that I would soon learn from my Black American family). The windows and doors were boarded up by then, but I knew a secret way to enter the house from underneath Mommysweet's verandah (on the other side). I came up through the dining room and then rushed upstairs to the secret hiding place where Mommysweet kept her shoe boxes full of diamonds. When I opened the boxes, the diamonds looked big and glowing, sparkling like ice cubes, some of them big as my eye balls. Obviously, being a child, I had no idea of the humongous fortune in the boxes. To me, they represented Mommysweet's pain and her beauty (without charcoal, Pappuh had taught me, the earth can't produce diamonds). For within their prisms, Mommysweet had entrusted all her secrets and prayers. I emptied them into a grain sack and ran back to Auntie Ramah's house before anyone woke.

After breakfast, Auntie Ramah did my hair up in what Black Americans call "afro-puffs" with a part down the middle (having this negroid hairstyle instead of being covered in a burka would obviously infuriate my Uncle Kar). She put a thin layer of vaseline on my face and fingered some in my nostrils for protection against the desert ride and scooped out some vanilla Halva/Tahinia (Sudanese candy paste for kids) and spread it over thin slices of bread so that I would have a sweet snack on the long trip to Egypt.

Auntie Ramah did not want to see Uncle Kar. She had put my bags on the front and had told him that I would be sitting there waiting when he arrived. So it was when she set me on the front steps with a jug of tea juice that we finally said our goodbye.

I gave Auntie Ramah the sack of diamonds. I lied and said to her, "Mommysweet told me to give these to you."

Her eyes filled with tears as she said, "Jiddi's rocks? I just assumed the soldiers had looted them. But here they are...with you. Come, Naima, quickly...we must go back to your house and honor your mother properly."

We went back to the house and stood on the banks of the Nile. We kissed each other and every diamond before tossing it as far as we could into the river of blood.

We said (in Nilotic Hebrew) the words of Queen Nefertiti's favorite hymn: *Khu sahu sekhem...enam betonim...onu ta ba*

My Auntie Ramah knealt down beside me, she took my chocolate hands into her orange-brown ones. She said these exact words, "No matter where you arrive in the world...you must never forget who you are. You were born in March, which is the only time that when the female crocodiles of the Nile build their nests. The day of Alu, Goddess of Trees--March 3rd, 1969. You are born under the crocodile and Goddess of Trees."

I didn't want to hear goodbye, but her stare commanded me as though I were expected to be fully grown for a moment. She said, "You are Naima...the one who is victorious; the one who is praying. Now *Say it.*"

"I am Naima...the one who is victorious. The one...who is praying."

Water stood in Auntie's brown eyes, but she wouldn't let it fall. She nearly barked at me.

"You are the *tima*...the African...the result of great fire. You come from a people...you come from a place...you come from a nation!"

I come from a people...I come from a place

I come from a nation!

"You are the Naima Sijira of Omdurman. Bint il Nil (daughter of the Nile)."

I am the Naima Sijira of Omdurman. Bint il Nil (daughter of the Nile).

When she stood up, her face full of rage and her bitter voice admonishing me, "Don't you ever forget what happened here!"...I suddenly saw her in the ancient image of the Nile's greatest queen...the one the southern blacks called Nuku, God's Wife of Amon...the black woman who ruled Egypt dressed as a man, built the world's greatest library and took only African men from her royal army to be lovers. Indeed, the one who is regarded by historians as the only brave and mighty warrior ever to rule Egypt as both Queen and Pharoah (sometimes wearing a beard)...Queen Hatshepsut.

I love you, Auntie Ramah.

Thank you for my courage; thank you for my "womanist" spirit.

I have remembered everything you told me.

I was alone in the world now.

Each day of my life...became a new heartbreak.

At the funeral, for instance, I found out that I was not an only child--I *had two brothers*! and they were both older than me. Their mother was a striking ebony black Ethiopian woman named Amina Kentworth (Afwerki). She had enormous eyes and kept her head shaved completely bald to denote Nilotic femininity. I would find out as an adult, from Uncle Kar, that she had been Mahdi Pappuh's mistress since around 1965, but had only seen him twice a year. I thank God that Mommysweet never knew. At the funeral, my brothers glared at me with a chilling hate--they resented me, I think, because Pappuh was always in my life and never in theirs. They were handsome boys, too. Very tall, as I am, with deep dark chocolate skin and fine boned faces. They were about ten and eight. As I was introduced to them, I tried to kiss one but his mother damn near slapped me...forbidding my uncles to even divulge the names of the boys to me. She said that I was not to be in their lives, *ever*. And to this day, I am not (although we know each other).

I watched the Arab townspeople carry Pappuh and Mommysweet into their tomb, and was finally hit, in that moment, with the realization that they were not coming back. They really were dead.

I cried all the way back to Grandmother's house and I cried all night.

There was nothing anyone could do.

My parents were dead and I had gained and lost two brothers all in one day.

I began to suspect that God hated me.

And then in a few weeks, I had proof that God hated me.

Grandmother Najet, being an Arab Egyptian woman who had spent decades carefully weaning the blood of darker races out of her family line (my late grandfather had been Turkish-Syrian Egyptian), felt that my complexion was a serious threat to the image of the House of Kolbookeks. People could see that I was actually related to the family and not just a servant's child or a slave girl. I had Pappuh's face, only 20 times blacker, and they could tell by my Arabic and the proud bearing and my aristocratic gait that I was "black blood" in the house, and that, of course, could bring Grandmother's pedigree down a few notches-- she wouldn't be able to turn her nose up at the Nubians and Black Egyptians she encountered in the community anymore.

So she decided that I should be...*let for adoption*.

Her own grandchild.

This is the only thing in my life that I cannot write about in detail, because...it is the one thing that very nearly killed my spirit. There are no words to describe how it feels to have one's own family scorn one's skin color, facial features and hair. To reject and withhold love based on a human being's failure to be something other than "fashionably ideal". And, as I leave this moment in my life alone (because I don't have the courage to explore the pain of it--which has not eased over the years), I will say that there is great wisdowm in the proverb--"*That which does not kill you...makes you stronger.*"

I was nobody's child.

A caucasoid man (the first white skinned man I'd ever met) showed up to take me away--and I was petrified! I remember being...so terrified and frightened. Clinging to my grandmother's leg, crying and screaming, begging the whole family not let the scary white man take me away. I was just a kid and with my fertile imagination he seemed mysterious like a space alien or some kind of jinn who ate the children that nobody wanted.

As it would turn out, he was a wonderful man and would become like a father to me. But still, the trauma and shock of it was cruel beyond words and has never left me. I kicked, screamed and hollered...but they still placed me in his arms and watched complacently as he carried me out of the Kolbookek house and placed me in his car and drove away--as though I were some stain that wouldn't come out of the carpet. And being black, I guess I was.

But the real shock...was that I was leaving Africa.

Boarding a great fire bird...*being taken from my body.*

MY NEW FAMILY
The Black Americans

"Having a childhood is a luxury...not a privileage."
--Kola Boof

<u>By</u> the time I reached America, I was a trembling, frightened wreck of a girl. O God, that day comes back to me now and I can hardly believe that I'm the same person. I had suffered a terrible year in London and was now eight years old (although, please remember, there is no way I can be sure of what my age is--because the Sudanese government and several people have disputed Auntie Ramah's claim, so I'm picking age 8). I spoke no English, all my hair had fallen out from nerves (see Unicef photo on internet) and I was painfully conscious about the the dark coloring of my skin. I had come to the place where I believed that all my suffering was because I was so dark. As I had witnessed all my life, blue sky never protects the darkest of people. They were the ones who were slaves or dying from poverty or lacked the self-esteem that was infused in lighter people or were put up for adoption by their family for being *"helplessly black"*. I had also noticed that it wasn't as bad if you were a boy with black skin--but if you were a black girl--there was a suttle lovelessness that pervaded your life. Or

77

at least that was how I saw the world through people's faces as I traveled outside Africa. And although my skin lightened about five shades once I'd lived out of Africa more than a year (the African sun makes us darker), I had still developed a complex about my color that I hadn't had when I was with Pappuh, Mommysweet and Auntie Ramah.

With my same white guardian, Owen McAnnis, still fighting to find me the perfect home, I arrived in Washington, D.C. the week after the Americans celebrated christmas in December of 1979. We flew to New York City and were immediately greeted by grim white people in blue coats with walkie talkies and security men. Owen showed them my paperwork and spoke to them in English. Good thing I didn't know they were sending me to have shot vaccines before meeting my new Black American father. My tiny body trembled as Owen handled the formalities, because I had never been surrounded by so many "caucasoids" before at one time(*the males grow fur on the top of their hands and on their backs like apes!*). There were at least twenty-five of them encircling us, and Mahdi Pappuh had taught me all my life that "the white gene" is evil and not to be trusted. So my very first impression about America was that it had too many caucasoids.

Owen McAnnis was different, somehow. As pale white and blue eyed as he was--as red as his neck was--I just didn't see him as white. Or at least not one of the white devils that North African culture warns against. For every since we'd left Egypt, Owen had been the only human being that I could trust and feel comfortable around. He spoke flawless Arabic and French. He made weird delicious foods like "grell chez sanwich", "pete-sa" and "fishemships". He taught me to ride on his back (like monkeys do!) and he often placed me on top of his shoulders so that in airports and on crowded London streets, the whole scary world was beneath me.

I lived with him at his flat in London first. He worked for Unicef and I believe he must have been a rich man, because he never had to go to work like normal people do. His whole life was spent studying poor people and watching out for the rights of little children like me. He had a girlfriend named Paula (whose Irish accent was so thick she sounded like a character from a fantasy leprechaun movie), and he and Paula were the strangest people to me, because their lives were completely immersed in all things African. On the walls of Owen's flat hung pictures of Masai tribesmen and Dinka masks and beautiful naked chocolate women bathing their children on the Congo river. Paula had henna designs on her hands, and although she couldn't speak any African (or Arabic) languages like Owen could, she knew a lot of African lullabies and would cradle me in her lap and hum them to me. Even with her small rythm-less voice, there was a great ethos of the ancestors within her white body and it comforted me.

Just as I had become attached to Owen and Paula, an Arabic speaking Ethiopian family in London adopted me (I have no idea how official or formal it was at the time) and I was thrust into their home like a sack of fava beans. I lived with them for almost a year before they set me on the stoop one afternoon with my belongings. They were appalled at how "intelligent" I was for a girl (the husband complained about it). They found it rude the way I would talk and talk and talk-- and ask them questions about almost everything. This was not proper girl-child behavior...and then when they discovered (from Owen) the circumstances of my parent's murder and the fact that Mommysweet had bore six stillborn boys in a row...and then a *living* girl--they decided that I must be a witch. No wonder the grandmother hadn't wanted me! They told Owen to fetch me at once! I had killed my own family, they told him, and I was obviously the reason their daughter suffered chronic ear infections the whole time I'd been there (from me running my mouth, I guess). The husband had been caught having an affair with a white lady. They blamed *me*. I will never forget the look on the Ethiopian wife's face as she stood by watching her husband tower over me, an eight year old child, accusing me of casting spells that drove him into the arms of the obese cockney housewife down the street. I remember the hotness of the tears that filled my eyes when he had knocked me across the head and into the floor, saying, "That's why your parents are dead now...you killed them...you pink-gummed Oromo bitch!" (they had black gums and Ethiopia is filled with Oromos).

It hurt...so bad...to be a child and to have no power over my own destiny and no one of my own flesh and blood there to protect me--so naturally I ran to Owen and Paula. Bloody-faced and crying.

The Ethiopians told Owen that if he didn't take care of me--then I could very well rot in the streets. They couldn't tolerate witchcraft in their home.

And that is how I ended up in America.

Owen had told my story to several Americans in Unicef and to military people he knew and then someone mentioned it to a Black American military man who lived in Washington, D.C. He and his wife had taken in several other children and were so moved when they heard about my plight that they decided to take in one more.

My belly was full of butterflies as the American officials escorted us through the airport and to a waiting car. From there we would go to a government building where I would be given the shot vaccines and be introduced to the American Black man who chose to be my dad, but all I really wanted in the world was to go back to England and live with Owen and Paula. They, however, had no interest in being parents to only one child. They traveled the globe--parenting thousands. And they also felt that I needed to be placed, specifically, with African or black parents. They loved me, though, and just knowing that they did was enough to keep a glimmer of my self-esteem alive.

"You're going to love America!", Owen whispered in Arabic.

I looked around outside and then looked around some more as the taxi took us to the next building. America seemed too huge to me. Too busy, but at least I had begun to see the Black American tribespeople lumbering on the streets. My eyes leapt at them, hypnotized and following them everywhere they went. They weren't as black as people in Africa, I noticed with a faint disappointment, and they certainly did look different from the African and Carribean blacks of London. But at least, thank God, I was in a country that had black people from Africa in it--even if they hadn't been home in over four hundred years. I don't know why, but I truly needed to see the sight of black flesh in order to feel some since of security. I think it was because of how Mahdi Pappuh raised me. Even with Owen and Paula, the fact that his flat was decked out in African photos and artifacts is what convinced me, on a daily basis, that the sky was not falling.

"Well, Princess...you're about to meet your new dad."

"No one can replace you", I said to Owen with tears in my eyes.

I took a deep breath and sighed heavily. It had already been explained to me that my new dad did not speak Arabic (nor any of his family) and that he had hired someone to live at the house who would interpret for us. As the car pulled up to the building, I instinctively knew that this was them I was seeing.

My new dad was very, very tall. Built like a boxer. He was the rich chocolate color that Mahdi Pappuh had always dreamed of being. Standing there, holding flowers. He was so nervous, I could tell, and that made me nervous. He leaned his head to see me as the taxi pulled up. He stared through the window, anxiously.

It was so scary to meet him!

81

"Here she is!", beamed the very lightskinned black woman next to him. This was not his wife, but the young woman who could speak Arabic and would become like a much older big sister to me. Her name was Amethyst.

I could not have known then how blessed I was--to have a Black father who wanted me. I didn't know anything about relationships between Blacks in America, so I took it for granted and assumed that he had sent for me because we were both Africans. As I got out of the car, my new dad walked up to me with a huge smile on his face and bent down and kissed me firmly on my forehead. He handed me the bouquet of flowers (of which I didn't know what to do with them--was I to chop them into a salad upon arriving home or was I to bury them back in the ground or make my deodorant out of them? *What did we do with flower bouquets?*). They sure looked fresh and beautiful.

I curtsied in front of my new dad, gracefully bowing my head, and then said the greeting that Paula taught me, "Hello, father. I am Naima." He grinned and seemed impressed.

"Naima...I am Amethyst", said the cream colored girl in Arabic. "Your father says that you're very beautiful...an African princess."

"All my hair fell out", I suddenly explained to them through huge tears. In Africa, I would have thought nothing of it, because a bald headed woman is considered the ultimate symbol of "femininity" throughout most of Africa--but after being around the blacks in England, I was so embarrassed to be nearly bald. The kids in London had informed me that I was ugly and that only women with long flowing hair were pretty. I had the tears in my eyes because Amethyst had spoken Arabic and was so pretty to me. Her white people's hair flowed down her back.

Before I knew it, I was talking and wouldn't shut up. On and on.

"She's a highly intelligent, very brave child", Owen told them.

82

Bless you Owen. Saying goodbye to Owen McAnnis was so painful and so traumatizing in itself that I don't even want to write about it.

I entered America as though I were some experimental microscopic organism being shot into the blood stream of a giant, resting Gulliver. My new dad turned onto the highway and from there we were speeding down the smoothest roads I'd ever been on. Gliding through an artery you could say--city to city, praire to sea coast, state to state. Amethyst was smart enough to calm my anxiety by feeding me African foods (a container of pan-fried perch with yams, red beans and rice, okra and cubes of watermelon with coconut flakes over it) and "Dad" would look at me through the rear view mirror every now and then and smile as though he didn't quite believe I was there. I would smile back, all the while wondering--what kind of African is he? He had dark chocolate skin, but his features were very strange to me. Amethyst, of course, I didn't even consider black. She was part-caste (compromised several times over). I remember staring out of the windows during the long drive and feeling really in tune with the earth and soil of the land. The trees here in America cannot sing, cry or speak like African trees (this country, like England, hardly has any birds in it), but they did have more to say than the ones in England.

America is a White country--even all the colors in it (for it has many) are diluted and neutralized by *"the thought"* of whiteness. Everything the colored races of America think in their minds...was thought *first* by whites, you understand. They have little thinking left over from their ancestral homelands. But luckily, God had arranged for me a very special blessing. I was on my way to the southern comfort of Washington, D.C. I was being taken in by the "The Soul People"...*honey child*!

It was nighttime when we finally drove into Washington, D.C. A city of white light. I remember gasping at the sight of the capitol building's dome. As we crossed over the Foufa Street Bridge and over Anacostia Park, I heard what I 've now come to know as hip hop music blaring, booming in the streets of "Souf Eeese." People were darting across the streets (crackheads and drug dealers), scantily clad women were dancing by themselves on street corners (which I recognized them from Omdurman)...and then you had other people waiting at the bus stop, on their way to work. Black women in nurse's uniforms were hurrying home after long hours at work, anxious to look after their children. This, I would learn, was the ghetto (the poor people). They had sewage systems and street lights, house lights, lights on cars, lights on buildings, lights on aircraft flying in the sky--you could look miles away and see lights! All the children had shoes on and the poorest of the poor drove automobiles--televisions flickered from every window in the poorest of houses and even the driveways were paved! (*now you know that's wealth*!). Everywhere you looked there was a place to get hot food--already cooked. They had liquor stores where children ran out laughing, munching Doritos! Each one had a bottle of orange soda all to themselves. I couldn't believe how rich this country was!

We turned off Good Hope Road and drove down a nice, clean residential street. It appeared quiet at first, but when we got to our house...you would have thought the entire block was there! It was like a party was going on. A child was hollering, *"Aint Claudine! Aint Claudine! ...dey heah!...dey back from Africa!! dey heah!"*

Of course, I don't remember exactly what people said verbatim and I wasn't speaking English back then--I've had to call up relatives and consult with them to map out (as best I could) the dialogue that was spoken during all of these scenes of my life as a child in D.C., but the feeling I felt was one of great love and excitement, and because I was to end up a patient in the hospital that very first night in Washington, it's important that I be detailed here.

Everyone was running out of the house as we pulled up. I recognized the faint smell of Gopi (marijuana). A huge spotlight seemed to have been turned on the car.

Dad said, "Yall don't scare the poor child to death. She ain't used ta niggas."

"Well she betta get used to niggas...her ass one", replied Aunt Zola.

My new brothers and sisters and my new cousins (the ones who were small children like me) started jumping around the yard chanting--"Ooonga boonga!"

I actually strained to try and decipher the dialect they were speaking! I thought they were speaking some kind of African language--LOL. My Cousin Rochelle ran up to the car window talk'n bout: "Oonga boonga, Pookey!" And had a damned bone tied up in her nappy head! I know her ass gonna be shamed when she read this book and remember that night. Old heffa!

"I gots ta go, Berthenia--the baby done got here from Africa!", yelled Nana Glodine (my new grandmother) from inside the house.

My new mother--Claudine Johnson--came out of the house with her hands folded over her heart. My God...it seems I can't write a single chapter of this book without breaking into tears. I remember my new mother was calm but looked scared. Everybody got quiet when came out. She called out, "Nay-eeema?"

Amethyst undid my seat beat and helped me from the back of

the car. There was so much light and I knew that all these people had gathered and were waiting just to see me, so I put on my best mannerisms and presented myself in standing position on the ground with all the bearing of a queen's child. My face leaned out as a Cobra's (Egyptian style) as I aligned my right knee, chin and shoulders in an Oromo virgin's pose.

Immediately, my new big brother, Todd, cried out, "eewww...she's *black*!"

To which Aunt Zola, seemingly in one motion, reached down and took off her house shoe and flung it, precisely like a boomerang, up against his own black nappyheaded self. She said, "You take your behind in the house 'n shut up, boy!"

Luckily, I hadn't known what he was saying. My new mother walked down off the porch and came up to me. She was nothing like Mommysweet. She was thick and shapely instead of skinny and her hair was permed and dyed auburn. Her brown skin glowed like molasses spirit and I could tell by her cheeks that all she did was talk, talk, talk! She bent over and said, "Well hello there, pritty girl. My name is Claudine Johnson and this is your new home. I'm gone be your mama now. I hope you'll be very happy here." Mechanically, she hugged me--afraid that I might reject her.

Because I had been in England, I curtsied and replied, "Hello, Mummy", as Paula had taught me.

Nana Glodine (my father's mother) came out on the porch. She was a big, wide dark brown church-matron type of woman. She said, "Claudine, don't she look jess lak Muskatell's baby sista that died from sickle cell? 'Memba dat pik-shur he kept on his wall down in Raleigh with the yella dress on?"

"Sholl, do, mama. Come on here meet your Nana Glo-dean."

Mother took my hand and we seemed to skip up the walkway to the porch. Everybody wanted to hug me, I could tell. I felt so *"welcomed"*--I don't think I've ever again felt that special. They really wanted me there with them.

As we reached the porch, Nana Glodine said something like, "Well, lookee here...come give yo Nana some shuga." And then she swept me up in her fat black arms and cushy bosom. She kissed me with huge, African lips all over my face. *"Mwa..mwa...mwa."* Then she let me go and looked me over with a big amused grin and said (I am told), "Uhn...uhn...uhn. Marvin, you betta watch this one. The good lord done sent her here to do someth'n. She got more than arms up these sleeves."

From that moment on I belonged to my Nana. She was from North Carolina, but she looked like a West African woman. In fact, I had started to notice that all the Black Americans had distinct mixtures of West and Central African features. Even the yellow ones had the forehead, lips, noses and body makes of the West Africans, particularly the world famous West African dukan cake or "mama bank" (booty). My Nana looked sort of like a very plump, older version of the beautiful movie actress Alfre Woodard. Ghanian-looking but Zulu at the same time like Miss Woodard is. This greatly relaxed me, because the large number of West Africans who lived in Sudan had always been very kind, honorable and morally well meaning people. They were known for their love of spirit, ceremony, dance and good music. Their ancient men were regarded (along with the Nubians and Congolese) as being the mightiest warriors the motherland had ever produced, so to be in the company of Black American men, I felt very safe and let go of my anxieties. No one could hurt me with Mandingos, Yorubas and Ashantis around!

The house became an odyssey.

Nana walked me inside and from crowded room to crowded room I met my new relatives. They were strange, strange Africans. They only spoke English and their range in skin color was truly bizarre as well. I wondered--how can they all be one family? There was no uniformity of color as there would be in a normal family. They had a portrait of Prophet Ciisa (Jesus Christ) hanging on the wall, but like in the Christian missionary camps, he was white and his eyes were blue--then again their food was decidely African (watermelon, yams, rice, fried fish, okra, pan-water bread they called "corn bread"). They even ate the Egyptian dish, Umfitit (chitlins), only the Black Americans make their chitlins in a pot of water instead of in a skillet of honey (*see my Egyptian Chitlins recipe on page 425*). At the kitchen table my uncles and aunts took a time out from their Bid Wiss game to holler, "*Well hello dare, precious! Welcome to America!*" Out of nowhere, my brother Albert (not Todd, the one who had complained I was black, but Albert, the bookworm) ran up to me and kissed me on the cheek--then shot off, lickety split, to another room before I'd known what hit me! My sister, Tamala, came up to me and handed me her dollbaby (which I'd always wanted one!). She said, "You gone sleep with me and Spring in our room."

She was just my age and had pretty deep brown skin, dimpled cheeks and big, shiny Shirley Temple curls. I wanted so much to communicate, so I said, "Kiar bisa usra...tofa eyoun sera; suluwee."

Tamala's eyes got wide with horror and she said, "*Girrrl...I know just what you mean!*" Then she ran off somewhere to hide.

Out back, there was a little unpleasantness, because Nana cursed at some of my teen cousins who were smoking marijuana. Several groups of people had been out back chatting and smoking cigarettes, holding drinks. They all cheered me as I was introduced.

I was introduced to my mother's arch rival and oldest sister--elegant, softspoken, size 4 Aunt Beverly. She was the "rich person" in our family, a college graduate who owned a big house out in Prince George's County, Maryland and drove a brand new cadillac every year. She worked for the government, and although she had three sons, she never married. I loved Aunt Beverly because she was the only woman in the family who always wore her hair in a short natural Afro (she now wears it long and locked)--she looked like an Ashanti princess (not watered down mixed like the Pop singer Ashanti, but like a *real Ashanti* woman--shiny jet black and thin with a bubble butt and high cheekbones). It was she, as a matter of fact, who paid for Amethyst to be my live-in interpreter and it was she who would pay for me to be in the hospital later that night--she was always paying for the family (or as she puts it, "paying to be *in* the family"). She had kissed me and said, "Welcome angel...it's a blessing to have you with us."

Uncle Booey, my father's brother, would always pay us children money if we danced or did something cute--so I got my first candy money that night. He kept gesturing until I figured out that he wanted me to *dance* in the middle of the yard with my new brothers and sisters (they were dancing to *"Rapper's Delight"* by the Sugar Hill Gang). Auntie Ramah and I used to amuse Mommysweet by dancing, so I promptly got out there with the rest of the kids and did the rain dance of Osiris (the welcoming of the snails following the rain goddess--the orgasm of Isis and fertility in other words), and for that...I got a whole dollar bill! Uncle Booey was impressed. He said, "Girl, you sholl is orignal. What was that--the dance of the veils? You in the right family, alright."

And so began my life in America.

But in my long smiling silences (dictated by my inability to speak English), my heart continued to break with the knowledge that Owen McAnnis had so easily left me half way around the world from him. Apparently, other humans didn't need like I did. My soul ached for Mahdi Pappuh and Mommysweet. I began to think that there must not be a God. And then I missed Auntie Ramah so bad that to think of her made me sick--I wanted to pee on myself, because my longing for her mothering was so ill repressed.

This is why I was so afraid to fall in love with the Black American tribespeople right away. I liked them, because they reminded me of the river people back home, but I also feared them, because I *needed* them and they, of course, didn't need me. At any moment, no matter how good and sweet I was, they could expel me from their universe and the thought of it hung in the back of my mind like a skunk's odor. I smiled at them with a kind of repressed suspenseful worry.

And then that very night...something terrible happened. Something that would damage my heart muscle and affect my nervous system for the rest of my life.

Mother decided to give me a bath before putting me to bed. This is always a good way for girls to bond with their clanswomen, and as Nana Glodine stood keeping us company and eating from a cup of bread pudding, Mother casually pulled away the fancy frilly ruffles that Owen McAnnis had dressed me in.

I did not know that, apparently, shortly after being born--my birth parents had taken me and had my vagina "circumcised"--as Mommysweet and Auntie Ramah and a great many Sudanese women's vaginas are circumcised (especially and mainly the Arab Muslim girls in Sudan) or infibulated.

"Something don't feel right", went my new American mother, as she felt a strange *"swelling of flesh"* (scar tissue) between my stick legs. Her face twisted up and she put down a towel and motioned for me to lay down on the floor next to the tub. You would have thought a lion cub was being born between my legs by the shocked expression on her face. She said, quite urgently, "Big Mama...what is this on her?"

90

Nana Glodine peered between my legs as though spooked. "Lawd Jesus...I don't right know what dat is. Reckon somebody been mess'n wid her, Claudine?"

"*Marvin!*", my mother screamed out, as tears beaded in her furious eyes. "Amethyst--*come here, hurry up!*"

I didn't know English. All I could see was that they were panicking, and I sensed very strongly that I had done something wrong. My little heart started beating wildly, because I had done something wrong and I didn't know what it could be.

Nana Glodine shook her head and went, "Uhn...uhn...uhn."

My mother began shaking and then was sobbing uncontrollably (I would find out years later that she had been repeatedly molested as a teenager by a minister at Bible Study and had attempted suicide when she reported it and no one believed her).

I heard my new father rushing up the stairs, two steps at a time. "*Claw-deeen?*"

I got so scared. My heart started pumping like mad. I started crying.

Amethyst rushed into the bathroom before father and my mother asked Amethyst, pointing between my legs, "Ask this child who did this shit to her!"

As Amethyst asked me in Arabic what had happened between my legs, mother forced my father to come and take a close look. He sid, "It looks like some kind of tribal designs, Claudine. It's probably normal. Africans put scars on their faces, you know."

"That ain't normal, Marvin. *That child ain't got no pussyhole!*"

He pressed with his finger gently. "I think she do. I think."

Nana Glodine said, "Brang me my coat. We best get this child to the hospital."

Amethyst looked up at my mother and said, "Naima doesn't understand my questions, Claudine, about molestation. She's drawing

91

a blank. But you can see the terror in her eyes...she's scared to even talk. She's petrified."

"That's because she's protecting him!", my mother screamed. "Scared to tell on that *white man*! That fucking Owen McAnnis bastard done raped my baby!"

"Claudine calm down", said my dad. "Big Mama's right. We better get her over to D.C. General and find out what this is."

And when they *rushed* my clothes back on me...and my dad lifted me up and carried me, half running, out to the car--that's when the chest pains started.

In Arabic, Amethyst had said, "We're taking you to the authorities!"

But I thought she meant that I was being given away again. *Put out* again.

There isn't any way possible to describe the hopelessness that possessed me.

On the passenger's seat, I clung to my mother, crying, digging into her flesh and burying my face into her bosom. I kept begging-- *"please keep me...I won't be bad anymore...oh, please don't give me away."* But I couldn't say the words. There was this fist clutching my heart. Squeezing it, twisting it. I was in so much pain I couldn't talk. It seemed that I could see Owen McAnnis and Paula in the dark hallway again of his flat--pulling my tattered luggage behind them. The Ethiopians, again, as Owen McAnnis carried my bags out of their home. Auntie Ramah setting my bags on the stoop for Uncle Kar to pick up. Grandmother Najet, her urine-colored face and light eyes, pressing down against my soul like a scarab's claw as the Arabic words poured forth as clear and thick as Egyptian honey wine--"Your mother's color is to blame. Black ruins everything it touches. You wouldn't be happy here with us. You look nothing like us...*Naima.*"

At eight years old, I had a heart attack, because I hadn't yet mastered how to be alone in the world.

On the tape recorded interviews that I made to write this book (I can't remember all this stuff on my own, you know)--my mother sounds just like a doctor as she describes what happened to me that night. She says: *"It was cardiac dilation or a cardiomyopathy. I read that medical report for ten years, because I was so afraid that it might happen again. I remember the doctors tried to claim that the heart attack was brought on by a combination of nutritional abnormalities and sickle cell trait* (a blood clotting disorder that I have as many Africans do). *Now that you've grown up and told us that you really throught we were taking you somewhere to get rid of you...it makes sense to me how your reaction was to have a heart attack. I always wondered why you've had no heart trouble since that attack. The doctors listed it as Idiopathic, which means--unexplainable. Truth is, they didn't know anymore than we did why an eight year old child would have a heart attack."*

The vaginal thing makes us all laugh now.

Mother says that the doctors explained to her and my dad about the practice of female circumcision and infibulation in Africa (which was not generally known about in America circa 1979). The doctors told them that at my young age, I probably had no idea that it had even been done to me. They told my mother that after my body developed more and my menstral cycle started, they could operate and "undo" some of the sexist tribal artistry (mutilation) that was done, truly, for African men's pleasure, and my new parents had thought that was a good idea...but I grew up and refused to have it undone.

"Why", they would ask me as a teen.

"Because it's the only thing I have that links me directly to Mommysweet. It's the mark they marked on her...I want it marked on me, too."

So I learned to live with the pain of it. And then, too, I learned to use it to manipulate and bend men to my own will. To "*pussywhip them*" as the saying goes.

But am I against this practice in Africa? Yes, most definitely. There are over 100 million African women currently afflicted with the horrors of Female Genital Mutilation, and as my sister, Waris Darie, has so eloquently come out against it--so, too, must I. I think it's a misogynist ritual and an abomination against the God in women. It should very surely be abolished and put asunder. I am only too lucky...too blessed...that in Mommysweet's particular culture, they do not remove the clitoris, or at least, she didn't allow them to.

For without my clitoris, I don't believe that I could have grown up and become Kola Boof. I simply wouldn't have *felt* like it.

The Stuff that Dreams
are made of

<u>But</u> I do have my clit...and I did survive to grow up. I have a poem in which I state: "America is my husband now...and he is good to me." This is really a true statement, because along with having my clit, I had America itself to help me become Kola Boof. This is the best country on earth for women, trust me.

I fell head over heels for a Black American boy/man--a student at Howard University and a rapper--his name was "Truce".

He could have told me the moon was made of blue cheese and I would have fought anyone who tried to tell me different. I believed everything he said. I expected to someday be his wife. My dad was my "dad", but Truce was my *daddy*.

I was a bad girl, too. An angst-ridden teenaged ghetto Isis. Neurotic. Angry, brilliant, sensitive...lost.

God, where do I begin?

There was so much that happened before the abortion and before I ran away to Israel and before Osama Bin Laden. It's like my life was always in a hurry, you know. Just fast, fast, fast.

I suppose for those reading this book one hundred years from now, I should go back a little and touch on the era in American history in which I lived, became a person. I call it the "Hip Hop Holocaust" era.

Arriving in America right after Christmas 1979...and immediately suffering a heart attack, I was released from the hospital just in time for my first New Year's Eve celebration...the ushering in of the year 1980.

This meant the beginning of the Ronald Reagan presidency, the beginning of the worldwide AIDS epidemic, which came about quite sudden and mysteriously, and of course, the beginning of the Hip Hop Holocaust...the rap music based social movement that would replace the 1960's Civil Rights and 1970's Black Power movements among the newly christened *"African-Americans"* (before that they had been called in this order...West Africans...niggers (slavery), negroes, coloreds, and finally, the best name for all of us worldwide...blacks). The Hip Hop Holocaust would signal the birth of a new ideology amongst American blacks, a new cultural ethic that would eventually migrate to blacks all over the world--a cultural ethic that now openly embraced and promoted materialism, misogyny, disloyalty and anarchy. Whereas the Civil Rights movement and the Black Power movements had unified black people worldwide and brought about independence and nation building in Africa and a huge renaissance in self-love, unity and empowerment and building up of moral character among the Blacks Americans, who in the 1960's and 1970's, were the mightiest most innovative black people on earth--the Hip Hop Holocaust destroyed all that. This was the music that eventually renamed the mothers of the men who performed it--*"bitches and Hos"*--and made it fashionable to be colorist (against black women) and self-centered (bling-bling). Already, the black community was plagued by drug dealers and gangs (in no part of America--do they respect the "elders", the children run the grown the people over here), so no one was willing to stand up to the Hip Hop anarchists. I call it a "holocaust", because it effectively killed the core community in Black America and completely bamboozled the black youth and separated them from their true worth.

I was there, a new American and a Black child in 1980, so my version of the history is not to put down my own Black American brothers and sisters, but simply to leave a written record of what I saw with my own eyes. What others praise and regard as a revolutionary new expression of the "black man's" experience in America...I regard, in retrospect, as a poison against the people, because it wasted the people's lives.

Nonetheless, I'm also being a hypocrite, because I was an active fly girl in the Hip Hop Holocaust myself. MC Lyte was my idol. I bought everything she put out and I remember now, with regret, how desperate I was to see her perform live in concert (at just thirteen, I showed my breast buds to a group of adult security guards, black men, who would let under aged girls into the concert as long as we degraded ourselves by showing them). I loved K.R.S. One and Public Enemy (Eric B. and Rakim being, in my opinion, two of the most important poets to emerge in the latter twentieth century), and I was a huge fan of Tupac Shakur, Young MC, Salt N' Pepa and later Lauryn Hill.

As a teenager, my only dream in life was to be a housewife (like Mommysweet and other respectable women of Sudan) and be married to Larenz Tate, my favorite movie actor back then. Or Tupac Shakur or Micheal Jordan or the writer Nelson George or John Edgar Wideman, and then later, Ed Gordan from BET News and Evander Holyfield, the boxer. In my dreams, I was always fantasizing about being loved and adored by one of these men and baring his children. I studied them and kept scrapbooks with their pictures and accomplishments, and I was constantly learning how to cook different recipes, all in preparation of being a "black King's" wife. It was silly, but since all the other teenaged girls did it, too, I didnt' feel so bad.

What I did feel embarrassed about was my insatiable love for white girl singers like Olivia Newton-John and The Go Go's. I couldn't even speak English when the Go Go's came out (1981), but for nearly five years straight, I drove the black people in Anacostia Park crazy by blasting, singing and dancing: *"Jump baaad...'an round...round 'n round and round....'n Wheeeeeee...We got the beat!...We got the beat!...ah, We got the beat!"*

And after overdosing on Olivia Newton-John (I still love her), I became the biggest Madonna fan in the world. My Black American family would be like, "What is it with these corny ass white girls? Shit, at least bust out some Teena Marie!"

I couldn't help it. As much as I loved Janet Jackson and Whitney Houston, it was Madonna that I considered to be the absolute queen of my generation, musically. I still do. She was unapologetic, political, the total consumate artist and a woman-identified woman. Despite the essay by bell hooks (another woman I greatly love and was influenced by) castigating Madonna for being an artist who pimped black culture, I feel that Madonna exemplified the African goddess concept of the female having "sexual power" within the society. She seemed to *love* being white, whereas the voice of my heart, Mary J. Blige, would often come out sporting fake blue eyes and long platinum blond hair. This image caused me to have less respect for Mary and to sort of pity her. While I love Mary's music (especially her classic CD, entitled simply *"MARY"*), I sometimes felt embarrassed to sit through her music videos. To me, she was so devastatingly beautiful and yet like Serena Williams, the tennis player, and Angelique Kidjoe, the West African singer, Mary fucked up her looks by violating and selling out her own flavor. Her self-hatred (or high esteemed blondness) reminded me of how Black mothers poison their own children by becoming walking billboards for the general society's message that whiteness is superior. And don't get me wrong--I'm not against hair extentions or beauty aids (I wear weaves), but Mary's <u>white girl drag</u> went on for decades, and although she was the voice of my heart, she seemed inferior. Madonna was better. Better than all of them. She wasn't weak or desperate and it wasn't until Black womanist artists like Lauryn Hill, Jill Scott, Res, India Arie, and Erykuh Badu came along that I lost interest in Madonna.

Lauryn Hill became my new #1 favorite (I even love her Unplugged CD--*it's a masterpiece!*) and I started listening to Anita Baker, Chrissie Hynde, Cassandra Wilson and to classic superstars like Aretha Franklin, Nina Simone, Sarah Vaughn, Barbra Streisand, Gladys Knight, Kim Weston (from the 60's), Dionne Warwick and especially Diana Ross, Donna Summer, Chaka Khan and Natalie Cole...*whew!*...and although Whitney Houston did take a disappointing fall and became self-destructive, I truly loved her more and more as her vulnerability and toughness showed through. Her music got deeper as she took more risks and I really started loving Whitney in the way that I love Bessie Smith, a sort of--*no matter what*--I love Whitney attitude, but still, out of all the 1980's and beyond women--Lauryn Hill and Madonna are the only two that I would label "genius". Oh, and let's not forget Grace Jones. She could barely sing and yet her music was so ahead of its time, and very often you will hear Black Americans refer to a woman as looking like a "Nubian Queen"--but Grace Jones actually *looks* like a pure blooded Nubian woman. She doesn't look West African or Jamaican. She looks like a Nubian goddess, and I've heard several other Sudanese say it as well. I was shocked when I found out that she's from Jamaica and isn't Nubian.

At fourteen, while in the midst of the new hip hop culture, the Madonna revolution and the Reagan-Bush Aids epidemic, I finally learned to speak the English language, *fluently*, and through the special language tutor that Amethyst arranged for me at Ketchum Elemntary's open space program, I met the man who would, by the time I was seventeen, take my virginity--my reading skills instructor, Truce Harding. He was a tall, handsome twenty year old economics major at Howard University and fronted his own rap group when we first met. He had a girlfriend who looked exactly like the actress Jada Pinkett Smith, only her name was Summer, and they used to pick me up on Sundays and take me to church with them.

I believe that Truce (who I originally called Mr. Harding) felt sorry for me, because my difficulties with English kept me from having many friends at school, and I also think that once he discovered that I was under the care of a psychiatrist and was considered "a troubled child", he felt as though he had to provide some sort of "Big Brother" role. By fourteen, I had already figured out from all that Mahdi Pappuh had taught me about "racial history" in Egypt and Sudan that there were two types of "Black Americans"...the _authentic blacks_ (Lauryn Hill, Denzel Washington, Toni Morrison, Michael Eric Dyson, columnist Alicia Banks, poets Mari Evans, Gwendolyn Brooks, Maya Angelou, politicians Winnie Mandela and Maxine Waters, Kalamu ya Salaam, Sister Souljah)...and what I perceived to be the _niggerstock_ (Beyonce, Russell Simmons, Bishop Desmond Tutu, Harry Belafonte, Sidney Poitier, the BET network, Kofi Annan, the Jackson family).

As I warned you when my autobiography started--you should not come into this book expecting to _like_ Kola Boof. My purpose as a literary artist is not to be liked, but to be understood--regardless of whether I'm right or wrong. I really could give a fuck. Like most little black girls, I spent my whole life being "dictated to" by American media and _nigger_ media about what to believe and think--and so now it's _my turn_, as an African woman and wombbearer, to do the dictating. If you don't appreciate my candor--then write your own goddamned book; this one is _mines_. So anyway--by fourteen, I was no longer insecure about my spoon-headed North African beauty or my blackness. I was

100

tougher. My sister Tamala and I had been molested (but not de-virginized) when I was twelve (by a friend of the family), and although I've elected not to write any details about that incident or the way it almost destroyed our family, I do have to acknowledge that it awakened a very twisted sexualized imagination within me. As my sister's response to the molestation was to become introverted and shameful of her body (which is the reason men rape women, to take away their sexual power and leave them in a long-term hindered state of shame)--my reaction was to mentally declare myself "ripe" and ready for a more leveled playing field with regard to sexual interractions with the male species. As a small child in Sudan, I had witnessed men kissing and groping child prostitutes (usually middle class mixed race Arab men with homeless pure African street girls). I had seen men masturbating between the legs of livestock, so I was definitely damaged long before the molestation and had developed a survivor's mentality in which I conquered sexual vulnerability by embracing the fact that as a female, I possessed something that could bring out the worst in a man--or the best in one. I also learned never to allow a man to strip away the potency of my sexuality or my sexual power--which is how men dupe women into becoming passive do-gooder servant stock.

As an emotionally damaged, sexually compromised (but not yet penetrated) fourteen year old girl, it became a kind of obsession with me ...to capture the romantic love of a man who wasn't related to me. It didn't matter to me that I was just a child. I wanted a man who would make me an African housewife like Mommysweet had been. I was not, however, interested in or would have ever thought it would turn out to be Truce Harding, because with his light skin and wild honey colored eyes, I had not initially considered him to be a desirable husband, and to be honest, I still didn't see certain people in America as "Black". Truce and Amethyst, although I adored them, were not black to me, and part of the reason I loved them so much was because

101

I pitied them in the same way that the Africans had pitied my Arab father. People in America should realize that when Africans refer to a Black American as a "nigger"--they are almost always referring to the ones whose blood is the most compromised, who've lost the Crown of the Black man (their hair being Euro-infected), whose skin is the lightest--because to the African mind, what is really being lost is the ambilical connection to authentic African people. In Africa, we use the term "Pogo-Nigger" for those Africans on the continent whose lives came to symbolize..."*the white man's victory/over black flesh*" (look at the Africans who bleach their skin and see Paris and Mecca as places to *run to*--to be saved; the Black movie stars whose mates and children MUST BE white or non-black in honor of their belief that white is more human; the rap stars whose music videos glorify the image of every wombbearer on earth but their own mother's womb, because they hate the truly black female, which is the surest way to kill Africa itself--*and that's what a nigger is*--a nigger's true goal is to erase himself and become the image of his master, because that's all he really knows or trusts is his master's world). So you can understand why I saw Truce Harding as being compromised and not really black. It's better to be with a *real* white man than a half-white one, was how I saw it.

But on the vine...it's meant for males and females to fuck and hopefully *love* no matter where they're from. And because I was an African, aloof and mysterious and cool towards Truce, it represented a challenge to him, and strangely enough, he was fascinated by my Africanness--to the point where I was sometimes the "*teacher*", and though we had years to go as "big brother tutor" and "naive baby sister student", I started calling Mr. Harding...*by his first name.*

It happened when I turned fifteen. Truce and Summer, who had become engaged by then, had gotten permission from Nana Glodine and my parents to take me with them to Buckaroo beach in Virginia. We were there for the weekend so that Truce could meet Summer's grandparents, and what stands out in my mind today, is Summer's comment to her grandparents that she knew Truce would be the perfect father by the way he cared for and doted over me, his little play daughter. She had chirped, cheerfully, "Truce tutors Naima in reading and she's become like a daughter to him. She goes everywhere with us, she's our baby."

I feel such a sadness remembering it, because I now realize that the reason Summer so often wanted me along with them was because she fantasized me to be the softspoken intelligent daughter that she would someday have with Truce. It's only now, so many years later, that I even realize how very close Summer and I had once been.

But anyway, in that painfully long ago moment when I realized that Mr. Harding had a thing for me, my reaction was to feel nauseated by how stupid I was, because there was this voice in my head that snapped at me--"*Of course, he wants you! You just now noticing that? The man is crazy about you!*" And what that voice really was...was my mind acknowledging, for the first time ever, that Truce Harding was a handsome, sexy, older guy who cared for me, genuinely sympathized with my life, and wanted very desperately, to fuck the shit out of me. And in that moment when his honey light eyes had revealed his heart, however briefly, I had let him kiss me and my insides had felt runny like eggs.

Summer wasn't around, because she was bedridden with cramps that morning, and Truce and I had went out swimming alone, and it was the first time he'd ever seen me in a bathing suit and I remember being annoyed, wondering--why is he acting so embarrassed about seeing me in a bathing suit? It's just a bathing suit.

But he acted strange that whole morning, watching me sideways and speaking to me in a deeper, more distant voice than usual. It was almost as though he were angry at me, and because I couldn't figure out what I'd done wrong, I felt very bad about it. He also seemed to be flexing the muscular plains of his body and sticking out his chest as though prodding me to verbally acknowledge that he had a great body, which he most certainly did. And then when I did say, "Wow, Mr. Harding. I didn't know you had a body like that"...he said, "What's up with all this Mr. Harding shit? You've known me nearly two years, Naima. Call me Truce."

My sister Tamala and I had already been molested.

When he was kissing me, I felt his finger slide inside my swim panties. But *before he kissed me*, and before I felt all runny inside like eggs, I had stepped on a jellyfish and gotten the sting of my life!

Immediately, our frisbee game came to an end, because I was screaming and hopping around with big tears in my eyes.

It seemed that in one swift motion, Truce had swooped me up in his arms and carried me across the sand to our beach towel, where I lay on my back staring up at the blue sky, as he elevated my right foot and massaged his spit on the jellyfish sting.

"You're not gonna die, Naima", he kept saying, and I cried, saying, "It feels like it." And then, somehow, he looked in my eyes and I saw him as a man for the first time, and...he kissed me.

And then I was crying for a different reason.

I was crying for Summer, who didn't deserve our betrayal, and I was crying for my own confused mind, because no matter how I had convinced myself that I had survived being molested at twelve and gotten past it, the truth was, I was now sick from it, and as Truce Harding pulled down my swim panties and began dragging his tongue quite skillfully between the crack of my firm little girl's peach, I knew that I was only getting sicker.

It felt so good. Having a man eat my pussy for the first time in my life.

In broad daylight with seagulls flying about and the sun shining and cars zooming down the Virginia coastline, as my eyes leaped like dolphins in the clouded blue seas of a clear Atlantic sky, I kept fearing that Summer would suddenly recover from her cramps and mosey on down to the beach with sandwiches for us. Thank God she didn't.

And then when my body spasmed and his very nose it seemed was competing with his tongue for space inside my melting sugar walls--I closed my eyes and prayed to God that I could just be dead, because I knew that Truce would not marry Summer.

He was mines now.

On the drive backhome, I sat in the back seat continuously asking myself, *how could I not have known all this time that we were in love?* (You know--stupid shit a fifteen year old thinks). It's been two years, I told myself. Two years of him tutoring me to read English and comprehend and appreciate the simplicity of it. Two years of playing checkers and nodding our heads in synch while he sampled and cut beats for his rap music. Two years of grabbing a hot link and cabbage together at Morgan's on Georgia Avenue. Two years of him making fun of my fascination with the inhabitants of Bay City on the daytime soap *Another World*. Two years of me riding on "Mr. Harding's back" and innocently giggling, completely unaware that he thought I was the most beautiful and unique girl he had ever met and that his dream in life, as he would later confide to me, was to have an African wife who catered to his every whim and bore him *Jackson-Five*-looking black children with big afros and rich dark complexions.

At fifteen--I just kenw I could do all that. I was so stupid, so naive.

He kept looking at me through the rear view mirror. His gaze devouring my then small young bosom while his heart called on my most private insecurities about how I looked or where I belonged.

We had insecurity in common.

As soon as I got home, before I rushed into my mother's arms or hugged Nana Glodine or kissed my father's cheek, I ran to the bathroom, bolting up the steps and stuck my head in the toiled and vomitted!

That whole evening, as I had dinner with my family and made polite chit chat about my outing with my reading instructor and his girlfriend (both of whom were deeply beloved and appreciated by my family), I kept seeing the face of the family friend who had molested Tamala and I. His dark brown flesh looked pourous as the inside of a meatloaf and his liquid black eyes seemed to regard our own dark brown skin as though we were made of nothing valuable at all. He was meat..and we were meat.

"Baby girl" asked Nana Glodine. "You alright?"

"Oh, yes, Nana. I'm just tired from swimming so much."

"Well at least she answers in English now", said my brother, Albert, and one of my other sisters, Spring, who I wasn't yet as close to as I was Tamala, had commented, "You still have the Russian accent, but you're speaking really well now, Naima."

I smiled proudly as Amethyst winked at me from the end of the table and it took everything inside me not to burst into tears as we all continued to eat the delicious meatloaf that mother had prepared for us.

I was so afraid for them to find out that I was not the perfect little girl--or even a decent one. And when I looked at the other end of the table and saw that my sister Tamala, who had once been a cheerful, talkative, outgoing, little brand new penny of a child...had now become a never-smiling dark older girl who stared only into the plate from which she ate, I felt so utterly helpless and filthy and thoroughly forsaken by God that all I could do was wish the moon would fall out of the sky and stop coming back night after night to lick its silvery tongue at us.

Instead, life went on.

Our parents, two hardworking conscious black people from the south, who literally forced themselves to remain in love so that they could raise their own children, adopt other people's orphans and provide food, shelter and unconditional love to a constant stream of foster children, year in and year out--never forgave themselves for what happened to me and Tamala. In fact, I think they spoiled us rotten as a consequence.

My brother Todd (not his real name) was the only one, out of eight children, who hated my parents. He hated them foremost, because they were black...which burdened him with being black. He hated them, second most, because they had given all their love, time and energy to other people's "*nappyheaded*" (as Todd would hatefully call us) black children.

Our father was a proud and serious black man from the civil rights movement. He believed that it was his responsibility as a man, and especially as a descendent of generations of slaves, to nurture and save the black community as an entity. He never wavered from that committment, and because of him, I continued to receive, right here in

America, the education about race that I had been learning from Pappuh Mahdi in Sudan. The only difference was, instead of learning about archeological artifacts and the history of the Nile, I was now being fed a steady diet of the history of the Black Americans (who to me, were West Africans). I had heard much of it growing up on the Nile from the black Zarpunni women, but never the specific names, laws (Jim Crow), details and incidents that jammed centuries of American rivers with blood and the plantations with chattel and the southern trees with a "strange fruit" as Billie Holiday sang.

For as identical as their experience sounds to the one suffered by southern Blacks in Sudan...it was still far worse than anything I know of in modern Africa. Slaves and oppressed peoples of Sudan retained their tribal names, father's languages, their mother's hymns to hum at night. But the Black American slaves had been truly gut-shanked into virtual "zombies". Their real names, their languages, their African religions, and especially--their umbilical connection to the authentic African womb--had been completely and unceremoniously circumcised from their brains first, and then from their souls. 400 years, you understand. There has never, in human history, been a more complete dehumanization of living people on the planet, because it's one thing to be conquered and put to death, but it's quite another to go on living, century after century, ignorantly regarding ones own flesh as nothing more than a "human stain"--your very mind and soul lost and bedamned in a wilderness of white lies--*forever*.

As my Black American father told me bits and pieces of it, I became obsessed with their history, and from the age of fifteen until my early twenties, it was all that I studied with any real commitment or passion. I studied it, because I already knew it.

I spent years in the psychiatrist's office. First with a white woman that I didn't like, but who meant well, when I was nine and ten. I didn't like her, because as I had come to notice about white women in the Black community--just as in Africa, they tried to co-opt and play the savior of a Black man or a Black child--but never the Black woman. This Arabic-speaking Irish-Scottish psychiatrist, who was guilt-ridden about the treatment of blacks in America and overly romantic about Africans, tried to compete with my new Black American mother for my confidence and my loyalty. It was as though she wanted me to see *her* as my mother, with me as her African rescue project (as white women are known to do), and then when I clammed up on her, she started flirting with my father, right in front of me on the days that he would come for me, totally disrespecting our newly formed bonds as a family unit and using me, a child, as her foil. She was a patronizing two-faced bitch with a big warm smile and a desperate need to be seen by Black people as some great all-loving white angel, so as you can imagine, I didn't get much psychiatric help, and after I told Amethyst about her flirting with my father, and after Amethyst confronted her (we never told mother), I never had to go back.

After the molestation, however, I was placed with an excellent...*excellent!* psychiatrist, Dr. Diallo, a Senegalese, who studied me from about thirteen until about eighteen. He was very laid back but strict, with a gaze so invasive it almost hypnotized me. He would often get furious and demand of me, "What are you leaving out, Naima?"

Of course, I never told him everything that went on in my life (such as Truce eating my snatch on the beach when I was fifteen). In fact, I never did tell him about Truce officially becoming my boyfriend when I was sixteen. Dr. Diallo was an old fashioned African husband and father, and he would have told my parents.

I knew, however, that Dr. Diallo was in tune with me, because he would say to me, "You have such a beautiful spirit, Naima...why do you think you're not a good girl?" That man could read me. He once told my parents, "She's a very lovely person, because she'd rather live in a make believe world. One that she herself can make up and control. It's not your fault that she's still anti-social after mastering English."

One day, he instructed me, "I want you to start writing a diary. Just notes each day to yourself about anything at all...anything you like. But it's not a normal diary, because at the end of each week, I want you to read the diary...and then take the pages for that week and burn them. That way you can let go of the days in your past and make room for new experiences, but with confidence."

Yet, because I couldn't understand or believe the life I was living, and because it was too painful for me to dwell on it, I never wrote about myself. Instead, I created imaginary friends to write about and that was how I physically began the process of writing things down, burning the first draft and then rewriting it the next week. The hunger for it, however, as a serious art form, came another way.

At fourteen, my Aunt Zola had left a worn paperback on our laundry porch, a book called *"Jaqueline Susann's Valley of the Dolls."* That was the first book I ever read in my life and it was the bomb! I read it four times that same year and probably ten times in my whole lifetime. It wasn't serious literature--in fact, it's widely regarded as trash--but it's also one of the ultimate classics in BubbleGum Pop Literature, gossipy, engrossing and fun to read, and because of that book--I assumed that all books were that entertaining and decided that I would make books my new best friends. This is important, because the second book I read literally changed my life.

It was called *"The Bluest Eye"* by Toni Morrison, and when I first saw the book (on my sister Spring's dressing table), I was both fascinated and frightened by it. The sad-faced dark girl on the cover looked like a Sudanese to me and when I flipped the book over and saw the author's photograph, her face startled me, because although she did not look exactly like my Auntie Ramah back home in Omdurman, she greatly reminded me of Ramah and other Sudanese women. Her yam-yellow lightskinned complexion and her thick West African facial features seemed to be calling me to the book and for a whole two weeks, before I ever read a word of it, I just stared everyday at Toni Morrison's picture and tried to remember where I knew her from, because I was sure that I knew her (or my people back home knew her), and to me, at that age, I thought that she was the most beautiful woman in the world. She soon replaced Diana Ross as my beauty ideal.

I read *"The Bluest Eye"* in one long, emotional, gut-wrenching night. And then I played sick the next morning so that I could stay home from school and read it again. As I have often stated in interviews...reading that book was the first time since I'd been in America that I felt that anyone had told me the truth, the whole truth and nothing but the truth, and if I should ever be a writer--that's how I wanted my books to read. Raw and truthful, yet tender. And *"The Bluest Eye"* is not, as my beloved Oprah Winfrey and others have described it--the story of a little black girl who wants blue eyes. Instead, it's the story of *"WHY"* a little charcoal black girl trapped amongst Black Americans wants blue eyes. And it is really, truly, the story of Black Americans themselves, as a displaced and psychologically abused people in this country. I realized, reading the novel, that I was becoming one of them and that I had been sent here by God to read that novel. I thought about it incessantly and realized that it wasn't just the story of the Black Americans, but was the story of all authentic Black people who had either been enslaved or colonized and were still living. It was definitely the story of the Nubians back in Sudan and their chronic self-hatred and it was what I had known even before my Egyptian grandmother put me up for adoption, but it had never been tangible or so clearly admitted to until I read Morrison's book.

So it was Toni Morrison who made me want to be a writer, because after you've read letters from a person in hell--you have to try to prove that there is a God by writing back. That's what real literature and art is all about--that endless search for sincerity. But frankly, back in those days, I never thought that I had enough talent to be taken seriously as a writer. I was fourteen, fifteen and sixteen, reading masterful works by Alice Walker (who would later have an even bigger influence on me than Morrison), Richard Wright, Sylvia Plath, Jean Toomer, Gloria Naylor, Gwendolyn Brooks, Mari Evans, Sherwood Anderson, Chinua Achebe, Mark Twain, Gayl Jones, Mariama Ba-- nothing I attempted to write was on their level of brilliance, so unfortunately, I would go on to waste my valuable time as men convinced me that I was pretty enough to be a model and an actress. In fact, I never went to college, because one morning when I was seventeen, I woke up in the body of a chocolate-covered Playboy bunny (which is a lot of easy fun) and I got sidetracked by powerful men. More on that later.

But thank you, Dr. Diallo. Thank you for trying so hard to help me discover my authentic self. God knows that I made all the wrong decisions.

For instance, I turned to Truce Harding when Amethyst left my life. Once I could speak good English and no longer needed an interpreter in the home, my Aunt Beverly was not inclined to keep paying for Amethyst to be there--and let me also mention, that I learned a lot of my English from watching daytime soap operas, most notably *The Doctors* and *Another World*, but especially *Another World*, where I loved Rachel Cory and Mac and Felicia and Cass and deliciously wicked Cecile to the point that they were like family to me. But anyway, Amethyst, had also met and fallen in love with a handsome Belgian pediatrician at Georgetown University and was engaged to become his wife. I remember the tears running down both our faces and the sweet coconut smell of her long, curly Spanish-like hair as she hugged me goodbye. Our whole family stood in sadness that day, because after seven years of living in the bedroom overlooking the driveway, Amethyst had become like a beautiful swan-like angel who brought good luck and tranquility to our home. My mother and Nana objected bitterly that she was marrying a white man, but they wished her well just the same and cried as she left us. Her pretty vanilla face folding into the melancholy museum of my mind as a yellow taxi carried her out of the ghetto and to the airport.

Truce Harding promised me that night, "I'll never leave you, Naima. One day you're going to be my wife. Then I can touch you...and make you a woman. Do you want to be a woman, Naima?"

I remember giving a captivated nod.

We weren't going together yet, because my parents would have put him in prison if they had known what he was trying to do, but we grew closer and closer in a very illicit and secret friendship that I became psychologically dependent upon. He was no longer tutoring me in reading, but because of him and Summer being so close to my family, we saw each other at least three days a week plus weekends. Gradually, as the months went by, Truce became cold towards Summer and she faded out of our lives without ever knowing how sick I was.

After the incident on the beach, it would be two years before he touched me again.

We didn't kiss or hold hands or play wrestle. He claimed he was waiting to marry me, because he required that his wife be a virgin on her wedding night, and I believed him. In the meantime, he explained that because he was already a sexually experienced adult male--his body needed sex. He said that he would have to see other girls, but only on rare occasions, to satisfy his sexual needs. To that I agreed.

I thought I was in love with him and I couldn't wait for the day when he would eat me out again. *That*...I could get addicted to. I was also fascinated by the power a woman has when a man so desperately desires her. Truce was dominant (which is how I like my men) and in control of our relationship, but as tthe same time, I knew that he was the one who was weak, not me. He had to have me. He seemed to regard my virginity as a conquest that would rank even more important than his graduation from Howard University. He always asked, "Do you love me, little girl?"

And I always cooed, "Yes...*daddy.*"

I couldn't wait for him to fuck me. I touched myself and dreamt about it every night for two years, and all throughout that time, when we would talk on the phone and he would whisper the question, "Whose pussy is that?", I would whisper back, "Yours...*daddy.*"

I couldn't wait to be his wife. Nana Glodine was already teaching me to cook smothered pork chops with macaroni and cheese and cheddar crab apple biscuits--his favorit meal.

When I turned sixteen, a series of shocking events transpired. First, Summer popped up at our house. She wanted to introduce us to her new boyfriend, and during the course of her visit, she revealed to my mother, Nana Glodine and I the reason for her breakup with Truce. She claimed that she had wanted to dust and vaccum his apartment at the college towers one afternoon and had dropped by while he was supposed to be in class, but when she opened the door and walked in, she found her openly gay brother, Russell, on his knees sucking Truce's dick.

Now that left us speechless, we didn't know what to say, but after Summer was gone, my mother telephoned Truce and had him come over to the house. She told him what Summer had claimed and he became indignant, dismissing it as a lie. He said that Summer was just taking revenge for him having called the engagement off. He kept saying to my mother, "Do I look like some kinda faggot to you, Mrs. Johnson?"

In the meantime, everybody was trying to fix Truce up with a new woman and this was how I came to discover the reason that Truce had never allowed me to meet his mother, Althea Countess Harding. Both my mother and Mrs. Harding tried desperately to fix Truce up with a new woman and I had to giggle in silence, because by then, Truce had officially made me his girlfriend by giving me his Dunbar High School ring and the very first O.G. Truce jackets that his rap group used for promoting their personal appearances around D.C. As his future wife, I felt confident in my position.

But then the bomb dropped when Truce revealed to me that he came from a special high society of upper class white-looking blacks who lived in Georgetown since the early 1900's. He called them "Boules" or "blues veins" and said that they retained their status by carefully marrying other educated, lightskinned blue veins (the skin being so light that you could see their veins through their wrists). His mother, he explained, was the color of light egg nog with "good hair" and was determined that Truce keep the Harding bloodline unblemished by marrying either ...pay attention...a non-black woman (*as long as she wasn't white*) or...an extremely lightskinned black woman who *looked* white. And they had been doing this for a hundred years and calling themselves "black" people. Anyway--Amethyst would have been perfect as Truce's wife, according to his mother's rules, but Summer, who as I told you was a dead ringer for Jada Pinkett Smith-- was considered a shade too tanned and too ethnic looking. As lightskinned as Truce already was, I found it remarkable that his mother admonished him on a daily basis about finding a wife with the proper genetics, and after having been put up for adoption by my own colorist grandmother, it delighted me that I would indirectly get revenge on snot-colored bitches like her--by producing *Jackson-5* looking babies to fuck up Mrs. Harding's daisy chain.

Truce's mother held a formal dinner to introduce him to a white looking mixed race debutante named Willow Wellington while my own mother introduced him to a high yellow, nappyheaded girl on our street named Rachel, and my father tried to hook him up with yet another lightskinned girl who worked at the pharmacy named Zenobia.

All around, color became an issue that gripped our family.

My brother Todd had been , for years, taking the subway out to Maryland in the great hope that he could secure himself a white girlfriend. He and his friends, his posse, would openly joke about using *"black Ho's with low self-esteem"* for sex whenever they could and then save their date money for white girls, because as my brother so often said--the best sex he ever had was with a black, nappyheaded round the way girl, but true love could only be found with a white one. In all honesty, I have to tell you that as much as my brother and his black buddies delighted in putting down black girls--the real fact is--they didn't know any black girls, because they wouldn't let themselves. And, tragically, America is overrun with these type of black males who make it a point not to know any black women--yet constantly demonize and degrade them. But anyway, Todd irritated my mother to no end by plastering his bedroom walls (a room that he shared with two of our younger brothers) with posters of Pamela Anderson, Brooke Shields, the Dallas Cowboy Cheerleaders and any other sexy woman who was non-black. He also constantly advised our younger brothers to "never date black women" and would call me and Tamala, the two dark skinned daughters (Spring was highest yellow), "nappyhead Ho's" (my oldest brother, Curlom, had punched him twice for it). My mother did the worst thing a mother could do by constantly nagging him, because eventually, it turned violent.

She found a truly sweet and pretty lightskinned girl at our church named Malika Simmons and kept inviting the girl to our house so that she and Malika's mother could get Todd to realize how worthy some black women (yellow ones anyway) could be, but he became increasingly indignant at being set up (which I didn't blame him, because he was a grown man now) and--he one day made the mistake of saying to my mother's face, "The only thing a black woman can do for me *is suck my dick.*"

Well.

My father came home from work and wanted to know why my mother was staring into dishwater with tears running down her cheeks and he wanted to know why Nana Glodine sat in the backyard coring apples at dusk, her dark elderly face steeped in heartbreak. *The only thing a black woman can do for me is suck my dick.* My sisters and I told my father, as soon as he walked through the door, what Todd had said to mother and Nana and my daddy dropped his lunch bucket and rushed up to Todd's bedroom.

Within moments, we heard the sound of our father bashing Todd in the face with his fist. He yelled out, "How dare you disrespect my wife and my mother, you sick twisted sorry motherfucker!"

BAM! "Don't you know the black woman is the queen goddess of the earth!?" My father worshipped black women.

BAM!

My mother ran upstairs screaming out, *"Marvin don't hit my baby!",* and Todd tried to fight back, but my father beat the living daylights out of him. We heard daddy say, "Pack your shit and move the fuck out, nigga."

By then we had all rushed upstairs to stop dad from murdering Todd, but Todd had grabbed a pocket knife from somewhere, and although blinded by tears of rage, was trying desperately to stab our father. He kept shouting, "I hate you, you monkey motherfucker...I hate all of you! *You're nothing but country-ass niggers!*"

My mother grabbed my father and demanded, "Marvin--let him go. Let him go."

"As far as I'm concerned, you're no longer my son, Todd", my dad stated resolutely, and even though Todd really did hate our family, I could tell that he was sorry for what he'd done, but it was too late. He had to go--especially before my oldest brother, Curtom, got home.

This, of course, wasn't the first time that our dad had been outraged by Todd's hostility against the women in our family. There had been another incident, years earlier, when Todd had been ashamed to have Nana Glodine pick him up from the private school that reliable Aunt Beverly (another black woman) paid for him to go to. He told our father, right to his face, that he was embarrassed of Nana, because all the white and biracial kids made jokes about her "spud" shaped nose and country accent. Todd said to our father's face--"But you gotta admit, dad...Nana's ugly."

He never seemed to realize how deeply that hurt our father, and for some odd reason, it never occured to him that dad would love his own country-talk'n, Baptist church-going, African-nosed chocolate to the bone mother more than anybody in this world. I guess because Todd didn't love our own wonderful mother, he couldn't relate.

And so he moved out and a year later--he found a white girl in Maryland who was willing to marry him, and to my astonishment, she didn't look a thing like the gorgeous white women who had hung on his bedroom wall like trophies. She was fat (something he mercilessly derided black women for) and her face, framed by oily, mousy brown hair, looked bloated and piggish. But she was white as a fish belly.

A year after that, my mother's heart really broke (all our hearts broke), because Albert--her good son who had always appreciated her struggle and loved her (and us) deeply--married a Korean girl who hadn't even finished high school and who had been known for sleeping around. Although black girls far outnumbered boys in our community,

Albert claimed that there just weren't any good black girls to choose from. I'll never forget the hurt I felt as I heard my brother rattle off what was wrong with _all_ black women except us--too much attitude; too materialistic; too uncultured; "dumb" and too fat.

Our D.C. area neighborhoods, however, were crawling (over populated) with a great many beautiful black girls, ranging all shades, who were intelligent, church-going, very friendly and open hearted (_white people see them all the time!_), stylish, as cultured as any black man and yet _less_ materialistic...than most black men.

So in my gut, I knew what the real truth was...black girls were _too black_--and out of desperation to have us accept his choice, Albert resorted to using the stereotypes that Todd had taught him to dismiss the over abundance of eligible black girls (tons of pretty black girls wanted Todd and Albert both)--to blame them for him choosing another race. And the sad irony is, my oldest brother Curtom, who father named after the Curtis Mayfield record label "Curtom Records", but who _looks white_ (he was adopted), was always pursuing and wooing black girls and was routinely rejected, because the black girls were so determined to prove their loyalty to "_the black man_", and like me, didn't see biracial Curtom as a true black man (*he became a brain surgeon and eventually did marry a beautiful dark brown sister). But in America, I realized that the color problem was a hundred times worse than it is in Sudan--because the black people here don't have tribes or secluded territory to run back to. They have no core identity to fight for.

For those reading this 100 years from now, let me say that all Black women come from African blood, so most of them don't have long, naturally flowing hair like the women in movies, television commercials and the women of the NBA. Most Black Americans don't seem to realize that _long flowing hair_ simply isn't a natural biological characteristic for authentic black women, and of course, there has _NEVER_ been a single Pre-colonial society in Africa, not even Egypt or

Ethiopia, where long hair was a standard of beauty (at least not before 1990), but in America, the standards for femininity were different, and I noticed that one of the major standards of Europeans was they considered *"dark"* to be masculine and *"light"* to be feminine. Therefore, the Black man's mother was automatically, because of her color, seen as less feminine than all other women--and more importantly, she was *"socialized"* to see herself as less feminine and so were her sons--to the point that Black Americans were brainwashed (and this is happening in Africa now, too). The authentic Black woman's short African hair (the crown and one true hair that only our race possesses) was portrayed as--an abnormality--when placed beside other races of women's flowing silkish hair. And so, in the Black Community, the <u>purest</u> black woman was the person who was looked down upon and as much as possible, disallowed (to borrow Toni Morrison's accurate word). And through her destruction and disallowment--the Black man was conquered and re-programmed and destroyed through his own desire to be competitve with the white man's standards.

All men rule through their women--and by helping to destroy the authentic Black woman, the Black man (during my era) lost his true chance at ruling himself or competing with the rest of the world as an independent power and world ruler. By choosing non-black women, he was always at a disadvantage--borrowing somebody else's woman and somebody else's genetics. Always beholden to some other man's race and will. But at the same time--duped into thinking that he had something great--as long as it wasn't black. So this time in history--his downfall was his own fault.

While Black men were celebrated no matter what their color was, their wives and girlfriends were usually "light-skinned" Black women. In fact, in every forum of Black American life that I had witnessed from the day I arrived, the females who were treated with the most respect and were allowed to hold positions of authority and were celebrated by Black men were overwhelmingly lightskinned, and before 2000, usually *less authentic* than the women they were born from. Many, many in the Black Community will try to deny my invectives--but one only has to pick up a history book of any type with photos or watch a black movie or the music videos that black people made to *see* with your own eyes that I'm telling the truth.

And because there are so many Black Americans who believe that bitch in New York Harbor is their real mother--and not--the African woman, they can't imagine why it's any of my business or why I would be so offended or would dare...would dare...have anything to say. But the fact remains--they came out of *my black ass*--I didn't come out of theirs. And my love for them needs no explanation.

NONE.

I love the Black Americans, because I love myself, and because although many other Africans are ignorant and disconnected...I am fully aware that in a symbolic sense, I am the motherseed of the Black Americans, the Jamaicans, the Haitians, the Brazil blacks, all Black people everywhere.

Being *raised* by Black Americans...forced me to see that race and color does matter, greatly.

So anyway, I wasn't surprised when our beloved Albert married a Korean girl and tried to explain it away by claiming..."*there are no good black women to choose*"...other than his mother, Nana and sisters. Millions of black men, nationwide, mostly through shacking up or moving to non-traditional neighborhoods, would soon be making the same stereotypical claims, and not only that, but many Whites and Non-

Blacks would begin to feel comfortable in making the same insulting comments about the Black man's motherseed and her experience being black and female in a society designed exclusively to accomodate the White man's mother. Black women were simply dismissed as "bitter" and "jealous". Terms that no one ever called Martin Luther King or Malcolm X when they had stood up in public and demanded to be treated with fairness and equality, and although millions of *Black* women had made it possible for Dr. King and Malcolm to achieve their goals, and had given their lives for the goals of those black men--there were no black men proposing a "revolution" to save the honor or rescue the genetic beauty of the Black woman. My soul shrunk and spasmed at the sight of Black men, who for 500 years had never protected Black women, suddenly rising up and protecting and defending the honor of the White man's mother, and especially if it was a black woman in an argument with a white woman--then the white man's mother had to be protected and shown favoritism. We black females were just "bitches and Ho's and golddiggers"--by virtue of our skin color and hair texture, and curiously--the White WOMEN who so often used the mouths they ate with to call us "Sister" while depending on us to help swell their numbers in their bullshit feminist organizations, were the first to join the black man in lying on and demonizing us--completely discounting and dismissing our experience after *hundreds of years* of living as slave women and molestation chattel in *her* putrid and overrated shadow. That's why I don't give a fuck what Oprah Winfrey says--the White woman is not my goddamned sister. Maybe my friend at times, maybe even a *beloved* favorite friend (as I do have white women in my life that I love), but as a group internationally, there is no sister in White women. I'm sorry, Oprah and Alice Walker and all the rest--but I come from Africa--I know what the word "*sister*" means. The white woman is the most selfish, pretentious two-faced bitch that ever set foot on God's green earth. Of all whites, she benefits the most from White

122

Supremacy--she protects it (by denying and protecting colorism--colorism being the root activator in racism and the thing she's *most afraid* to talk about). She promotes her agenda in non-black communities whether they be Black, Latino, Indian or Asian--under the guise that she's our savior--and at the same times preaches "one love, one humanity".

The White man (who has singlehandedly turned this planet into a living hell--*but still*--is no more devil than any of the other men on earth), has conquered and pimped this planet for the wellbeing (by any means necessary) of his White family--has forced the whole world to bow at his white mother's feet and has treated his white woman better than most other races of men have treated theirs--and yet how many times have we witnessed a white woman sit up on our livingroom sofa--because she's bored and has no culture of her own--sit up and vow her allegiance to black people by making hateful jokes about *"the evil patriarchal white man"* and his iddy-bitty white dick? Be honest--how many times have whole livingrooms full of black people and *"A"* white woman sat up and laughed their ass off while she bemoaned the *"dickless, no-fucking bore"* of a white man and how she's been his "slave" and "second class citizen" for thousands of years and how she's about to do us morally superior black folks a big favor by giving us her life--all that bullshit.

Of course, black folk are always gullible and stupid enough to feel some victory in watching her stabbing her own father in the back, watching her go where she can have her asshole licked by self-hating black men, because the white man has earned the right to think he's too superior to stoop that low--but somehow, neither she nor the black people see the *circle of self-destruction* as they take "racism" and <u>make it worse</u>--make it worse by splintering and complicating it and creating more deceit and confusion rather than embracing the truth--that black people already have their place (Africa), already have their savior

123

(the temple of what's most familiar) and are most beautiful--*most beautiful*--when sporting their own god-given black faces.

They don't need her (the white woman) for shit--and she knows that--so her greatest fear is that they (the niggerstock) will someday wake up and realize that it's her who needs *them*.

<u>WORD:</u>

People in America are so afraid of the truth, and because of that, they try to categorize me as some crazy militant African who "hates" white women and hates white people. That's camelshit. *Total camelshit!* I am not militant; I am not bitter.

I'm just not a nigger. I have no desire...to be white.

I love God. I *believe* in God.

I love all races of human beings, including my white brothers and sisters, and I believe God requires that we love each other--*I truly do*--but I'm nobody's goddamned fool and in order for anyone to read and comprehend this book--they're going to have to understand the complexity of where I'm coming from...because I don't hate anybody for their race, sex or sexual orientation. Just because a Black woman loves herself and tells *her truth*, as she experienced it, in public does not mean she's bitter or hates anyone--and white people and black men make those accusations to silence a Black woman, to keep her from standing up for herself, to control her. But you see, I'm not from here--I have no problem killing the white man, the white woman, the black man...*anyone*...who's against Africa and against the birth of my sweet black babies that *GOD gave me*! to protect.

I am an African woman and the Black man (in general) has "<u>betrayed</u>" the Black Woman--so my loyalty now is to my womb. It's not that I don't love black men (I truly do--he is the only dream I've ever had)--but I just don't have the same respect for a black man who wants to be white, who neglects black children and sells out Africa,

124

and I am apt to say shitty things, as I rightfully should, because no matter how much the White woman's image is risen up by the Americans and the authentic Black woman's image "disallowed" and misrepresented by a watered down mulatto...no matter how far away the Black man in America gets from his true identity and his natural mate--the fact remains that *I* am the Black man's mother and that *I* have been his god-given wife, queen, concubine, daughter, sister, aunt and the voice of his heart for 26,000 years, and before the living...*tima sijil*...the alight of nature's mind, heart and scrotum of God, from where our images were dreamt into being--we, the Africans--the genesis of vision itself, by God. I am the African woman.

I don't need your fucking permission to kill or give birth to my man. I am the black woman, and every God there is became a God through me, because there was no place else...to come from.

I know who I am. I'm not America's nigger, not your bitch, not your HO--you better know...what you *used* to know.

If you Americans call yourselves human beings--then you should understand that.

And when I speak of the White woman, it is not with jealousy or hatred or bitterness...but with truth, love and *pity*. As my Aunt Kem and so many other African women taught me when I was a little girl growing up in Sudan: *"Take pity...on the white woman. Everything she has, including what she thinks of herself...is at the expense of someone else."*

And the African women were right.

 *virginity*

Anyway, I began bringing these issues up to Truce and he was embarrassed (as are so many Black people worldwide) and in denial about them, seeming to believe that only his "high yellow" mother or only his Georgetown family were colorist and not the entire culture. Despite his mother's admonition that Summer's Jada Pinkett Smith looks were too ethnic and neither light or neutral enough for a proper Boule family--he insisted that I was beautiful and that my dark brown complexion and Nilotic ethnicity were completely accepted and desired by him. He felt that I was too analytical about our "secret love boo" and that love would conquer all.

O

When I turned seventeen, we ended up kissing in the back of his car one night and found that neither of us could wait any longer--I laid on my back and caressed, with an excited fear, the hardness of his thick, throbbing penis as he finally got it out and positioned it between my legs, and then as he tried to penetrate my virginity--I screamed as though I were a dolphin being harpooned! The pain was so intense that seizures gripped my brain and my eyes rolled back in my head and my flesh turned like rubber and Truce found his penis not only bruised by the tightness, but also, trapped inside.

"Let my dick go!", he hollered in agony, but the seizure had me paralyzed. I could have very well swallowed my tongue.

I had to be hospitalized that night, because neither of us had realized the special difficulties of Nile River vaginal circumcision. To put it in the vulgar words that Truce used--"Your pussy is so tight, it's barely there!"

My menstral cycle changed after that and I began to experience an elongated period (five to seven days long) and severe cramping (I wasn't pregnant). On many days, I could not get out of bed, and yet, I couldn't tell Nana Glodine or my mother what had happened.

But it kept happening. The kissing; him sucking my titties. The fingerbanging.

All that and I still wasn't de-virginized.

Obviously, I had to learn how to perform fellatio (sucking a man's dick). According to the prognosis that the doctors gave concerning my sexual future, I would have to develop alternative ways to please a man, because intercourse would be painful if I wasn't willing to have some kind of operation to correct the stitch ritual. But, tearfully, I tried to make the doctors and my parents understand that the vaginal cut/stitch was the only thing I had that connected me to Mommysweet, and that I couldn't change it. I told the doctors that I would just have to live with the pain, and that's what I've done all these years.

I became an expert at giving Truce head. I really enjoyed it, too.

But then, eventually, after many, many attempts--he finally got his penis inside me. I thought I was literally going to split open, and he couldn't really move it around, but it was inside me and it felt like his entire knee and thigh was up in there. As he struggled to pull it back out, I fainted.

"Damn, that's some good pussy", he would always whisper as we plied it open little by little, week by week, and then he would bury his face in it and eat for hours, loving it more and more with each passing month.

And then one day, out of the blue...he was able to fuck me at a pace, and I remember digging my fingers in his back and crying, moaning out loud as he held me down and bucked inside, stabbing and stabbing. I screamed and screamed, shouting his name as hot tears ran down my face and into the carpet of his apartment at the Towers across from Howard. Someone called the police, because they were convinced that some college kids were slaughtering an animal in one of the apartments, perhaps as part of some silly satanical ritual. In no time, the police were banging on our door. It was embarrassing and I remember how stupid I sounded telling the police, "This is my future husband."

By July of 1988, my *"future husband"* would be facing twenty years in prison and my whole family would come crashing down around my ankles. It started, first, with the murder of my brother, Todd. White police officers found him dead on a dark road in Maryland with a bullet in his head. They tried to claim that Todd was the victim of a drug deal gone wrong, but no one in our family was willing to believe that Todd had ever picked up a drug, and the autopsy proved us right. Nana Glodine insisted that the police themselves had "lynched" Todd for marrying a white girl, but there was no way to prove it, and quite frankly, there were only four people in our family who even cared that Todd was dead--my mother, Nana Glodine, Aunt Beverly and Albert. Only they went to the funeral. My father was angry about the circumstnaces surrounding his son's murder, but still, he confided to us that in his heart, Todd had been dead since the day he'd been kicked out of our house.

Two weeks after Todd's funeral, drama hit the family once more as Albert's Korean wife caught him in a motel with a white girlfriend that she trusted. Our whole family took a switch to Albert's ass and roundly condemned him, because his wife had just given birth three months prior to a healthy baby boy, but then in the midst of a heated argument, his Korean wife announced that Albert was not the father of her baby--*Albert's best friend Kozy was the baby's daddy*! I thought my mother, who was in love with the baby then, would have a heart attack. The Korean sister-in-law disappeared but left her baby at my mother's house and hasn't been heard from since. I for one thought the whole thing was immature and hilarious, but before I could have a good belly laugh...my ass my next.

The police picked up Truce Harding for statutory rape. The victim was a thirteen year old girl from the low income housing projects in Berry's Farm, S.E. All around our neighborhood, people kept exclaiming, "...*thirteen*!" and shaking their heads in disbelief. The blood in my heart turned to ice water when I discovered that she had a one month old baby, which DNA tests had proven was fathered by Truce, and that her mother claimed that Truce had been dating the girl for well over a year by then.

I layed in my bed for a week and couldn't move before Nana Glodine burst in one day, my tattletale sister Tamala trembling behind her, and demanded, "Is that nigga been mess'n wit 'choo, baby girl? Neh you tell Nana da truth, heah?"

Nana Glodine immediately called a family meeting. "I want that boy strung up by his balls, you heah me Marvin? All these years we been trust'n that no account weasel, think'n he was some kinda read'n teacha!"

"I'll take care of it, mother." My father was diabolically upset.

My mother chimed in with, "I want his ass *up under* the jail, Marvin!"

I got a terrible whipping that night for not telling that I was being molested again. I had not seen it as molestation. Nana Glodine picked the switches (thin vines) from the backyard and ripped off the leaves herself. Nana was like an African woman--she believed in burning the hair out of combs and making gravy out of the pot liquor from greens. So she sure did hand my daddy those switches and told him, "Whoop her tail good". Then my father, tears streaming down his cheeks, gave me the first beating of my life. I barely cried, because it was mild compared to what I had seen other kids get, and for the look of disappointment in my father's eyes, I deserved it.

I wouldn't cooperate with the police. My parents reminded me that Truce didn't really love me, because he'd been seeing this other girl for over a year and telling her the same lies he told me. I knew that better than anyone. Truce Harding had ripped the very life out of my soul. I had trusted him with my virginity and in return he left me a whore and a fool, but still, I wouldn't cooperate. The police played a demo of one of Truce's rap songs for me and my parents. It was called something like *"Jailbait Ho, Be My Queen"*. With tears in my eyes, I kept insisting, "I'm not like that project hoochie. I wasn't molested. I'm engaged to be his wife."

"That'll be enough for the jury", the police told my parents.

Two days later, it was discovered that Truce had also been having sex with one of his backup singers, a girl I knew named Shanika. But I had no idea that Shanika was only sixteen. I had thought she was a grown woman--like me.

I tell you, I was sick.

I packed up a duffle bag and ran away from home, because I couldn't bare to sit in a court and testify against him. I didn't like the police (because of their routine crookedness in the black community) and I didn't trust the legal system. I took all my allowance savings, which over the years had amounted to nearly seven hundred dollars, and I hit the Greyhound with my friend Audrey. For legal reasons, I can't tell too much about her, but she was young and black like me and she was basically the child of a single parent who didn't love her.

In running away, I worried about my mother, of course, because she had taken ill after Todd's murder. I wrote a note saying:

Don't worry. I'm fine with friends. I can't put Truce in Prison. Will call you after you calm down.

And that was when my life seemed to take flight without me.

Me and Audrey got off the bus in a place called Lake Fairfax, Virginia...and the local firemen were holding a beauty contest...and I strolled into town *and won*! I kid you not. They had this big circle of cars, jeeps and vans with their headlights turned on--and all the girls had to parade in front of the headlights with bikinis on and stuff. It was like being a hoochie in a music video, and adding to the fever of my teen girl rebellious tension was the fact that these were all White men--which was like landing on Mars for me and Audrey. Those White men wanted to fuck us so bad. They put a sash across my perfect-breasted, plum-booty, tiny waisted bikini clad cocoa body that read: *Miss Fire and Safety--August 1988*. I had won!

Efrem Nelkin, the forty-three year old businessman who would soon replace Truce as my lover, watched from the Budweiser and Heineken filled judge's jeep as they crowned me with a dingy yellow and black fireman's hat. I had immediately noticed Efrem Nelkin's icy blue stare, because he had been the only judge who wasn't clapping when I had won. He was the only person in the entire "headlight" pageant who seemed to be literally hypnotized by me, and another shock for me as a ghetto girl--was discovering that white men are less colorstruck than Black American men are. They love dark girls.

I was seventeen and the *attention* from these foreign-yet-familiar by way of t.v. white men was so intense that it was palpable. I'm a naturally sensuous person (I just am), but because of all the attention, I think I was fantasizing that I was a white blond girl.

Of course, Black Americans are "domestically <u>conservative</u>" people, devoutly connected to "church", to "sexism" (as are Africans) and especially scapegoat and loathe the black female in comparison to their excuse-making for black male human frailty, so this is the part of my life that hardcore Kola Boof fans don't like to read about...because of Efrem being a White Jew; because of my racially motivated abortion. But what can I say...you plan your future and life steps in.

The fact that Efrem was a married man and was old enough to be my father is not something I'm proud of at all, but still, I can't forget that it was Efrem Nelkin who plucked me from the apple tree and then planted me all over again.

He brought the whole world out of me.

Goddess of Trees

CAIRO, EGYPT
1994

BintSaro, my very kind maid, poured me a lime margarita and lit me one of those long, brown cigarettes I used to crave--a MORE green, imported from America. I blush now now remembering that I actually used to smoke cigarettes (starting with Virginia Slims, then Benson and Hedges Light 100s, then KOOL Super Longs, then MORE, then back to Benson and Hedges Light 100s, then Marlboro in the Red Pack, then GPC in the red pack). *Truly*! It seems like another life.

I remember Egypt and how different it looked to me as an adult. I remember standing naked on my penthouse terrace, sipping the lime cloud margarita, puffing my cigarette, running my hand through my hair and thinking that I was very right to have aborted Efrem's baby, because after all, why bring a child into the world if I myself would not be braveenough to stay in the world and look after it?

This particular night I'm telling you about--this was the night that I tried to kill myself, which by the way, is also an act that requires enormous courage or insanity (or both).

"If there's nothing more, I'm leaving now", said BintSaro.

"Of course, darling...goodnight."

I had kissed her on the cheek, intimately.

"Are you alright, Miss Kitar? You're so dramatic this evening. It's like a play."

O ⅃

Egypt was red that night.

The vermilion sky seeming like paper mache against the sand colored poor houses, the eggshell white city buildings, the palm trees. Every blood in the world seemed to be splashing inside the bellys of Cairo's fat, lazy mosquitoes, but then again, it might have been the fact that I'd had twelve margaritas that day. I was drunk and feverish.

Todi (his nickname), a high ranking *black* member of Egypt's government as well as the man wo paid for my penthouse each month, arrived around ten thirty and slipped out of his shoes, fixed himself a White Russian and then sat in his favorite chair while I knelt naked between his legs and gave him "American" (Egyptian slang for "blowjob"). He hummed along to my Al Green songs and slid his vodka-covered fingers between the crack of my ass while I sucked. The alcohol burned my pussy, but as usual, I was grateful to perform fellatio and not have to endure the pain of intercourse.

I stood up with tears when it was over, because I couldn't quite understand how I had ended up where I was.

I was lost. I was without God. I had fucked up my life.

~~

After Todi's orgasm and my pretense at being grateful to taste it,

135

he told me that he had a present for me. He reached into his briefcase and came up with a movie script. Only the year before, March of 1993, I had turned twenty-one and received the declaration making me a Citizen of the United States of America. Two months before that, I stood in the crowd at President Clinton's inaugaration as my heart and mind soared with pride at hearing one of my idols, Maya Angelou, read her now classic American poem, *"On the Pulse of Morning"*, and also a sense of wonder at seeing in person what a classy, beautiful and stately woman Angelou managed to be--even in old age. Like me, she had no college education and yet had endured the experience of growing up a misplaced child, taller than most other girls (which was a complex for me, too, as by age twenty, I surpassed six feet in height) and her romantic past, to be polite, had been marked by prematurity. Angelou wrote of being an unwed teenaged mother, a runaway, a cook, an exotic dancer and a "pimp" long before she had reinvented herself in the mold of her authentic spirit and found purpose in her life by tapping into the talents of her soul--something that I thought, I too, could do.

I determined that I would create black women movie stars.

So I had copied Angelou by running off, back to the land of my birth father's family and his ancestors. Being that I spoke Arabic and was half Egyptian, I thought that I could outrun the racism of Hollywood and American Nigger media (light skinned or biracial women being overly represented, beautiful authentic black women of *child-bearing age* being disallowed as leading ladies). By becoming a filmmaker in North Africa, the qualifications, I imagined would be far less exlusionary than the ones that seemed to keep me from expressing my opinions (purely in the syntax of an African woman) in America. My dream was to become the female version of Senegal's legendary director, Ousmane Sembene (the greatest Black filmmaker the world has yet produced), but of course, being female, I was told that I would have to start first...as a model and actress. So that's what I tried to do.

Todi handed me the script and I flipped through it while he explained that he had spoken to the film's Arab director and tried to persuade the man that a Black African woman could be cast in an Egyptian film without playing a maid or a small child. Todi told me that the director agreed to screen test me for the role, but made it clear that the part I was testing for--a school teacher--would have to be changed into a prostitute if a Black woman was to be cast. I would also have to do a full frontal nude scene.

His words cut like a knife, but I was of the belief (back then) that if a pretty black girl could only be allowed to play the prostitute today--then possibly later on down the road, another black Arab speaking girl would be allowed to play the decent Egyptian school teacher and not be judged by her color.

And besides, I had already played the topless, oversexed dancing girl in two other low budget films since arriving in Tel-Aviv, Israel (1994), supposedly to be a model,. I had appeared as a clown figure in an Egyptian television commercial that Todi talked his friend into letting me have. In the commercial--my wig gets snatched off (by the child playing my son) just as I look into the camera and give a big, jolly "Auntie Pogo Nigger" smile to the lovely row of dignified, stick-figured olive colored Arab mothers sitting on the park bench. This, of course, is the world famous joke image that is regularly presented of the black man's dark skinned mother (they darkened my skin for the shooting). Whether it be in America, Egypt, Brazil, Puerto Rico, Korea or Sweden--this bafoon image of those women who give birth to black children comforts people.

Todi stood up to leave. He said, "Don't trade your pussy for the screen test, Naima. You're too good for that, you understand?"

I started crying after he left. A senseless, cerebral howling that was not, as one would imagine, rooted in self pity or any manifestation of thought whatsoever. It seemed to be hormonal, because it wouldn't end and it exhausted me yet wouldn't allow me to sleep. I drank liquor and cried for hours, and then just before the sun came up, I took several palm-fulls of sleeping pills and other pharmacy drugs. I wanted to die with a man's penis inside me, because somehow, in my sick, twisted sexually abused mind, I thought that a man's dick inside you represented some tangible proof of possessing his heart. I wanted a man to love me, emotionally, romantically and spiritually, and so I endured the pain of inserting the dildo, because it would represent what I had always longed for--a man's undying love.

Blah, blah, blah.

BintSaro found me in the morning with blood all over my sheets.

At the hospital, they broke two of my teeth and fractured my jaw while pumping the drugs from my stomach.

The paramedics had tied me up in a straight jacket and erected me like a bongo in a corner of the medical rescue wagon. The floors of the wagon smelled like piss.

"Keep your shit inside your ass!", one of them yelled at me.

I cannot prove it--it could have been a nightmare caused by the drugs--but I would swear to God that the men attending me in the hospital room were poking their fingers in my vagina and praising me for being *"properly cut down there"* while pumping my stomach. I remember that I cried and cried, but they wouldn't stop assaulting me. I was a young pretty black woman in distress in Egypt. One of them kept pulling on my titty and sucking it.

Only years later would I realize how shocked and fascinated people in Arab countries are when they come across a "dildo", especially if it's race specific, as my black one was. The sight of it absolutely stops them in their tracks, their minds do cartwheels and their eyes just glaze in disbelief, so perhaps that was why I was assaulted--they thought I was a mentally ill girl who wanted it.

Luckily, I passed out.

Something miraculous happened while I was asleep. I had a dream that Nana Glodine was sitting next to my bed, singing one of her church songs (my favorite one by her, *"My Soul Looks Back and Wonders...How I Got Over"*)...and for the first time in my life, I did not dream in Arabic--I dreamt in English!

I woke startled, because it truly felt like a turning point. Sort of like having your period for the first time. *I had actually dreamt in English*!

Todi came to see me. He said, "Nefertiti..." (For some odd reason, White and mulatto Arab men *always* call the black women in their country *Nefertiti*--even Egypt's President Mubarak would later give me and other black women the same tired nickname--ask Condi Rice. It's a habit with those men when they see a pretty black woman). Anyway, Todi said, "Nefertiti...why are you so bad always?"

I stared at him for a moment and then feeling the pain, I passed out again.

Truce Harding came to my mind later that night as I lay in my hospital bed smoking a cigarette and sipping white wine from a paper cup. I realized how much he had hurt me and I felt regret about the fact that he had gotten off scott free from the child molestation and statutory rape charges. I heard my mother's voice again--telling me that the thirteen year old girl had given birth to a boy and that Truce and Summer had gotten married after all (her claim about Truce and her gay brother notwithstanding). Somehow, he had wrecked my life (and the 13 year old's life) and yet managed to go on with his own.

I took a drag on the cigarette and thought about the whipping that my father had given me and the way he had looked at me while doing it. I had let him down, and I finally realized that this was the real reason that I was not in America with my family. I could not bare for him to look at me as a disappointment, so I had bannished myself and had been running away for eyars.

"Every day of your life, Naima...is a rehearsal for the next one", my Black American father had taught me growing up. *"Black people don't have the luxury of wasting time--you're not white--your fuck ups and mistakes count forever. You're smart, I expect a lot from you."*

I remember pouting as a kid, because he forced me to clip out at least one newspaper article *every day* and write a one page report on (a) what the article was about and (b) my personal opinions on whatever the issue/subject was that was raised in the article. He gave us math quizzes at the dinner table and expected us to know intimate details about the lives of Frederick Douglass, Malcolm X, Fannie Lou Hamer and Nat Turner. He cooked a huge breakfast every Sunday morning and personally bumped and styled my press 'n curl before church and never allowed mother or us girls to wear pants--*ever*.

My handsome, lion-like Black American father wore the pants in our home and was unquestionably the ruler of the house--but had never been an oppressor. He was a keenly responsible person and I remember how loved and protected I felt when he called me *"baby girl"* or said, *"Where's daddy's African princess?"* And all while I was growing up, I remember him saying, "You're Marvin Johnson's daughter--you're too good for that, Naima."

"But dad...all the girls are doing the butterfly."

"You're Marvin Johnson's daughter, you're too good for that, Spring."

"Dad, can you buy me Snoop Dogg's new CD?"

"You're too good for that bullshit, Tamala."

On the suicide bed in Egypt, now fully adult, I cried for hours and hours--sobbing profusely, loudly--because I had let my father down and was scared to go back to him for fear that he'd take one good look at me and detect every sinful thing I'd done. Not to mention Nana Glodine and the eye in the back of her wig.

I was scared to go home, because it would kill me if they stopped loving me just because I was a bad girl.

Images of Tamala and I being molested when I was twelve rolled into my mind like a fog and I could once again feel the hot urine of our family friend pelting against my scalp and rolling down my face and rolling down my sister's face as he pissed on us and moaned out, in spasms, "Oooh, babygirlsbabygirls."

I did not cry.

I thought of Tamala's wedding pictures back at my Cairo penthouse. How sweet and kind her dark brown face still was. How sparkling and joyous her eyes burned beneath the white wedding veil in one photo. She had made it look like she was healed, I thought. Clutching the arm of her tall, handsome black husband.

I thought of my dad and I sitting in the basement on saturdays and singing along with his jazz records: *Straighten up 'n fly right.*

Nana Glodine would fix potato salad while mother bar-b-qued some hot links and chicken and Uncle Booey would come over and pay us kids to dance.

"Soul Train's coming on!"

"Naima, grab my comb out my purse and come here and let me do something with that head, child."

"Claudine, yall's African is gitt'n just as tall and skinny. Lawd have mercy, how tall is she gone be?"

"Ain't she jess da prettiest thang?"

And somewhere in the middle of that day, we children would be smacking on NowLaters and flip-flopping as a tribe down Good Hope Road, on our way to the indoor swimming pool at Anacostia Park.

"Don't chall let Albert go past five feet, and Naima you keep your behind out of twelve!"

"I know how to swim, mother!"

"*I said*...you keep your behind out of twelve feet!...and *do not* take that cap off your head while you swim'n. And Spring--you stop flipping your hair around like some white girl!"

"Mom, I can't help it if I have long pretty hair! It gets in my face."

"No, it's those black boys that get in your face after you advertise yourself, flipping your perm around like a white girl."

"O.K., that's it. I'm not taking you guys to the pool."

"*O, Spring come on...pleaaase!*"

In Egypt, even my suicide was...unsuccessful.

People who know me today (2006), can't believe that I ever lived, romantically, with a White man--and yet for five years, before trying my luck in North Africa, I'd been the mistress of Efrem Nelkin--and mostly happy about it.

As I started telling you before, it was him, one of the pageant judges who had rescued me that afternoon near Lake Fairfax...as my victory was revoked after the white girls complained and boo-hooed that I simply wasn't as pretty as they were. And lucky for them, after being asked to show identification, it turned out that I wasn't old enough to even be in the pageant, and my win swiftly nullified.

"Miss Fire and Safety can't be seventeen--*and you're a black chick, too!?* You want us white boys in jail, plus on t.v. for racism?"

Efrem and I became like eels under mud. His tongue down my throat; fucking me everywhere. And at just seventeen, he got me my own apartment in Virginia and I didn't contact my parents until the very end of 1988, at which point George Bush was the new President and I was eighteen. I lied and told them that a girlfriend and I were roommates and that we had good, stable jobs. I called home every day, and although my mother would eventually track me down and show up unannounced, I never told them where I was calling from.

My poor mother and Nana Glodine--God please forgive me for all I put them through, because I can never forgive myself. My father was angry and wanted to send me money, but I said no. He always challenged, *"You're stay'n with some nigga, ain't you? How old is he?"* And then after he'd advise me to wear condoms, I'd hang up in his face. I was a terrible daughter.

Efrem gave me a used Volvo as a house warming gift for my new one bedroom apartment and I would wait for him to leave and go back to his wife and kids before I took myself on long drives through the Virginia countryside. I had no license, but at seventeen, I could pass for twenty-one. My body had developed into a super tall, ultra-lean dancing "S" with perfect baby fat chocolate titties and a lush rear end that was shaped like a prized golden onion.

Efrem bought me loads and loads of books. He gave me cash every time I saw him. He loaded my apartment with all the exotic and hard to find ingredients that I would need for practicing my greatest love--cooking--although he rarely ate what I cooked. When we made love, it always came as a shock to me, because growing up in the ghettos of D.C., black men (*the whole black society!*) lectured females constantly about how we were raped in slavery times by the white men and how the white man "has no dick and can't fuck". White men, our community taught us, were devils (just as Mahdi Pappuh and the Africans had taught me back in Sudan) who wanted to enslave our souls, breed our children into a "pale confusion" and separate us from our natural mate--the black man.

But Efrem was an expert lover--tender, masculine, completely passionate yet sensitive and *patient* regarding my difficulties with penetration. He could bring me to orgasm using just his penis and the intensity of his kiss was the proof that I was beautiful.

I ignored the endless Black American women who would saddle up to me and whisper, "*They used to rape us!*" To me, it sounded silly, because I was from Africa and I knew full well that black men had been raping and genitally mutilating black women for centuries--as well as selling us to Arabs and Easterners as concubines. In fact, the very first slave trade (East Africa, year 700) had begun with the sale of black women, by Black Kings, exclusively, for hundreds of years before any "*male slaves*" were sold, and even today in many of the poorest areas on the continents--African fathers pressure their daughters to put ads in newspapers soliticing for "European husbandry" or "Arab husbandry". I had lived in Sudan amongst tribes where black men kept plates in women's mouths so that only the males could eat, and where they used black "wives" as work mules to farm their land and do heavy labor. There were whole villages where the men laid around in the sun all day while the women cooked, built the huts, carried the water and raised both livestock and children.

And more than that--I knew damned well that Black men in America had betrayed the Black American woman in every way that a woman can be betrayed--and so, too, had African men always been whorish, selfish and took it as their birthright as men to betray and humiliate black women without even a second thought. The more the White man raised up the White woman on a pedestal, Nana Glodine had told us girls--the more the Black man (as a group) lowered the black woman into a ditch and endeavored to pass the Mulatto/High yellow woman off as *"the black woman."*

This, after all, according to my Auntie Ramah and Aunt Kem back in Sudan--was one of the main reasons that European, Arab, Indian and Asian women loved coming to Africa--to be gaped at and treated superior by Black men while African women were treated as invisible servant wives or trusty mules that weren't going anywhere.

I was not--at seventeen and eighteen--bitter in any way against "black men"--I loved and desired black men and thought of them as the ultimate men, but still, like most black females, I knew by my brothers and by boys at school--and especially by black men in the media and in sports--what the facts were.

"You're nothing but a white man's whore!", the Black men began shouting at me as I shopped in town for lip gloss, and I would hiss back at them, "I'd rather be a white man's whore...than a piece of gum stuck to the bottom of a black man's shoe!"

"Cocksucking sellout nigga bitch!"

"Yoh mama, motherfucker! *Tiku abeed Tabu!"*

And in my silver Volvo, I'd speed away hot as a hornet.

As so many Holy women of the Nile River had decreed for

for centuries and taught their daughters, I too believed that our loyalty as African women was not to the Black man--but to our wombs. Or as the Nubian women say, "Only our children can be trusted with our hearts."

But few Black women thought like me. I had witnessed that the majority of them, in both Africa and America, would take any amount of abuse, mistreatment, "conning" and exploitation just to spend a single day with a Black man. There weren't enough to go around in America, and though it's denied--a great many black men didn't like black women who _looked_ like black women--so those men who were the most disconnected from their true selves had free reign to do as much harm in the community as they wanted to, using women for sex, impregnating and deserting them after promising them a chance at true love--and although black women talked a lot of tough girl smack--most held tightly to the dream of a Black Prince Charming. As a group of women, racially, no women on earth love their men more than black women love black men (when black men allow themselves to be loved by a black woman, that is), and I dare any woman of any race to claim otherwise, because she would be a damned lie.

We are the only women on earth who refer to our men as "_our men_". The whole planet sees us at each other's throats, constantly bickering and cursing one another, and of course, nothing on earth is more demonized and lied on than a black woman--but in our own natural surroundings (Africa), in our true flesh, there is no love...none on this earth...more potent and other-worldly than Black on Black love. Nobody can love like two blacks together can--_nobody_.

But in America, two _authentic_ blacks together--is taboo.

Efrem detected early...that I was psychologically _damaged_.

Within the first three months of me living at the apartment, he had to buy me a new mattress, because my problem from childhood--bedwetting--had returned.

I felt so ashamed, but I couldn't control it.

Can you imagine a seventeen year old wetting the bed?

Sleeping in the fetal position, clutching my pillow.

My hair started falling out again. Not noticably to him, but noticably to me. I wet the bed, my teeth hurt and my hair was coming out in the comb.

"Why do you cry all the time? You're so sensitive."

And I really played the role of Mommysweet when I was with him. It seemed that I didn't have much to say.

But as the "sex marathons" died down, Efrem became intensely interested in who I was. He was fascinated by black people period, and with me being African--it was like I was a prized study project. He wanted to know every inch of my conscious and sub-conscious personality.

One night, I just...opened up to him...

For instance, telling him about the time that my head doctor, Dr. Diallo, telephoned my parents to tell them that I was being traumatized by the straightening of my hair with the straightening comb.

I had never seen black women with straightened hair until I came to the United States--and because I was so extremely intelligent, but could not communicate in English--I immediately realized that the straightening of our hair in the kitchen by Nana Glodine and mother--was a CODE. A message that we were not in safe territory.

Dr. Diallo: "Mrs. Johnson. Naima thinks that your straightening her hair is a secret code telling her that you're all in danger."

Mother: *"Whaaaat?"*

Dr. Diallo: "You're not allowed to show your real hair, you have to hide and disguise it. She takes that as a serious message."

147

Dr. Diallo thought my bedwetting (I was about 9, 10, 12, 13 then) was due to adjustments to American culture such as straightening my hair. He felt that I was in a constant mode of panic, but when Amethyst and my Black American parents confronted me, asking me if I was upset about my hair being straightened--I didn't want to be *different* from them and I didn't want to make them feel bad. They were such wonderfully loving people and had recently gone through the agony of a family friend molesting Tamala and I--and although I can't tell you too many details about the molestation, I will tell you that my father almost went to prison behind it and that because of who the person was--our family was utterly ripped apart for years and years. My dad had hunted down the man who molested us and nearly beaten him to death. So with all that, you can understand how important it was to me that I not to be a pain, and then my mother was always worried about me having a heart attack.

So I denied having a problem with my hair being straightened, and by the time I was fifteen and sixteen, *I really did like it*! (because boys started complimenting me and I learned that long hair on a girl was--not just important, but...*crucial*...in American society) and for the rest of my life I became accustomed to having my hair straightened and styled up like a White person's--although, unlike a Black American woman, I never got over the nervous panic and feeling silly that accompanies my hair being done like that--because I know what it means (that authentic black women are not welcome here)--yet even today--as Kola Boof, the Afrocentric womanist writer--I will occasionally wear my hair straightened (permed, weaved) Europa style, not usually, but every now and then.

And when Efrem seemed to really and truly understand that--I told him more of the things I'd been carrying around. Like for instance being constantly annoyed by my very light skinned sister Spring's insistence that I couldn't possibly think that women like Grace Jones or the model Roshumba or the singer Cece Winans were world class beauties (which I did).

"You're just saying that!" she would hiss, and when the singer Mariah Carey came out (I'm a *huge* Mariah Carey fan), she dared me to say that Mariah Carey wasn't a pretty girl. Prettier, in Spring's words, than that *"man-looking"* Grace Jones. And when I told her the god's honest truth--that I preferred Grace Jones's beauty to Mariah Carey's-- she shoved me and we had a fist fight. It was awful, because I love Spring. But it wasn't really just my sister so much as it was that...*most Black Americans*...had drastically different ideas about what is beautiful than I did, so that whenever they asked for my opinion about beauty and I gave it--they looked at me as though I were crazy; as though I couldn't possibly believe that (Evander Holyfield, for instance) was the finest man on earth (which I did and do believe). And as you can imagine--many people that Black Americans claimed were *"black"*-- were not even black to me (deep chocolate skin and thick healthy African hair being the most prized beauty to my eyes), and therefore, in the cases of people like Mariah Carey, Alicia Keys, Prince, Vanity and Rosario Dawson--they look alright for their *type* of beauty, but they just don't look like *"my people"* (black people*)*, and because of that, I'm not able to see them as THEEE MOST Beautiful ...so I was always the "weirdo" in the bunch, always being accused of being *"jealous"*...jealous...of those kinds of people just because I found them attractive but didn't fawn over their type of mixed looks.

On top of it--the beauty of *those kinds of people* was forced down our throats by slave tradition and mass media 24/7 in the Black American community, so it seemed to me like an invasion of blackness (an *invasion* of blackness), rather than a variety.

What *I* thought was beautiful...was rarely if ever celebrated.

And as I had let go and told Efrem Nelkin all of this--he not only understood, but for the first time...I had been able to *tell somebody*.

And that moment was enormous for me, because when you attempt to *truthfully* discuss this color issue with the light skinned Black Americans--they become very emotional and upset. They see it as the ultimate rejection. They see it this way: *If you don't see me as a Black person, then you don't love me.* Which is not true. I deeply love many many light skinned and biracial people who, to me, are not black (although, like most Africans in America, I lie to their face and say they are to get along)...but the truth is the same in America as it is back home with the African mulattos--we who are black, do not think so little of ourselves that just anybody can be us (*we who are black*...do not think so little of ourselves...*that just anybody*...can be us)--and when Efrem Nelkin had responded, "That makes total sense, I agree"--it made me feel truly visible in America and I bonded me with him.

And from then on, I was able to post my Mariah Carey pictures on the wall and play her CDs and love her for who she was and not pretend that she was me--or worse, be reduced to invisiblity while the colorist American society pretended that she was me.

My mother was the first to find out that I was living with a white man. I'll never forget myself standing in my little kitchen chopping fresh rhubarb stalks and braising the rhizomes in honey water for the cobbler I was making as a hard spring rain fell across the complex--and then there was a banging on the door.

I had turned down my soap opera (*Another World*) and went to the door, "Who's there?"

"*Your mother!*" And I had froze in shock, because the voice was unmistakably hers, and on top of it, she sounded angry. How had she found me?

"Naima--open this goddamned door!"

And although I was about to pee on myself, I had undone the lock and opened it.

It was my mother, putting her umbrella down and pushing right inside my apartment as though she lived there herself. We had been talking on the phone maybe once every six weeks, and I'd done all that I could to assure her that I was alright and safe, but somehow, it had all been part of her plot to track me down.

"Mom, I..."

"Is you liv'n with a white man?"

Her eyes had never looked so cool and beady in my memory, her usually pretty face crusted with rage, and I couldn't answer the question--I was silent, but then, my shame and the tears swelling in my eyes answered for me.

And them--*WHAM!*

The force knocking me against the wall and down on my knees as the umbrella became like an extention of her arm--the wet wirey bat wings splashing my flesh as my mother beat the shit out of me, shouting and screaming, *"Got-damned WHY--N--CH!! What the fuck is wrong with you!? Is you just a Ho or what, Naima!? Don't you know what these cracker motherfuckers did to us in slavery!?"*

I had cried, "Mama, no...please, no!"

But across my back and the back of my head my mother beat me as I cowered with my face to the floor, and then when she got dry-throat from cursing me out, she called the police and tried to force me to come home with her, but I was nineteen by then--I refused to go with her. I told her, "I am home."

"This is going to *kill* your father! Is that what you want?"

The police asked if I wanted to press charges for battery and other stuff, but of course I told them no.

That night, I spoke with my dad on the telephone and he surprised me by saying that he loved me and that he stood by my decision to do whatever I wanted to do with my life. He told me that he was sending me some money (which I declined) and that if I ever wanted to come home, I could with no problem. "You're daddy's babygirl no matter where you are or how old you get, Naima. If anything goes wrong, you call me right away."

"I will dad. I promise."

"Here--your grandmother wants to say something."

And then I lost it. I broke down crying as soon as I heard Nana Glodine calling me by my nickname.

"*Spoon*? *Spoon*--dis Nana. You read'n your bible 'n gett'n your bath at night, shuga?"

"Yes, Nana."

"Alright, den. You know you in my prayers and you know your Nana *looves* you. You hear me?"

"Yes, Nana."

"And I don't like you be'in away from home lak diss--you need to brang yo tail home sometime. You 'sposed to be my Spades buddy. 'N I ain't got nobody to talk to bout my stories no more. You get yo-self cleant up 'n brang yo tail home, you hear me?"

"Yes, Nana."

"O-right den. I loves you, precious."

"I love you, too, Nana."

"Here Yo daddy back."

My family never did found out that Efrem was married.

And as time went on, Efrem began to convince me that I was a writer. He knew a great deal about the middle east and about my culture and was the one who impressed upon me that I could use my talents and my passion to stand up for Sudan. He insisted that I was beautiful and "brilliant"...and would always say, *"You're going to be somebody important one day, Naima. I've never met a girl like you before"*...and for those five growing years, he insisted that I wear my natural hair, and on cuddling nights, he would read my Alice Walker books with me and argue with me about the difference between feminism and *"womanism"*--Walker's philosophy about the ethos, purpose, integrity and spirit that motivates Black women's lives, the author's vision providing a kind of saving grace for lost girls like myself. I mean, according to her (and I pointed this out to Efrem)--I could reinvent and save myself no matter what self-destruction I'd done against myself-- there was hope for me. But still, Efrem and I were devils.

He was married with two sons and a daughter...and because I knew from the beginning that it was wrong to be wtih another woman's husband, there is no way that I can ever justify our relationship. I betrayed another woman, my own spiritual sister--a sweet looking white christian lady, who to my eyes, appeared to be a loving mother and a bearer of good will to all in her community, yet in her own bed, while she was in the hospital having a hysterectomy, Efrem had fucked me into a delirious sweat, practically pounding the imprint of my buttocks into the mattress where his wife rested every night--her tiny fallen blond hairs mixing on the pillow with my springy African hair. His moans intensifying because, as he'd tell me later, excitedly, he could smell her scent and mines mingling like wind and flowers. So this was pure evil, you see. I had betrayed the principles of womanism, because a man had picked me from the tree of life and made of me any pie that he liked.

And that's what happens to a *weak* woman.

Before I left America (with a gay business associate of Efrem's) and went to Tel-Aviv, Efrem dumped both me and his wife. He had found his ultimate dream woman--a very young Black American girl from Ohio who was the spitting image of the British supermodel Naomi Campbell. He married this girl and moved his business up north so that they could *"live their lives"*, and I sold the Volvo and went and lived with my parents and Nana Glodine for a few months before drifting back and forth between Amityville, New York and Martha's Vineyard--eventually living with a Black American marine biologist named Simon in Oak's Bluff. A perfect relationship that was tragically ended because I could not endure the size of his penis.

These were truly the years that I was *lost*. Partying every night and making it a rule to have serious relationships with multiple boyfriends (*when no man is offering true love--have yourself a harem*) when I lived in Amityville and Brooklyn. I was not yet Kola Boof.

I know a lot of people reading this book want me to address the controversies surrounding the abortion I had of Efrem Nelkin's baby--and I most certainly will cover that in depth in this book, but for now I want to tell you about my return to North Africa and my terrifying experiences with Osama Bin Laden.

The hospital in Cairo was discharging me, and no matter the suicide attempt, my spirit was filled with optimism, because I had slept and dreamt yet again in *English*! This, to me, was a good omen. I thought it symbolized some sort of transformation.

I would be twenty-three (I guess, who knows) and twenty-three is the number of years that it takes before Alu (my Nilotic birth mother--Goddess of Trees) bestows her powers on all those who are born female in the month of March. This is the only month in the year, mind you, that the female crocodiles of the Nile will glaze their nests. This is the month of newly born boys, honey wine and pan fried perch.

I could feel the power of Isis reordering my journey and the Cushite blood monthlies of the Nile coursing beneath my flesh like rivers from rich soil. Through my dead father, I was an Egyptian, and because of America and the Black Americans, I was unique--not just young, black and beautiful, but sassy, sophisticated and assertive. Oromo moon and red sunrise burst the semen of all my ancestors within me like a white stone of courage. There was still the chance, you see, that I could become...myself.

Because of my Alice Walker books, I wanted that.

And I took a cab to the penthouse and found, waiting for me, a long letter from Todi informing me that he was ending our arrangement. Naturally, I would have to vacate the penthouse--a new girl, a Syrian blond, would be moving in. He wished me well and wanted me to know that...a friend of a friend...was casting an American film production in Morocco. Some sort of biblical mini-series that I should audition for.

He left me a plane ticket to Marrakech, several thousand dollars and a beautiful postcard on which he'd jotted down in red Arab ink: *"It's a man's world, Nefertiti. Be careful."*

An Evening with Osama Bin Laden

O

The Dinka women of Sudan say that the devil is the most beautiful man you'd ever want to lay eyes on. They advise that this is how you will know him. Of coure, I never took those words seriously until I encountered my now infamous ex-lover, Osama Bin Laden.

When I first met him in a Moroccan restaurant in 1996, he certainly was a handsome man--and on that first night, he would also prove that he was Satan come to life. I still suffer paranoia and even mattress-ruining night sweats concerning the months that I spent as his mistress in Morocco. For whenever I remember that evening at the restaurant--I am besieged by nightmares even while awake. I can see Osama's guards, his henchmen, coming up to me and my date (a handsome black soccer player from Senegal). I can hear their guttural Arabic intonations (clip riffed and practiced, as Osama spoke his own special version of Arabic)--his men instructing me, not asking me, but instructing me to come with them to Mr. Bin Laden's table. I remember telling them to go to hell. Who in the hell was Osama Bin Laden anyway? I didn't know his tall, overly-gowned basketball-player looking ass and I didn't care to! I remember my date, his dark black face flooding without anxiety as he realized, before I did, that these men were killers. Gangsters. In fact, it was the head waiter who told me that I had better do as the men were telling me to do. The waiter told me that Mr. Bin Laden was to be "obeyed" and that I might find my legs broken if I tried to advance my American attitude. The waiter,

156

I could tell, felt genuinely sorry for me (that I had been picked), but he also made it clear that this man, Osama Bin Laden, was under no circumstances, to be denied.

Osama's men escorted my date out of the restaurant and I never saw him again. It was only through a friend, years later, that I was told that he had married a Dutch woman and was not dead, as for so long, I had feared.

It's so terrible, really. People in America ask me--"Why didn't you just run away? Why didn't you call the police?" But *hello!*...in most North African societies, it just doesn't work like that. Women have no real rights in these countries--it's the rights of their husbands and fathers that protect them or it's their standing as Muslims, but as just women out and about, they have no rights. I was seen as a temptess and an infidel. I was a woman who dared to travel in their society alone, dressed in sensuous American clothes with my head uncovered and flaunting my Black American womanness, which they both despise and lust after, mightily. Although I spoke Arabic and made sure to remind them that my father had been an Arab Egyptian, it made no matter to them. I was trash in their eyes (and unlike Osama's sister-in-law, Carmen Bin Laden, who has tried to insinuate that Osama would never be in the company of an infidelic woman--the fact that I am *Black* made me something of a Non-woman animal *sex servant* in the eyes of Arab Muslim men--and the rules that applied to good decent White Arab Muslim women like Carmen were not applied to my black flesh). So, you see, there was nothing I could do when Osama decided that he wanted me. I had no money, no resources! I had no man of power to speak up for my wishes. Osama was a man, an Arab, a Muslim and in Morocco, he considered White. I was nothing but a woman, a lost one raised by filthy Americans, and worst of all--*black* African.

I was escorted to Osama's table. He stood up. I think he intended to be charming, but he could see the fear and loathing in my eyes. I can't deny what a handsome man he was--at least six feet six with a light salmon-orange zest complexion and very sexy negro-like facial features (*see the footage of him in my online video documentary*), dominated of course by generations of infused Arabic blood and desert sun. His hair was more like a pure Hebrew's (knotty) than like a pure Arab's, although, that comment alone would make Osama want to kill me. And I remember thinking that he had the most beautiful lips (for a man), and remember being overwhelmed by the largeness of his hand when he took my own hand (to kiss it)...but then, also, I remember being frozen in terror by the blunt deadliness of his eyes. He has cold, clinical brown eyes that look right through your flesh, as if lusting for the vital organs beneath it. His gaze, quite honestly, reminded me of a rat's gaze. I didn't like him.

He assured me that no harm would come to my date. He told me in his special Arabic, "I just don't think that guy's right for you. He looks like a monkey." Osama's men laughed and Osama's eyes kept falling on my cleavage. I could tell that he was intrigued (not repulsed, Carmin) by the large fleshy prettiness of my natural breasts. I almost cried and peed on myself, because I knew that no matter how many Bette Davis and Barbara Stanwyk movies I had devoured as a teen, I was powerless and men can be merciless when women have no power, no protection. I knew quite well of soldiers merrily raping women in Sudan when I was a girl. I ahd seen homeless children in Tel Aviv, Cairo and Kenya routinely used as sex slaves--and grown people just walked right past it like it was nothing. So I knew that I had better not get smart-mouthed with this Osama guy.

"What are you called?" he asked me.

"Naima Bint Harith."

He didn't seem to believe that.

"What are you eating?"

"Lion's meat", I answered, but when Osama heard that his face twisted up with disgust. He told me, "From now on, you are never to eat lion's meat. And from now on, you are to see no other man but me. Do you understand?"

In his eyes right then...I could see that he was fucking me.

Immediately, there was water standing in my eyes--silvery tears of fear. If I had been a smarter girl back then, then I might have realized that bursting into tears only turned him on. He loved it and demanded of me again, excitedly, "Do you understand?" I had nodded, the tears then running down my face, because I knew in that moment that he intended to take me sompeplace that night and fuck me. Maybe even let his men have some. I couldn't stop shaking. Amid the huming of their strange phones, he instructed me to sit down at his table.

I could just feel that I wanted to throw up! I sat down and immediately began squeezing and contracting my vaginal muscles, nervously.

"Why are you shaking?", he asked.

And that was when I broke down crying and pleaded, *"Please don't hurt me. I'm a good person. Please don't hurt me."*

It became quite a scene, as I half intended, because people all over the restaurant were staring at our table--my loud, child-like sobs carrying like a singer's voice. I have to say that there have been very few instances in my life when I have ever been as humble as I was at that moment. I silently begged both Jesus and Mohammed to rescue me, and for a moment, Osama seemed to take pity on me. He took my bony hands into his big cold ones and said to me, "I would never hurt someone who was weaker than me, Naima. You're a woman; you're scared for your boyfriend. I understand. I will not hurt you."

As I have alluded to before, there is one thing that I have come to know in my life about many Arab men and some African men, particularly men that I've known personally like my Mahdi Pappuh, Hasan al Turabi, Moammar Khadafi, my children's father, Aquaman and Osama Bin Laden...they detest people who *cry*. The sincerest sight of it makes them loathe you all the more. It makes them feel that you should be given something to cry about, and even though Osama had been very tender only moments before, he was still annoyed by my tears. So he slapped me.

Hard as hell across the face! It stung so painfully, the entire left side of my head lit up and enflamed with his rage. He shouted, "Why are you still crying, stupid one!? I just told you that no harm will come to you! You want my foot then?"

Suddenly--I was gone.

I had jumped up and ran out of the restaurant. I don't think I've ever moved so fast in my life...and I remember the shock I felt when I got about three miles away and noticed that Osama's bodyguards weren't following me. *Jesus-Mohammed*! The most shocking sense of relief came over me! I got in my car and drove west like a bat out of hell, thinking to myself--*Naima, you've gotten away from that towel-headed, gangbanging bunch of sand niggers*!

I lived, in those days, in a quaint little sea side place called Sofitel Cottage Thalassa on the corner of Ejema El Fna about a hundred miles from Marrakech in Essaouira. I didn't make much money from acting back then, but I pooled my resources with my various roommates so that we always--us girls--managed to live nice and comfy. I would recommend Sofitel Cottage Thalassa as a good place for any young woman to stay in Morocco, although, I hear it's gotten quite crowded. But it was far better than most and it was affordable in 1996.

Anyway, that night, I guess for the good, my roommate didn't come home.

I went in exhausted from the long run and the general state of terror that gripped my bones. The first thing I did was run a bath for myself (which in Morocco the water is always cold, especially at night). I felt really nautious, because they don't have sewage sytems there like

I had gotten used to in America, so driving with no top on the car as fast as I had through the night streets of Marrakech and later the beautiful coastal village Essaouira had caused the stench to irritate me. Everything seemed like it was moving in slow motion. I lounged in the cold bathwater for about twenty minutes and then I changed into a flowing silk Joan Crawford-like robe, my favorite kind, with the fanned sleeves and shoulder pads. Back then I weighed all of about 115 pounds--I was just a bean pole with big tits and a round little bubble butt.

Out of the blue, the hotel's manager started banging on my door! He was calling out to me, "Hey, black girl! Black girl!" (And to the Moroccans, who are light cinnamon brown to custard white and generally don't consider themselves black or African, I was indeed *black*).

When I went and opened the door, it felt as though a cold bolt of lightning went straight through me. There was Osama Bin Laden and his seven-man posse. They looked at me as though I were a kitten they'd been looking around for and found.

Osama was so friendly. He said, "Naima--why did you run? I just think that you're lovely and I find you intriguing. I wanted to be your friend."

I summoned my American side and said, "Well, I don't wish to be friends with people who bully and intimidate me, Brother Bin Laden. Now if you don't mind, I want you and your men to leave me the hell alone. I just plain don't like you, O.K.?"

Tima father; سخخسحخحردس. Why did I ever tell that man that?--he looked as if I'd just spit right in his face. He told the hotel manager these exact words in Arabic: "Take yourself to bed and hear nothing for the rest of the evening."

At that very moment, a kind of terror came into my body that I cannot describe with mere words. I was so frightened. I was certain that he was going to kill me...I was just frozen in the doorway and I

161

couldn't move, because I knew that if I moved one inch it would only piss him off more than he already was.

He stepped into my room and told his men to wait outside. We were chest to chest, his eyes looking down at me, as he closed the door behind him...and immediately, a hundred ideas went through my head. I thought--*maybe you should lie and say that you have AIDS, girl*, but then I thought--no, he'd kill you, put you out of your misery. I thought maybe I should get on my knees and beg for mercy, but I had basically done that at the restaurant in Marrakech and that was too wimpy for twice in one night. Finally, I thought that my escape from death would have to be to seduce him. He wanted to fuck me really bad...that was my only good card in the deck. So I stretched up, real quick, and kissed Osama very softly on the mouth. It was a chaste kiss. One that pleaded for mercy, and in my eyes, I tried to convey all the surrender that I could muster. *Get it over with.* I saw that my kiss had arrested his anger instantly, so I exhaled. I thought that by allowing him a sexual conquest, I could save my life.

I undid my robe and let it slip down to the floor, so that he could see what a shapely bone I was. I took one of his giant hands and placed it between my legs--but he complained that I was dry. Then he told me, "Put your clothing back on. I don't want this acting that you do. I want to see the real you, Naima. Put your clothing back on and serve me something to eat."

God, I'll never forget. I made a pot of tea and served him chunky crab salad (from crabs I'd caught myself a few days earlier) on the home baked Italian pita crackers I'd made. I served him thickened Tofu with dates, sooch and sugar in it. Everywhere I went--his eyes followed my buttocks. I could not understand him, because his lust was so thick you could cut it with a knife.

He smoked a little marijuana from a gold Huka, sipping his tea and instructing me that I was always to keep hot tea for his Kif-canbo (marijuana). He smoked it rolled as a cigarette, as well, sometimes, and told me that he didn't like the burn in his chest and felt that the tea cured it. To me, his beard smelled like one big reefer patch.

"Why do you wear braids?", he asked. "You're a Nubian woman?"

"Because they're beautiful", I'd replied. "No, I'm a Sunni Egypto Gisis-Waaq. My Pappuh Mahdi was an Egyptian Muslim."

"So your father married a monkey?", he asked casually, because *some* bi-racial children in North Africa (and many Palestinians) speak of their one black parent that way. It's just part of Arabic culture and it wasn't out of the norm to ask it that way.

I ignored the question, and Osama told me that he didn't like women's hair braided. He said only monkeys braided their hair. He told me that the singer Whitney Houston was the most beautiful woman he'd ever seen and that she never wore her hair braided. He said, "I want you to fix your hair like hers from now on."

(This was back in 1996, long before Whitney Houston's public troubles and she wore her hair straightened and flipped around her face in very cute short styles).

I said, "My hair is too long to fix like hers."

"Then wear it like a European woman's", he snapped. "I can't put my fingers through it when it's braided."

You must understand that this was a very unusual request from a Muslim Arab man, but then again--I was being "fetished" and not seen as a "woman". My sexuality was like midnight bream, safe in the dark, and the standards applied to other women were not being applied to me. I was trash to someone like him.

But anyway, I had long since stopped straightening my hair, so I realized as well, that if he was going to run his fingers through it, I would have to get a chemical relaxer and straighten it. I didn't have the money and told him this. He said that he would pay for it. He said,

"I will be financing your life from now on, Naima. Simply tell Master what you need."

He asked me to hit the marijuana Huku, but I explained to him that I couldn't handle drinking or marijuana. I told him that I had a weak system and couldn't stop laughing (to the point of tears and vocal pain) during the one time, as a teen, that I had tried to smoke pot. Luckily, he didn't insist. He told me that he was from America, too, and I had thought he was joking--but then he laughed and talked in depth about his favorite t.v. shows...*The Wonder Years*, *Miami Vice* and *MacGuyver*. He said the U.S. government was made up of "fanatical crusaders" and that he'd once trained secret agents for the C.I.A. (I'm only reporting what Osama told me, I have no way of knowing what the hell he was talking about--the U.S. government later told me that Osama has *never* lived in America). He even said that he'd had a white blond girlfriend back in some state I wasn't familiar with.

I felt like a prostitute as he began telling me about his mother and what an "unusual" woman she'd been in their Arab world. She was Syrian, according to Osama, and wore her hair exposed in public, loved caviar and squab, loved homemade African-styled Sooch (it's like a honey-based Sangria) and dressed in expensive European designer fashions. He described his mother as being something of a feminist, and although his father had impregnated over twenty other wives, Osama said that he was his mother's only child and that she had spoiled him but at the same time neglected him by leaving him to be raised by Saqq (governess), tutors and lackeys as she jet-setted around the world. He struck me as having an inate personal like for strong, smart women--but at the same time loathed and felt threatened by his feelings because of the religion and the culture he'd been created by. I was bored, but I was listening (happy that I was no longer in danger) as he asked me if I personally knew Whitney Houston in America. I told him that I didn't. He said that he had a paramount desire for Whitney Houston, and although he claimed that music was evil (I would later find out that he was associated with the Wahhabit Muslims, who are strict and don't allow music of any kind), he spoke of someday spending vast amounts of money to go to America and try to arrange a meeting with the superstar. It didn't seem impossible to me. He told me that he'd once been a "mindreader" for the U.S. government. He told me that he was attracted to me because I was Sudanese (the country he was currently living in, he said), and he asked if my vagina was circumcised, which I declined to answer on the grounds that "infidel women" have the right not to reveal their age or such other essentials, even in an Arab nation--to which he blushed and laughed. He told me that he owned many expensive Arabian horses and that he was going to name one *Naima* in honor of my body. I tried to feign being flattered.

He went once again back to Whitney Houston. He said that he wanted to give her a house, a mansion really, that he owned in a suburb of Khartoum called Al-Riyadh City. I would later learn that Osama owned more than twenty mansions in that very wealthy neighborhood and that he had at least twenty-five children by more than a few wives, some of them stationed there. He explained to me that to possess Whitney he would be willing to break his color rule and make her one of his wives--he said that he would just have her tubes tied. Of course, I tried to hide my outrage at his racist remarks, but it would come to pass that for the entire six months that I would be trapped in his palm, Whitney Houston's was the the one name that would be mentioned on a constant basis over and over. How beautiful she is, what a nice smile she has, how truly Islamic she is but is just brainwashed by American culture and her husband (who Osama spoke about having killed as though it was normal to just have women's husbands killed). In his briefcase, I would come across photographs of the star (as well as copies of *Playboy* magazine), but nobody in the west believes me when I tell them this. It's like they have this totally bogus image of Osama Bin

Laden. Anyway, it would later get to the point where I was sick of hearing Whitney Houston's name!

By virtue of color, there was to be no consideration of marriage for Naima, thank God. I was to be Osama's mistress and the more we chatted, him eating and me serving and him going to the bathroom an awful lot, I thought--the more I tried to accept the fate that he had chosen for me. He was obviously Arab Mafia (or at least that's what I thought that first night) and I couldn't afford to make a run for it. I'd already witnessed first hand what happened to blond white women who'd come to Arab countries alone, been "*courted*" by Arab Mafia men and then tried to make a run for it. He was also, very rich, so I would probably be comfortable and even a little bit spoiled if I put out right. As it was, I'd been able to use my infibulated vagina to play the role of the young inexperienced "virgin" (over and over and over again)--and because of the tightness and my American boyfriends easily believing that each of them was the first, it just sort of ended up where they felt I was a "good girl" and that I deserved everything I wanted--*and it wasn't prostitution*--it was having a boyfriend, which is what women do. So like I said...being with the one with no power and no protection...I thought that if I put out right, then Osama might come to be less gruesome. And he was handsome--rare was the Arab captive girl who could count on that large comfort. Tall, confident and manly with the softest lips. I began to fantasize that maybe I could even bring out the true romantic in him--and then just as that thought went through my head--*rape* went through is.

He had been there for about an hour of soothing tea and bland conversation, and I had gotten too comfortable. I think I asked him about my date, the soccer player, and I indicated that I cared for the man and was worried about his safety. Osama told me not to worry, saying my friend had been told to get lost and had done so without putting up a fight. I nodded sadly. And then Osama surprised me with some bit of information he'd been given about me. He asked, "Why would you love a man anyway? You're one of the top paid prostitutes in Marrakech, right?"

I was stunned speechless. I said, "Prostitute?"

"Well, of course. How else would you pay for a place like this?"

"I am not a prostitute", I said hotly. I told him about my trifling work as an actress and model and that I had a roommate. I told him about my incredible life growing up in America and then returning to Africa as a traveling dancing girl cum vagabond. But, of course, there is always that perception on the part of Arabs, Berbers and some Europeans that if a Black African woman is traveling without a man amongst them and is pretty to their eyes--then she must be a prostitute. In fact, this is how they justify their attraction to her, and if their sons and brothers should rape her (as often happens), then this is what they claim--that she was a prostitute and had therefore wanted it.

"I am not a prostitute", I told him.

"All African women are prostitutes", Bin Laden replied. "And the whole race of African men is the *abeed* stock. Did you notice how that monkey fought for your honor, fought to defend you? You're the mother of his race, aren't you?...I said...your black womb is the beginning of him, right? You're the mother of his race, aren't you, and yet he doesn't give a shit what happens to you." The cruelty and the insanity of his words cut me like the razor sharp fins of a devil fish. I felt ashamed because I wasn't brave enough to do what my heart told me to do--slap his face. I would later be even more shocked when I learned that some of Africa's most powerful black men were close, close friends with Osama Bin Laden. He ended, saying, "Your people are like rats plaguing the earth. Surely you know that, Naima?"

I remember that I replied, defiantly, "The black man is the only true King the world has ever known. Mohammed was a black man and so was Prophet Ciisa (Jesus Christ)...and yes, I am the black woman. I am their mother."

This made Osama stare at me for a long moment. He didn't say anything, he just stared. Then he reached over and parted my robe just above the knees. He grabbed at my dark legs and rubbed them, saying how soft they were and how nicely shaped they were. He marveled at how long they are (I am over six feet tall with 50 inch legs), but when he put his hand between my legs and tried to caress my inner thigh, I crossed my legs and pushed his hand away.

He laughed. His eyes said--*this is more like it*! He scooted over, sitting very close to me and pulled my face to him, as if about to kiss, but, instead, he *bit* my lips. Bit them shut. I tried to scream from the pain, but it was like my mouth was stapled shut and his hand was groping at one of my breasts, squeezing it. He stopped biting me to say something (at which point I jumped to my feet) and he marveled, referring to my breasts, "Your big cow boobs are real!"

My mouth was in such pain! I held it as hot tears fell from my eyes. Osama got up and eased me back into sitting on the couch. He was very gentle. Then he took some kind of garment from the side of his robe, it looked like a purple velvet towel. He started to fit it over my head and I thought it was a hat of some sort. The inside of it was made of silk--but then he pulled it downward, over my forehead and my eyes--it was a sack, I realized, and I tried to fling him away with my arms, but he overpowered me. He had managed to pull the sack over my head and then pulled a drawstring at the neck. I was so terrified that I kept screaming for help. He said, "Yes...scream, Naima. You have a lovely scream." He slapped me but I didn't shut up.

A moment later, I felt an object being rubbed up against my mouth. Of course, I couldn't see it through the sack--but I knew it was the head of his penis. It felt like a doorknob, but I knew it was flesh. Plus, I know men. He kept rubbing it against my mouth until I stopped making noise and sat there quietly. I tried to hold my breath at times, because the stench from his scrotum was foul. It was as though he never washed, and I also squinted my eyes tight, because I had heard many stories about how some Arab Muslim men liked to urinate on a woman (for instance in Egypt, Syria, Afghanistan and Saudi Arabia, it's not uncommon for a wife to drink her husband's urine in her morning tea as proof of her devotion--many Arab Muslim wives have told me this in Arabic, proudly). He said, "You like to obey your master. Isn't that right?"

I was too afraid to respond. He said, "Call me master, Naima."

I remember that I called him master.

He asked me, "Do you like what I'm doing to you?"

I said, "No."

Then he tightened the drawstring around my neck and ripped my robe open and yanked it down off my shoulders, pulling and pulling so hard that I got fabric-burns on my buttocks. He seemed to be very high for someone who had only been smoking marijuana, because even though he had a velvet bag over my head (which blinded me), he kept saying, "Close your eyes--I don't want you to see me."

I thought I heard him disrobing, then he took my hands and raised them to his penis--he made me clasp my hands around it and I was instantly terrified by the size of it, because Osama is huge. It's long and skinny when it's limp, but it's even longer and gets thicker when it's hard. It has a dark brown dot (a spot) on the center of the shaft about half an inch from where the skin pulled back from the head of it. I knew already, that he was the type of man who liked to use it to hurt a woman.

I was right. For in one fast move Osama forced open my legs and attempted to ram his penis inside me. Unfortunately, he had to make the attempt several times, and kept shouting out (to his men outside), how delighted he was to find that I was a circumcised woman and Sudanese and black enough to have whore's blood. As you already know, the tightness of it killed me as he stabbed inside, but this is what would make me valuable to him as a mistress, because like so many Arab and African men, he preferred inflicting the abuse, debasement and ritual woman-hating that is enjoyed when beast-fucking an infibulated female.

I cannot describe the feeling of violation that I felt--having my personal space invaded and being helpless to defend it or having my head tied up in a bag as a man who had described my race as a plague of "rats" violently fucked me all over my couch and then on my floor. I cried and cried, but the tears only encouraged him.

When he orgasmed inside me, he bit my left shoulder hard, I think to silence his groan and draw blood. I screamed, of course, crying more and more. Then he undid the drawstring, which had made deep grooves in my neck, and removed the bag from over my head. I didn't dare look at him, but I could breathe again.

At that point, I didn't care if he killed me or not. I lay there crying.

Osama stood up, wiped off the tip of his penis with the velvet bag and told me to get up off the floor. As I struggled in pain to get up, he told me that he wanted me on my knees. I raised up on my knees, trembling. He took the dried head of his penis and pushed it against my mouth. I opened my mouth and took it in, not the least bit surprised. I started to suck it, but he stopped my motion with his hand.

I looked up at his tall, skinny naked body. He looked malnutritioned and banana-colored without clothes on. He told me to look into his eyes and I did.

He said, "You belong to me now. I'm your only man. I expect devotion from a woman, Naima."

Then he began to urinate in my mouth. I knew better than to spit it out or jerk away. I let my cheeks fill up with the hot urine, and then, luckily, when my cheeks were full, he stopped and pulled it out.

He went to the bathroom and finished urinating in the toilet. And while he did that, I got up and spit out his urine in a vase. I know that he heard me, because I crashed into a table and gagged after spitting.

When he came back, I was laying on the sofa, his semen dripping out of me...and my vagina so sore and inflamed that I could not sit on my bottom. Osama smoked some more marijuana. He talked about his children and the fact that he'd missed an appointment with his *"doctor"*--Ayman Al-Zawahri--just to do me.

I will never forget the humiliation that I felt (still feel) when I asked him, in the most pathetic voice, *"Can I wash myself and put my panties on now?"* His men out in the hall had burst into laughter--that cruel, persecuting laughter that only men are capable of. I still, after all these years, hate myself so much whenever I remember that one small, debilitating moment--*"Can I wash myself and put my panties on now?"* To this day, after being rescued by the perfect black man and having the most wonderful children, I still find myself sometimes having to get drunk to get the sound of my voice out of my head.

But that night of madness did come to an end. Osama and his men left.

I took another cold bath and went to bed. But I couldn't get to sleep at all that night. I lay in bed contemplating slitting my wrists, because Osama had told me he would be back. And before the week was out, he did come back twice--one afternon he showed up with his men to take me to some wooly-haired "Lilith" women who straightened my hair and styled it in a flowing body wave (and we had sex that night, only it was pleasant). Then another night he showed up wanting sex (his men escorted my roommate from the building)--again, it was quick and pleasant, without the urine, the biting or the violent thrusts, so in lieu of a nervous breakdown, I began to tell myself that he was rich and I could adjust to being a gangbanger's girlfriend as I'd seen frightened girls do back in D.C. My car vanished one morning, and when I reported it to the authorities, they told me that I had never had a car and was *imaging* things. It was so...horrifying! And I had no one back home who could afford to transport me out of Morocco, and quite frankly, I never told my family about what was happening to me. I didn't feel I had a right to tell them something this horrible after I'd been such a bad daughter. I was young and pretty back then--I looked *way better* than I do now--and I wasn't Kola Boof yet, I was Naima--I was stupid and believed that beautiful people always land on their feet. Scary but *exciting*. And I reminded myself that it wasn't all that bad. Osama, in fact, had been treating me quite autonomously.

But then one afternoon--his men showed up without him.

They said they had orders from Osama (who had left the country *on business*) to move me to a better location, a hundred miles away in Marrakech, a place where I would have my own luxury suite. They also stuffed a wad of money in my hand and said that Osama wanted me to buy a new wardrobe. They informed me that a blonde Arab-speaking English woman would be taking me to the dentist to have fillings (tracking devices) put in my teeth.

I thought, briefly, about downing a bottle of sleeping pills and going for an ocean swim, but who was I kidding--I hadn't the courage to have my stomach pumped again, so I grabbed my purse and got in the car as told. And that was the beginning of my tenure as Osama Bin Laden's mistress.

As the car glided along the narrow stone streets, I sat numb and unafraid, patiently sipping a chilled vodka Tabrihana and enjoying the luxury of the plush, air conditioned ride. Resigned to it.

The Devil's Pass Key

<u>My</u> life, literally, became locked away from me and only Osama possessed the key. He installed me in one of the most beautiful and prestigious getaways in all of North Africa--the famed La Maison Arabe of Medina--the breathtaking walled city of the ancient ruins of Marrakech. It's actually a Moorish estate (a bed and breakfast back then) hidden at the end of a secret road that leads into the central abdomen of the Medina's fortress. I cannot describe it to you other than to say that I have never lived anywhere more heartstoppingly grand and that one must see it to believe it. It is guaranteed to take your breath away.

On moving in, I was told that Winston Churchill had once occupied the room that I was to live in and that other people like Princess Diana, Mick Jagger, Anwar Sadat and Denmark's Queen Ingrid had either dined or slept on the premises or both.

Osama and I lived there at the same time that Prince Fabrizio Ruspoli was renovating and upgrading the place into the more Hotel-like property that it has become today. I think his partner was a man named Philippe Kluzelle and I remember them to be completely wonderful, friendly people--totally welcoming and a teensy bit curious about who I was, because I had arrived without Osama and lived there quite a few days by myself (a kitchen worker thought that I must be Whoopi Goldberg, while another said Naomi Campbell). Still, no one asked me any questions--and when Osama finally arrived, no one asked him any embarrassing questions either.

I felt like a Queen. The La Maison Arabe is a hidden, magical, ancient oasis encompassing luxurious gardens, courtyards, mystical ponds, day-skies of blue diamond and evenings of orange sand--truly the ideal place for a love affair. My room was decorated in breezy silks and priceless antiques. The bed itself looked like a giant cushy seashell and the bathroom was ornamental to say the least. I had my own terrace and whenever I became hungry...the kitchen was given orders to prepare whatever I requested. Osama is not a man who reads a menu--he insists that you cook exactly what he wants. Not only that, but when Osama found out what a great cook I am, he made arrangements for me to sometimes prepare him meals in the kitchen. I love it, because I love cooking. God, I can't lie. Those first few weeks, I was genuinely excited and hopeful about my fate as his mistress. Although I'm now a womanist who thinks it's shameful, I remember back then feeling really beautiful and *desired*. Like I said, it's stupid to feel that way, but that's how it felt. There was a certain erotic charge about being a powerful and handsome man's captive and being catered to by his servants.

Each morning I was served ostrich eggs and golden deep fried locusts or crepes stuffed with Apricot couscous and berries in cream. At lunch, I would have a crab salad or a piece of broiled fish with yogurt (in Arab countries, we eat yogurt with our meals the way that Americans eat salads and Osama especially loved my yogurt dishes) and I'd go out amongst the ruins and write poems and stories. Always about Islam and color; war and slavery. The blue doors to the yellow houses on the narrow streets of Essaouira. And for dinner I'd have a green ruffage salad, couscous with baked lobster, spicy red lentil soup or roasted ground nut eggplant or when Osama was out of the country--a thick juicy camel steak braised in goose fat.

My first night in my room...I wore one of the sexy negligee's that Osama had commissioned for me to own. In fact, indoors, I was always to wear sexy negligee's (American getups) that showed off my

174

breasts, my ass. I kept my nipples dipped in honey, as Osama instructed, and I eventually acquired a straightening comb and a few jars of Ultra Sheen creme satin-pres via airmail from a "sista-friend" in Anacostia Park (Washington, D.C.) to keep my tresses as silky and shiny as I possibly could. But on that first night, I had the place all to myself and it was like living in a dream. Osama had arranged for there to be a gift on the bed for me--a ruby sapphire necklace and a pair of twinkling diamond earrings. A giant Owl with a purple bow around his neck was sitting on a bottle of $300 perfume, which I don't remember what it was called, because I never did wear it--I preferred Musk oils or Poison by Dior back in those days. What really touched me was that on the wall there hung a painting of a beautiful dark child, a Wolof-looking girl with a long neck and spidery West African braids. Braids that made me smile. There was also a note that read: *"I'm sorry if I ever hurt you or scared you, Naima."*

I took a long, luxuriously hot bath that night and ate crab legs and garlic-seared Blow fish for with a pungent red wine (I drank two bottles in fact). I had Caramela Kola (the national desert of Sudan) for desert and then layed across my plush, heavenly bed and fell asleep wearing my sparkling necklace and diamond earrings.

~ • ~

Three days later, I felt boxed in and bored. Osama still hadn't shown up. The estate was unnervingly quiet, because there was only a few rooms and there weren't many paying guests, and then when there were, they were usually filthy rich Europeans or Saudis, both of whom traditionally come to places like La Maison Arabe so as not to have to look at a black person's face in the first place. Jut imagine how startled and annoyed they were to happen upon me--a glamorous looking black woman living on and floating around the premises without a man in charge of her. The managers would always tell people that I was a celebrity from America (I heard people whispering, "Whoopi Goldberg" or "Naomi Campbell", alternately)--and after all, Osama did have his guards watching over me. They circled the place like vultures literally 24/7 and had *told me* that my tooth fillings were tracking devices.

It felt like being in prison by the fourth day. There wasn't anywhere I could go, because I didn't have a car and the driver for the estate told me that he'd been instructed not to take me anywhere. He said that Osama's men were to drive me if I needed anything. So I put on my Muslim woman's outfit (which was required whenever I went outdoors) and went and asked them if I could go back to the modern part of Marrakech and see a movie or have lunch. They told me no. They said that Osama had given strict instructions that I was not to wander off the premises.

When I asked them where he was, they told me that he might be with one of his wives or with one of his other "dependents", and of course, that left me cold--to realize that all of this pomp and circumstance, the sweetness of it, didn't mean a thing, I was still just *one* in a stable of *whores*. Son of a sandnigger bastard! I realized then that he must be Donald Trump-sized rich instead of just Mafia rich, which are all the kind of men I would never date willingly, because men with too much money are guaranteed to never grow up and never know any God whose love can't be at least rented. As a rule, I don't care for men richer than me. The guards went on to brag about Osama's "uncountable" wealth and his "Arab women", who, according to the guards were far more beautiful than my black "abeed" ass could ever hope to be (yeah, right).

I returned to the estate with my heart and stomach full of stones. For it occured to me that I might never be free again. That he might keep me there, trapped in an ancient paradise, until I was forced to run for the Bad Doukkala (an entryway that leads out of the Medina) and be shot in the back trying to escape. I yanked the burka from my head and ran inside weeping.

Every day that came and went was just a little more snickering than the one before it. One of the managers commented that he worried about me going batty--*"all the time you spend alone"*--but then he wouldn't really chat for very long either. There was no one to talk to and my poems were beginning to torture me!

One day without even thinking, I wrote across my mirror--*"Isolation."*

The night was black with a hump in its back.

Osama's phone had a dial tone, but it never rang. If you dialed, it would click back to a dial tone. I couldn't call America.

Six days...seven days.

Ten days. No one wanted anything to do with me.

One morning, I woke up and started crying. I screamed and threw things around the room. The guards and managers came to see what was wrong, but even when I turned belligerent and demanded that someone call that *"Bastard motherfucker!"* and tell him that I wanted to speak to him, they simply hurried a look-see and departed unimpressed, as though my behavior wasn't the least bit unusual.

I remember rolling on the floor naked, crying uncontrollably and screaming expletives to the top of my lungs, my silkened hair gone wild and nappy at the roots. But no one came. Osama never called.

A few nights later, I was sitting naked in the middle of my giant bed. I had taken a long bath and was lotioning my body, when all of a sudden, the doors to my room *flung open*! (as if they'd been kicked open)

--and in marched a dozen Arab men! I screamed and grabbed the big stuffed Owl to cover the front of me. They were carrying suitcases, baskets, trunks, there was a strange phone static I'd come to know. Not one of the men looked at me, and at the rear, entering slow and cool...was Osama Bin Laden. He was walking like Hitler with his hands behind his back, his eyes first finding me...and then *on* me.

It was the only really good night the two of us would ever share. I don't know why that is. But the sky beyond the terrace was like spilled sand, vermillion in color, and the moon was full and round with dazzling ivory light. It hung in the red heavens like a pearl of perfectly formed semen, waiting to drop.

Please...*please* understand, that in 1996--there was no way for me to know who this man would become. I didn't even know he was a terrorist, and although he'd raped me, I was a person who was used to being violated and then denying it. I'd watched Mahdi Pappuh and Mommysweet murdered in the privacy of our own home--I'd been molested and knew of so many other girls that were molested, it seemed to be a normal occurence in our community--and I'd been a runaway girl who *enjoyed being lost*, who catered to men in exchange for shelter, food and whatever education they could give. My gut feeling is that people don't speak truthfully about the types of reactions there are to sexual violence (rape) in real life, and I think people's religious piety and morals are the cause--so please understand that I scarcely had time for that shit. I dealt with and survived in the real animal world. And people are animals. They fuck, pray and make bombs.

Osama waited until his men were gone...then he walked over to the bed, and I scooted to the edge, and he pulled me upward and dove his tongue inside my mouth, and we kissed long and deep, passionate as any lovers would kiss. It was the beginning of a bumpy night--a hot polluted flesh and devil cat-wishing night. Neither of us could get enough of the other. I was so glad to no longer be in isolation. I went with it and before I knew it, I was being lifted up off the bed and possited down on the dresser. He fucked me there on the dresser first, and then he put me back on the bed and we stretched out as he bound my wrists together over my head with one hand and he buck-fucked inside me again...and then I got on the floor, on my knees, and swallowed him whole...and then he spread me on the carpet and he baptized me there, too.

It would be at least a year before our tastebuds could detect sugar again. We locked up time, discovering that we're both Pisces. Slithering the entwining sorrows insatiably. Better than sex. *March 3rd*, I said, as I took my sugary cat and glazed his face.

March 10th, he said. Pisces, the Egyptian crocodile.

And the fact is...we went there, *"together"*, at least once.

And when morning came, I giggled and played with Osama's nose. I started calling him by a nickname--"Somi". I outlined his soft, gum-pink lips with the tip of my finger. I pressed my thighs together as his hand rummaged around the wet sticky folds of my kitten's face. I called him "Master" and asked him what he wanted for breakfast. He said cubed watermelon (which is his favorite fruit), some cold sweet porridge with perch crumbled inside it, a good piece of Kubutz, some yogurt and a cup of tea. I floated off to get it.

When I came back, Osama was on the house phone (strange, because he usually talked on a transistor) laughing and talking.

Of course, I thought nothing of it. I did not know that my doom was upon me, lurking about the other end of the line. I set the tray of food on the dining table next to the terrace windows and I removed my robe, because Somi preferred me to never wear anything but high heels and honey on my nipples when we were alone in the room.

Suddenly, by intuition, I sensed that I knew who Osama was talking to.

A swift, paralyzing panic washed over me. I was crippled by

terror and astonishment, because you see, although people of today call Osama Bin Laden *"the devil"*--those of us from Sudan know who the devil really is, and I must reveal with more than a little regret that I had once been desperate enough to entertain him as well.

"Don't be silly, Hasan. You are like a father to me. Allah has placed you in my path to guide me and to mold me. I do for you, because you are my teacher. We must honor you."

I could see my rich brown breasts in his liver spotted, wrinkled brown hands again.

He liked squishing them together. Until it hurt.

He was Hasan al-Turabi, leader of the National Islamic Front and easily the most powerful man in Sudan not to mention one of the three most deadly and diabolical men in all the Arab world. Where others ate apples...Hasan ate skulls. He had started out as a kind of brilliant Professor, educated in Britain and France (where he'd met my father, Mahdi Pappuh, during an anti "damn" rally at the Sorbonne in the mid-sixties), but had become a major political force in the Sudan, and because of his committment to his own visions (namely, it was him who made Sudan an Islamic sharia-ruled nation), was in and out of Khobar prison his entire life--years at a time--because other leaders feared his popularity and his ability to mastermind real change. I had been Hasan al Turabi's mistress in 1995 (the year before all this was happening with Osama), getting cast in several hideous Arabic B-movies as a result of our relationship, and had left Sudan for Libya because of a conflict with his son, Isam, and his wife, Wissal.

I almost peed on myself, because I couldn't believe that I had been right. How could they know each other? And that was such a stupid question, because actually, why wouldn't an Arab billionaire gangbanger with a special fondness for Sudan be in league with the movers and shakers of its always corrupt government? Apparently, by their phone conversation, Hasan was being elected to the position of

Chief Speaker in Sudan's Parliament and there was opposition. Someone needed to be killed, and although Somi was very sad about it (you wouldn't believe what a tender, sensitive "boy" Osama can be when it comes to murdering a fellow Muslim), he considered Hasan's will his will and would bless whatever means it took for the Speaker seat to be secured. As Osama was telling Hasan on the phone, it was only natural that they should be Devil and son...and I, the most unlucky little black African poverty-stricken actress/model/concubine who should have kept her smart ass back in America, had defied the bounds of natural coincidence and wound up with more power, more danger, more devil and more dick than any single woman should ever have to dodge in one lifetime.

I went into the bathroom so that Osama wouldn't see the look on my face.

What on earth was going on? Had it been Hasan Turabi who told Osama to look for me in Morocco? Had he, my former sugar daddy who could play with my tits (but because of religious piety restricted his sixty-something year old self from fucking me) arranged for Osama to track me down and do what he hadn't been able to do? God knows men are like that.

And then I wondered, too...whatever became of Isam? Hasan's beautiful son whose root beer brown eyes once held me on the staircase and followed me in the garden of the al-Manshiyyah estate and yet never brushed against me without some sad secret music. Dark, sensitive Isam who out of loyalty to his mother pretended to hate me. Pretended to think of me as nothing but some exotic African nigger whore with an American accent.

Isam...Isam, who once said to his father, "The whole row of them is pretty--but Naima's the only real jewel. The rest are just costume pieces."

Stiff, clean white uniform. Captain's hat. Shiny black boots.

181

Isam.

But what I remembered most about him...was that he never once touched me. Nor I him. Not even our fingers by accident exchanging a glass. Only our eyes, our...*suspicious*, tragic people's eyes. So sad.

Isam.

As Osama hung up the phone, I wanted to die. He called out for me.

"Yes, Somi?"

"I'm having a very special guest stop in next week."

Oh my God. My sugar daddy from the previous year under the same roof with my new self-appointed "Master"? Two men, both of whom I believed were capable of slitting a girl scout's throat, the scout cookies spilling at their feet, with nary a second thought. I stared at Osama with my mouth hanging open, waiting for him to let the cat out of the bag. Why surely any minute he was going to reveal that he already knew that I had been one of Hasan Turabi's "*nieces*" for a while in 1995? But he didn't say anything like that. In fact, the more I looked at him...the more I realized that he didn't know a thing about it, and therefore, I was in big, *big* trouble.

What if Hasan walked right in the door, took one look at both of us, and then burst out laughing? Who would Osama take it out on? Why me, of course!

Men don't like to be embarrassed, and if you're to feed them a biscuit that's been dropped on the floor, wiped off and kissed up to God, they'd better not know it.

"Yes...that was the great Hasan Turabi on the phone. He's like a father to me. I look up to him in everything I do."

Then the other boot dropped. The *real* boot.

Osama Bin Laden said, "My closest friend in the world...is Hasan's son--Isam. The two of us share a great love for horses. He often helps me to pick out the best ones for purchasing. He's coming here the week after next."

I wanted to faint, but there was no time for it.

I KNOW THE ROOMS
IN HELL BY HEART

"If you cannot sing, Naima...then recite for me a poem."
---Isam al-Turabi

I know the rooms in hell by heart. I know the misery of a music hardened into ear wax. I know not only how it is...to be filled with nothing...but to be covered in it, too. I know too much...to be accepted by you.

This is one of the poems that I wrote about Osama Bin Laden during that time I was with him in Morocco. And yet, it was inspired by Isam, too. One of them abusing me, sadistically, and the other being curiously infatuated with me.

Osama Bin Laden was in Morocco for primarily two reasons. To hunt wild game and to hide, I would later learn, from people who were trying to kill him.

On Fridays, Osama, his gang and I (about ten of us) would go to some mountainous or forested location and hunt for quail, snipe, teal duck and wild boar, sometimes camping out, or--whenever we went deep sea fishing, which was something Osama and I were both pros at, we'd stay at the Doumss hotel in Dakhla, and Osama would eat at the Samarkand Restaurant and just stare out at the ocean for hours and hours. Or talk on his transistor. Dakhla is near a military base and most of the women in that town are prostitutes--they sit painted in the windows and even in that Muslim country, everyone knew and accepted that it was a prostitute town--so Osama's men would forage the local women and have a good time. But it was the hunting that Somi loved best, and he loved to be in the midst of old oaks, or him and his men making tea by camp fire and praying out in the open under the blue blue skies before going out to bag snipe (a kind of water bird) along the "oueds" (rivers)--and snipe was Osama's favorite, because he said he loved the challenge they gave even the best hunter.

Osama very rarely ever ate meat--but after I literally conquered his men with my delicious snipe recipe, he'd have a little of that. My secret was one that Mommysweet had taught me as a little girl--using the cheese from water buffalo milk (if you can get it) in place of cow or goat's milk cheese. They all taste different, the goat's milk being the sweetest, but the water buffalo cheese is the best for cooking, because it traps in the flavors. So I'd take the birds (they look like killdeer only they have an orange spot cover on the back) and I'd get them all plucked and greased with palm oil (stuffing them with chopped onion, garlic, a few salted pond rocks and couscous) and then wrap them in very thin shards of Robiola cheese (made from the Water Buffalo milk), thin slices of Prosciutto and cabbage leaves, all tied up with string. Of course, you season your layers to taste. But it was with that recipe that

Bin Laden's men warmed up to me a little. They just *adored* my cabbage baked cheese snipe with sugar-water porridge.

It got to where I really looked forward to my Friday hunting trips with Osama and the men. That part was fun.

The abuse by Osama, however, started long before Isam arrived. Osama's hand would be resting in my hair, his eyes glued to the pages of his Mohammed Quttub books while I read Galway Kinnell. And we would be laying there in bed and out of the blue he'd say, "African girls are good for a man's lower pleasures, but what need have you of a womb? Does your race really want hair like this?"

And, of course, I would feel so insulted--not just to the heart, but to the soul.

"I like my hair", I usually responded. And then I'd go back to reading Galway Kinnell's bone white stanzas--only I wouldn't be able to make out the words for the tears standing in my eyes.

Other times he would humiliate me by making get up and dance naked. It was such a strange thing, because for the most part, Osama believed that music was evil and I remember how angry he'd get if any guest at the estate played music (Isam, for instance, did enjoy music)-- Osama would cover up his ears and not uncover them until he got the managers to have the "poison" silenced. But then he'd become this other guy who wanted to hear Van Halen or some B-52's. To this day, I hear the song "Rock Lobster" in my sleep. I would be jerking around like a white girl (because, he would instruct me, *"dance like a caucasoid girl!"*) and his eyes would track my jiggling tits from one side of the room to the terrace to the other side. Constantly telling me not to turn around , because in his opinion, "Your ass is too big--show me the front."

Osama had no preference between being either vicious or tender, you understand. These were like the two sides of his face and by a mere wrong step you could find yourself facing either cheek at any moment.

After the dance, which always exhausted me, he would have fellatio. Only the head of it was to be sucked, and then when he orgasmed, he would smear it all over my nose, eyelids, cheeks and mouth. I hated it, but he'd take his time and carefully look at each feature and then smear the sticky jism on me as though anointing me. Then he'd slap me across my ass and tell me to go wash my face. "Naughty girl--you make me do bad things."

Whatever romantic energy we felt on his first night at the estate--it was all gone. It never came again. It was replaced by pure servile servitude. We possessed the right chemistry for what people call a love jones, but I believe that Osama was frightened by it, because he had assumed that he could control how he felt about a woman whose skin was black. That's really the truth, you know. He initially had not intended to keep me for so long, even as a mistress--I believe he saw me at the restaurant and was attracted by the rarity of seeing an African woman who *looks* African in town and then decided he'd bully some sex out of me--but keeping me this way, no. It surprised even him that he was doing it, and then sometimes, ever so briefly, he would talk to me or touch me in such a way that we both knew that he had intense emotional energy towards me, probably a mixture of lust, racial hate, exotica, ideation, power-over-child syndrome, suppressed traditional western romantic motivations--and don't forget his quasi-feminist mother who'd bore only one child and refused to wear a burka...all this to say, that truly at heart, Osama Bin laden was a "deeply religious" hopeless romantic, a dreamer and a fanatic, a person emotionally out of control but intellectually unwavering in his committment to his political and social "obligations"; his beliefs.

Anyway, I had to think of a way to escape, because once Isam Turabi arrived--there would be no mercy on my past. Osama would find himself in an embarrassing situation and would likely take it out on me--with violence.

The sand in the hour glass was running out. The tarantula turning gray.

And as each leg of the tarantula dragged our days towards misery...I began to learn bits and pieces about who my mysterious lover and master really was. There was a man named Bakr Humayd (or Abu-Humaid) who Osama kept in touch with by phone almost daily. Bakr, I believe, was the person who oversaw the running of the vast corporate empire that Osama owned and I never could tell where in the world he was calling from--only once, I heard Osama say it was Kanhahar (a place I'd never heard of--it's in Afghanistan)--but it was by listening to their exchanges that that I came to know that Osama's homeland, Saudi Arabia, had withdraw his passport because of his intense dealings with the government of Sudan--a government that the Americans and the Saudi Arabians regarded as "terrorist" or at least that's what I heard Somi allude to (I was never into politics or kept abrest of world news, mind you, back then). I also overheard bragging, on Somi's part, about how he had played a role in an assassination attempt the previous year (1995) on Egypt's president, Hosni Mubarak...yet another man that I had known personally. Of course, that revelation startled me, because it confirmed my suspicions of Osama being a member of the Arab Mafia (which would later be called "al qaeda" by Americans), which was not back then the same as being a terrorist, but close enough.

These small facts for the time being would have to do, but they were just enough to frighten me into *not* trying to escape. I told myself, instead, that I would just have to throw myself at Osama's feet, on his mercy, and tell him everything about my travels in Tel Aviv, Egypt, Libya and Sudan, and how I had been a poor vagabond girl at the mercy of all his powerful friends...Hasan al-Turabi, Hosni Mubarak, Moamar Khadafi (and others that I didn't yet know were also aquainted with Osama like the Sudanese diplomat who would go on to write a newspaper article about me in London, Gamal Ibrahaim, and the rich oil tycoon, al-Namyri, and one of Bin Laden's closest friends, Sheik Omar Bakri). Of course, no man likes to think that his *whore* is really a whore...but what else can you do?

I decided that I would wait for a moment to come when he was tender and calm, and then I would dramatically throw myself at his mercy. I would even present him with switches with which to whip me--because Osama didn't know how to whip with switches--so that was better than his fists or sticks.

That special moment came about a week before Isam was to arrive.

Osama was laying in bed, reading the Koran, and got a cramp in his foot. He used to get them a lot, actually--the most painful, muscle-bending cramps that would take hold of either foot and twist it, bend it into positions from which he couldn't wiggle it free. It hurt him so much, in fact, that during these cramps, we were commanded never to look at his face. He was too ashamed for anyone to see him on the verge of tears or in a position of defeat. Luckily, I knew how to get rid of those cramps, immediately, and I heard him screaming my name that day. I was out in the garden.

"Come Naima!", he called in pain. "It's my foot again! I can't undo it!"

Two of his guards in the hall were calling me as if they were the ones dying and I had arrived finally with very hot water--a bowl of it for him to stick his foot in and a glass of it for him to drink, which was to shock his nervous system into letting his foot go. Of course, I have other secets, but I'm not writing them here. The hot water is enough. But in no time, his foot was free and his toes wiggled.

He lay back on the bed as I massaged his foot, saying, "Oh, Naima...if not for you, I would be fully humiliated by those attacks. You may be black, but you're a good woman."

I stopped massaging his foot right then, pulled away from him and stood up with my back to him. He asked, "Naima...what's the matter?"

"I'm not a good woman, Somi. I don't deserve a good man like you."

"What's this nonsense, girl? Turn around. Show me your eyes."

I turned around. I told him, "I was at al-Mashiyyah, at Hasan al-Turabi's house last year." His eyebrows went up and his staring was intense but not the kind I expected. I said, "I counted on Mr. Turabi for financial support, Osama, because I was very poor. I was trying to do modeling and ordered a few people to put me in their movies. He invited me to important parties and we went away together for a weekend in Kenya. But he never..."

Just as I was about to say, "But he never touched me for sex. He never fucked me"...Osama raised up as though he were a dragonfly raising from the surface of a lake and his head moved like a cobra's as he hissed, "...LIAR!"

Liar.

The way he said it, I almost believed that I was a liar.

"You dare scandalize the name of one of the purest holy men in the world today?"

"Somi...I", I was so scared that I started peeing on myself.

"A dirty, worthless, cocksucking, dickloving, lying little American cunt like yourself?"

His fist hit me square in the face! I fell unconscious.

When I woke up, I was in the hospital. I had a broken nose and a fractured rib.

This was my big chance to escape...to be free!

The nurses brought the police to my bed. The older policeman held my hand as I cried and patiently explained to them that I was an American citizen and that I was being held captive by Osama Bin Laden, a very rich and powerful mafia guy who kept me like a prisoner at the La Maison Arabe. I told them that he had raped me and that he beat me up.

"Hey listen", said the younger policeman. "You shouldn't be drinking. You should watch your step and stop falling over things. You keep falling into things, you're going to hurt yourself."

The nurse in the doorway, a pretty white Arab girl, put her hands over her mouth and quietly laughed into her palms.

Of course, I was shocked.

To hear something like that in response to my truth, it was like being socked all over again. I wanted to die, because I had been raised on *"the truth shall set you free."*

I passed out again. When I woke the next time, I think it was very late at night.

I heard Osama talking to me. He sounded so close.

And he was holding my hand. Telling me that the very first time he ever saw me...was at a party. In Libya. Moamar Khadafi's hotel by the sea. He even described to me the dress that I had on that night and how none of the men wanted to dance with me because I was too tall and tanned even blacker by the Libyan sun.

He said, "You were out on the terrace and you looked so handsome and sad at the same time. Like you wanted to jump into the sea and swim away to some other world that none of us knew about." Now mind you--it's been so many years, I really don't remember verbatim what Osama said to me, but I'm reconstructing, as best I can, what I recall the "essence" of it to be. He had said, "I am a poet, so I knew that you also wrote poetry. I could smell that you were some kind of artist. I saw how you avoided Moamar (Khadafi) each time he patted you on your ass. You were sweet and humble when you denied him, manipulative, too, but any man could see that you weren't a whore. I know that about you, Naima. You're not a whore. I know about women like you who don't belong anywhere and have no money and no power and no man. That's most women, Naima. I understood and I watched you that night. You were so in love with my friend...Isam. And he was so in love with you. His eyes followed you everywhere. That's why I noticed you...and wanted you, too, that night. Aren't you glad, Naima? That he's coming to visit us? I think he still loves you. Don't you still love him...Naima?"

I know it was real, but I must have blacked out, because when I came to again...the light was on and three of Osama's henchmen were standing around my bed. They'd forgotten all about how much they loved my cabbage baked cheese snipe. One of them pulled the covers away from my body and hiked up my gown so that my legs and thighs were exposed. I started screaming out for the nurse, the police...but it was no use. The man took a belt and began whipping me hard across my legs!

"You bitch! Don't you ever talk against the Falcon!"

I screamed and promised that I wouldn't, but he wouldn't stop cease the lashings and I slipped out of the light and into the warmth of some lost evening. I could hear music...the breeze of the sea brushing against my flesh like a flirt. Brazilian bossa nova floating on a North African night. I was there again...in Tripoli.

They call her "The White Bride". Bone white buildings, palm trees. Tripoli.

It was August 1995.

Moamar Khadafi's pre-Revolution Day Ball.

Isam al-Turabi watched me from across the room. His stare owning me.

He claimed that he came all on his own, but I knew damn well that his father had sent him to watch after me. It's a long story, but Hasan Turabi had financed my trip to Tripoli so that I could make a screen test for a popular Turkish filmmaker. While there, someone at the studio told all the "actresses" on the premises that Khadafi was throwing a big, glamorous bash and that he needed wall to wall pretty girls at the party. This is so routine for Egypt and Libya's governments--they do it all the time. Actresses under the age of 25 are paid a fee to attend a government party--just as I had been paid a fee, initially, for going to a party at Hasan al-Turabi's house and for going to one at President Hosni Mubarak (of Egypt's) "retreat" on the mediterranean (in fact, President Mubarak made me a regular girl for his parties at *Sharm el-Sheikh*). This is how party girls make their money, you see. And let me just say that in my own case, I never turned a trick--but as Marilyn Monroe would say, *"Ouh Piggy!"*--I always met my sugar daddies this way. You just go to the parties and if a rich man or politican likes you, then you might choose to have a relationship with him. I assure you that my being the only noticably black girl at many of these functions is what made me stand out and attract attention from Hasan al-Turbi (who from a distance looks like a dark skinned black man),Moamar Khadafi and al-Namyri. It's not at all that I was so beautiful as much as I was the most coco-luxurious, nilotic-looking woman in the room. Most of these girls were underaged white blonds from Turkey or pale Italians, white skinned Arab girls, even a few anorexic Koreans, so surrounded by them, I came off as having a lot of

193

sophistication and flavor, and on top of it--I was always mistaken for a *"Black American woman"*, which, just slightly _above_ having a blond haired blue eyed white girl, had become the #1 sexual fantasy for Arab and middle eastern men (you have no idea how big Janet Jackson, Vivica Fox, Naomi Campbell and Whitney Houston were in the Arab world and central Europe in the 1990's, and before them, Diana Ross), so I was quick to speak in English and roll my eyes and rock my head a certain way when I wasn't getting my fair share of attention.

But alas...there was Isam at the ball. One of the few Arab men who didn't see me as some sort of exotic dark sex toy. He sipped a sweet coffee and acted his usually snobby self, ignoring the partygoers and the ostenstatious beauty of this paradisical, chandelier and golden glassed hotel right on the cobalt blue beaches of the White Mediterranean. God, it was breathtaking! Tripoli being one of the most beautifully sensuous cities on earth.

I remember that Isam and Moamar Khadafi were wearing the same white captain's uniforms that night, hat and all--and Moamar, as the world knows, is the Armed Forces leader and dictator of Libya, so his outfit made sense, but why Isam was dressed that way I don't know. Isam was, to my knowledge, an engineer, an award-winning horse breeder and one of two spoiled rotten sons of a wealthy, powerful politician. A devout Muslim (as virile devout Muslims go). He was also dark for an upper class Arab (as I told you, his father Hasan was a black man), and like Osama, who despised being as tanned orange as he was, being "dark skinned" was something that Isam had serious hang ups about no matter how silly it sounds.

Moamar Khadafi approached me and without even looking, I could feel Isam's eyes encapsulate my entire being as though I were a Sudanese mummy being preserved under glass.

I must tell you--amongst the "party girl" set, Moamar Khadafi was known quite internationally by the nickname *"Princess Tiny Meat."*

It is said that some of his boy servants made up this name for him, and that's why I giggled when he came up to me to chat, because he is such an animated, jubilant yet diabolically dangerous character. He comes off like a comedian, but he'll kill you. Believe that. "Naima! How do you do that?"

"Do what, Master?" (they love that shit)

"Look so stately and unconcerned with riches. You behave like a politician's wife instead of a party girl. You watch the room as though you're planning to write a book."

"Oh, I'm just a good actress, sire."

Moamar is the funniest looking man. I think he's had some major plastic surgery, because his skin looks leathery and old, but then, his entire demeanor is one of youth and vitality. It's as though he's suspended in his thirties forever, but something beneath the flesh screams sixty! He looks like that Peanuts cartoon character--Snoopy with a bowl on his head. Seriously. I will say, however, that I shall always appreciate Moamar's seeming lack of race prejudice towards Black Africans. He really did consider us his flesh and blood and he was one of the few northerners that I believed whenever he said that.

On that night, he wanted me to go out to his limousine, because he had written a very important book--his own bible!--and he wanted me to have a personal copy, he said. Naturally, I feared that it might be a lead in for rape, but being that he was the leader of armed forces and beloved dictator of the nation, how could I possibly get out of going? I mention this, because this is what I hated most about traveling in North Africa amongst powerful men. They can rape you at any moment and in that part of the world--there's really no such thing as rape. Almost any woman who ends up raped is basically considered a whore who wanted it, and in my case, paid party girl--I was almost inclined to agree with them, because I didn't actually have a lot of respect for what I was doing. I want readers to know that. I felt ashamed by what I had allow-owed myself to be reduced to, but at the same time, the adventure and excitement and the glamor was addictive. And I had also lied to myself about the situation and thought I wouldn't get too dirtied up by the men and would end up a successful serious actress, later a filmmaker. It's so hilarious now when I look back and realize what a starry-eyed, risk-taking woman I was in my twenties, but then again, I was trying to find out who I was as well. I don't hold that against myself and I still like the old Naima.

We went to the limousine.

On the way there, Khadafi had his arm around my waist and he was asking me if it were true that I been to President Mubarak's parties in Egypt. I could tell, by little jokes he made, that he wanted know how big President Mubarak's penis was. He asked me if I had ever had sex with Mubarak. I told him the truth--no, I hadn't. In fact, I explained to him that Hosni Mubarak had been one of the most humble and respectful *"cocks of the walk"* I ever came across on the party circuit (then again, I have a friend who says he just isn't into black women and that's why he was so respectful to me). Anyway, Mubarak had a lot of class, I told Khadafi. He wasn't immature, fondling the women guests and didn't make his nation and his position look comical by trying to advance public whoremongering. At Mubarak's gatherings, the party girls were for the guests and not for him. He kept his own "booty" stashed on various yachts in the mediterranean.

With that said, Khadafi got a shitty attitude and snatched his arm from around my waist. He looked angry, as though he'd fix me for being so high and mighty by raping me. I tried to distract him from his anger by saying that it would save my life to be given the honor of reading this bible he had written. Khadafi fetched it from the limo. It was called Kitab al-Akhdar (*The Green Book*). Actually, it came in a three volume set. I acted as though I were holding the actual tablets of the ten commandments in my hands. I had to divert his anger.

"I call it the Third International Theory", I remember him telling me, proudly. "This will be the saving grace of the world, Naima. I will save our poor mother, Africa, and her dark beauty will rise from the ashes once more."

I could tell we were bullshitting one another. Khadafi just wanted some pussy.

He reached out and pulled me to him and started to kiss me.

"NO!", commanded another man's voice, thick as steel.

Khadafi and I both jumped, a little startled, and saw that it was Isam al-Turabi.

Isam had his hands deep in his pockets. His rage-filled eyes targeted Khadafi. He protested, "...foar de kofje net eamelje!"

Translation: *Not the wine before we have coffee.*

Khadafi pulled out a gun and clicked it. "Who the fuck are you, boy?"

"I am Isam al-Turabi...the son of Hasan al-Turabi, the rudest man in Khartoum."

Khadafi knew immediately who he was dealing with--the son of Koranic jihad's most mercilous and malicious goliath. All of these powerful men in North Africa know each other. Khadafi didn't want to fuck with Sudan's Turabi.

"That woman", said Isam, "is an employee in my father's house."

Khadafi laughed and said, "There's room in the limo. You look like a handsome young man. We can both fuck her."

Isam said, "I think you should let her go. I don't think my father would like this."

Done. "How is old Turabi lately? One of my wives is related to his mother."

Khadafi snapped his fingers, announced that he wanted to dance and hurried back to the party as though we'd been holding him up. I braced myself and said "thank you" as Isam came over to see that I was alright, but he spat at me, angrily, "You need to get yourself a new life. You hang around these big cocks long enough you're going to get what you deserve, Naima. You may not live through it."

He took my books. "Come on now." He almost touched me, but he didn't.

On the way back into the hotel, I felt safe and protected. I knew that he loved me. It's just something you can feel when a man really loves you. But I couldn't understand him at all--he was always, always mad at me. Always looking down on me.

Only a month earlier, I had left his father, Hasan, asleep in a hotel and gone over to Isam's horse stables in Khartoum. His family was really proud, because he had won the Cavaliers Federation Championship trophy (again!) for the Arabian horses he bred. By the time I got there, it was dark of night and Isam was grooming one of the horses. He looked up and saw me approach.

"What are you doing on my property!?", he had raged.

"I came to confront you about your father, Isam."

"You're just a sorceress!", he scolded. "Don't bother, Naima, because your spells don't work on me."

He was right, because I came to him wearing a short gray fox coat with nothing else underneath but flesh. I had on silver high heels and a wet mouth.

"You oughta be ashamed, Naima. Why do you cheapen yourself?"

"Isam...your father has never once broken his marriage vows to your mother. I just want you to know that, because he feels very bad about how you treat him. He's not a fornicator, Isam. He's never ever fucked me. I promise you."

He was angry but interested. "Oh no--then what are you for?"

"I'm just company, Isam. I laugh at his jokes. Because I'm a Black African, I'm less human in his eyes, therefore I can't judge him.

Don't you see, he's an old man who needs his ego stroked. He thinks I'm pretty."

Isam said to me, "The one thing I will give you, Naima...you talk truthfully about any and everything under the sun in a natural way. I've never met a person like that before. I admire that about you."

I went up to him close knowing full well that the artful cleverness and sexual tension that so magnitized us would neutralize him. I told him, "I know you want me, Isam. You can't deny that. I want you, too."

He tried to look away, but he could not break my stare.

"Isam...I'm not the devil. *I just look like her.*"

The windy night found me naked as though just born. My coat in the straw.

"Why won't you claim me, Isam? We both know I belong to you."

His dick was hard as a rock in his trousers, my knuckles brushed up against it--but didn't quite touch him, just before he moved back, and he was quite petrified at that moment, so he couldn't find his words right away. Certainly, I had pushed the envelope. Women in our culture were not to engage a man so aggressively, but I felt certain that the American woman's characteristics worked like magic on Arab and African men, no matter how it frightened them. I made tears in my eyes and asked him, "How can I go on living if you never touch me, Isam? How can I stay beautiful if you never kiss me? How can I call myself a woman if you never...*enter me*?"

"Naima!", he nearly shouted, his breathing labored although he hadn't been running. "You must cease this cruelty at once. Yes...I do want you. I have very deep feelings. I admitt it. But my hands. My hands belong to Allah." He raised his hands in the air as if I had pulled a gun on him. "I cannot touch your flesh with them and yet uplift the pillars of Islam, too. This is my faith. This is who I am. My wife must be a virgin and it's her that I wait to touch. Please understand."

Of course, I was quite frustrated. I was not disrespectful enough to grab him and kiss or force him to touch me. But I asked, "What can I do in this moment then, Isam? I'm surely dying from our passion. It eats me alive and has nowhere to show itself."

"Sing me a song", he said tenderly. "When I was a child, there was a Dinka woman who took care of me. I remember how dark and beautiful she was and her voice used to be like a magic carpet that sent me riding on clouds. Sing."

"I can't sing", I cried.

"If you cannot sing, Naima...then recite for me a poem."

"I can't talk", I cried. And with that, I jumped on the barrels and mounted his prized Arabian horse. I took the reigns and rode off into the dark ever-clear...my fully naked flesh galloping, my breasts free and bouncing like cannonballs of jello, my tight tiny pussy wetting against the hot hairy barebacked horse, my tears and clamped mouth alit as the wind blew through my hair and eye lashes. And of course, Isam leaped on another horse and came thundering after me.

And then there we were. Entering the grand ballroom with all the mysterious elan of Cleopatra and her asp. For this was the tarantula and the hourglass. So that night had not gone down inside me. O firebirds of the Nile. Blood and moonlight at brown feet? What did they see, these whispering Arabs who watched us climb in from the street?

Raven's wings and red skies--ancient nights thta still called upon me? The passions of a dark brown sepia soldier--the quickened pulse of a queen's dark lumbering isolation? Evenings of the Sun. O enchanted Nile. How had I not sang my lullaby? Surely, they recognized the breasts of the mother. Yes, this is the thing. That unsettling remembrance that goes down best with warm rum. They, too, knew the rooms in hell by heart.

The music before it was ear wax. Khadafi's ballroom and the pretty black girl from Sierre Leone who was standing in front of the band and elegantly singing the words of the ballad like oars of paddling dreamtime. Words that tore me apart.

"God has made the night for lovers--take now my hand."

Isam al-Turabi.

"So many mansions in this heart of desire/ please understand. My heart can't beat without you...baby you knowwww."

Isam looked at me. His stare said that he loved me. He always forgave me. Always.

"Angels in a world of fire...never let me go!"

I came to.

My legs and abdomen were covered with welts from Osama's men whipping me during the night, but the nurses still prepared me and discharged me.

As Osama's men drove me back to the Medina, I thought about Osama's voice the previous night until it was real to me that he had been there. He knew all about Isam and I. He himself, unbeknownst to me, had been watching us that night at the ball in Tripoli. How ironic and man-like, I marveled. Scooping me up in Morocco and knowing all along that his best friend and I were in love.

"We'll stop in Marrakech before the Medina, Miss Naima."

"What?"

One of the men handed me a white square. It was from Osama. I opened the small envelope and read the note (he'd scribbled it in his hideous attempt at English):

I want you to look impressive when Isam arrives.

Classy but feminine, Naima. Sensuous.

I want you to look American.

Hope you're feeling better.

We're having a lot of guests.

I purchased a white crepe figure-8 strapless evening gown made of antique lace, a simple but stunning white pearl necklace.

Diamond earrings shaped as fat and full as tiny comquats, because fruit should always adorn a woman.

And on my lips--I wore honey over a faint splotch of raspberry powder.

Osama's Lake of Fire

"He who thinks about consequences...is not a hero."
                              ---Osama Bin Laden

The two of them would be sharing a room during Isam's visit--bunking together like boys having a sleepover. Then after Isam's visit, they would be leaving for Khartoum. I, of course, would stay put and wait for Osama to get back. Although Isam hadn't yet arrived, the house, indeed, was full of Osama's friends.

A screening room was set up and the silly films of Egyptian comedian Adel Amum (hope I spelled his name right) were played non-stop. He's like the Jerry Lewis-Eddie Murphy of Arabic cinema. Osama loved his ridiculous movies. I myself would usually sit alone, ignoring the men, and read my Alice Walker books, my James Baldwin essays, my Buchi Emecheta short stories and my Sylvia Plath poems. Garrison Keillor helped me to smile through many a trying moment--and there was this one friend of Osama's, his "doctor" Ayman al-Zawahiri. He kept pinching my butt when I would walk by or knocking my books out of my hand and when I told Osama--Osama only laughed and winked at the shithead. Osama's brother was there, too. Umar Muhammad Bin Ladin (the family spells their name Ladin). He kept taking polaroids of us all (which I would kill to have one of those pictures today--but how could I have known that Osama would become the most famous man in the world?), and even though he couldn't stand my guts (Osama's brother, Umar), he would rave on and on about my cooking. God knows I was cooking day and night, and that at least, pleased Osama. By then, I was terrified of Osama. I could see in his eyes that his violence was on a ledge waiting to pounce on me at any moment. I was very afraid.

Three men particularly close to him--Tahir, Abdullah Azzam and Sayyed Qutb (who Osama was very angry at)--were there at the estate and through these men I learned a lot about Osama's trips outside Morocco and about who he was to the world.

Although it isn't generally acceptable for females to take part in Islamic men's conversations, and especially though the men never share any pertinent information with the womenfolk, I did get to overhear juicy tidbits about the vast sums of money (millions and millions!) that Osama had spent on my country, the Sudan. It seemed that he loved all things Sudanese and had built roads and infrastructure in my country. Tahir bragged that Osama had virtually paid the bills for the Sudanese government on more than one occasion, for instance paying the cost of imported oil when the government was short on hard currency and that Osama had paid off the completion of an airport in Port Sudan. I was both impressed and flabbergasted! Especially when Osama's friend Yunis Khalis from Iraq backed up those allegations on another day, speaking to someone else, and especially after I'd fished for info from Osama's guards and gotten even more details.

I almost went to Osama and told him that I was proud of him, but then I didn't, because I realized that I'd probably get my ass kicked if he knew I was listening to the men's conversations.

Other--even bigger things--came to light. I learned that Osama wanted people (dangerous people on the outside) to believe certain things about him. For instance, that he's left-handed (when in fact, I've seen him write with his right hand--late at night, he would compose the most intricate poems, and he used his right hand). But then, suddenly, he was pissed off at his friend Sayyed Qutb, because Sayyed had revealed to someone in Khartoum (or perhaps it was Kandahar) that Osama could write with his right hand.

I don't know *why* it was so important--but Osama wanted people to believe that he was lefthanded, and he was capable of writing in both, but I thought his scroll with the right hand was better.

He was also angry at Saayed Qutb for failing to show up at a prayer gathering for his favorite holiday--"Eid al-Adha", which is the Feast of Sacrifice and takes place on January 21st. There was a bronze object that Osama and his "friends" referred to as "The Emir" (which was also a nickname they called Osama sometimes), but the bronze dagger-like Emir was connected to a secretly held "black box" (as they called it) that was kept in the wreckage (or perhaps a whole airplane) that was stationed on a runway at the Khartoum airport. I don't know what was in that wrecked plane or why a certain length of the air strip was so crucially important--but I do know that the men acted as though the fate of the entire Arab world rested on the contents of those two mysterious objects--"The Emir" and the "black box".

Through Abdullah Azzam's chit chat, as I was cooking and serving and pretending to be dumb but listening--I discovered that Osama and Hasan Turabi owned vast fields of land where they grew marijuana crops and that Osama was "casually" partnered with a few other gentlemen in producing heroin for traffic to Turkey. Apparently, to Osama's surprise, the heroin business was booming and he was debating whether or not he should sell his cut of the biz and get out of it, as he said the drug business wasn't holding his attention.

One afternoon, when I had served him and the other men spinach yogurt, Osama made me suck his penis in front of the other guys. He laughed and muttered racist comments as he humiliated me by having the other men watch--and by ordering me to make loud slurping and sucking sounds so as to titillate his guests.

It was a nightmare, because as I sucked Osama's penis, Ayman (Osama's doctor) came and slapped me on the ass and fingered me.

After Osama orgasmed, he made me suck the other men's dicks as well--Ayman al-Zawahiri, Abdullah Azzam, Sayyed Qutb, Tahir and one of his Syrian guards, Ibis (who was so sympathetic to me that he faked an orgasm so that my degradation could end).

"Isn't she amazing?", Osama had enthused as though I were a pet doberman making its master proud by the tricks I performed.

I truly hated Osama Bin Laden with all my heart.

When the impromptu sex show was over, Osama talked to his posse about *"making people think things"* to throw them off track.

He told the men that he wanted people to think that he suffered from serious kidney problems--far more serious than the occasional lower back pain and urinating that I mentioned earlier. He wanted the rumor to spread that he was on dialysis machinery, and just when he'd said that, Ayman al-Zawahiri warned him that if he put this in the universe, then it might come true. "You already have sensitive kidneys as it is, my brother", Ayman had said.

"Hey--you're dismissed", Osama said to me.

I went upstairs to wash out my mouth and try to fix my hair back in place. The tears had long dried.

The estate was flooded with women at this time, mostly White and Arab "girl-toys", but none of them were nice to me or helped me with the cooking and cleaning up after the men. This I resented greatly. Unfortunately, I got into a fight with the stupid blond girl who had come with Muhammad al-Faysal, a very rich banker from Sudan. She was a German girl named Letty. I asked her to help me with something and she told me that *I* was the maid, not her. The truth was, her man Muhammad had been making passes at me and she felt threatened by that. Arab men have two major sex taboos--caucasoid blonds and koolox (*"nappy goddessa black"* African women). I was the only black woman on the premises (and black women, anywhere in the world, are the easiest to rape and not pay for--because in many cultures the black man's mother is not even considered a woman, but is a mule to be victimized), so naturally many of the men kept a watch on me. Osama damned near acted as if he might let one of them fuck me (now that they had violated my mouth), but if it came to that, I intended to have a surprise for all their greasy towel-headed asses.

I ignored Letty's assertion that I was the maid. I tried to ignore Letty in general, but then one day, she and three other women approached me out by the pond. All four were tall European blonds and they had one universal, *sisterly* message for me--"Stay the fuck away from our men, nigger bitch!"

What? As loud as I screamed at night from Osama's bed chamber because he wanted his friends to *hear* my screams--hadn't these skanks realized that I could barely take Osama's dick let alone the rod of somebody else's man? And wasn't <u>my man</u> richer than all theirs put together? What in the hell were they talking about?

The Bosnian one had the nerve to poke me in my chest, talking about, "You monkey girls are..."

God help her. I must have reached out and knocked the living shit out of that bitch so quick, I couldn't even understand why my hand was stinging. And then Letty was next. She ran at me screaming--I kicked her right in her low fat stomach and grabbed her by her hair, ripping off her blond wig! The bitch was a damned short-haired brunette! I flung her weak nasty pale Charlize Theron-looking self into the pond. Julianne ran her flat ass in the house.

Hadn't these whores heard me when I said I was raised in a ghetto in S.E. Washington, D.C.? Had they no concept of what that meant just by seeing the way my face had turned into a man's? And more importantly--had *I* forgotten what kind of tough kick-ass Black American people I had been raised up by? Had I forgotten the time that a whole baseball team of white girls had got in my sister Tamala's face at King's Dominion and me, Spring, Tamala and our friend Shontay had beat the fuck out of those bitches--and when *"Jesus Christ"* showed up (inbetween socks, they had started calling on Jesus), we Johnson sisters had whooped the shit out of his black sell out ass, too!

Had I forgotten where I came from?

Had I wimped out and let Osama beat me down to the point where I had forgotten that without his guards, I could probably take his bony ass if I really wanted to?

I became emotional and went the fuck off. "Come on wit it, you nasty caucasoid dog smell'n *skank-ass Ho's*! Naima Bint Harith is the queen of this motherfucker, who's going to dethrone me--*Bitch*!?"

The real problem was that they all wanted Osama. That's truly what it was. And also, they had to be <u>scanned</u> to go in and out of the mansion, but I didn't. All hell broke loose.

Everybody's man was upset and offended--*that uppity African bitch had actually disrespected decent, privileaged white people!*

Unfortunately, Osama wasn't home. The men were running around trying to figure out what happened. The European bitches were crying, screaming and grossly over-dramatizing how badly they were hurt. They wanted my black ass <u>kicked</u> and they intended to pull out all the stops to see that it happened.

I went to the kitchen and grabbed the biggest butcher knife on the estate.

By the time Osama's henchmen and some of his rich friends caught up with me in the hallway, I was shaking like a leaf and sobbing like a maniac. God in heaven knows I had just had enough. I was somebody's child, too, after all. I was a human being. I had cooked, cleaned and fed all their greasy Arab and nasty White dog smell'n asses and this was the fucking thanks I got?

I hollered, *"Yeah, that's right!--I'm the goddamned queen of this motherfucker. Osama didn't tell you?"*

Very unfortunately, one of Osama's men called me an "ignorant monkey bitch" and came rushing towards me--I stabbed that motherfucker right in his throat! *Sweet Jesus, it felt so good*!

He fell. The women screamed in shock!

"Who's next" I asked. "Who wants some American dick?"

The next thing I knew, the place was swarming with police officials. I put down the knife and gave up. *I hoped to God they put me in prison*!

I fell asleep on the dirt floor of the jail (they never did wash the blood off me), and in the morning, two of Osama's men were there to fetch me. I couldn't believe it. Shouldn't I be going before a judge or something? I had stabbed a man--in the neck, and had been high with pride all night, because I was certain I had killed him.

That greasy fat towel-headed motherfucker was deceased!

The Jail Matron said to me, "Next time, don't be so temperamental, young lady."

What!? I thought surely these people must be crazy!

Osama's men walked me to the car. They were so different than before. They actually seemed a tad subservient, respectful and even protective towards me.

Osama, I knew, was behind this and would be waiting for me at the estate. That's it, I thought. He wants to punish me himself.

When we got to the estate, Osama walked up to me and kissed me very gently and for a very long time on my forehead. He said, "Naima...I am truly sorry they disrespected you in your own house. That is never righteous. I have kicked everyone out and hired a staff to clean up their mess."

He then presented me a thin, kind-looking white girl. "This is Pretoria. She's going to be your maid from now on. Pretoria...Mistress Naima."

The girl, who was about nineteen, curtsied and said in a sweet voice, "So pleased to meet you, Mistress Naima. Shall I get you some tea?"

I became...*extremely* afraid at that point, because I basically don't trust anyone who isn't a black woman. That's stupid, I know, but at the core of my life's suffering, that's how I am. I felt more than ever that Osama and I were headed for a deadly confrontation, because I had made up my mind that when the very perfect moment arose, I was going to rebel and rebel and loud and violently--totally off the hook. With this kind of man, I realized, there was simply no other way.

Osama Bin Laden was not famous back then. He was not the ultimate Cobra, the most wanted terrorist--the most feared man on earth. He was just another coldhearted thug ass gangbanger like the kind I'd grown up around in Washington, D.C. A woman beater. Just another sexist psycho-nationalist religious sorry ass motherfucker.

210

I became nautious and threw up. I was running a fever.

"Quick...get her inside."

Pretoria supported me by positing her small body under one of my arms. I could smell her hair. It smelled like lavender. That touched me and made me weep.

"Where is the man I stabbed?", I asked after Osama and Pretoria had me in bed.

"Fishing. Eternally", said Osama with an amused grin.

"You're always leaving me here alone", I mumbled. "Flying off to Afghanistan, Sudan. You never take me with you."

"Mistress Naima--will there be anything else?"

"No, Pretoria, thank you so much--you can go."

Osama came to the side of the bed, right next to me, and presented me with a round, large ebony-wood box. It was about the size of a hat box. He said, "For you...Naima."

"Why are you treating me nice!?", I demanded out of fear, but he only laughed and said, "Please, silly one. Open the box. This is how I feel about you, Naima."

I raised up to full sitting position and took the heavy box in my lap--Osama gave me a solid gold skeleton key with which to open it. I don't know why, but for some strange reason I immediately hoped that there would be a bucket of Kentucky Fried Chicken inside with an order of macaroni and cheese. I was starving!

I unlocked the box and carefully lifted the lid. Brilliant light beamed across my face. My God, you talk about beautiful. You talk about art and craftsmanship!

Two things happened immediately.

First, I realized instantly that I was pregnant with Osama's child. And not only that...but I saw...Osama standing virile and barechested in a lake of fire, as though he were satan.

I looked at the gift and then asked Somi, "What is it?"

He said, "It's an ancient water box. All the way from Yemen. Here, let's take it out."

Osama lifted the beautiful box out of the round dark ebony and my eyes were just flabbergasted by its beauty. It was incredible! He explained to me, "It's made of crystal and inlaid with golden plaques--notice the ancient writing on the plaques. They speak of a beautiful queen who is pregnant with her true love's son." The solid gold legs of the box were covered with sparkling diamonds and rubies. Osama said to me, "This is a replica of the same water box that King Solomon once gave to the Queen of Sheba."

Of course, inside the box, was the shining pretty marrow of clear water.

"Water from the Nile", Osama Bin Laden said. "I had them go to the river bank right beside the house in which you were born, Naima. It's the blue Nile. Don't you recognize it?"

"Yes", I lied through tears. For the water sparkled like Mommy-sweet's diamonds. Streaks of light and silver and faint blue sky. The hint of the women's menstral blood. The sound of my parent's own spilled blood running into the earth. Yes, I recognized it by feeling, I thought, by spirit, by sensuality. Like him, I was a dreamer.

"Thank you, Osama."

"Good. Now get some rest. Isam will be here tomorrow. You'll want to look your best for the man you really love. He doesn't have a clue that I've got you."

Isam.

No. My heart dropped. No, please...no.

O

Deep in the night, when the locusts were blowing off the mediterranean and splashing across the skies of Tripoli--I was being tormented by a nightmare. I saw Osama again, standing in the middle of a lake of fire. He raised a spear over his head with one hand and with the other he beckoned for Isam to join him in the lake. They were like boys; best friends. Their closeness sealed by something more powerful than the flames--and yet I couldn't imagine what it was that sealed them. It was more than brotherhood.

It stabbed me and I woke up in a painfully agony!

Osama's penis. He had lunged inside me while I slept. He stabbed again!

He began fucking inside me. The pain so intense that it nearly shut down my central nervous system, because I had no warning and hadn't mentally braced myself for the impact. I cried weakly, because I feared my maid would hear.

I held on to the bones of his skinny back and tried to brace the attack.

I cried out, "Osama...I don't love Isam!"

But Osama banged violently anyway...until he drew blood.

Butterflies dominated the air in my strange stomach. I heard his voice in the entry hall and I wanted to run. He sounded so happy and I just knew that the sight of me, and especially the ironic nature of my now being his best friend's whore instead of his father's whore would make him want to shake his head and ride off into the night air--but quick.

Suddenly, Pretoria came searching for me. "Mistress Naima...Mr. Bin Laden is wondering where you are. You have a guest."

I took a deep breath and walked out along the cavernous corridors of the estate dressed glamorously in the low cut tight-fitting antique lace gown that I'd bought in Marrakech. I recall that Osama and Isam were so goofy and excited to see one another that night--chattering like teenaged boys around a campfire. I walked in slowly.

Isam al-Turabi caught sight of me.

In less than a second, his happy, animated face turned into one of stone-still shock and utter disbelief. He went silent, staring as if he couldn't believe it.

It suddenly dawned on me that Osama had waited an eternity for this moment. Oh yes. *This...had been it all along*. Osama watched the face of Isam al-Turabi as intently as a wife watches her husband when he's being caught in a lie about another woman.

Isam's shocked stare turned to rage as he realized that Osama must be fucking me now. "What are you doing here!?"

I looked to Osama, because I hadn't been coached on what to say.

Osama laughed very heartily and said, "Isam...loosen up. Didn't I tell you that I had a sweet little darkie bitch on the estate? I told you about her. A nice African whore to suck my toes and wipe my ass." I had never seen Osama this crude, carefree and juvenile. He laughed with an animated freedom that just wasn't his own. It was almost as though he were a westerner.

Isam turned around and stormed out. He was so hurt.

"*Isam!*', called Osama behind his back. "*Isam!*"

But he couldn't stop laughing, he was holding his gown as he might pee on himself. His face red and tears nearly in his eyes, Osama Bin Laden was laughing and having the happiest moment I'd ever seen him have.

I hung my head in shame. Filled with regret.

Later that night, Osama came to my room. He said that Isam was back and that they were having dinner in another lavish bedroom suite that Osama and Isam would be sharing as roommates for the duration of Isam's visit. He told me, "I want you to wear this around your neck."

He handed me a leash--a leash that you walk a dog with.

I looked up at him as though he were crazy. He said, "Take off all your clothes and put this around your neck. I want to walk you in the room and let Isam see you."

Was this the moment, I wondered? Should I jump up now and go the fuck off and start kicking and screaming? I wanted to...but I was scared.

I sat there looking up at him as though he were insane. I told him, "I will not do this, Osama. This is *sick*."

He immediately knocked me across the mouth hard!

He said, "You think I won't kill you, bitch? Is that what you think?"

I started to say something else, to beg really, but then he lifted up his right leg and kicked out his foot so fast that I couldn't get the words out. His foot struck me hard in the face and I flew backwards off the edge of the bed crashing into the table by the wall. He came over to me--I was holding my face and bleeding profusely.

He said, "You wish for me to stomp you like the worthless rat you are, piece of trash?"

I was crying. Shaking my head no.

"Then take off your clothes and put on this leash, bitch."

I could not believe that this was happening. I just could not believe it. For I knew that at any moment, Isam would come to my rescue and defy Osama. I just knew it.

Once Osama had me on the leash, my body naked and bent down on all fours like a dog, he took a tube of lipstick and made a circular "O" on my buttocks--a bullseye. He yanked the leash forward and I walked with him, trying to keep up, but I couldn't move as fast. He kept yanking it.

Finally, by the time we reached the room that Osama was sharing with Isam, I was so humiliated and so completely broken down that I wept like a baby. I could not believe that a human being was treating another human being this way, and in particular, that one person found so much joy in mocking the forbidden love that was shared by two others. I could not believe that I had attracted such evil to myself. The leash was yanked again and I saw Isam on the bed, the room lit by candles, his dark brown face apalled.

Osama was laughing more freely than I'd ever seen him laugh.

Isam shouted at him, "Stop it! Let her go!"

He had been curled on the bed sipping wine, the whole room pregnant with the stench of marijuana, but now he leaped off the bed, furiously. *"Don't treat her like that!"*

He snatched the leash out of Osama's hand and finally...for the first time ever...touched me, because he had to pull me up to standing position--his gingerbread colored hands clutching my flesh.

Osama, meanwhile, had fell on the bed laughing uncontrollably. Isam turned to him and yelled, violently, "I will never forgive you for this, you twisted bastard! This isn't funny!"

I lay in my bed the rest of that night--totally and completely terrified for my life. For now that Osama had detained me long enough to embarrass his beloved Isam with my presence--what else was left to do with me? I had served my purpose. Osama thought me a whore, an infidel, a rat. There was no reason for him to let me live.

The next day, Isam insisted that he and Osama go away to Sudan to attend to some horse business (they bred horses as a team). I dutifully packed Osama's luggage--shaking in fear every moment.

Right before they departed, he kissed me on the mouth, as a man would do when parting with his wife, and told me, "I shall return in about three weeks."

This wasn't unusual, because out of the six months that I lived at La Maison Arabe, Osama was only there for four of those months. He had business in Sudan, usually, and other times I heard him mention taking trips to Kenya, Afghanistan, Egypt or Greece. One of his daughters had gotten married and he'd gone to that.

"Have a safe trip", I said trembling. I didn't know what else to say. I became hysterical, crying in fear, "You and Isam have a good time, because you deserve it. You're such good men."

Even after the jeep was long gone, I was shaking like a leaf. Just sick with terror. I could still hear the sound of their partying from the night before. The both of them laughing hysterically, play-fighting and jumping around the room like teenaged boys. It frightened me more and more each day to realize that I had absolutely no idea who Osama Bin Laden really was whatsoever.

The pregnancy symptoms became a reality. I had to be about six weeks.

I worried, of course, that he would react to the pregnancy by killing both me and the baby, so I decided not to tell him.

~~~

Three weeks later, he came home in a good mood.

Isam wasn't with him. I didn't ask any questions.

I cooked a Libyan dish that Osama likes. No meat. Just tomatoes fried in garlic, milk and tofu with a thick blackened gravy poured over cous cous and his beloved yogurt. He often said I was a better cook than his wives. He always wiped up the plate with Khubz bread and would usually have seconds and thirds. For desert I served up his favorite--watermelon peppered and chilled lightly in tamarind juice.

Osama Bin Laden *loves* watermelon. He loves it.

But anyway, he got terrible cramps in his left foot.

I did the hot water thing and massaged his foot.

He told me about his new girlfriend--a pretty blond French woman who lived in Crete. He said that he'd be going away for the weekend to visit her. I said nothing.

When we laid down in bed that night, I could tell he was already fucking her.

I hated him.

Whenever Osama went away, I was glad, but at the same time, I was faced with an intense loneliness. For without him on the premises, no one would talk to me, because he had instructed them not to. I tried to forge a friendship with my maid, Pretoria, but it turned out that her primary job was was to jot down everything I said and did and report it back to Osama--and one afternoon, I even walked into the bathroom to find Pretoria on her knees sucking Osama's dick. So there you had it old girl.

I took refuge, naturally, in books. I scoped the estate's library and read people that I wouldn't have ordinarily read like Willa Cather, Henry James, Wole Soyinka, Naguib Mahfouz and one of my now all time favorites--Mark Twain, despite the silly controversies over his use of the word nigger, I loved him.

I wrote poems, because I couldn't sing of my sadness, and I wrote little short stories so that I could enterain myself all the way through it.

Osama had four wives and twenty-five children, but I never saw them or heard any details about them. I began to understand that I was also a mythical person in his life. Owned and tucked away like a sack of corn meal in a cabinet.

I fell in front of the sun and let my soul seep into the earth.

I couldn't go on this way.

Pretoria figured out that I was pregnant. She obviously told Osama, because they arranged for me to have a miscarriage. I know they did, because I had noticed that my daily porridge had a funny taste in it for a few days, which I thought was the pregnancy effecting my taste buds, but in reality I was being poisoned. One day I had the worst stomach pains. I had a terrible fever. I went to the bathroom and the fetus slid right out in the commode. A little boy, I believe (as of 2006, I've been pregnant six times in my life and they've all been boys).

I cried for a few days non-stop like I had when I had went through my abortion, but deep down inside, I thought it was for the best. I wouldn't have been able to stand it if he had looked anything at all like Osama Bin Laden.

What I couldn't abide, however, was that Pretoria had poisoned me. I confronted her and she denied it, but I fired her anyway. She called Osama in Khartoum crying about it and I snatched the transistor from her. I told Osama, "I want this bitch out of my house, today! Either she's leaving or I am, and I hope you choose me."

Pretoria packed her things and was driven away by the guards.
~~~~

I made up my mind that I was leaving, too. Osama came home exhausted and worried about his dealings, but secretive.

His eyes were bloodshot and he wouldn't eat anything.

I gave him a back massage and brushed out his hair (he had terrible split ends that I repaired with egg). I told him, "Somi...it's not fair the way you took over my life. You're holding me captive and I don't want to be here. I want to leave and go back to America."

He stared at me, probably stunned that I would risk a violent reaction. But, of course, there's also a tender boyish side to Osama.

"Did you ever love Isam?", he asked softly.

"No", I said. "I was infatuated by him, but I never loved him. Not real love."

"Well he loved you, Naima. He really...*loved* you."

Truth was, I no longer believed nor cared. Osama saw that in my eyes. I hadn't met my children's father, Aquaman, yet--so I hated all men following the days in North Africa.

Osama shocked me by saying, "At the end of the month, Naima...you may leave. I will give you some money to get yourself started. You may take all your gifts with you. I will pay for your transportation. Where are you going--New York?"

"No", I said with tears in my eyes. "London or Spain first."

"Whatever you wish." Then he rolled on top of me and put his knee between my legs. I would soon learn that the reason he was so agreeable about my moving out was because he had been planning on moving his blond French girl in...but who cared, I was free at last. *Free!* She could have his psycho ass.

~~~

Unfortunately, our parting would not be sweet.

Osama could not let me go without inflicting one last scar. One last humiliation.

It was June 1996. My bags were packed a month early.

The plan was...he was supposed to be going to Afghanistan for the rest of the month, and during that time, I would quietly slip out of the country as I pleased--never to see him again. I would not be poor, as I had been when I came in, because Osama had already handed me an envelope with more than twenty thousand dollars in it. As well as that, I would retain my Bin Laden jewelry collection and the gifts he gave me, plus have my "fillings" removed.

As usual, before going on a business trip, Osama had guests come over. One of those friends was a Black man, a Senegalese employee and a good friend of Osama's named Babba al-Khadir. He was a Muslim also and had been educated in Cairo, Egypt where I believe he wrote for Sudan's "Khartoum Magazine" under the pen name Ibrahim Eddy. Like so many Black Muslims (and Palestinians) in North Africa, Babba Khadir did not like to associate with Negroes or Nilotics of any kind-- unless they were highly mixed race or rich ones from America. His woman that he brought on his arm to the estate was a White Turkish girl. Still, I was so happy to see any kind of Black person (Isam didn't count, because he was Arab brown) that I went all out on dinner. Osama laughed at me and told the man, "My mistress is delighted to be serving a black man tonight. She rarely gets to see her own kind."

Of course Babba was gracious--but I could tell that he hated his color being noticed or related to other blacks.

His white Turkish woman sat next to him looking like a broke prostitute. She had a scar over her top lip and looked kind of cross eyed. Her hair hung brown and oily and her white flesh had that "smudged" look. I tried to make friendly chit chat with her, but she had a nasty attitude (as so many white women do in Africa). In all fairness, it's probably because she was well aquainted with Osama's four wives. So her loyalty was to his wives and not his whore.

I cooked Shya (lamb cooked over coals) for dinner and served it with onion pie (talk about delicious), Fassikh (tuna cooked in onions, tomato sauce, peanut sauce and hot spices) and Aseeda Dukhun (a rich Sudanese porridge that specifically goes with meat). I baked my own American Wonder Bread (which for them was a treat) and served up vanilla ice cream on pancakes with peaches over it for desert.

I put an incense burner in a corner of the dining area and burned sandalwood. I felt good because I thought I had created an enjoyable dining experience for everyone.

Osama gave me one of his religious speeches. The kind that for legal reasons (and for court purposes), I have not been allowed to write about in this book, but I recall him saying something like: *"Taghut* (satan) *will always assemble the non-believers, that is not our concern, al-Khadir. What must be redeemed is the sanctity of Palestine. All of the thieves against Ummah must be brought into the light and made to see their ways. Allah has entrusted us with this, my brother. The Jews shall not violate Al-Aqsa."*

I never knew what the hell Osama was talking about and I certainly never imagined that he was a terrorist--mainly because I would never imagine back then that anyone was a terrorist. I was Americanized and therefore very naive. I just thought he was rich, influential and liked putting on religious airs.

They talked for hours and the white Turkish woman and I sat next to them for hours, patiently breathing and holding our ladylike demeanors (we were both covered as Muslims).

Somehow, as it was very late in the evening and the men were laughing and talking about horse races, Osama suddenly asked Babba al-Khadir, "What do you think of Naima? Is this a lovely African girl like I said?"

Babba smiled uncomfortably and nodded that I was. He hated black women, but what else was he to say to his boss?

Osama told him, "She's got incredible breasts. Beautiful and natural. Naima--show him your breasts."

I felt my head caving in. I froze.

"Do you want to see her breasts, Babba?"

He scooted to the edge of his seat and nodded vigorously that he did. The white woman didn't look perplexed in the least.

I did not cry. Instead, I became filled with rage. I told Osama, "I am not showing this man my breasts."

"Come on Naima, show him how lovely you are. He's ten thousand miles away from Senegal, he's not seen black breasts since he was a boy."

"*Fuck you!*", I winced, furiously, ignoring the surprise in his eyes. I was so outraged that I had forgotten what a man like Osama could do to me. I shouted, "When you show him your goddamned dick, Osama, I'll show him my titties!"

Osama then pulled up his gown from the floor and whipped out his dick. He was lit up with laughter.

Babba and the white woman burst into laughter. They seemed shocked but suddenly wide awake and dangerously amused.

(According to Carmen Bin Ladin, Osama never behaves this way around his family members, and I've had many of his Muslim friends say the same thing. But this is how he was when in my world. He was a devout party boy.)

"I showed them my King, now show us your breasts."

I shook my head that I wouldn't do it. Tears filled my eyes.

The white woman spoke to me at that moment. I could tell by her voice that she feared what would happen to me if I didn't show my breasts. She said, "Naima, you're such a beautiful woman...if I looked like you I would be proud to show my breasts. Go ahead now. Show the men your breasts."

I cried trembling as I undid my top garment and took out my breasts.

Babba spouted, "Oooh...very nice."

Osama decided to punish me for defying him. He ordered me to suck his dick. The head of it was hard and bloomed like an umbrella. He wanted Babba and the white woman to watch me suck his dick.

This, however, was out of the question. Osama was White. Babba was Black. I could never, *ever*...suck a white man's dick in front of a Black man. I would rather die first and I told Osama, "Go ahead and kill me, because I cannot do it."

The white woman offered to suck Babba and I shot her a single *Mama* glance that paralyzed her, shutting her stupid ass the fuck up.

Of course, even people reading this book will not understand, after all the other humiliations I'd been through, why I couldn't carry out this one last act to save my life...that's only because people don't care to understand the obvious. I am an African woman. And everyone--the white man, the black man, the white woman, *everyone on earth*, has attended my rape for centuries. Black men had sold black women as slaves to the Arabs and other easterners since year 700 and White Arab men had violated African women for centuries--our entire culture, the whole African race has been bastardized and obliterated forever by the white man's penis. Of all the women in the world, the ones who look like me are the most unprotected, most disgraced, most violently abused and sexually compromised women on earth.

No...I would not and *could not* suck a white man's dick in front of a black one. My two abusers, historically. I'd rather die first.

If you've got a soul--then it makes perfect sense.

But alas, the moment came at last. Osama Bin Laden reached out laughing to grab or smack me. Something in me snapped.

I stood up and I swung...*I swung* on him!

He fell backwards.

The white woman screamed.

I kicked...I swung...I ran. I ran around outside amongst the ruins, and from a distance, as I'd run into the night yard, I could hear Osama and Babba laughing ferociously. Merely tickled by my show of defiance, and that was the last time I *felt* him with me.

I hid crouching all night outdoors in the ruins, terrified that Osama would get his electronic pad and locate me by the tracker fillings he'd had put in my teeth (and many of the guards' teeth), but luckily, he was too busy laughing, smoking pot and partying.

When morning came, they left the country. Then I collected myself and left as well, just as we'd planned.

Be and Be NOT Afraid

FIVE YEARS LATER...2002

 Connie Chung and the New York Times.

I never wanted the public to know that I had crossed paths with Osama Bin Laden, and especially after Osama became world famous (which was the most unbelievable shock to me), I didn't want to bring shame on my Black American family by having it discovered that I'd been his mistress or ex-girlfriend, but the problem with being a public figure (even as obscure as I was) is that people will OUT you. And that's what my former maid, Pretoria, and my former roommate in Essouria set in motion as they tried to pitch cheap stories about Osama and I to the British press in the spring of 2002. They were desperate for money and would make up any outlandish lie (even fabricating nude photos)--but those outrageous lies, for which those women were never paid a dime, managed nearly to destroy my life.

British news people began looking for Naima Bint Harith--they contacted the United States Government for information about "Bin Laden's mistress", which caused the government to become very suspicious of me and classify me as a "possible terrorist." You have to understand that I had reinvented myself by 2002 and was now known as Kola Boof--a feminist poet, novelist and freedom fighter--the highest ranking female Secret Agent in the SPLA (the Sudanese People's Liberation Army), as I was now fighting to eradicate and draw attention to the slavery-genocide that was taking place in my country as an effect of the civil war that had broken out between the Arab North and the African South, and because I was the daughter of an Egyptian and was half Arab and born Muslim--it was a shock to Arab Sudanese that I would take the side of the African South and denounce my Arabic name (Naima Bint Harith) and crusade as "Kola Boof" for the Dinka, Nuer, Shilluk, Nubian and other Southern Cushitic tribes.

My short story collection *"Long Train to the Redeeming Sin: Stories About African Women"*, was an especially volatile book causing the following responses from Arab media:

●

"Death to Kola Boof! She is the devil's daughter--America's newest prostitute! She's a disease that needs to be cured."

--Alray Alaa'm Weekly (Sudan)

"This woman is dangerous."

---Sunni Men's Bath Press (Sudan)

●

In 2003, my publisher in Rabat, Morocco, would be firebombed for even publishing the acclaimed stories and I would be dropped from his roster out of fear. Along with all that, I would be threatened by my former sugar daddy (Isam's father), who had basically become Sudan's Vice President but then been put under house arrest (at which times I'm not sure), Hasan al Turabi.

Hasan threatened to have me killed and so did his friend, the Sudanese Diplomat Gamal Ibrahim, who would go on to write a rather famous article about me in London's top Arabic newspaper--London being the home base of many of the most powerful Sudanese political players whether Arab Muslim or African Southerner.

So, you see--before Osama Bin Laden's name ever came up in 2002, I was already involved in mounting political danger concerning the books that I wrote, and because those books were just then being released in the United States and being promoted on the internet--it would eventually make it look as though I were trying to stir up publicity about myself in order to sell books.

A closer look at the facts, however, proves that nothing could be further from the truth.

For instance, the moment the Bin Laden rumors started, I immediately gave an interview to Britain's top daily newspaper, *The London Guardian*, in which I vehemently denied ever being Osama's mistress. I did admit that I had known him, but I made it clear that under no circumstances had I been romantically involved with the man and that it was all just meaningless gossip. Please go on the internet and search up my initial comments regarding Osama in the London Guardian--you will see that I was in no way trying to make money off his name. That's his niece, Wafah Dafour's style, not mines.

I had reinvented myself by then as a totally...*totally* different woman than the sexpot actress Naima Kitar in North Africa. It wouldn't make sense or be of any advantage to my political causes in Sudan or my black womanist literature to have this kind of scandal break--to be labeled "Hitler's girlfriend"and a HO. Americans HATE Osama Bin Laden, and especially in New York City, the book publishing capital of the planet, he is loathed with a passion. So it would have been plum stupid for me to advertise a relationship with him.

Of course, at that point, few people in the media world knew what I looked like and the name "Naima Bint Harith" conjured up images of an olive complexioned Arabic woman with flowing silky black hair, Cher-like with seductive brown eyes.

They didn't realize that I was a black Arab woman.

Meanwhile--the U.S. government suspected me of being a terrorist and under the Patriot Act, I could lose my citizenship and be deported. I had no choice, you see, but to reveal to the U.S. inspectors that I had been Osama's mistress against my will and that my loyalty and my love lay completely with the United States (which it does). Luckily, to back me up on that fact was the word of Prince Fabrizio Ruspoli, the owner of La Maison Arabe (where Osama had kept me, but is now a hotel resort), and it was Prince Ruspoli, I am told, who told the State Department guy that I was not happy to be at the estate, that I appeared to be a "sexual servant" and that I had been clearly afraid for my life and clearly fearful of Osama Bin Laden. So as you can see--I was an African mother trying to protect her children by protecting my citizenship, but things would get much worse.

~~

Once I admitted to the media that I had been Osama's mistress, the media discovered that I was a black woman, and worse--one who *looks* black. They thought first of presenting me as a bimbo--like the type Bill Maher routinely dates, and that type of image would have come and went, but my activism and literary works ruled that out. Media attention would only lead Americans to my body of work and my outspoken beliefs on race, sex and religion, thus forcing them to seriously "affirm" an African Goddess Image in a society where only mixed light-nearly white black women are allowed to be portrayed as having "cosmopolitan" life experiences or being "desirable fodder" for rich men. I was not the right *image*, you see. It was constantly said that I wasn't "*pretty*" enough, and in my novels, I had openly attacked White Supremacist culture and was just as "<u>weird</u>" as Osama himself, so they immediately began to do two things--(1) discredit and dispute my story and (2) not report my story; make me invisible.

The Bitch Shoots Guns

On August 21st, 2002, I was involved in a shoot-out about 50 miles outside Los Angeles.

I cannot say too much about it, other than it took place on Indian Hill Road in San Bernardino, California--I guess at 8 at night, I don't remember--and I had been meeting with U.S. government agents, because my children, their father and I were living in hiding by then because of the death threats pouring in from Sudanese officials.

I was armed, which was illegal for me to be armed, and although I was arrested for shooting a gun, there was no record of me being arrested (I was taken to the Pentagon in Arlington, Virginia)--which is why I can't say a lot about it. Luckily, my Black American military father has some pull at the Pentagon, and I was comfortable.

A group of Arab teenagers (white ones, probably from Anaheim) had pulled up in a mini-van cruiser that warm California night and opened fire on me and the men (paper-pushers) I was with as we strolled under the cover of trees, darkness and parked cars.

"Traitors of Allah must die!", the boys shouted in Arabic as they took shots in the dark--and just as the lone white agent shielded the paper-pushers and pulled out his gun, huddling everyone into the ground, I pulled *my pistols* out, kicked off my heels and ran towards the vehicle shooting MS style--aiming my bullets into their mini-van by standard Marine wrist harpsicord technique, immediately deflating their back tires, which made them give up shooting and commence with shouting *"let's get out of here!"* as they burned the pavement leaving heavy splatches of blood behind, driving as fast as they could to get away from my sprint-gallop and precision-perfect aim.

Days later, an editor at *The New York Times* would comment to my publicist, "OH, this is unbelievable! *The bitch shoots guns, too!?* You people will do anything for publicity. No--we are not sending any reporters to check out the shooting incident. We don't even *believe* the shooting incident took place! And this woman is naked on the back of her books for crying out loud--she's a clown!"

"She's an attention whore", added a black male journalist at the popular Eur-Web Urban News.

Women at Spelman University, the high yellow and token brown afro types who wear Chanel suits with kente cloth tossed over one shoulder--the same mulatto academics who brag endlessly about *bare chested* African Queens Nzinga, Nefertiti, Yaa Asante and Sojourner Truth--bitterly objected to me speaking on their campus: *"Why is she naked on the back of these books--this is the 21st century!?"*

Apparently these stupid women feared I might show up on campus bare breasted and address the daughters that way.

I was <u>disinvited</u> from speaking.

"Your client's a joke", said an editor at ESSENCE magazine-- purportedly the definitive magazine representing the voice and face of America's *"black women"*. "She's getting death threats, she's been in a shoot out, she was Bin Laden's concubine and she's naked on the back of her books. She's too much for ESSENCE magazine."

These American people had no concept of my culture or what I was struggling to represent as an African woman *artist*. To them-- breasts are sexual appendages and are used for getting attention, and the fact that I have such beautiful nearly perfect breasts (by *their standard)* was proof that I would do any and everything to get attention. Right now (2006), more than 100 million African women still go topless outdoors at some point in the day each and every day, and for 26,000 years, the authentic Black woman has honored God by baring her breasts in the sun, and yet--these highly educated academics and newspaper people couldn't see it as a womanist cultural statement--as a statement of African pride. I didn't have flies coming out of my mouth or sagging stretch marks, which would have made it acceptable.

While all of that was going, I really was being threatened by the terrorist government in Sudan and my children and I were living in hiding, under protection of the U.S. inspectors.

THE PENTAGON:

For days I was questioned.

When asked if I knew anything at all about where Osama Bin Laden could be hiding, I stated what I had heard on the Arab grapevine as an agent for the SPLA:

ı*Osama's in the Baluchistan region of Pakistan, in the Toba Kakar Mountains of South Waziristan."*

It was all I knew via gossip, but amazingly, it turned out to be very accurate within the next year.

I told them it wasn't true about him needing Dialysis machines. It was my opinion that Osama wanted people to think his kidney problems were more serious than they were. I told them everything I knew. They had a psychologist to pick apart the words and meanings in my novels and poems, and though they recognized that I was against the Arabs and terrorism--they were highly disturbed by my afrocentrism. They tried to persuade me that I should be more "inclusive"; more "assimilationist"; more "one love" oriented, but I am not niggerstock, and that became a major problem with my protectors. My inability to "*serve a larger purpose*" by erasing myself. They ordered me that under no circumstances was I to speak to the press.

But you see, I feared the U.S. government--*I didn't trust them in the least.* And because of that, I wanted there to be a record of what happened to me if I suddenly died or disappeared.

I disobeyed the government's orders and spoke to a Black woman reporter from the Washington Post--Lynn Duke--who was very sweet and wanted to help me to tell my story, but the thing was--she didn't believe much of it--for instance, I had thought I was being protected by the "F.B.I." and had told her so, but the F.B.I. doesn't protect people, and when I gave Lynn a list of names--the 8 people who were protecting me--she contacted the F.B.I. and they told her that they had never heard of me (or the people on my list) and that I didn't exist. I tried to direct reporters to the U.S. State Department, but they gave a firm "No Comment" and later followed that with *Kola Boof does not exist*--which started a major, major rumor that White College Boys had created me on the internet and that I was not a real person, but a computer generated image that didn't really exist. Lynn Duke and other reporters asked to meet with me, to disprove the "internet rumor"--but I was living in hiding and could not get clearance to meet with anyone. This made it look as though I really might be a hoax, and people like Lynn Duke naturally came to the conclusion that I was seeking media attention and were disappointed in me, and another black woman reporter--Pam Noles at the Los Angeles Times, refused to even hear my story when I telephoned her (and she lied to a black women's rights group, claiming she had tried to interview me), though she helped to spread the rumor that I was a "hoax" and didn't really exist. I would later learn, however, that her loyalties were with Muslims friends.

"The State Department says there is no Kola Boof" came the emails from reporters at Newsweek and Wall Street Journal.

"Meet with us in person if you really exist."

"I can't! I'm in government hiding!"

Black Issues Book Review flat out refused to take my publicist's telephone calls, and when she finally did get them on the phone, they said, "This woman is pulling a hoax on everyone."

On September 15th 2002, however, the proof came at last that I was not pulling a hoax.

Sudanese diplomat Gamal Ibrahim was so worried by the growing number of Black Americans who were responding to my stories about slavery and genocide in the Sudan that he wrote a full article denouncing me in London's top daily Arabic newspaper, "Alsharq Al-aswat". This, of course, was unheard of. An entire article in a political Arab newspaper devoted to a *"woman"*--that in itself, as many analysts commented, stood as a death threat. For as much as Condoleeza Rice and Hilary Clinton have rankled the nerves of so many in the Arab world, neither of them have ever been the subject of complete articles denouncing and demonizing their characters, and you would especially think that Condoleeza Rice would receive such attention before I would, but it was me who was being called "mentally unstable", "a liar", "a traitor" and a "prostitute" in Ibrahim's lengthy article that called on me to be *"watched"* by the Arab world.

Still, the American media refused to acknowledge that I existed or that my plight was real, and on September 26th, 2002--word came from London that a "fatwa" (an order for assassination) had been placed on my head by Hasan al-Turabi in Khartoum and by Gamal Ibrahim and Sheik Omar Bakri in London for the crimes of "blasphemy" and "treason". This, of course, was an illegal fatwa, because none of these men are Islamic Scholars, they are government politicians--but still-- they had a Sharia court issue an order/warrant for my beheading.

There was still no coverage, no reporting by the media. No one cared. And it was very surreal--these monumental death threats from the world's most proficient killers and yet <u>no one believed me</u> or cared about my children or even cared to *look into it*.

I had become good friends, by that time, via email correspondence with three legendary black men--Professor Derrick Bell, a bestselling author and activist at New York University, Keith Boykin, a former aid to President Clinton and the first openly gay black man to work as a Presidential aid in the White House (Derrick Bell, for those who don't remember, had made national headlines in the 1980's when he protested the absence of minority women on the law faculty and took a two year "sit-out" for which he was eventually dismissed)...and through my work as a Secret Agent for the SLPA, I had become very close to Washington, D.C. radio personality and former head of the NAACP, Joe Madison--a brave heroic black man who actually went to Sudan and purchased slaves from the North Arabs and then took them back to the South side and set them free. On top of that, it was Joe Madison, before anyone else, who had brought the plight of my people to America's attention through media and constant picketing and protesting at embassies and oil companies.

These three men, along with my SPLA comrade, Deng Ajak in London, and a fellow black woman writer and activist, Ajowa Ifetayo--became advisors as well as friends, and it was around this time that the Southern civilians of Sudan began calling me "QUEEN KOLA"--an assignation that I was seen as a *good daughter* for sacrificing so much to bring liberation and justice to my people.

I had no idea that *The New York Times* was about to attack me so viciously that it would nearly destroy my career, but I was starting to be made aware of the all out war between Conservative Republicans and the Democrats in the United States and how my story was not one that the heavily Democratic media wanted to focus on--despite the fact that I'm about as Liberal Democrat as they come.

Through Keith Boykin, Joe Madison and others, I learned that the coming war in Iraq, the Palestinian middle east saga and the ousting of the Republicans from the White House were such high priorities for Democrats in the media that the last thing they needed was a Black African mother of two highlighting the atrocities in "Arab Muslim" Sudan (the media was not yet covering it) or speaking out against Arab Muslim Imperialism or pointing out the anti-black, anti-woman violence that so thoroughly pervades Arab Muslim countries.

A friend at NPR Radio warned me:

"Democrats don't want an African woman talking to black voters about terrorism, evil Arabs and the oppression of Black Africans by Arabs right now, Kola. Your *'fatwa'* and your life story could push black voters to identify with President Bush and the Republicans. You make it seem like invading Iraq would be justified."

SHUT THAT BITCH DOWN:

In October 2002, a reporter from *The New York Times* contacted me to say that Gerald Boyd, the "Senior Editor" of the newspaper (a black man), felt that Kola Boof was unfairly prejudiced against Muslims and Arabs and that she needed to be "confronted" (*these were his exact words). I told the reporter to tell Gerald Boyd to "kiss my black ass", and I declined to be interviewed by the paper--but then a week later, Julie Salamon, a regular features writer for the *TIMES* called to say that she had been commissioned to write a feature article about me whether I cooperated or not. I spoke with Ms. Salamon in snippets on the phone, very little, for about four weeks. It was my hope that if I answered their questions and presented my case, politically, they would write a fair and balanced story rather than the "confrontational" attack that I felt was being hinted at by the Boyd aid. But when the feature article ran on Dec. 11th, 2002, it was filled with the most shocking lies and distortions about my character--for instance, I am only quoted one time in the entire article saying: *"I can't deny that I'm a conniving person."* Which is something I would never be stupid enough to say about myself in an interview, but of course, because it's *The New York Times*, people still believe that I actually said that. Then as well, the newspaper claimed that they weren't sure that I was a real person (despite the fact that I'd done a 90 minute photo shoot with them the day before the article ran). They didn't use a single shot from our photo session, but instead took a movie still from one of my old Arabic films and *"darkened it"* and used that as the lead picture--with a childhood photograph of me they got from Unicef on page 3 of the article.

Along with these deceitful things, they misquoted Deng Ajak, my SPLA commander in London and reported that they had interviewed the terrorists Hasan al-Turabi, Gamal Ibrahim and Sheik Omar Bakri and that these men had claimed that there was no fatwa issued against me and that none of them had threatened my life.

Now please keep in mind--Hasan al-Turabi is such a dangerous terrorist that the rulers of Sudan put him under house arrest to keep him from killing, and in 2005, Sheik Omar Bakri threatened not only to kill the President of Pakistan for giving "the west" information about where Osama Bin Laden might be, but also threatened my life again--giving a public speech in which he claimed that I'm a "cannibal" who eats human flesh and stating that he would have me killed if I ever released my autobiography, *"Diary of a Lost Girl"*.

The New York Times portrayed these men, all three of whom are killers and close friends of Bin Laden, as upstanding, trustworthy politicians and referred to me in the article as "a prostitute", "a hoax", "a liar who will stop at nothing to get publicity for her books". To top it off, they suggested that I don't even exist--which would mean that my children (whose lives were in danger) don't exist either.

Once the article was published, the roof caved in.

Aquaman, which is the nickname I call my children's father, left me, because he couldn't stand to live under protection of the government and resented that he alone wasn't enough to protect his wife and kids. Not only that, but he was angry at me for writing the books I did and for being an activist--all of which I was before he met me, but I'd mislead him into thinking that a writer writes late at night and that the extent of my career aspirations would be nearly anonymous. I would be a stay at home mom and homemaker (which I am) and not allow my career to interfere with our family life--but with all the controversies I was involved in, and then after finding out that I had been sexually involved with Osama Bin Laden--Aquaman left me.

HUMILIATION:

Everyone, of course, from coast to coast was saying that I was a liar, a hoax and a con artist after *The New York Times* article came out, and naturally, I became desperate to defend my honor, to find some forum, some way of telling my side of the story and respond to the hatchet job that *The New York Times* had done, but no one would allow me to be heard. People, like for instance Natalie Danford at Salon.Com (yet another "white woman" who wrote that I was not a real person and didn't exist)...just liberally brushed aside the reality of me and my children's suffering and made all manner of insensitive and ignorant comments.

Hillel Hitalie of *Associated Press* and I talked on the telephone for several weeks when I was considering bringing a lawsuit against *The New York Times*. Hillel was extremely kind to me and I adore him, but still, he did not allow me any rebuttal against the *Times* article.

Paul Brown at *The Los Angeles Times* told my publicist that I didn't exist. Journalist Neal Pollock wrote an article about how he couldn't stop laughing at my name--he actually wrote this on the internet and it's still there. Editors at ESSENCE magazine and BLACK ISSUES BOOK REVIEW not only refused to give me a chance at rebuttal, but were scornful towards my publicist, Yi Nee Ling, and basically made the comment that I was "African" and *not one of them*, and to let her own people (the Africans) worry about her.

My mother and sisters cancelled all their subscriptions to ESSENCE and I've bad mouthed BLACK ISSUES BOOK REVIEW every since, but the ironic thing is, it still hurts--as a black mother who was in very real danger (and may still be)--it hurt really bad.

Keith Boykin agreed with me, that I should sue *The New York Times* in order to get the opportunity to rebut their hatchet job, but Derrick Bell, who had defended me and said good things about me in *The New York Times* article advised me not to sue the newspaper (he said that there was no way I'd be able to win against such a powerful and wealthy enterprise and that they could use their position in the media world to further hurt and humiliate me--not to mention, the network of good old white boys could destroy my career).

And it was during this time in 2002 that the Dutch filmmaker, Theo Van Gogh, contacted me to say that he did believe me, because he'd heard Muslim extremists all over Belgium and the Netherlands professing that *"Kola Boof must die"*. Theo told me to ignore the cruelty of the American press and offered to send me money to help feed and clothe my children, but I turned it down, as their father was more than financially supporting us and always had taken care of us. But I will never forget the love and kindness that Theo Van Gogh extended to me as I struggled with my Dutch in our conversation and he made quirky comical phrases in English and we lamented the great suffering that one does when they dare to reveal injustices in the Arab Muslim world. Sadly, on November 2nd, 2004, a Muslim extremist shot and stabbed Theo as he was cycling to his home in Amsterdam. The murderer would later say in open court, while clutching the KORAN, *"the law compels me to chop off the head of anyone who insults Allah and the prophet."* He actually said that.

And every time I think of a human being actually muttering such sick, fanatical, satanic jibberish--I feel so ashamed that I was born human and born Muslim and so betrayed that God isn't powerful enough to defend shim-self and needs psychotics to do it.

God bless you, Theo Van Gogh.

For being so incredibly kind to me and for getting the Dutch press to write about me and report my story. For caring about my sons and for believing in me.

God keep and protect you, Theo.

tima usrah

(*through fire comes the family*)

OSAMA BIN LADEN IS NOT DEAD:

I began to think I'd never be free. I found a dead bird on the windshield of my car one morning with a threatening note.

It was still 2002.

My parents were forced to move out of our family home in S. E. Washington, D.C., because of *"suspicious"* people making crank phone calls and leaving strange notes. My sister Tamla had to move, as well, and all the way in Sudan and Egypt--several of my uncles; men who had disowned me years ago for reasons mostly having to do with religion, were jailed and beaten just for being related to me.

And then a new accusation started. Because I'd left from Osama with more than $200,000 in gifts, and had sold the Yemenese water box for a fraction of its cost ($60,000) in London, and because I had lived relatively high on the hog after leaving Osama, it was suddenly being said that I had wanted the relationship with Osama and was happy in it and that I had been *in love* with him.

An Egyptian newspaper reported that I'd been spotted shopping in Milan with two of Osama's best known bodyguards in 1996, and someone claiming to have been a worker at La Maison Arabe went on the radio in London and said that Osama and I had been involved in a whirlwind romance and that I was just bitter because he'd refused to marry me. I just want you, the reader, to know in case you hear about these rumors--that they're not true. And all of that I could handle--but not the bombshell about my oldest son being fathered by Osama.

Miss Connie Fucking Chung--CNN:

My publisher, an Ethiopian businessman named Russom Damba was firebombed as the new year--2003--rolled in.

Arab Muslim extremists, upset at him for publishing my short story collection *"Long Train to the Redeeming Sin"*, firebombed his printing press in Rabat, Morocco which caused Russom to drop me from his company, The North African Book Exchange--a company that he'd originally started just for me.

There was never anything romantic between Russom and I (at 70-plus, he was more like a grandfather in my life), but the rumors abounded that I had *"fucked"* him to get my books published, and as you'll soon see, that nasty rumor was to follow me at other publishing houses as well.

Although about 100 newspapers worldwide reported the bombing of my publisher, in America, only *The New York Post* did.

In fact, it was *The New York Post* who telephoned me concerning my oldest son, who was only 5 years old at the time. The principal at my son's school had called the police because a reporter was on the premises of the school attempting to take photographs of my son!

Apparently, despite the dark chocolate complexions of both my sons, there were rumors floating in the media that my oldest was the result of my affair with Osama. You may as well know that I would later discover that my former publicist, a disgruntled ex-friend and ex-employee, Yi Nee Ling, had been telling this lie to the New York Times and other media, and when I explained that my child was only five years old and was therefore too young to be Osama's son--members of the press (the National Enquirer and the Globe, for instance) challenged me, saying that 5 was too young for a kid to be enrolled in elementary school, and on the strength of Yi Nee Ling's misinformation, they believed that my son was "7" and that I was lying about his age.

It became violently ugly (right there at the school) with *The Irish Examiner* reporting the following:

> But when recent media reports about her past sparked
> rumors about her son's paternity she decided to remove
> him from school.
> "I am fighting to protect the lives of my children", she said,
> explaining that a photographer had been seen outside the
> school attempting to take her son's picture.
> **"Osama Bin laden is not my son's father, and I shall rip out**
> **the throat, in one bite, of anyone who tries to photograph my**
> **babies."**
> Boof has US Federal protection after the Sudanese-based NIF
> issued a fatwa against her because of her writings condemning
> female castration and stonings in the country.
> She was recently dropped by her publisher, Russom Damba, after
> his printing press in Morocco was firebombed. (Irish Examiner)

Out of the blue, I received a blessing from God that I never in a million years expected--a check was sent to me by the boxer Mike Tyson for over seven thousand dollars. It contained a message instructing me to get my son out of public schools and into private school to keep him from being traumatized by the insensitivity of the media. I was shocked, because I had never ever met or spoken with Mike Tyson at any point in my life--and to this day--I have not met him in person. So, obviously, this was a sincere gesture of genuine kindness from a black man who was concerned about the welfare of young black boys, and because of his good deed, I was able to enroll my son in one of California's most secure and exclusive private schools right away--and my son has benefitted from this ever since.

I realized then that I would never be free of Osama.

A woman named Betsy Goldman called me on behalf of CNN's *Connie Chung Tonight* television program. She was very nice, extremely professional and wanted me to do an interview with Connie. I said yes. But then the next night, another call came in from a producer at *Connie Chung Tonight*. She said that it was her job to do preliminary questions, and she had the nerve to say to me, "Now Kola, I'm not accusing you of lying or anything--but Connie was wondering why a man of Osama Bin Laden's stature and wealth would choose a black woman for his mistress?" *RING-ring*. <u>I was so shocked</u>. I told her, "I don't know too many white women whose vaginas are infibulated--maybe they're all working over at ESSENCE magazine, but infibulation is a requirement with Osama."

She asked, "What does infibulated mean?"

Anyway, they wanted to have my son on the show--his little innocent chocolate angel face on screen for all America to scrutinize and demonize. I said absolutely not, and Derrick Bell told me in an email that he would have lost all respect for me if I had taken my child on national television. I asked the Producer, "With all the people in this world that are threatening to kill me, why would I allow my children to be photographed or seen on t.v.?"

Other media criticized me as well for not making my family and personal friends available for interviews and for being so reluctant myself to participate in them. I had turned down appearances on *Good Morning America*, *EXTRA* and had declined to be interviewed by *Playboy* and *the National Enquirer*, because the white press hated me and were only interested in making fun of me, and in order to get an interview with me--I had rules about how I was to be presented.

But no one seemed to care when I explained to them that my uncles in Egypt and Sudan had been jailed simply for being related to me or that my Black American family was in danger and that many of them had moved out of Washington, D.C. The press refused to understand that this was a serious concern--the protection of my loved ones more than my own protection.

Anyway, the producer insisted that I bring my son on the Connie Chung show to visibly prove that he doesn't look anything like Osama and I flat out refused.

"I don't want my son exploited."

The Producer, who wanted to make it seem as though it wasn't about my son, said to me during a subsequent phone call, "Well, Miss Chung thinks that viewers might find it unbelievable that a man of Bin Laden's religious background (*O pull-eeeze!*) would have a black mistress and one raised in America at that."

The following day, Betsy Goldman called me back and told me that if I wasn't willing to have my son on the show...the events of Jan. 7th 2003 being the "topic" of the show...then they were cancelling my booking.

As if I could give a shit. I said, "Fine."

But because I'd always been a huge Connie Chung fan, I shook with rage for about three days--totally freaked out that someone of her position and background could make such assinine comments about "race". I just had to confront her about it!

I wanted to know...*WHY?*

And over the next few weeks, I sent several messages directly to Connie Chung, both in writing and by phone, expressing my hurt feelings behind the things that her producer alleged that she had said, but I have never--in all these years--gotten a response. No denial of the comments, no apology or claim that it was a misunderstanding, so naturally, I took her silence to be a confirmation...that she had said the shit and that she was standing by it.

As my Black American mother would say: *Uhn.*

There's a name for women like Connie Chung, but I wouldn't use it outside of a kennel.

Or on second thought...yes I would.
Cross-eyed unemployed <u>bitch</u>.

FOX NEWS came after me next.

And I say *"came after me"*, because that's exactly what it was-- they wanted to discredit my story and dispel the notion that I was some female Amiri Baraka espousing Conservative Republican views on the issue of Arab Muslim extremism--when what I really represented to FOX NEWS and the rest of the "conservative media" was yet another uppity black woman writer, promoting abortion, attacking christianity, and telling Black Americans to eschew assimilation and get "blacker".

Anyone who has actually watched the interview that FOX NEWS did with me remembers two things--(a) just like the New York Times, they *"darkened"* my image on t.v. and had me sit at a very strange angle that was unflattering--and (b) they kicked me off the show before my interview was even finished.

So for all those Democratic Kola haters in the liberal media who claimed that FOX NEWS liked Kola Boof and wanted to confirm her story--that's camel shit.

I was treated horribly by FOX NEWS.

For two weeks...*two weeks*...FOX NEWS assigned more than 25 "fact checkers" in North Africa, London and Spain to investigate my story (and of course, by then, an April 9th report on the floor of the United Nations had confirmed that the Sudanese government had put a fatwa on my head--so that much they knew), but many other details...such as my relationship with Bin Laden and other essentials, they were determined to discredit and make me look like some *"deep dark scary"* militant jigaboo woman (view the tape online).

"This is going to be worse than the New York Times", my handlers worried, and so I insisted that FOX NEWS allow me to appear in their national news "Special Feature" about Kola Boof--to refute whatever claims they raised and to defend myself.

The U.S. government had removed all public records of my adoption and my 1993 citizenship declaration, so I was forced to show them my passport to prove that I was Naima Bint Harith.

If you watch the show, you can see how terribly nervous I was (because I had come in fully expecting a fight)...but to my shock...FOX NEWS had been able to confirm just about every aspect of my recent life--the fatwa and the affair with Osama Bin Laden (again, Prince Fabrizzio Ruspoli confirmed that I had lived with Osama and a cook at the estate also confirmed it, although her life was threatened afterwards). At last, my experiences had been validated, and no matter how rude I was treated by FOX NEWS (as I said, they kicked me off the show right after announcing that they had confirmed my story), and no matter how conservative and right-wing their network is, I will always be grateful that they took the time, spent the money, and *by accident--* ended up proving that my story is true and that...I do exist.

I am Kola Boof.

Make Way...for Kola Boof!

"Be and be not afraid"
            --Tracy Chapman

● ●

<u>In</u> 1997, when I wrote the two word poem "Kola Boof" and decided to take it as my pen name--I believe that it was my way of escaping my Egyptian grandmother's evil light skinned face and the cataclysmic pain that she had inflicted upon me for being a little black girl. For most of my life, and especially as an artist, I have tried to analyze the source of my enduring sorrow (that one hurt that I can't remember, but is there at my core--making me an artist, making me love art) and I have come to the conclusion that...*once someone abuses us*, we can never really stop...

...being abused.

So instead of completely healing, I try to catch the music from it, to create perspective out of sorrow. I try to fix up the wound so that it's beautiful and singing--but still a wound, still oozing. I just want to find the God in me, to love and to hate as much as it takes to bring about change in this world, and to find the thing that every artist and lover of art alike is in search of...sincerity.

In spite of everything, I really, really love myself. I do.

One day in 1995, a special flower bloomed open inside my head. I was traveling back and forth between the United States and Egypt and I realized that I was no longer just an African. I was something *mixed*--and I'm not talking about the blood of my White Arab father--I'm talking about being mixed in a much better way. I had been raised and grealty influenced by Black Americans. Not via media--but in the actual home of a blue collar Black American family, daily, until I could mimic and imitate them to a tee--read their thoughts, understand their thinking, sing in the choir with the church on sunday, talk just as they talked. I had become a *hybrid*, a fusion of Nilotic Black African people and Black Americans, specifically the Black Americans of North Carolina, Georgia, Tennessee and places like that. I was *mixed* in a very tangible way with these two cultural realities, which truly for a black person...is the <u>best</u> of both worlds.

And by 1997 when I was arrested and kicked out of Morocco for leading a feminist protest against the stoning of a group of *lesbian* Arab Muslim women (I was unsuccessful, as the lesbians were buried up to their necks and stoned in their heads to death as planned), I fully realized that no matter how tight and sweet my pussy was, and no matter how much I had grown to love having sex with men (in spite of the pain), I would have to stop being a dick-teaser/dick-pleaser sexpot of a girl...and become a woman. A real woman, like the kind that my heroes Nawal El-Sadaawi, Gloria Steinem, Ama Ata Aidoo and Alice Walker not only were, but had had the courage, against all manner of death threat and intimidation, to write about. A *"womanist"*, to use Alice Walker's word, with a purpose in life.

But before that, I had to make peace with my mental canvas.

~~

The first thing I embraced was Dr. Diallo's assertion that I was not "mentally ill" but was--"*too mentally aware*". Somewhere between 1991-1993, he testified before a D.C. Immigration/Naturalization panel (as my Black American father was fighting for my U.S. citizenship)...that by staying with the bodies of my slain parents overnight, I had *sat down and visited with death itself*, and in doing so, had traumatized myself to the point of being fearless and had turned myself into an "exhibitionist". He said that orphaned female children have a tendacy to herd and *mother* other children--and could be over protective of not just other children, but of "rules and standards", and he said that in adulthood, female orphans will herd and *mother* group associations to the point of preaching or being over-bearing, but will be superior builders and strategists, strengthening and providing foundations upon which the people she touches can better stand.

"None of this is grounds to deny citizenship", Dr. Diallo told them. "If anything, this girl will become an over-achiever--*slightly eccentric, yes*--but highly valuable to any society that will have her. She is much stronger than your average human being. Naima is not bipolar, she is not schizophrenic, she is not anti-social or a danger to herself or others--what she is...is an exhibitionist; accutely sensitive, fearless and has sexually splintered manifestations of anger and rage due to a molestation and due to racial and cultural displacement, much of which was healed by placing her in a black family. As a small girl, she witnessed her parents murder and stayed outdoors all night with the bodies. From that moment on, her mind was blown wide open, which can give the appearance that she's crazy--but she's no more crazy than you or I. Naima is *passionate*. She feels very deeply."

In 1994, before being dumped by Efrem and leaving for Israel, I'd written the novel "Flesh and the Devil" and attempted to find a publisher in the United States. That was the beginning of my horrendous difficulties with White women--as most of the editors at the major publishing houses who were assigned to read, evaluate and aquire new works by women authors were nearly all white, and right away, there was a general consensus among these women--"*You are brilliant!*" Viking. Riverhead. Seven Stories. Putnam.

I couldn't understand it.

They constantly praised my talent and were astonished upon learning that I had no formal education whatsoever--yet they couldn't publish me.

"Your work is too disturbing."

"In the slavery scenes, all the white people are evil--there's not a single good white person being shown."

"The female characters are too dark for American readers?"

"Why are the white men being castrated?"

"Naima--if you look at Terry McMillan and Toni Morrison and Alice Walker's success, it's been built by the steady support of white feminist book buyers. They write the same things you write--the same themes, the same issues about being a woman of color..."

"*I am not...a woman of color.*"

"--well, about being a strong black woman."

"*I am not...a strong black woman.*"

"OK--anyway--your books turn white women off. Your anger and the underlying separatism."

"*I am not a separatist...and there's almost never any white women in my books!*"

"Well--we're looking for black authors who have the ability to transcend race."

Transcend race. We can't have nudity.

Transcend race.

"This is a time of coming together, of finding common ground as Jesse Jackson says. There's nothing wrong with you telling your stories of slavery or black women being raped and dehumanized by white and black men--but you don't have the forgiving tone of most black women writers or the empathetic understanding of an Alice Walker. You've got the little blue black girl dousing the light skinned children with gasoline and burning them alive in a classroom (*Long Train to the Redeeming Sin*)--then later in the same story, she's walking on water with Jesus Christ and has apparently gone to heaven. You've got a white man castrated by another little black girl in the same story and she also goes to heaven. You've got a wedding scene between two homosexuals that uses African wedding vows (*Flesh and the Devil*). You've got a black woman beating the crap out of a white woman--a white woman raping a black woman. Your leading ladies are so incredibly dark skinned that it's hard for Black American women to identify with them...and you harp on color...too much writing about black hair and dark skinned beauty--this is not the 70's."

I changed the leading lady in *"Flesh and the Devil"*, RooAmber Childress, to a mulatto girl with green eyes, yellow skin and flowing auburn hair and changed the villain from a blond white woman to a sexy Puerto Rican--but they still didn't want the book.

"You're one of the most interesting new writers we've read, Ms. Bint Harith, but your themes are too confrontational."

In 1995, *"Flesh and the Devil"*, a book I'd written *for* the Black Americans as a love letter that first documented their lives as Africans before dramatizing their journey through slavery to the Western Hemisphere--was published under the name Naima Kitar *in Arabic* by the tiny now defunct Feza Press in Morocco. So, of course, no Black Americans got to read or know of my book honoring them from an

African woman's perspective, but at least I was published somewhere on the planet.

I was not topless on the back of the book, however.

By 1997--I'd gotten the bright idea to direct a movie. A remake of the Somerset Maughn classic *"Rain"* (which had been filmed in 1932 with Joan Crawford and had deeply affected me), the story of the prostitute Sadie Thompson and a male Religious Reformer's frustrated quest to transform her into a nice docile christian woman--even to the point of *"raping her"* as a way of forcing her to turn over her sexual power as a human being to mankind and to the church.

From the moment I saw that film as a teen, it haunted me.

In Rabat, Morocco, I approached the wealthy Ethiopian businessman Russom Damba about financing my remake, but after reading my script--he was incredulous as to how anyone from the Arab Muslim world could wish to glorify a whore.

And this is <u>*crucially important*</u> for people to grasp if they want to understand who "Kola Boof" is--because at that point in my life, after being mutilated vaginally in Africa, molested at 12, raped several times as an adult, raped and held by Osama Bin Laden and exploited by the producers of the B-pictures I'd been appearing in--I no longer believed in the concept that women can be whores.

I saw my mutilation and my rape for what it is.

A tool for conquering a woman's ownership of her sexuality...so that men could own it. Through rape and Men's religions (Christianity, Judaism, Islam) women were made to feel dirty about their sexuality and to cover themselves up (for men) and suppress their sexuality so that MEN (and those who believe in the superiority of men) could call them *"respectable ladies"*..."*good decent women"*..."*clean*".

It was all such camelshit--another form of slavery. The concept that men could fuck around as much as they liked, lie to, impregnate and then abandon their women and children, sleep with ten females a week (playa, playa), transmit and carry veneral diseases, let drag queens suck their dicks in dark alleys--and still be respectable--in fact--be patted on the back and looked up to for being whoremongering dogs --while females were expected to *"cover up"*--their virginity placed above their human worth...say it again: *their virginity placed above their human worth*...and the entire prime of their lives often wasted...used up...as they compete to be the most respectable "Lady" in the community, the most deserving of having a MAN, the one with the most self-hating, anti-woman moral beliefs (for instance, the R. Kelly Child Pornography case where millions of black women actually demonized the 14 year old female victim, but defended R. Kelly based on the fact that he was a *"genius musician"* and *"a brother"*--calling the little girl a "HO", but not being women enough to ask the question-- how, where and from whom does a 14 year old *learn how* to embrace molestation? And what grown man had fucked her at 11 and 12 so that she could be a sexual performer by 14? And why were we, the mothers of the community blaming a child for its own corruption?).

Men are men. Women are HO's.

I couldn't tolerate the sexist camelshit.

I told Russom Damba that I could never go back to Christianity or Islam and that instead of *"covering up"* and relinquishing my sexuality after being raped by men--I was determined to flaunt my sexuality even more, to embrace and use it.

To own it.

To live my life. To put my sex in the service of me for my own selfish agenda and enjoyment. I could give a fuck about men validating my respectability or the society considering me a decent woman. Like any man, I owned my sexuality and I lived my life. I had men on my own terms, and this to me was freedom and allowed me to use my sex as both a power *over men* and as a comfort to those men I wanted to comfort--just as <u>MY</u> God and the universe had intended.

I came to understand that religion itself is not God, but is the institution (the *institution*) through which mankind worships and studies God. Therefore, like any other institution of law and higher learning, it is created and shaped by human beings, by human behavior and by human insecurities, almost entirely by MEN, and in my remake of the film *"Rain"*, I wanted to take the story a step further by having Sadie Thompson start her own religion. A women's religion loosely based on the ancient Nilotic religions of my own direct ancestors, the Cushites and the Egyptians, but most assuredly, a rebuke of the men's religions that currently dominate the world--impeding peace and spirituality (you can't have spirituality without sexuality); impeding justice and preventing men from nurturing, respecting and understanding women by disallowing women to be fully developed as sexually autonomous human beings.

I wanted to demonstrate that the only reason that we hate and demonize so called *"whores, HOs and prostitutes"* is because these women (the smart ones, not the dumb ones) dare to own and legislate their own sexuality and are not dependent on males for their self-identity. This, of course, is similar to being a lesbian (the only women I've ever been jealous of, because I'm not able to be a lesbian myself)--men feel threatened by it, because they lose phallic power.

"I can't finance this movie", Russom had said to me, "But what about a book? Your writing skills are absolutely stunning. I've always wanted to start a publishing house."

And thus began The North African Book Exchange (1997), with me as its sole author the first few years, causing people to gossip that there was sex between Russom and I--but the truth was, he and his wife were like grandparents towards me and were greatly intrigued by my history and my work as art. They weren't particularly religious people and didn't necessarily agree with me, but they felt that I should be heard, as Russom said, "For art's sake". I wrote the two word poem, "Kola Boof", originally intending it to be included in the poetry collection I was putting together to serve as the debut of the new me--but then I liked it so much that I decided to take it as my pen name.

The book itself, *"Every Little Bit Hurts"* (released years later in the United States as *"Nile River Woman"*) was sort of a remake of another black poet's book--as I'd been greatly influenced by the legendary Mari Evans and her classic 1960's collection *"I Am a Black Woman"*--which is probably one of my all time favorite poetry collections. If you read the very first poem in *"Every Little Bit Hurts"* (aka *"Nile River Woman"*) and then immediately read the very last poem in the book--you will get what the book is about, and for those who haven't read it yet, I must warn you...it's my angriest, most lethal book. Chock full of anti-Muslim, anti-Arab Afrocentrism and epic celebrations of womanist religion and female sexual power.

The pornographic poem *"Cleopatra"* (*Nile River Woman*) is one of my many salutes to 1930's Oscar winner Hattie McDaniel, but people never realize it. They assume it's about me.

By 1998, the book was so powerfully whispered about in North Africa and Ethnic Europe that even with only 700 copies sold, it moved Osama Bin Laden to telephone me in Spain and say, "If I had the time to waste...I'd come and slit your throat myself."

He (and a lot of the big boys in North Africa) were shocked that one of the palace *hostesses* was actually becoming something.

People who love my poetry ask me about my process of writing it, but there is no process. The only reason I write poems...is because I can't sing...and in the middle of trying to sing to get the spooks or the rainbows out of my head, I end up writing a lyric that passes as a poem of some kind.

And it's because of Curtis Mayfield that I'm a poet. Because of him writing songs like *"To Be Invisible"* and *"The Makings of You"*-- that I'm a poet. And because of Mari Evans and Sylvia Plath and Nina Simone and Maya Angelou and Alden Nolan...I said Alden Nolan and Lucille Clifton and Jessica Care Moore and Wanda Coleman and Toni Morrison, who to me is a musician, and because of my very favorite poem, *"Be Nobody's Darling"* by Alice Walker and because of Burt Bacharach and Hal David and Eric B. and Rakim.

And because of Audre Lord saying to black women: "Our silence...will not save us."

Because I can't sing/I'm a poet.

When I'd had my abortion, I remember it being a bright sunny Virginia morning and me driving myself for what seemed hours to a clinic in Maryland and no words for a poem would come. Efrem Nelkin was more than happy to pay for it, but never knew the true reason I was aborting, and I'd pulled the car to the side of the road repeatedly, because of the tears blocking my vision. I was so scared.

The nice white lady told me to take off my clothes.

Then they put my legs in stirrups, which were uncomfortable, because my legs were so incredibly long.

They inserted a huge needle into my vagina, giving me a shot in the cervix--and then I felt nothing. Nothing at all. They performed the abortion and I bled a little for about two days, but not a lot.

Which brings me to another memory--that of being a little girl in Omdurman, Sudan and my father, Pappuh Mahdi, raisng me like the son he'd always wanted--teaching me how to build boats and shoot guns; telling me emphatically that, "*A Queen is not a Queen...until she knows how to kill.*"

It was the seed, you understand, of why I had the abortion.

The two of us, rising before daybreak, so that Pappuh could go down to the Nile river and say his ablutions before morning prayer, and then after his prayers, the fishing ritual...Pappuh and I singing the special songs for Fayoum, the ancient gathering place of Sobek, the Egyptian Crocodile God. The two of us wading into the river to catch breakfast--Pappuh's very favorite being the Tilapia fish rather than Nile Perch (which can grow 6 feet long and weigh 400 pounds), and then maybe twice a week, we would catch a crocodile--two or three feet long--which required, using Pappuh's pistol or any gun, a special technique in order for the fired bullet to penetrate the extra tough hide.

It hurt my tiny wrist to shoot the crocodiles, effectively killing them, but Pappuh made me do it until I was a pro, and Mahdi Pappuh would talk to me quite in depth, and he would tell me the mantra of the old Arab Egyptians (which most Arab boys are taught): "Crocodiles who swim up North are *pure*. Crocodiles who swim South...are mixed breed. Never ingest the meat from the mixed ones."

And so we would only kill the crocs swimming north.

Hook-shanking their rough prehistoric skin, ripping off the body suit (which Pappuh would sell to "*Kwawaja*"--caucasoid tourists) and flaying the beautiful bone white meat beneath it--the back strap and the tail filet--Mommysweet roasting, pounding and cook-frying the morning coffee before adding ginger and hot water to the syrup, and Pappuh pounding into my head each and every day: "*White Supremacy*...is this world's only true religion. Everything else, Naima, is just a decoy to hide that fact."

Carefully, we would cook the crocodile meat (and it's very easy to cook), seasoning the fresh white filets and frying them about three minutes on each side in peanut oil...but *careful*...careful not to let the meat sit in its own fat, which becomes a curse.

"They weaken the African and steal everything from him", my white Arab father would preach as Mommysweet and I cooked. "...by separating him from his own people. They teach him to hate himself and to destroy himself by removing his own crown."

We would eat breakfast and then take a boat out to Tutti Island where we'd sit around the conical tombs of our great warrior Mahdi, or if it were Friday (on Fridays they shut the city down), we'd go to the Souq and listen to the Sudanese drum recitals. But Pappuh would be telling me, "The knotty hair is the African man's crown. It is the _Proof_ that he is the unique one made in God's image, the chosen one spoken of in religion--the _Proof_ that his people are the chosen people. No other race on earth has this hair but God's son, the Black man, wrote the ancient Hebrew Cushites. Do you understand, Naima?"

"Yes, Pappuh."

"Without your African hair, the one true hair--you are defeated. And that is what this whole game on earth is about! The Serpent must trick the black man into relinquishing his crown."

"Yes, Pappuh."

"To seal the black man in poverty and death, to keep the black man from being born--to ruin and bastardize your hair as so many of the Ethiopians have been ruined and bastardized. To own Africa by erasing the Black man and raping the womb of the black woman. It's been going on for thousands of years now--do you hear me?"

"Yes, Pappuh."

"You must fight against White Supremacy--by giving birth only to your people...*the black people*, Naima. And the blacker the better. This is why I married your mother--because I'm a bastard!"

And I would start crying, weeping, *"Don't say that Pappuh."*

But he would keep on. The sweat pouring from his brow and the chapped lips turning nearly blue from his heroin fix. His sunken eyes lacerating my flesh as he demanded, *"White Supremacy...is this world's only true religion. Everything else, Naima, is just a decoy to hide that fact. I'm counting on you to fight against it by giving birth to your own image--and your children doing the same, and so on. When you let the whites erase you with their blood--you are defeated!"*

All the way to the abortion clinic, I had heard my dead father's words over and over again. His admonition that I must not be a pawn in the game of the Non-Blacks. The game of removing the crown--*the proof*--from the scalps of the chosen people, the black race.

And for that reason--I could not have a white man's baby.

I am already half white Arab, and at the roots of my own nappy hair, there is evidence that I am...*not authentic*, not pure.

So it terrified me to be pregnant with a child that would advance the White Supremacist World System that has been destroying African people and eroding the Black man's power for centuries.

Black Americans spoke of mixed children having *"good hair"*, but my children would have to settle for *"God's hair"* (the Proof), and in order to produce such hair, I would have to love my own reflection--a black man. Only then, according to my Arab Egyptian father, could I win the game against the White Gene, not only for myself, but for my entire race--for my people and for Africa.

~~

Of course when bi-racial people heard about the reason for my abortion, they called me a racist--but the truth is--I love all of God's creations, of all creeds and colors, the whole planet of animal life and mankind, God requires me to love and value everyone, because we are all, in a sense, connected to each other...but that doesn't change the fact that White Supremacy (the belief that *"light skin"* is superior) rules the planet, continuously favoring one side of the human race while slowly erasing the other...and as an African woman--the mother of all human beings, the lowest person on the food chain, the one who is the most despised, lied upon, unprotected by her own son-seed and betrayed simply for being both dark skinned and female--I have to choose justice (not idealism) and have sense enough to stand for the love and respect of my own womb and my own ancestors and for the acknowledgement of the deliberate _holocaust_ that has enslaved, raped, robbed and massacred untold millions and millions of African people at the hands of assorted Non-Black peoples for more than a thousand years.

That is not racism; that's self-respect and self-preservation...and as a black woman, the one human on earth who has been put last and betrayed by everyone on this planet including the black man, I don't owe any loyalty to any goddamned body. Fuck the bi-racial people. I am not a woman of color, I am a *Black* woman--a wombbearer and a daughter of the earth's first garden, Africa and the Tima (the result of great fire--the black people).

We who have been niggerized, bastardized and removed from our own legislation, our own land and our own glory--and yet still, for the most part, have not lost our crown (the Proof), which is why the game of the Serpent has not stopped.

As controversial as my books were considered by the Arabs, Muslims and traditional African sexists circa 1998, I was never considered a serious threat to the Arab Muslim Imperialists of North

Africa until I began developing a following amongst Black Americans in the United States. Only then did the Mullahs inject real passion and fire behind their death threats and their propoganda against me, and you must understand...that the Black Americans are a crucially important "Demographic" to the Arab Imperial world, because Minister Louis Farrakhan has spent his life selling their loyalties (the Afro-Americans) to the Arabs and the Muslims, under the guise that the Arabs are *"our brown brothers"* who are oppressed and wronged by the White Devil man just like Africa...but that's camelshit. The Arab Muslims are the exact same oppressors as the White Europeans, and not only that, they're worse--the Arabs and Muslims are, *without peer*, the two greatest oppressors of African people in world history. They are not our brown brothers and sisters as the Black Americans like to romanticize, but are the bastard children of ancient African women--bastard children who hate Africa and hate black people and hate their own brown skin and will pimp, exploit and use black people's energetic loyalty for as long as black male leaders sell us out and offer us up as fool suckers to be licked. No nation of black men on earth has ever been more abused, more violated or more dehumanized than they have by the last *thousand Years* of Arab Muslim racial (colorist would be more accurate) and religious slavery, genocide and oppression...and if I, an African mother...had to choose between an Arab Slavemaster and a White Caucasoid Slavemaster--I would choose the White man--because at least he can be impressed, seduced and mentally manipulated.

Obviously, it seems that I hate the Arab Muslim people--but I don't hate them. I'm just...*extremely angry*...pissed off at their deeds and practices and at the lie that they are the black people's brother and ally. I am extremely angry at the satanic evil they reign down on Sudan and Mauritania and the corruption and brainwashing and mafia-like violence that they fill Africa with. Of course, I have love for Arab

Muslims--because I am half Arab and was born a Muslim and I love Allah and I have people in my life (Said Musa, Carol Chehade, my Uncles) who are Arab Muslim and I truly, truly love those people with all my heart. My brother is a Muslim and he means the world to me. But in the political sense, I cannot support the Arab Muslims, and in fact, for the good of Africa, I fight against them. From Nigeria to Khartoum to Egypt, they really and truly are destroying the African continent and the Black Man should stop trying to hide behind and claim every colored person as his "brother and ally"...because the truth is...those of us who are Black have no brothers and sisters but each other. Not the Latinos, not the Indians, not the Asians, not the Arabs--all of them got together (along with the White man and our ancient sell out African Kings)--got together and created a "nigger".

They all took part. Every fucking one of them.

And they all would do it again--in a heartbeat. So we need to recognize that when your skin is Black and you possess The Proof on your head--you have no family but your own.

Whether you like it or not, you're part of a war to save Africa and the Black race. *People of color*...are not black...and they have always chosen the White man's mansion over the Black man's hut, and while I love the Black Americans with all my heart, I know better than them, and because of that, I have an obligation to tell them the truth.

And the truth is--when you're black you don't have no friends, and you can barely trust your family. So cease with this bullshit of trying to claim everybody with a tan (and straight hair) and focus on your own bloodberry--the black people of the world--and unify and cater to them before you go kissing the asses of all these honorary white fuckers who claim to be "dark". A Latino is nothing but a white man with a taco. Asians are nothing but white men with chopstix.

But anyway, it was when my books began to reach Black Americans that I was classified as a serious threat by the Arab Muslim

Imperialist world.

Between 2001 and 2003, my book "Long Train to the Redeeming Sin" was released in the United States and was immediately Reviewed and recommended by the nation's leading African-American online bookseller--(www.aalbc.com). Of course, the owner Troy Johnson had never heard of me or read any of my work, and frankly had had no time to form an opinion about me, but by accident--he made me an overnight sensation on the campuses of Howard University and UCLA--and his web site quickly became one of the first in history to demonstrate that the internet was more than just a middle class way station, but was a revolutionary new way to market books and break in no-name authors like Kola Boof, and in fact, the cult following that began around "Kola Boof" was so impressive that it drew the attention of *The New York Times*, who used Troy Johnson and (www.aalbc.com) as a back story in their article about me, rightfully heralding the marketing prowess of this powerful new beast--the internet--and me, as its first bonafide literary star.

That was all good--but then came war.

I had been invited to appear on singer Stevie Wonder's Los Angeles radio station KJLH following the 2003 North African firebombing of my book "Long Train" and became such a ratings hit (they did the whole 90 minute show around my story) that I was invited back for a second 90 minute interview, and during that show--a very wealthy Black American businessman in Bel-Air, California by the name of Cornel Chesney called in saying he was apalled at the treatment I was receiving from White media and was outraged that I'd been firebombed--and offered, on the air, to start a publishing company just for me! It was so shocking and fairytale-like, but that's how DOOR OF KUSH BOOKS came into being, and for the second time in my life--*a black man*--had stood up and determined that I would not be silenced and that my books would be published.

Unfortunately, people claiming to be members of the Nation of Islam contacted Cornel right away and tried to convince him that he shouldn't back me--and on nearly every radio interview I've ever done, people claiming to be NOI members have called in to harass, heckle and at times "threaten" my life--but Cornel Chesney refused to go back on his proposal. He set up shop and made me my own boss. I was not only to oversee the American publication of my own books, but was made aquisitions editor and given the power to publish two other authors--Chris Hayden and Diane Dorce. Of course, consequently, the rumors began right away--from New York to D.C. to Los Angeles--that I was being fucked by Cornel Chesney, a married man, but nothing could be further from the truth. Cornel and his beautiful wife, Samia, became like a brother and sister to me, our children doing things together and all of us attending church and sharing holidays together. There's nothing whatsoever about this black man that is dishonorable and he has never once disrespected me, and so it was very painful to have people constantly calling me *"the Diana Ross of the publishing industry"*--which is certainly not to say that I view Diana Ross as sleeping her way to the top, I do not--but after Russom Damba and then Cornel Chesney, that's what people kept calling me, especially in New York--where it matters.

And although (at the time this book went to print) I'd never met Troy Johnson of www.aalbc.com in person and had only spoken to him by phone twice, there started to be this constant question floating around the industry--*"Why is Troy Johnson risking his life to make Kola Boof a star?"* --because with each new release of one of my books, Troy would feature me on his web site, and eventually--he gave me my own discussion board (THE KOOL ROOM), but what people didn't realize was that my publisher, Cornel Chesney was giving Mr. Johnson "free copies" of all my new releases and having me autograph them for Troy to sell and keep 100% profit from in exchange for <u>exposure</u>.

So you see, it was purely business. Troy was being PAID to promote me. And with all these men...Russom, Cornel, Troy, Robert Wright...it was business and not a single one of them ever acted interested in me or came at me like that... nor I them...and during all of this, my complete love and devotion was and has been to the most wonderful man on earth, my children's father, Aquaman--the only man I've *ever* loved. But unfortunately, it's very hard when you have a colorful past like mines and you have no formal education and you're in the high hat snobby genre called "literary fiction"...and in 2003, those rumors about me "sleeping my way to the top" went to a new level when in the midst of all the controversy and suspicious scrutiny one "lying non-existent black publicity hungry African harlot" can stand-- a real cool literary white boy (and I mean an *authentically cool* literary white boy)...the author of *"Happy Baby"* and *"Looking forward to It"*...Stephen Elliott...asked me to submit a short story to his ground-breaking anthology *"Politically Inspired"*. To my shock, Stephen Elliott, who was teaching at Stanford University, was a huge Kola Boof fan (he'd actually read my books and knew quite a lot about me!), and like me, he'd also been orphaned, only he'd ended up shuffled through the system and greatly abused, and the anthology was for charity--as Stephen was very adamantly against the war in the Gulf and wanted desperately to help feed and buy medicine for Arab Iraqi children who'd been orphaned or displaced by the war in Iraq. I, of course, would have rather put my energies behind the genocide/slavery in Sudan, and as a conscious Black North African, saw the Iraqi Arabs as my enemies, but still--little Arab children are innocent and not responsible for the sins of their parents, so I was glad to help and to prove that I didn't hate all Arab Muslim people by being associated with the project.

The nasty rumors about me using Stephen (who to this day I've never met in person, although we live close in California) didn't start up until industry people noticed that my scandalized name was being published by Stephen in the same company as Charles Baxter (a nominee for the National Book Award), the legendary Stewart O'Nan,the infinitely gifted Z.Z. Packer, Anthony Swofford (who was all the rage that year), the legendary Elizabeth Tallent (twice selected for the Best American Short Story) and the cutting edge Michelle Tea- -just to name a few. The book received a starred review from KIRKUS and several people in New York, including Derrick Bell and an editor at *The Paris Review* said that my contribution ("The One You Meet Everywhere") was the best story in the whole book.

But how did _she_ get in the book, people demanded.

Isn't she that provocative African who's been trying to use Osama Bin Laden's name to get famous?

At a Manhattan dinner party, an editor from INTERVIEW magazine actually said to my agent (without knowing it was my agent), "Isn't Kola Boof that lying whore who was featured in the New York Times? How did she manage to get in *that* book?"

And according to my agent, someone from NEWSWEEK (a magazine Stephen writes for) replied, "She must have driven up the coast and sucked old Stephen off during one of his poker parties."

Ha ha ha.

It didn't help, of course, when word got out amongst the Black literati that the romantic lead in Stephen Elliott's autobiographical first novel, "*A Life Without Consequences*" (2001), was a black girl with very large natural breasts. Well, what a coincidence!

And to this day, because very few people in the industry have actually read my work--yet quite a few of them know my name or have heard some negative story about me (she's an overly ambitious attention whore, a LIAR, a prima donna), there remain a lot of people who don't like me, don't respect me and plum don't understand what I stand for. I'm an oddity. *Naked on the back of her books*. Not interested in multiculturism (unless it's to *fuck white men* who can help her career).

And once people start saying these things about you ("*she's the Diana Ross of the publishing industry*"), it's very hard to create a new image of yourself. But the fact is--Stephen Elliott was a fan of my work and asked me to be in the book because, in his own words: "*Kola, you write like a singer. Your stuff is really powerful. I loved* 'Long Train'." We have never met in person, and although we did use to chat on the phone quite a bit--flirting with each other in a "*smitten cousins*" sort of way--I was *pregnant* during that time and was happily in love with my children's father (although we miscarried a week before I appeared on FOX NEWS) and Stephen was also deeply involved with some woman and never once--not once--did we act serious about our flirting.

And I'm writing about all this to *irk* him--exactly why--you'll find out in a minute. But the fact is, I think Stephen Elliott and I are both *masochists*, cut from the same cloth (we're both insecure, sensitive people), and because I wanted to be spanked and he wanted to be spanked, we were more like "gossipy girlfriends"--and sadly--we didn't even get to stay friends (we originally thought we'd be friends for life), because I wasn't the "peachy keen" little Black American I-Got-A-Donkey-Button for the poker 'n beer party in Iowa next week "type" woman that he's used to kick'n it with--that's #1--and because people who were displeased that he was furthering my career by legitimizing my work, filled his head with negative comments about me (*Haven't you heard? She's a Republican Hoax man!, a LIAR and a separatist, dude--she hates white people!*)...the camel's back came breaking when someone (I don't know who) attacked his good friend, the sexy dominatrix Mistress Morgana...and Stephen blamed me.

Stephen had already fired me once, but then rehired me during the writing of "*Politically Inspired*" (in fact, I had been asked to submit a story after Z.Z. Packer said that she couldn't do the project, but then after I wrote my story--she came back and Stephen said that my story was better than hers, so he kept both stories), and after that bit of drama,

I was used to his thin-skinned temperment, but I had _not_ attacked Mistress Morgana (apparently someone had written vicious remarks about her fiction abilities on an internet web page), and because I was known for writing all kinds of wild shit all over the internet--Stephen convinced himself that it was me, Kola Boof, who'd done it, and even after I swore to him that it wasn't me, and even after I telephoned Mistress Morgana and told her that I was _so sorry someone had attacked her_ and assured her that I had nothing against her and would never do something like that--Stephen didn't care...and the truth came out (in my opinion) that he'd just been looking for an excuse to end our friendship, and decided to use that as the reason. Naturally, because I really adored Stephen and had enjoyed having an intellectual buddy to chat on the phone with about all kinds of issues that most people don't normally discuss--I was devastated--and took it especially hard, because this was a time in my life when I was living in hiding and had little contact with the outside world, had just suffered a miscarriage, was being gossiped about and lied on by all manner of industry and press people--and it felt worse than being accused of stealing--if felt as though Stephen were taking their side against me, no matter that I'd shared so many inner truths with him and trusted him so implicitly-- he was adamant that I'd attacked his friend and that I was a bad person (_a gifted writer_, he said, but a bad person) and zapp--I was dismissed for supposedly attacking the dominatrix.

I'm crying just remembering the unfairness of it and his cowardice in not just coming out and admitting--_"you're not a popular person Kola; none of my friends like you"_--which is what it was. He had idolized someone that his type of people didn't approve of.

But anyway, the moral of the story _IS_...I've never slept with anyone to get my work published.

And as 2004 saw the release of three of my books in the United States, wealthy Arab-American companies in the United States (the kind that make large financial contributions to the campaigns of so many Black American politicians) began a smear campaign to deter Black Americans from reading my literature--and the Sudanese government itself issued Press Releases in New York attacking my credibility and assailing me as an African woman, with David Hoile, their head at ESPAC (European Sudanese Public Affairs Council), erecting whole web sites just to slander and discredit "Kola Boof" as both an author and an activist--by any pasted together lie necessary.

In some ways it worked, because none of the Black Book Distributors in the United States would carry my books and complained that I was..."*unfair to the Islamic brothers and sisters*"...forcing the black owned and operated DOOR OF KUSH to distribute my work only through white channels like Baker and Taylor, Borders and Barnes and Noble. In fact in New York City--fans looking for my work complained for the entire year of 2004 that they could not get Clara Villarosa's Hueman Bookstore in Harlem to even special order my books (only as this book was going to press did Harold change that), and by default-- The New York Public Library ordered and stocked 60 copies of my books in their system--just so my readers could have a place in New York to find my work. Quite bravely, Karibu Books and the now defunct SisterSpace Bookstore in my hometown, D.C., carried my books from the very beginning, as did Dr. Rosie Milligan, but many other major black bookstores, like the Afrocentric bookstore in Chicago and the Knowledge Bookstore in Toronto and the black woman-owned A Different Light, also in Canada--not only refused to carry my books, but refused to special order them as well...and in Los Angeles, for reasons having nothing to do with Islam or my politics...the greatly famous ESO WON books refused to carry or regularly stock and carry my books (they did accept and sell the free complimentary copies that my publisher sent them)--but many notable people (such as community speaker James Hampton) reported that the owners of ESO WON had tried to talk them out of reading my books--and then refused to order them.

Supposedly, these owners at ESO WON, James Fugate and Thomas Hamilton (both of whom I know personally, because I shopped at their store for years, always pretending to be a Black American and alway chatting with them) were disgusted by the topless images on the back of my books and felt that my books were divisive in their blatant exposure of *colorism* and were put off by the overall feeling that I was _against_ light skinned black people.

"You don't want to read that crap", they said to James Hampton. Or they laughed in customer's faces when they requested my titles and told them that my books were out of print.

None of the major newspapers or publications in America, black or white, were willing to review my books--and even though it's customary for an author's hometown newspaper to acknowledge its local talent, *The Washington Post* (even after I had 6 books published in 8 countries) never once printed my name, never acknowledged that I am a local girl done good--and more shockingly, when I came to D.C. and did book signings at Karibu and spoke at the University of the District of Columbia, *The Washington Post* refused to carry an anouncement of my events--which is extremely unusual, but then the *Los Angeles Times* also refused to post my events in their Calendar on all the occasions that I signed books in that city. A smaller, more "right wing" newspaper in my hometown, *The Washington Times*, did, however, write about me (when the fatwa was issued) and did request a review copy of my work, although no reviews were written.

As hard as it was for me to comprehend, being friends with Keith Boykin made me understand that I was still viewed by the left as an artist whose rhetoric could create black voters for the Republicans, so it was important to liberal media that I not become too famous. I was told, "Your story makes people worry about terrorism."

"But they *should be* worried about terrorism--there's a fatwa on America!", I would retort, truthfully.

"It's more than that" Ajowa Ifetayo would say. "It's your image."

And then Derrick Bell would send an email explaining something to the effect of--"A black woman in America has very few identities to choose from. She can be a nurturing Mammy...a tragic Mulatto...a Comical Whoopi type...a bitter domineering Sapphire...an oversexed babymaker...*but she can't be a Kola Boof*...eating lions and crocodiles and going topless and abolishing religion and always talking from a dark skinned face about how beautiful it is to be black. That's akin to an African goddess; it even scares most black folk."

I was forced to become a STAR.

In order to not be silenced by all my many enemies...I had to be very unorthodox in how I marketed myself (playing *up* the glamour), inventing colorful sound bites about Osama, *thickening* my accent (because people who came to my book signings were disappointed if I didn't speak with *"enough"* accent), constantly taking pictures and constantly doing the one thing I detest the most--interviews.

And God knows I give good interviews, but more often than not, I end up dividing the audience, because I don't know how to make people like me. I only know how to express my passion and to be candid, which is often by accident--because the Americans can speak and understand English faster than I can. So before I have time to edit what I'm saying, I've pissed off a whole slew of folks.

But as all these forces were working to silence me, to make my work *go away* and discredit me--I had to keep building my name, and what those who called me an "attention wore" didn't realize is that I was fighting for my career.

For my place.

You *have to* understand that.

And for the first time in my life, I was developing a weight problem. Getting fatter and fatter.

I didn't even realize it was happening.

All my life, I'd been either pencil thin (and I mean *skinny*) or I'd been semi-voluptuous, but never larger than a size 8 dress and a 38C cup bra. I'm over six feet tall, so I can carry a lot of weight and still look slender, and because of that I'd been used to eating whatever I wanted to and getting away with it all my life--but as the years of my sons and I living in hiding went by (we were under government protection a total of 2 years and 10 months), and as my depression regarding all the people in media and publishing who were trying to slander or derail my career engulfed me, I was steadily packing on the pounds and just couldn't see how "thick" I was getting until I was given clearance to make my very first American personal appearances tour in the late summer of 2004.

I kicked it off in my hometown, Washington, D.C., by doing a morning radio interview on the popular black affairs program *"Our Voices with Nkenge Toure"* (on which my adoptive Black American mother also appeared--*you can listen online) and then speaking that afternoon alongside my hero Joe Madison and politician Walter Fauntroy out in front of the Sudanese Embassy (actor Danny Glover had already been arrested for standing in the doorway to protest the slavery/genocide taking place in my country).

You won't believe how shocked the crowd of demonstrators were when six bodyguards escorted me up the steps of the embassy--for two reasons--#1, a great deal of them had thought I was just an "urban legend"--a fictional character made up by pranksters on the internet. #2, the black women in the crowd, who were mainly the ones who'd followed my career and kept abrest of my situations through an underground network of black activist sista-girls, just couldn't believe that I was so chubby and average looking!

"THAT'S Bin Laden's former sex kitten!? The one who used to play in movies? NUH-uh!!"

As I waited to give my speech, the whispers found me:

"Girrrl...her ass done put on some weight."

"I didn't know Kola Boof was a real person."

"That is NOT Kola Boof!"

"Whew lawwwd, she got some ass on her."

"She's a writer, you guys...not a supermodel! Be nice."

God!

I've never been overweight in my life--so dealing all that day with the sudden realization that I didn't look like myself (the photos from the event shocked the shit out of me, see the back flap!)--was a humbling blow. But, of course, the show must go on.

I tried desperately to ignore the teenaged black boy in the front of the crowd (wearing under his jacket, a t-shirt of Kola Boof topless!) who sneered at me in disgust as though I'd shot down all his fantasies of what I was supposed to look like (Naomi Campbell, Janet Jackson)--and feminist readers have to remember that I have all types of fans, and one of my biggest groups, whether we like it or not--are certain afrocentric men who support my work and my politics simply because they love my breasts and know about my history as a "sexual pleaser" of men, and because their radar can detect women like me (freaky women), the content of my message is ignored and they focus on the "Goddess Image" that's been created by African mysticism--they delight in knowing that my husband is a black man and that I love being a mother, and they write to me asking questions about my professional cooking. In many ways, to these particular men, and Chief Elder Osirus Akkebala admitted it while we were on a radio show together--I am like Queen Nzinga (the African warrior queen who led armies of men into battle *topless*, and during her rule, kept more than a thousand of those men as her concubines).

So by speaking in public for the very first time (people had waited years to meet me in person), and arriving as a *chubby* woman with fat arms and a fat face, I had let some people down--and before I could get out of D.C.--they made sure I knew it, and all through out that five city tour (Washington, Philadelphia, Memphis, Chicago, Detroit), I was fasting, taking laxatives, wearing bigger clothes (sexier tops, long loose skirts), packing on make up and doing everything I could to look more like the glamorous Kola Boof that I had created through my own backfired internet image making--and having once been a model and actress, the fact that I'm vain didn't help. I can't describe the pressure to you, but somehow, I found my voice--and because I looked so dumpy and unattractive to myself, it was a new voice--richer, stronger, more focused, more serious.

Without my looks, God had taken me to a deeper place.

And although I worked hard to lose that weight (I walked 5 miles a night and swam each day, only lightly cutting calories) and try to keep in shape now that I'm close to 40, that was a major turning point for me, because I realized that something I've often written is very true--"Beauty is not a virtue; it's a trick, a crutch and a temporary piece of *luck* that later mocks you. Beauty is not God at God's best."

~~

The spoken word is more essential than the written, and as people in the crowd held up signs that said *"QUEEN KOLA"* that day in font of the Sudanese Embassy, I began to tell them about the charcoal-skinned men and boys of Sudan, chained to the back of houses and fed by both white and black Arabs out of doggy bowls (there are no plantations in Sudanese slavery). I told them about the sodomization of hundreds and hundreds of Dinka, Nuer, Shilluk, Azande and other South Sudanese boys by both white and black Arabs in Sudan. I told them not to believe the images of Sudan on television where only black Arabs were being shown--and pointed out that the Arab government in Khartoum adopts its "sociological standards" from the white Arabs in Egypt, Saudi Arabia, Libya and the rest of the white Arab nations, and I pointed out that my own father was a white man--not a black Arab--and that most of the members in Sudan's parliament (whatever you want to call it) are white Arabs, not black.

When you meet Sudanese President Bashir and his co-horts (Turabi, for instance)--these men appear to be some type of "black" people with very straight, slick hair. But they are mere puppets for the rest of the white Arab world. Determined to Arabicize the rest of Africa through nations like Sudan, Nigeria, Mauritania and determined to make Africa an Islamic continent--ready and willing to do the bidding of the white Arabs (I said *white* Arab Muslims) of the middle east and southern Europe.

These people pimp, exploit and con the Black race.

"We're all brown brothers." That type of bullshit.

The Palestinians--who, nowhere in the world, have ever got in the street and marched for any *Black* causes--expect me to support their struggle against Israel just because they've been wronged (and it's true, the Palestinians have been greatly wronged)--but yet and still, they will not go against the Arab imperialists who rob the oil from Sudan, they will not go against the Arab imperialists who lynch black men in Khartoum (cutting off black men's hands, filling up Sudanese jails with black men on trumped up charges, castrating and kicking holes in the stomachs of these South Sudanese African men). The Palestinians will not join me in denouncing the regime in Khartoum.

As bombs were dropped on the heads of hundreds of thousands of South Sudanese Africans and as Arab militias (paid by the Sudanese government) raped untold numbers of South Sudanese women, rode into villages on horseback murdering thousands of women and children and capturing twice that many to be sold as slaves in the kitchens of Arab households all over the middle east and North Africa, and as 2 million South Sudanese human beings were displaced...and _driven_ from their land and their country and billions of dollars worth of oil that rightfully belongs to them...our brown Palestinian brothers in Port Sudan and Khartoum and in Palestine itself...laughed and made abeed (slave nigger) jokes to their own kind.

But, of course--when they need parity in Washington, D.C. or at the United Nations, they _kiss up_ to the ignorant masses in Black America, many whom are PAID to support the Arabs, and many of whom wish they had olive skin and "good hair" like those poor mistreated Palestinians, and they count on Farrakhan and the Nation of Islam and Amiri Baraka and Jesse Jackson and even my beloved Alice Walker to promote their stories of suffering and injustice--and they, the Palestinians (along with so many other Arabs and Arab-Americans) sit their asses up on Oprah Winfrey's stage, on national television, and give sob stories..._fucking sob stories_...about how much they have in common with the poor mistreated "Black man" and how they have to stick together--"as brown brothers"--against the evil White Devil--yeah, yeah--all that fucking CAMEL SHIT!

But they never seem to mention how terrified they are back in Palestine of becoming "black again"--and how they sterilize African women in Palestine to keep them from reproducing "abeed stock" in their downtrodden population. And they never seem to mention how they talk about black people in the privacy of their homes--they never mention how they threaten my life and my children's life (their brown sister), just because *I can't stand* their greasy two-faced towel-headed hypocrite asses!

No, no. You never hear that side of the story. You never hear the truth about how they really feel and think about "the monkey race." And how they have to manipulate and keep us down and keep us in our place and keep us...as an ally.

A sidekick to their imperialism.

Or how they enslaved...enslaved East and North Africa for over one thousand years. How they imported *Swahili*...an Arab slave language and forced our children to learn it--and how one thousand years later, the whole planet thinks Swahili is an African language.

No, they never find the integrity to put their bloody hands on the table and tell the truth about where the *smell* is coming from.

Whining rat-hearted sandnigger anal-sex lov'n motherfuckers!

Kola Boof, I am calling to inform you that we are going to kill you.

YEAH FUCK YOU, motherfucker--fuck you!
The Palestinian people cannot tolerate you speaking this way.

YEAH FUCK YOU!!!! Eat my goddamned pussy and lick my motherfucking black ass--*FUCKYOU!*

In June 2005, my book signing at Zahra's Bookstore in Los Angeles had to be canceled because of a bomb threat by people claiming to be Palestinians--and in September 2005, I received more threats after getting into a heated battle with Palestinian supporters while being interviewed on Air America Radio (The Dr. Firpo Carr Show) in Los

Angeles, but both my husband and my children (of whom you'll be reading a lot about in the coming chapter), told me not to back down, and that they were proud of me for ignoring both the Palestinian callers and the Black American supporters of Palestine and speaking up for African women and North African people.

But you see, Arab *"brown brothers"* get stunned as hell when a black nigger won't accept their dirty Arab blood, slavery, genocide money and do their bidding against the Great White Devil.

I'm not on their side.

Dear Amiri Baraka and Harold Pinter--I prefer that Great White Devil motherfucker. Red, White and Blue. *GOD BLESS AMERICA!*

I don't give a fuck how Black Americans feel about it.

I support no Arab governments, nowhere on the planet, whatsoever. <u>None</u>. What a farce to call America *evil* and not Arabs.

I'm an African woman. The Black man's motherseed.

I'm on *my* side, the side of the South Sudanese.

My own people.

The Black Africans. We who call ourselves <u>*Black*</u> and not Arab. I don't give a damn what my mothers Oprah, Maya Angelou, Alice Walker or my love Mumia Abu-Jamal or anyone else have to say. They need to go live in Sudan or Egypt as black folk. I can't support Palestine. Whether they've been wronged or not. I can't support Palestine.

3rd cataract: I can't support Palestine.

From March 1998 to May 2004, I worked as a Special Agent for the Sudanese People's Liberation Army--primarily providing "Spy Detail" for the "drum" of three of South Sudan's top military heads: Paul Malong Auan, Commander P. Yaka and Commander George Athor. Of course, the details of what I'm about to tell you are very ugly, but I was young then, childless, single and very determined to do whatever I could to save my people. I'd been walking up to my flat in Brixton (London) on a day in late February, 1998 when out of the blue, an extremely tall, handsome charcoal skinned Dinka man (about 6'7) tapped me on the shoulder, startling me of course, and asking, "Aren't you Kola Boof, the poet from Sudan?"

"Why yes."

"I heard about the reading party that the white women threw for you the other night. Collen Merrick is my friend."

"Oh, Colleen!"

He nodded, saying, "My name is Achwil. I'm with the resistance. Garang."

There was fear in his eyes as he stared down into my dark brown face--that special intimidation that the charcoal South Sudanese can often feel when they're in the presence of an "Arab", which is what I was to him, a Black Arab.

"It's good to meet you Achwil. I'm very impressed with what the SPLA is doing."

He stared so deep into my eyes that the bottom of my feet suddenly felt very warm.

"My father, he's dead now. But he used to take me to John Garang's house when I was a little girl. He was in on it--the creation of the SPLA before it was even called that."

Only a few days earlier, another of Mahdi Pappuh's aquaintences, who was also a leading Commander for the SPLA, Arok Thon Arok, had been killed when his plane crashed in Nasir. I had been deeply saddened by it and wishing that I could do something to help the South win the war against the Arab North.

I sighed. "What did you want to talk to me about?"

I had noticed the scar tissue going across Achwil's throat and was eager to know how he'd gotten such a dramatic slash.

When he came in and I served him tea with baked bread covered in bacon strips, sliced tomatoes and cheese, he told me the whole story of how he'd been a slave in the north when his white Arab master had slit his throat in frustration, because he'd come down with a flu (he'd been living for three years chained to the back of his master's house and fed from a doggy bowl). Amazingly, when they dumped him on a donkey cart to be taken to the river to bleed to death, the old black fisher-woman driving the cart rushed him instead to a band of local black washerwomen she knew and they'd cleaned and stitched him up back up, after which he'd run back to the South and become a part of the Dinka men's armed guerrilla resistance. And then before he'd been a slave, he'd been orphaned during the infamous Ad Duayn Massacre when more than 1,000 unarmed Dinka townspeople had been murdered by the *murhaleen* (the same Arabs who killed my Pappuh Mahdi and Mommysweet)--all 1,000 of them--charcoal skinned fathers, mothers and their children, doused with gasoline at the rail station and burned alive...for *"being too black"* and non-Muslim and to get back at the SPLA for some earlier battle.

"I'm twenty-five now. Been in England three years."

I cried and cried, softly commenting, "I'm just *so* sorry."

He never smiled. He didn't trust me. But there was something he'd been sent to "find out". He said, "You're Arab, but you're for the South Sudanese."

"Yes", I nodded. "Oh definitely yes."

"You were raised by the Black Americans."

"Yes."

"You write books. You're very smart."

"Thank you."

"You're not like the normal village women."

"No, sorry."

"We need women for the SPLA. But it's not a clean job."

Of course, I don't remember all of this verbatim--but it basically went just as I'm saying.

"You are lesbian", he said intensely (and disapprovingly).

"Oh--no, I'm not! That's Colleen and her friends. We're all friends, but I'm not a lesbian. I make love only with men."

"Where is your man?"

"Uhm. He's at work." Back then, I was going with a very handsome Nigerian poet from Biafara, and it was semi-serious. I mean, I believe we could have ended up married if not for the SPLA.

"A Nubian? Or a black Arab?"

"No, Nigerian, from Biafara. He's a poet, too."

"This is his flat."

"No, this is my flat. He has his own."

He didn't look as though these were good answers. He said, "We need women to carry out assignments for the SPLA, but they can't have a man. Men want their women home and their food cooked."

And after a full week of Achwil and I meeting each mid-day to talk for hours and hours about the war in Sudan and our backgrounds in that country, he suddenly asked if I'd be willing to come with him to a very secret place--blindfolded.

"Are you willing to die for the Africans of Sudan, Naima?"

I said yes.

When we arrived at this place on the Thames river and got inside and upstairs, he removed the blindfold, and there were two other black charcoal men in the one room flat. One standing against the wall with his arms crossed and the other sitting on a crate where he'd been strumming a guitar (I would learn later that a white British guy, also a member of the SPLA, had been guarding the hallway and front door the whole time I was inside.

The two Dinka brothers, Achwil and Thardel both, were about 6'7, but the mean hateful one, Rain Naath, from the Nuer tribe, was about 5'11, which is considerably shorter than I am.

He looked at me as though I were a piece of a shit and then said, "Miss Kola Boof. The writer. The Arab."

"Well to be so Arab, the Arabs sure don't like my books", I said defensively.

"She's an American citizen with an American passport", said Achwil as if those were high tech weapons.

But Rain Naath walked up to me. His black as a crow flesh glistening with a sheen. He got within less than an inch of my face, so close I could feel his skin without it even touching me, and he sniffed me and said, "You even smell like a dirty fucking Arab."

"She's here for initiation", Achwil said. "She's willing to die for our people."

Initiation?

I was suddenly very terrified, because I'd heard all manner of initiation rumors over the years. Men having to survive knife fights against a gang of other men or having to be branded with hot pokers or having to have their fingernails pulled out with pliers or teeth pulled--no anesthetic, no pain killer--just raw, gratuitous pain, and because I'd once worked as a hostess for Moamar Khadafi and knew that his personal guards were all women and that his requirement for them joining his army was that they had to have survived being scarred and wounded, nothing was unbelievable to me.

But I was about to be initiated the old fashioned way--having a train pulled on me--and although the SPLA will claim I'm a liar and making up stories, it happened just as I'm telling you.

The eyes of Rain Naath bore into me with a hate so lethal, I felt my soul wrapping around my heart as it broke to brace the melancholy.

Rain said, "The only thing lower than a Murle girl...is an Arab girl. So get on your knees, soldier. Put your hands over your head and get down on your knees."

The guy with the guitar, Thardel, stood up and came over.

It dawned on me what was about to happen and...I felt the most incredible rage towards Achwil! Betrayal that he hadn't warned me or given me a choice about this.

My whole face twisted up in anger and I hissed, "What if you motherfuckers have AIDS!"

"Well, you're willing to die for your people, right?"

"Put your hands up. Get on your knees soldier."

Tears filled my eyes, as I realized that I would have to break up with my Nigerian boyfriend that night. I'd have to. Because I just didn't feel like going through the drama of explaining to him what had happened to me and why I'd had to go through with it. He wouldn't have understood that the lives of millions of children in the South Sudan depended on my sacrifice and my ability to think like a man.

And when I slid to my knees with my hands in the air, I noticed the mattress pallet that was on the floor and I just...could not *believe* that this was happening to me.

I wiped away one especially huge tear that dragged down my cheek like syrup, but then suddenly--Rain Naath's charcoal dick slid into my mouth and Achwil bound my wrists together within his fist, all of them excited about seeing the dick in my mouth.

Of course, an infibulated girl usually has to be very good at giving head, but I did nothing for Rain. He had to slide it in and out himself, I wouldn't even re-wet my tongue, and that made him take it out so that Achwil's could go in. And having him go in made me burst into full sobbing, because I had thought he was my friend.

"It's the initiation, sister. You're either for the Arabs or the South. Come on now, prove it."

I hate when black men call me *"sister"*. Prove it.

I had to prove that I wasn't just an Arab Northern black Muslim girl talking shit, but truly *down* for the Dinka, Nuer and Shilluk.

Through my sobs, I began sucking Achwil's penis, steadfastly, and then Thardel, and then they stopped and stood me back up and had me undress myself and lay down on the lumpy mattress.

I hate London, because it's so could and gray.

But then Achwil was covering me. So very warm.

To you, who are reading this book--I'm just a black girl who was in a room with three black men. But to us from Sudan, it's so much more complicated than that. To us, I was a symbol of the bastardization that all niggerstock (worldwide) are taught to covet; a prized representative of the mothers of the invaders--a reddish mahogany brown colored naked Arab girl, at the mercy, at last, of pure blooded black African men--men who would ordinarily be considered *beneath* my blood, beneath my <u>mixed status</u>, inferior. Men who might even refuse to speak to me on the streets of Khartoum for fear of Arab retaliation. But there in that one room flat--they were getting revenge by re-casting me as the one *beneath*, the one with inferior status.

Achwil, who I'd welcomed in my home all week and cooked for and trusted like a brother and had spent the whole week feeling in awe of and protective of--was banging me, squeezing my breasts and hollering, "She's infibulated. It's so good, brothers!"

And then he lay next to me, holding my hand, as Rain Naath entered and fucked inside me furiously, causing Achwil to shout, "Take it easy, *she's infibulated--dont' hurt her!*"

Thardel took his turn, and he was gentle, but by then the lily-pad exterior of my circumcised vagina was swollen to three times its normal size, filling with fluid, and the soreness and bleeding of the interior was invasive enough to numb my hips and lower thighs, the freezing tingling regions of my middle becoming rubbery that I imagined I might be permanently paralyzed--they were too big.

Yet I truly understood that I had to be marked.

Gang raped out of my Arab tribe and into theirs.

Men who are on the bottom, riddled with poverty and displacement (in this case, kicked out of their own land and spit on and dehumanized by their enemies)...need to feel like men. And very tragically, exerting power and dominance over females is a way for them to feel like they are really truly men.

"You're no more Arab, oyeeee!" shouted Rain Naaf as began taking a second turn inside me.

He grabbed the wound between my legs and said, "This soil is the property of South Sudan now, oyeeee?"

"Yes", I cried softly, kissing him and embracing his hot flesh as he fucked inside me. "I belong to Dinka men and Nuer now."

To which Achwil and Thardel laughed and clapped, victoriously, as Rain's banging shot literal sparks in the top of my skull. And then Achwil and Thardel took their turns again, and then all three of the men squatted around my face and hair and jerked the staffs of their penis rods until they ejaculated hot sperm across my cheeks, my lips and eyes, my breasts, my hair and neck, my ears. Thardel exploding first and then Achwil and Rain nearly together a moment later.

And then all of them hooting and hollering with cheers--their arms pulling me up into sitting position as they put a beer bottle to my mouth and I, with sperm dripping down my face, drank from it.

"Oyeeeee! Congratulations!", grinned Rain. "You're no more Arab girl--you're in the SPLA now! You're a soldier!"

All around we drank from the same beer bottle, and as Achwil took a hot wash cloth and wiped me off, Thardel played and sang a traditional Dinka song on his guitar.

Rain made a telephone call and simply said, "She's in."

The white British guy in the hallway was brought in and introduced to me. His name was something like Ian. He was very handsome and had just begun staring at my breasts when Achwil quickly covered them up.

"You're a brave woman", Ian said as he squatted down next to me. "Your first assignment isn't easy by the least."

My first assignment?

He offered me the clove cigarette he was smoking, but I declined to take a toke. His blue eyes waded into mines, sailing, and I took that moment to make an announcement.

I asked Thardel, who was sitting back on his crate singing and strumming, to kick my purse over to me, which he did, and then after I was standing back up and had my blouse and long skirt back on, I pulled a pistol from my purse and I told the men, "I'm committed to revolution my brothers, but let's get one fucking thing understood right now. This will never happen again. The initiation is over, and I will never have sex with any of you...again...*ever*. So don't be stupid enough to approach me, because I will kill you...or die trying."

"But Achwil is your boyfriend", Thardel whined like a little boy.

"No he's not!", I spat with annoyance. "I don't have any boyfriends. All I have is rapists. I've had enough *joPepp* (dick) to last me a lifetime, so don't even waste your time thinking about Kola. I'm in this for the people of Sudan, for the children who are being enslaved and slaughtered. I'm not interested any fucking men."

Rain Naath was very gracious for the very first time. He said, "We understand, sister--oyeeee. The initiation is over."

Achwil, who was relieved by Rain's reaction, smiled and told me that my code name as a Special Agent would be "Nya Miuokda". He explained to me that Nya means "the people's female" and that <u>Miuokda</u> means *"it's our oil"*, and in actuality, "Operation Miuokda" (*operation it's our oil*) itself was to become one of the major ongoing missions of the SPLA special forces, to fight for the land in the south that was being given away to foreign oil companies by Bashir's Arab regime in Khartoum.

Rain wrote my new name down on a piece of paper for me so that I would learn it. Nya Miuokda.

Achwil then told me that a person from Higher Intelligence within the SPLA would be coming to London to set up my first assignment and that the person would identify himself by saying to me: *"Did you know that Anwar Sadat's mother was Sudanese?"* (which is true).

To which I was to reply: "No, I don't like Arabs."

You really must understand the seriousness of this.

Rain Naath explained to me that the major Canadian oil company, Talisman Energy, and Sweden's big one, Lundin Petroleum, were paying "multi-million dollar *gift* checks" to the Sudanese government in exchange for Bashir to "<u>clear</u> the oil areas"...of people and villages. And accordingly, the North Arab government had been air bombing whole villages of innocent non-Muslim, charcoal Black Sudanese, Cushitic tribal people who had lived in those areas more than 26,000 years. Along with the air bombings, "Black Arab" militia men were hired by the government to go through those regions on horseback and randomly shoot and kill as many people as possible.

I went back to Brixton that afternoon and took the longest shower, followed by the longest bath that I've ever taken in my life.

I cried.

A lot. Because I was sad to have to break up with my Nigerian boyfriend, and when he came to call that evening, I'd fixed him a chicken dinner, but did it the way one prepares crocodile--taking the skinless chicken breasts (I hate chicken breasts, but most people love them) and mixing them well in a bowl with one tablespoon tumeric powder, two tablespoons chili powder and two tablespoons coriander powder (this is really an easy recipe). After covering the breasts with the different powders, I'd heated a wok pan with extra virgin olive oil and sliced onion and tumeric powder by itself, browning the onion and powder about 2 minutes, and then adding the breasts and cooking them on medium heat, about a total of ten minutes. And then I'd boiled some linguini, strained it and poured melted butter and garlic salt over it. The last four minutes of the chicken frying--I poured in a half cup of red wine and then placed the breasts on the pasta bed.

I served him a spinach salad and Gish (half a glass beer, half a glass apple juice and a ginger stalk) with it.

He loved the meal, having me bake some more slices of garlic bread as he had thirds, and then we sat in front of the telly, and as I cried on his shoulder, I began to tell him that I couldn't be his girlfriend anymore.

I reminded him of all he and I had discussed that week--me meeting Achwil and feeling very strongly that I had to join the SPLA, and of course, he hadn't been happy about that prospect, but he'd truly understood my obligation (being that he himself was from Biafara), but then--when I told him that the men had initiated me by pulling a train on me, and that I hadn't fought against it, but went with it--to prove that I was down--he began beating me!

In the mouth and face with his fists! Beating me!

I knew my jaw was broken and that the upper teeth on my left side had been loosened and I could feel my right eye swelling into a muffin, all vision shut out from that side as blood gushed from my nose and my busted mouth, but still, he wouldn't stop beating me...and calling me "bitch" and "whore"...beating me.

Until I made it to my purse and got my pistol out and *POP!*...it was so much more than scary, it was ugly--having to shoot someone as they rush at you like a rabid dog--and I'd had no choice.

"Goddamned son of a bitch...*fuck you!*" Pee-yune!

He rallied, haul-assing in the other direction, trying to find my front door, his big feet ass tripping all over each other as his own voice suddenly shrieked like a woman's--and then he found the nob and he was out of there, running down the street, wounded.

I called my lesbian friend Colleen and she rushed me to the hospital where they kept me the next three days.

When I got out of the hospital, I went to my first "get together" with some of the other soldiers of the SPLA in London. Unfortunately, I looked fucked up in the face--and apparently several people at the gathering assumed that Achwil, Rain and Thardel had done this to me during the initiation, and heavy penalties were imposed on them by a mysterious Dinka man who was always silent but always watching everyone. Of course, I went to him later that week and cleared my three buddies of having done anything wrong. I explained that my boyfriend had beaten me up, because I'd allowed myself to be fucked by other men in order to get clearance to join the army.

"Good daughter", he'd remarked.

But the party itself had been sad, consisting of a bunch of men and boys, not just Dinka, Nuer and Shilluk, but other non-Muslim black tribesmen like Anyuak, Toposa, Jur, Mundari and Azuak (they don't allow their tribeswomen to attend). It was so tragic.

The level of depression and mental illness--not natural mental illness, but the kind that is brought on by intense trauma. The kind that I have suffered from all my life. Almost all of these people, just like me, had witnessed loved ones being murdered right in front of them. Most of them had watched on as Arab men raped their mothers, wives or sisters, and many of them were alcoholics.

Deeply bitter, disconnected and wholly out of place in gray, smarmy white London.

I remember we ate boiled eggs and drank beer and that I...as Agent Nya Miuokda, read a poem I'd written for them. Something that contained:

> drums hanged to the trees
> Bahr Lol river (kick de football)
> Vnudin River (catch your Papa's skull)

And then we'd all taked about the chemical warfare that the Arabs had been testing on South Sudanese--which is why I know about terrorism. The chemicals they'd drop into the well water or the strange powders they'd use wind fans to blow over a certain area (one whole village of southern blacks had itched for a week--to the point of scratching their own skin off, and those who still had skin were covered in strangely permanent burns--I fear this will happen in America).

Later on as a Special Agent, I would hear white Arabs in places like Jordan, Syria, Iraq, Afghanistan, Egypt and Saudi Arabia make comments like..."it really works--they tested it on the *South Sudanese*". And that, of course, was when the photographs first began trickling into the western media. Pictures of blue black South Sudanese and the strange eye afflictions, the mangled limbs, the scalp infections, the bio terrorism scars; the chemical exposure--that nobody in America cared about and still don't care about.

But I cared.

A black Kenyan woman with skin as luminous and shiny rich as a vat of chocolate pudding--I'm talking hands down one of the prettiest women I've ever seen in my life--walked up to me in a pub in London several weeks after I'd joined the SPLA and smiled and said in a voice that was smoother than warm cognac, *"Did you know that Anwar Sadat's mother was Sudanese?"*

I recognized the Nairobi accent and the smell of acacia honey and the glossy brow, poised with African violet.

But I hadn't recognized the secret code.

She said once more, "Did you know that Anwar Sadat's mother was Sudanese?"

And then my mouth turned into a huge "O", and I said, "OHHH!...uhm...no, I don't like Arabs."

The classy secret agent lady suggested that we go someplace and have a chat, but I was so completely mesmerized by her beauty that I could hardly get my wits about me. She was one of those chocolate women who looks like a doll come to life, not really a person, but like a stop-motion animation puppet--moving about and talking.

She told me her "agent" name (but lets call her *Swan*) and reiterated that we should leave the pub and go to her hotel room.

"Oh, of course, yes", I said, sounding like some teenaged girl newly employed by McDonalds and not yet accustomed at how to do several things at once work.

We went back to her hotel and there was a very tall and handsome charcoal black man in the room. He had a British accent, but told me that he was from South Sudan and that he was a Nuer, but that he'd been raised in England his entire life, yet hardly lived there.

The three of us had room service (I had prime rib) and drank wine and they explained to me what my assignment was.

Swan said: "You're to play a Black American woman--a geologist named Katrina Wexler. She's also an anthropologist."

The Nuer man told me that he would be training me for the next two months (an entire eight weeks) on exactly everything I'd need to know about Higlig PX-40, a dossier of classified scientific findings related to the earth-soil, water toxins and plankton-mineral contents of several oil drilling refinery stations throughout the south Sudan, but the combined reports being called Higlig after one of the major drill towns that the SPLA wanted to eventually destroy."

"They're killing off innocent South Sudanese villagers to build their oil drilling operations--so it's up to us to bomb and destroy their oil sites and reclaim the land that rightfully belongs to our black fathers. The thing is, Agent Nya Miuokda...we have to understand exactly how to exert the most extreme damage and how the oil flow is processed, how the mining complex itself operates."

Swan said: "This mission Nya Miuokda...is going to take you up to eight months and will require intense training."

Gradually, I became the Black American anthropologist and geologist Katrina Wexler, and as a woman born and raised in Dayton, Ohio--I had no emotional or political concerns about any of the conflicts that were taking place in the Sudan. I was just a nice Black American science lady who wanted to educate the oil companies on how best to comprehend the indigenous Petrophysical and Earth/Wark Lithologies of Planktonic Upper Africa, and in turn, how to effectively integrate Calibration of Porosity Logic with modern American "Variance of Porosity"--to not only yield the greatest results from their various drilling operations, but also for the health of the landscape, the reservoirs and the surrounding wildlife.

It was worse than having to know Algebra or Physics, but I had to know my shit or I'd be dead in the water.

Somehow, I became very adept at making it appear as though I was an expert of Petrophysical Lithologies and Porosity Logic, and because of my father's archeological work and him taking me as a kid--I was able to speak quite convincingly as an anthropologist having great knowledge of the Sudan, but little interest in the people.

As I so often said to the oil companies: *"My job is to make your company* richer--*for a price."*

As I write this book, you must understand that there are many things that I cannot divulge--#1, for reasons of protecting the SPLA and the SPLM (the movement) and their ongoing existence, despite the fact that we're at peace now--and #2, because I don't want to be sued, I don't want lawsuits by these (relative parties--on either side) claiming that I owe reciprocal information or returned monies.

I did my jobs--the exact work I was paid to do for the oil companies.

And *while I was doing my job*, I also extracted valuable information for my people, the slave babies and the slave mothers, the limb-less black fathers and the lost boys and lost girls of Sudan, for the Sudanese People's Liberation Army. In July 1998, I landed in

Port Colborne, Canada (Talisman Oil) and worked as an analyst and consultant to Nathan Quimby; in September, 1998, I landed in Stockholm, Sweden (Lundin Petroleum) and worked consulting Dr. Einojuhani Gustafsson (of Helsinki, working in Stockholm); in November, 1998, I landed in Nairobi, Kenya (China National Petroleum Company) and worked with one of the most racist women I've ever met in my life, Dr. Yok Yung...and I did whatever I had to do; *whatever it took*...to secure the information that would help the SPLA to bomb and implode the oil fields of South Sudan and to force the North Arab government into disarray--*by any means necessary.*

Exactly one year later--all of my clients knew that I'd given detailed introspective information to SPLA Special Forces; information that need not ever be compiled again, because once you have it, you always have it--and because the oil companies have known since 1999 that I mapped them out for the Africans, I'm not revealing anything here that could derail or diffuse any future espionage on the part of my comrades in the SPLA. Everything I've written...is generally known.

In March of 2004, speaking by radio in Tel Aviv, Israel (I'm not allowed to reveal the details of this last assignment or who gave clearance or how it was set up or followed through), I completed what would be my final mission as by then the highest ranking woman in the SPLA--Special Agent Queen Kola.

I appealed to the men of Israel to understand my desperate need to acquire guns and ammunition for the South Rebel Army and used our mutual hatred for the Arab Muslim Empire as the thing that should move them to act in my favor. Truly, I had (and have) no interest in Zionism, and I fully recognize that Israel is a white racist nation (not nearly as racist against blacks as most Arab socities are, but still racist and still white), but the thing is--my people were being bombed and shot down in their villages and left homeless in the wilderness and there was no one else that was willing to supply us with arms, food, shoes for the babies and medicine for the sick. We had nowhere else to turn, but to Israel--who has often been an ally to the South Sudanese, because of our shared non-Arab, non-Muslim status in the middle east, because of Prophet Ciisa (Jesus Christ) being a Black Jew, because the ancient Cushitic language is Hebrew and because there are 2 million Black Jews in the Sudan and Ethiopia, and because despite what the Black Americans try to perpetrate--the Arab Muslims are not our *brown brothers* who love us, but are the chicken bone that is caught in Africa's throat, and after enslaving African people for over a thousand years,they still refer to us as monkeys...still bomb, murder, steal our land, *rule* our land and starve our children (white racists of Israel do not bomb, murder, steal our land and starve us in Sudan)--so I am very proud that I took that opportunity to do what needed to be done, as my great hero Malcolm X would put it--*by any means necessary*.

And many Black Americans, who truly are ignorant about our situation as pure Black non-Muslim Africans in our own country, have viciously criticized me for having anything to do with Israel...but as I always say...if my dear father figure, <u>Minister Louis Farrakhan,</u> can align himself with the genocidal Arab regime in Sudan and the government of Libya...then Queen Kola can align herself with the enemy of those governments...ISRAEL.

Another sad reality is that many Black Americans see themselves in the Black Arab (Kola Boof's color), but *cringe* when they see the pure Charcoal Black South Sudanese, and therefore, will cry about what's happening to the Palestinian, but care nothing for the blue black child. So I am for the true Black Africans...not the Arab Invaders.

(*The speech I gave in Israel is printed in full on page 434.)

Because of me, *an African mother*, more than $600 million worth of guns, ammunition, food, clothing and medicine were channeled through the South Sudanese military check points of Buoth, Waniek and Pariang, and because of me, the armies of Commander Paul Malong Auan, Commander George Athor and Commander P. Yaka--never fell to the Arabs and were never uncloaked.

There was a bit of major ugliness, when I distrusted Commander Lam Akol over the incident where SPLA soldiers (all Shilluks) from the village of Akrooa massacred 31 innocent people (Nuer civilians) on Akrwa Island--the type of self killing that I feel is so typical and ignorant of the Black race in general and that I could not abide, but for the most part--I am extraordinarily proud of the accomplishments of my comrades in the SPLA.

Only because of the <u>sexism</u> of my brothers in the SPLA, the fact that I haven't been given recognition for all I've done to combat the Arab regime in Sudan, and because I'm a soccer mom now, did I decide to downgrade from a Special Agent to a soldier/consultant on call--and accept the sexist moniker "Queen Kola" instead of an official military title--Commander. But it's O.K., really.

One of the proudest moments of my life was when they read my poem "Choll Apieth" at the funeral of our great leader, the Martin Luther King of Sudan--Dr. John Mabior Garang--a poem (*see page 440*) that I'd been asked by the SPLA to write especially for his funeral. It was their way of acknowledging my contributions, despite the fact that I am perceived by many at the top of the SPLM as a "crazy woman", "a disobedient woman (a feminist) corrupted by America", and as a wholly unpredictable wild child--one they can't control.

But I will always cherish John Garang, truly Sudan's best son, and I will always admire the beauty and wisdom of his widow, our great mother of Sudan, Rebecca Garang, and I have great faith in our new leader, Salva Kiir Mayardit, and in men like Pagan Amun and Deng

Ajak (my hero, my inspiration in London)--I miss your guidance so much Deng Ajak, and I bless those <u>Arab brothers</u> who supported me in the SPLA, my two loves, Monsour Khalid and Said Musa.

And, of course--it's no secret that I was completely against the Muchakos Peace Agreement and that I am diligently hoping that the South Sudan will secede and become its own nation in 2011.

Many are saying that the peace agreement won't last...especially now that John Garang died under such mysterious conditions (his airplane crashed shortly after the peace agreement was signed and he was sworn in as Sudan's very first Southern national Vice President)...that it's impossible to expect the peace to last.

But I will stand with our mother Rebecca Garang's call for peace and wait to see what happens, and hopefully, like I said, the South will become its own nation in 2011.

I've just told you what it was like to be a Secret Agent for my people's liberation and how punishing that was--but in the summer of 2004, just weeks before I spoke on those steps at the Sudanese Embassy in Washington, D.C. with Joe Madison--there was another event that was even more painful, in fact so painful that it ended up changing my perspective on some things, as I was suddenly faced with something I'd never even thought about or expected to find out...

the possibility...

that the iconic women writers I'd idolized all my life--Alice Walker, Toni Morrison, Gloria Naylor, Maya Angelou--<u>didn't like me,</u> and quite possibly didn't want to be in the same room with me.

I can't tell you how stunned I was--but now you'll have to switch back to Kola Boof, the struggling literary writer.

It all started one June morning when Derrick Bell sent me an email, suggesting that I speak at *The Yari Yari Pamberi International Conference on Literature by Women of African Ancestry*. Derrick is a Professor at New York University, which is where the one time event was to be held for five days that year (2004), October 12th--16th, and he was so excited about it and sent me the name, email and telephone number of the woman coordinating everything, Laura Rice, and told me to contact her and say that he had recommended me as a speaker for one of the many author panels they were planning.

I then turned that information over to my publicist Kate Wilson and my friend and editor Nafisa Goma, and they (I believe Nafisa) contacted Laura Rice at New York University by telephone. She didn't know who I was, but said that she believed that on the strength of Derrick Bell's recommendation, and because it was still early enough (June), I would probably be added to one of the 40 author panels being presented that week. She asked Nafisa to send copies of all my books (Nafisa overnighted them) and told Nafisa that she would speak to the event's Director, famed author Jayne Cortez (the person with the last word), and get back to us by the next day.

I had not originally been all that excited about the event--but once I found out that Alice Walker would be speaking on one of the panels, and that Toni Morrison was coming and that Maya Angelou, Gloria Naylor, Octavia Butler (whose work I love so much) and the heroic black filmmaker Julie Dash were going to speak on panels, and that my idol Iman was hosting a panel...I got very excited about possibly appearing there and looked into the event...and then...*lawd have mercy*...I discovered that the hero of my life, the greatest black filmmaker in history and the one artist, who above all others means the most to me--Mr. Ousmane Sembene of Senegal--was going to be feted with an awards dinner at the event and that Egyptian feminist and writer, Nawal El Saadawi, the woman I had patterned myself after, was going to be on a panel--I just had to be included!

The event was being given by the Organization of Women Writers of Africa (headed by Jayne Cortez and the legendary Ghanian writer, Ama Ata Aidoo), so it never entered my mind that there might be any controversy about me being included, yet the next day, when Laura Rice at NYU got back with Nafisa Goma, she told Nafisa that she'd spoken to Jayne Cortez and that quite frankly--there were people who were already scheduled to speak on panels who *didn't want to come* if I was going to be there. Naturally, it hurt to hear such a thing, but there were two concerns--#1, that my presence might attract violent demonstrations by the people who had firebombed my publisher the year before....and #2--that I myself would stir up people with a dramatic, fiery condemnation of the Arab Muslims and make comments that weren't in line with the thinking of the rest of the so called "African women" writers. This was the summer of 2004, mind you--the summer that the U.S. government declared that there was indeed a "genocide" in Sudan (slavery had already been proven)--but because the _government_ declaring such a thing was the Republican regime of George Bush-- many of these so called "African women writers" turned their back on the very real genocide of charcoal black Sudanese as a way of inserting their hatred for Bush and his war in Iraq. At the United Nations, Kofi Annan took the side of the Chinese government, the racist French and the oil companies by claiming that while there were "blatant human rights violations in Sudan"--there was no genocide being carried out by the Arab government--and because of that blatant lie by Mr. Annan, many Black American movers and shakers felt justified in overlooking the situation in Sudan, caring only for Iraq. As a further shock--these female icons at Yari Yari were going to screen a film about "The Lost Boys of Sudan"--but as usual, there was going to be no panel, screening or discussion of the Lost _Girls_ of Sudan or of the widely reported national gang rapes that were sweeping the South Sudan that summer and being carried out by the black Arab militias that were financed and given their instructions by the government in Khartoum.

Because Laura Rice felt that I, as a lost girl and Sudanese woman writer, was the perfect person to speak about these atrocities--she told Nafisa Goma that she had pressed the issue with Jayne Cortez and that a special meeting would be held--not with the board of directors, but with the advisory panel--to decide whether or not I was to be invited to the 5 day event and in what capacity I would be asked to participate. Personally--I would have liked to have helped salute either Ousmane Sembene or Toni Morrison at the Awards ceremony. I told this to Nafisa, who relayed it to Laura Rice--*that I would like to either give a short speech on what the films of Ousmane Sembene have meant to me as an African woman...or to "sing a Nilotic song" for Toni Morrison, or to speak on one of the globalization panels about the Sudan and be allowed to speak up for the Lost Girls at last.*

As Nafisa told her all this--I listened in on another line.

Laura Rice, who I perceived to be a studiously considerate and intelligent young woman, said that the advisory panel was meeting in person and that she was flying there and would use my published literary works as well as the recommendation by her colleague, Derrick Bell, to secure a spot for me at the Yari Yari event. She would not disclose exactly who was going to be at the advisory meeting (other than Jayne Cortez and Ama Ata Aidoo)...but on the Yari Yari web site, I found a list of all the members of the advisory panel:

Gloria Naylor...Maya Angelou...Sapphire (whose book *"PUSH"* really touched me)...Paula J. Giddings...Rosa Guy...Paule Marshall...Maryse Conde...Ama Ata Aidoo and Jayne Cortez.

Four days later, Laura Rice contacted Nafisa Goma to say that the advisory panel had met and had decided that I should not be invited to the event in any capacity--but that I was welcome to *"buy a ticket"* and attend with the general audience just like anybody else.

Well, naturally I was devastated--I mean it was very possible that the women who'd inspired me to become Kola Boof--*didn't like me*--so I cried and then I had Nafisa Goma telephone Laura Rice and tell her that I was furious with rage, but they didn't care.

And, of course, when the phoney ass Pacifica Radio star Amy Goodman (this bitch chose not to acknowlege my children and I living in hiding and our lives being threatened, because as her producer Jason said--"Amy isn't interested in your story"--to which I had rightfully replied--*"If I had a big black dick like Mumia Abu-Jamal, she'd have me on her radio show every goddamned day and her fat, phoney white ass would be all over me and my* black *babies, and she'd be beside herself trying to find out what she could do to help the people of South Sudan!"*) and such male figures as Walter Mosely, Manthia Diawar and Max Rodriguez were invited to speak, it only added insult to injury.

So I learned yet another truth about America...that even what the richest, wisest old Black women stand for is often just pretense and "show"--and that not everyone is truly allowed to have a voice, but only those who tow the status quo.

~~

Several months later...after I was dis-invited the second time from taking part in a writer's event on the campus of SPELMAN college...Derrick Bell got so angry and fed up, he flew down to see the President of Spelman College <u>in person</u> and voiced his concern that *"academic"* black women were misjudging Kola Boof and not even reading my work or checking to *see* what I was about...but rather listening to the people who were dismissing me and my children's reality (and the importance of my work), people like Amy Goodman and those jerks at *The New York Times* (newspaper of record, my ass). He was also appalled at the different prejudices that *Black Women* held towards me for being an "uppity African" and going topless and for saying things aloud...that they, with their kente cloths tossed over the shoulders of their Ann Klein suits, hadn't the integrity to say.

And in no way did (or does) Derrick Bell agree with everything that Kola Boof says or stands for--in fact, he disagrees with me on a lot of issues, and he's quick to put his foot in my behind if he thinks I'm being wrongheaded, he really is like a grandfather to me--but I love him so much, not only for defending *my honor*, but for defending the honor of all women, something he has strived to do all of his professional life. If you are reading this, 100 years after it was written, then please note that he was one of the greatest men that ever lived, and because he allowed himself to get to know me, he got to see what a sweet and complex person I am and that I am not *scary*.

I was lucky to have such an icon of respectability who would take up for me, and when other black women writers would not even acknowledge that I existed (as writer Jennifer Williams said, black women at book club discussion meetings *"whispered"* my name), Derrick Bell defended me and did it in public.

Wild crazy stuff happened to me between 2003 and 2004. It appeared that Halle Berry wasn't going to reprise her role as "Storm" in the X-MEN 3 movie sequel and a producer who heard about me through the internet, contacted me to see if I'd be willing to audition for the role. At first, I considered it--but then Aquaman pointed out that in order to play Storm, our sons would have to see me with blond hair flowing from my head. I talked to the producer and asked if perhaps the character could have locs and a more appealing hair color, but there was no way that they were changing Storm (a mutant, supposedly part Kenyan woman with blond hair, blue eyes and Eurocentric facial features) into a more African looking woman, so I declined to test for the part. And around that same time, another producer from Fox Searchlight Pictures asked to see the manuscript for my life story (this very book) and seemed very excited about the possibility of turning it into a movie. I really wasn't happy about the prospect of seeing my life made into a movie (especially since it would focus on Osama Bin Laden)--and mainly because it would be impossible to do it right--but I needed the money, and although I am a huge fan of Halle Berry (I actually loved her in *"Dorothy Dandridge"* and cried with her when she won the Oscar--just as I cried with Vanessa Williams when she won Miss America)--I felt that Halle Berry was all wrong for the role of Kola Boof. And the fact that she's bi-racial and not black (not to mention <u>too short</u> and doesn't have *"the proof"* growing from her scalp), had an awful lot to do with it for me--but the producer explained that Halle was the only bankable black actress in Hollywood and in order to get financing, we'd have to make it work.

Luckily, the negotiations stalled (*someone called me a racist*) and I went back to pursuing my writing career.

Which was going as well as could be expected considering I was on the super-tiny no frills Door of Kush label, where three of my titles (*Flesh and the Devil, Long Train to the Redeeming Sin* and *Nile River Woman* were released in the spring of 2004, but given no publicity, and as I mentioned earlier, were blocked from normal distribution in the black community, along with black stores not carrying me, while the major trades such as Publisher's Weekly and Kirkus refused to give any of my titles even the "Forecast" mention that all books usually get--so I was still not doing well enough to be considered a mainstream author...BUT...because of the <u>quality</u> of the writing, and because of the controversies surrounding me, I did became two things--(1) an underground sensation with *young* black women, college kids and black gay readers--and (2) the most gossiped about, debated and argued about new writer that the black literati world had seen in years.

Very big fish in the literary world were suddenly finding my work and the word began to spread that I could actually write.

And there were these people claiming to be related to me--a man in Virginia came forward to say that he was my "father" and that I was a terrorist working for Osama, while yet another man in Georgia came forward to say that he was my cousin and that I was an agent for Bush and the U.S. government--out to destroy the black community, and then a man in New York tried to claim he was my cousin and tried and to sell "fake" nude photos of me and Osama Bin Laden to the tabloids. Rumors abounded in London that I'd once been a cannibal (eating the flesh of other human beings) and assorted men claimed to have photos of me sexing 3 or more men at a time--photos that don't exist, because other than the one time with Osama and the other time at initiation, I've never willingly engaged in something freaky as that. Not with 3 men at a time, anyway. *Ha Ha!*

It was a wild, difficult, very painful era--these years of trying to establish myself as a writer in America--and I was desperate and had to do many things that I didn't like doing, but somehow I made it through and I did it...as myself. Without political correctness, without whitening my image, without the moral laws of Men suppressing my sexuality, without any formal education whatsoever and without support from the media or the literary establishment, black or white, I dared to come as my African self--with all the goodness and badness I had--and when they threw me against the wall with that slanted pitch of theirs, to their utter dismay, *I stuck!*

I NEVER MARRIED
MY HUSBAND

My dear baby boys (neither of you yet 10), I've promised you that when you turn 21, you can read mother's autobiography (although I suspect as teens you'll probably sneak and read a copy, so *shame on you!*)...but of all the chapters, this is the one I'm most excited for you to read, because your father...was such a wonderful man, in fact, in my whole life--he's the only man that I ever loved, and I'm praying that you'll both turn out something like him.

He didn't pick me...*I* picked him. He was walking home one sunny California afternoon, coming from a five mile jog around the park track and minding his own business...I turned the wheel of my car and ran up on the sidewalk, instantly cutting off his path. I had only seen him for the first time two seconds before from the back, but he struck me as being a Sudanese--very black, very tall, very slender and extremely muscular. His head was Stevedore-shaped like a Nubian's. I stared at him from behind the wheel, my eyes literally eating him alive and my face permeated by a nervous grin. In my head, I thought: *What in the fuck are you doing, Kola? How are you going to explain that you're not some Ho looking to get poked?* Luckily, he was so shocked and flattered by my actions that he grinned right back at me and said, in the sexiest Belizian accent, "DAYUM girl...what's up witt dat?"

I was so shocked at what I'd done that I couldn't speak, and he leaned into the window on the passenger's side and looked me over head to toe. I could see then that he wasn't African (it would turn out, of course, that he was from the Central American nation of Belize). He said, "Dayum, *girrrrl*--where you com'n from look'n all cute?"

Your daddy was so *Ghetto* and it just lit me up inside!

And I still found myself paralyzed, not able to say a word, because people all over the block were looking at me like I was crazy. And that's how we met--on a ghetto street in Los Angeles with me looking like some desperate fool.

I think he felt sorry for me, probably thinking that I was some lonely black woman who hadn't been able to get a man and had finally snapped and just decided to run one down! Lol.

He invited me to come inside his apartment, which was half a block down, to have a health shake and chat for a minute. So I backed up my car and followed him to the security gates behind which he took the wheel and parked my classic 1967 Stingray (you know how mother likes her classic cars) behind his own shiny red sports car. It was when I saw his car and the decent appearance of his apartment that I knew that he at least had a job.

Goodness! Your father was such the perfect gentleman. He made me a strawberry "trainer's" milkshake and tried to show me how to work out on his Calistenics equipment. We sat and laughed mostly, as though we'd known each other forever, and he was really fascinated about me being from Sudan, although back then, he really didn't like Africans and told me as much, but there was such incredible playfulness and ease of atmosphere right away. It was one of the strangest moments of my life, because I had ordered it.

I gave him my phone number and started to leave. He told me that he thought I was beautiful (and back when I was young, I really was hot). He told me that he feared that because he was a blue collar government electrician and going to engineering school part time, I wouldn't be interested in him (he didn't own his own business yet as he does now). There was such a tenderness in his eyes and such a boyish charm about him--not to mention that kingish walk of his and just the fact that he was so handsome to me. His accent was plaintiff, and he spoke very intelligently (as though he was well read), and everything he said with that accent--especially my name--sounded like poetry. In fact, I fell in love with him because of the way he talked. Everything about him reminded me of a dream I'd either had or should have had. He walked me to my car, saying that he'd never met a woman like me before.

We didn't want to go away from one another.

But I did. I flew off back to London (where I still training for my first assignment for the SPLA). It was May of 1998.

Your father called me in London and we talked for hours. Then I called him from Rabat. I phoned him from Madrid. I didn't tell him a thing about the SPLA or what I'd been through with Osama, but he told me about the fact that he'd recently been dumped by a woman who he really thought he loved--in fact he worshipped her. I would later learn that she was one of those ultra-fine high maintenance women who can't love a man unless he has a certain degree, makes a certain amount of money or drives a certain kind of car. She worried that her children with Aquaman (I call your father *Aquaman*--because he loves to swim), might be born too dark, too *foreign* looking, he told me. She basically used him to pay her bills, and even though he knew that, he loved her and couldn't resist her.

Because of the atmosphere you've been raised in, this may come as a shock to you, and of course your father would never admit to it

--but I've always known that his real attraction was for extremely lightskinned black women with long Spanish-like hair and Caucasoid-like features, and because this woman was that type of woman...I, your mom, didn't think I could compete. When I came back to Los Angeles, your dad seemed so sad and so depressed over being dropped by her, my intellect told me that if she should ever come back...he'd dump me in a heartbeat. So after I saw her picture, I decided not to talk to him anymore. I didn't want to get hurt, and besides, there were always many other men who wanted me.

Months went by. I'd gone to Canada and Sweden to spy on Talisman oil and Lundin oil for the SPLA, and then dropped back into London, and one day, I came home to my flat--and there was your father, standing in front of my door, waiting for me.

And that was the first time we ever kissed. I walked up to him, ina state of disbelief, because I couldn't believe he'd come all that way just to see me--and we didn't even speak. We kissed, and then we went inside my little bedroom and we took off our clothes and got on my rickety cot and we made love--for hours.

In so many ways, your father saved my life with his love. He was incredibly smart and was the first man I'd had who could talk and really express himself, and it was him who rescued me from a terrible pessimism about men. As was my M.O., I lied to him, claiming that I was a "virgin"--and men always believed it once they penetrated me, and your father was no different. A tear actually ran down his cheek when he thought he'd actually met a *virgin* who wasn't a teenager and that he'd been the first.

He was so tender and so caught up in the apparition I was creating just for him that night. The truth is--I hated men when I was young. I saw them as rapists, users, abusers or sell outs, and I didn't believe in love--I really didn't. I used men for sex, because beyond needing that intimacy, I didn't trust them and I feared their betrayal.

But, alas, Arnofo, you were conceived during those four days that your father visited me in London (as you know, it was him who named you boys, not me), I try to keep your ages secret. But anyway, your father made love to me four days and nights straight it seemed. I wasn't even officially his girlfriend yet, but there was something between us that was truly bigger than the whole world outdoors.

I was like a fish that stopped swimming
                    after I met your father.
My tail waving slowly
/into the belly of the whale

swallowed up
swallowed whole
a blue sky love--the last thing I'd expected
Your father's beautiful sperm (his own fish)
spilling, filling my ocean
'til like dolphins/the two of you leapt from our dreams
More perfect than Quasars
Until he and I were one blue world. Complete.
All my life I had been merely a female.
Your father made me a *woman.*
He made me feel something other than pain.

It was senseless, soulful and illicit. Neither one of us had any real money, but it felt like we owned heaven. I made him simple things to eat like cheeseburgers and beans and franks, and he raved about it, and we danced around my little room in a kind of timid loneliness. We were wounded children from very ugly, insecure backgrounds. Two black people from foreign countries whose glory days as Americans were to be sweet, for sure, but still never anything less than...*lost*...no matter how tenderly we tell the story, because all black people--all over the world--are lost. I remember Aquaman holding me close as we danced to the Prince song, "Truly Adore You"...and that was the beginning of our not letting go.

Your father went back to California. I stayed in London and worked on my writing and went to Kenya to spy on the Chinese for the SPLA and tried to get financing for a film that I wanted to write, star in and direct, a remake of *"Rain"*, but of course nothing came of it.

I never told your father I was pregnant.

Sometimes he called, sometimes I sent him poems about my feelings. About how I could feel he himself growing inside of me, but I never told him what the poems meant.

I gave birth in Washington, D.C.--and, of course, although I pride myself on people often commenting that you, Arnofo, look like a miniature Denzel Washington, and that you, Wombe, you look like a miniature Tupac Shakur--it's really your father that you both look like, exactly like. Nothing like me.

Your Grandma Claudine nearly put her foot in my ass. She said, "You mean to tell me you ain't even told that nigga that you was pregnant with his baby? Girl, what is wrong wit' choo? You are the craziest damn child I got!"

And your Great Grandma, Nana Glodine, shook her head and said, "Chal, you is more then a notion."

So I called him up and said that I was coming to Los Angeles.

You know your Grandmother Claudine. She was like, "Are you sure he's the baby's daddy? Don't take yo ass to Los Angeles if he's not, Naima."

Of course, mother hadn't met him yet, but she flew me to Los Angeles.

When I got to his front door--I presented you to him--and he was shocked as hell, but he shocked me right back by asking me to be his wife. Your father's like that, because he's very christian, you know, and because I'm "pagan", he's already trying to out-shock me and make an honest woman of me. You slept right between us that night...your little perfect chocolate self...and from then on we started living with him.

Things were pretty rough at first, because your daddy had several girlfriends. Notably a black latina named Phoebe. She was crazy about him, but he had mainly kept her for sex. As soon as you and I popped up, he broke up with her, yet she carried on for weeks showing up at the house to cry and throw tantrums. I felt so sorry for her, and at the same time, your father's friends (mostly Belizians) hated my guts. They were used to seeing Phoebe with your father and remained loyal to her for the first year of our relationship. They blamed me, exclusively, for the fact that Aquaman mostly stayed home now and didn't have time to play pool, drink beer or shoot hoops.

Phoebe, bless her heart, moved to Moreno Valley and got herself a true relationship, but still, for an entire year, all of Aquaman's family and friends continued to refer to me as, "...that African bitch."

I wanted Aquaman and he wanted me, but I was also a very smart girl, so you see...I did the right things that a woman can try to keep a man interested. For instance, I used my cooking skills. I came up with at least three or four delicious recipes that he absolutely loved and couldn't imagine life without. But the trick was--I made sure that these were recipes that no other woman could cook, and believe me, I'd had to go through at least 30 recipes until I found those select 3 that he just absolutely loved and couldn't go without. So that was the mainline hook I put in his ass. I also kept my body in shape by jogging three nights a week and doing at least a hundred crunches every day. I've never been the most beautiful woman--so I've always engaged your father in stimulating conversations. I learned to play Chess (his favorite game)...and even though I'm famous for being a womanist and a freedom fighter...I tolerated his sexism. For instance, whenever we visited his Belizian buddies or uncles, I did as he asked and did not speak while in the presence of the men unless spoken to. If his friends came to our home, I whipped up snacks and served them with a big smile and lots of cheery hostess banter. It wasn't very Alice Walker-like behavior, but it also wasn't hard or annoying for me. There was always a part of me that fantasized about being like Mommysweet and the other wives back in Sudan--catering to their men, as African women are so famous for. I knew that your father had a lower self-esteem than I and I knew that it meant a lot to him to appear as the King of his house in front of his friends, so it made me happy to act the part of the dutiful, submissive wife, and of course all your lives you've seen me catering to your father and calling him "daddy"--rubbing his feet and serving his plates--but it in no way meant that I didn't believe in the womanist values and opinions that I've always extolled in public. I want you to know that I am *both* women. There was no contradiction. I was both a feminist and I loved catering to your father.

And I was also a sexual athlete. You will someday grow up and read this memoir--my soul book--or I'm sure that someone will throw the details of my sexual history in your faces...but I have faith in you. You will remember going to the river with me all throughout your childhood and me baring my breasts to pray. This is a very human, healthy, natural part of women--our sexuality, and you will appreciate that I raised you to respect and admire this in women. A female is a sexual being just like a man is. Her life is to be lived to the fullest. And regarding your father, I always strived to make the art of my sex as pleasing and unique as I made my cooking.

I want you to know that no other man ever made me as happy as your father has. He is my one and only true love, my best friend, my greatest lover, my Black king. He treated me like a Queen, giving us this beautiful place to live in, filling our lives with comfort and male leadership and love, and that I have no doubt you'll remember.

But even still, like so many other young black women in America...*I never married my husband.*

And I realize that even though you don't notice that we aren't legally husband and wife right now while your little boys, once you're grown men, you'll want to know why.

~~

As of 2006, there was an "outdoor" set of reasons and an "indoor" set of reasons.

I never maried my husband, because I was never truly free. There was slavery in my homeland, the Sudan. There was genocide and I was a soldier, even if it was undercover and mostly spying and speaking out, it required an obligation from me that your father didn't appreciate and resented. <u>So I wasn't free.</u> I had to be for my people. And if that wasn't enough, there was plenty of shit going on right here in America that I was consumed by. The assimilation of the Black Americans was in its beginning stages and the bling-bling self-destruction of the Hip Hop Holocaust had taken over the black world, defiling all of us, so I had to invent images of myself and tell stories about our people in such a way that I could challenge and bring introspective criticism of black complacency as it related to Black Americans--and because your Egyptian grandfather had imbued me with superior knowledge, it was my obligation to fight against the assimilation of the Black Americans

314

with everything I had. Of course, your father thought I was crazy and wasting my time--but being victorious wasn't the point. The point was that I had tried to lead them back to their authentic selves, their own ownership. This nation had taught them to committ mass suicide and I had to create alternative messages, and I swear to you, my sons, there was nothing tougher in this country than being a black woman who *looked* like a black woman, who looked un-mixed and had *"the proof"* growing from her scalp, and like most black women in this country, I was not truly *free* to marry.

White women, Latinas, Asians, Bi-racials or any "straight-haired" women--those women were free to compete and were most often affirmed by this society, but not the authentic black woman.

So, you see, although I had time to stop and have babies--there was just too much fighting for me to do. Too much was wrong with the conditions for black people (those of us who wanted to stay black and to provide for our black babies). It was a constant battle.

Your father greatly respected me and admired my courage, but he also resented my devotion to our people as a race. While he was very proud to be a Belizian and proud to be a black man, he did not feel particularly responsible for what happened to other black people and blamed my activism on my mental difficulties.

We fought terribly over my appearing topless on the back covers of my books, because he didn't want other men looking at "his titties" as he put it. Your father read many kinds of books, but he never read any of my writing and he had very little interest in the Sudanese culture from which I had come. Although he was a pure blooded Garifuna (the African people of Belize) and spoke the Garifuna language fluently, he never would teach it to me or to you. He even got agitated when I took lessons to learn to cook his Belizian food that his Aunt used to cook him. He felt cheated by my interests outside the home, and just so you'll know, it was your father who paid for our lives, one hundred percent, as I never made any substantial money from the sale of my books, and was completely dependent on your father (which is what made him most comfortable). It was your father who worked like a dog and supported me and supported you both (I, of course, have been a stay at home mom and *"housewife"*, cooking, parenting, swimming and chatting on the internet in the day and writing my books at night--only leaving occasionally to do work for the SPLA)...and even when we split up...he gave me his house and ranch (which is mines until the two of you reach 18) and he continued to pay all of our bills without ever having been asked for a single dime. Even as I was writing this book, he was paying for my car to be fixed and paying all our expenses. I never asked him for a loaf of bread, and yet I paid for nothing, sons. So you can see, your father did not mean to have a <u>working</u> woman, and as I began to become famous, that was part of the problem.

For years, we were like butterflies holding a seyonce. Enchanted by our mutual love jones, and at one point in 2002--I had agreed to marry him, but then I backed out when he insisted that I move to his house in Belize and give up "Kola Boof", who he despised almost as much as he loved and adored "Naima". Of course, I couldn't live with your father on the turf of his sexist uncles, and Grandmother Claudine warned me, *"Don't you let that man take you down there. He'll be whoop'n yo ass 'n treat'n you like all kinds of slaves. You slave enough for _____ as it is. Don't you step out this country with no nigga."* And then once the death threats and firebombing of my publisher kicked in, and the story came out about me being Osama Bin Laden's former mistress (which I'd never shared with your father), and when we had to live under virtual house arrest and be protected by the government--Aquaman could not help but lash out at me for endangering all of our lives--and then when the gun battle happened in later summer, 2002, and I was taken away to be interrogated--he snapped.

My work and my commitments and my passion for the things I believed in were ruining our lives, he said. And he was losing control of me and I was becoming more and more "Kola"...and less and less "Naima", he claimed. So he left us.

Certainly, you've heard my mother and your auntie Spring and aunt Tamala whispering things about your father *"cheating like a big dog"*--but that's not really true at all. It was me who brought women to your father. And I really think you need to understand a thing...about my vaginal difficulties. Frankly, the circumcision that was done to me was harmless, because my birth mother, Mommysweet, did not allow them to remove my clitoris--they simply made "tribal markings", scarring my outer lips as the face of the singer Seal is scarred about the face. But the <u>infibulation</u>, the *sewing shut* of my vagina opening and the manipulation of vaginal muscles--left me mutilated in such a way...that I had to endure a very painful sex life in which I was a perpetual virgin each time I laid with a man, and even after having two babies, I am still like a 12 year old down there, but in all honesty, my sons, like 100 million other African-born women, I accepted it and I became accustomed to it. Your Black American grandparents wanted to have it corrected when I was a teen--but I wouldn't let them. It was the only thing I had of my birth mother. *I had to honor the ways of my mother-roots.* I wanted the mark...to be marked on me. And so as little boys, when you would run to our bedroom door crying and upset, because you thought daddy was hurting me--we were making love. And we both loved to make love with each other. I was not suffering.

But during pregnancy...I could not have sex. In fact, for an entire year going in and after pregnancy, I could not bear for your father to touch me or penetrate me. I could not give him head or be anywhere near his penis--I can't bear to smell a man when I'm pregnant. And because I come from a culture where it's perfectly normal for pregnant infibulated women to have "co-wives", I insisted that your father allow me to bring other women into the house--young African college girls who needed free room and board and who completely understood and honored the infibulated woman rites of co-wifery--to live in my home as *my friend*, handmaiden and confidant (not the husband's) and to make my pregnancy easier by performing whatever chores I was not up to-- and as you know, I won't let another woman cook and clean in my house--so I needed the co-wives (I had one while I carried each of you) to be sexually available to your father.

And at first--he was totally against it. Because he is a Christian and is pruddish, and more than that--he felt embarrassed having permission to cheat (although, I don't consider co-wifery to be cheating), and he felt very awkward having a young pretty woman living down the hall in the guest room...waiting to abide him on whatever night he wished...but eventually...as I nagged him and promised him that I knew that he loved only me and that it would nothing more than sexual release--he went to the co-wife. Of course, after sexing the co-wife, the husband must wash off and return to the bed of his wife and sleep there. And during the day, the husband and co-wife can have no interaction without the wife present, and we followed those rules.

Now, of course--your Grandmother Claudine and your aunts criticized me for allowing this. They insisted that he could just wait the 12 to 14 months that it would take before I could have sex again. But I refused to have the man I love wait, and the reason I refused, is because I do not believe that I myself could go 12 to 14 months without having sex with a man, and as I told your Aunt Spring--if Aquaman was to be hit by a bus and paralyzed and could no longer fuck me--I could not go without sex. So why would I want to be silly with this American "romantic" bullshit and insist that he go without pussy for a year? No. I would rather *pick* the woman myself and have him sew his oats in my own house where I can know everything.

And please understand one thing...if I was <u>not infibulated</u> and could have normal sex like other women...there is *no way* that I would have ever brought co-wives into our home.

I am completely...completely against the practice of women sharing men and women being part of harems and accepting situations where the man has multiple wives. If a woman can't find a man who's offering her love and commitment, then I feel that it would be much smarter for a woman to have *"multiple boyfriends"* (as I once did when I was young)--and to put her career and her education and freedom first. It makes no sense whatsoever to be involved with a man who has multiple wives, but in America--a lot of lonely black females find themselves the victims of black men who convince them that they don't have any other options or prospects. That's camel shit. In all honesty, females can get a lot of their intimate and emotional needs met by having healthy, nurturing friendships with other females--and then using men for their sexual needs. I'm not talking about lesbianism here (although, if a woman is *able* to be gay, which I never was, but always wished I could--then that's a solution, too)...but what I am saying is this...if no man is offering a woman love, and for whatever reason, she doesn't have any prospects romantically--then I see no reason that she can't just have close female friends for emotional plug in and "use men" for sex--until she happens upon a better situation.

I don't believe in this bullshit about women being "whores", because they're sleeping with more than one man. If it's good enough for men and they're laughing and congratulating each other for their "variety" of conquests--then lonely women should be able to have their cake and eat it, too. Fuck men's respect and fuck the society. Women are human beings and they have needs, and since the playing field is not even in this colorstruck, sexist, "looks oriented" American society--then I would rather see black women getting *some* enjoyment and pleasure out of life, rather than sitting in a corner eating themselves into oblivion and watching their youth fade away.

Let me tell you something. Your mother always...always...had her some dick and someone to talk to and someone to go out with and someone to help pay my bills--and it wasn't always the same man. And until your father came and rescued me and cared about my heart and challenged himself to heal me--I didn't let these selfish sexist motherfuckers worry me. I lived my life and I gave as good as I got. Luckily, your daddy offered me love. Not every woman gets that offer. So, please my sons--don't be out here putting women down, and *especially*, don't be out here putting down black women--because it's hard for a woman in this world. This is a <u>man's</u> world, and these motherfuckers don't give a shit about us--they walk out on babies and all. And the lowest thing you can be in America is a black woman with *"the proof"* growing out of your scalp. Even the black men in this country, dark as tree bark and carried 9 months in a black woman's womb--generally believe that the race of women they come from are the most inferior on earth. They affirm the white man's mother and try to *lighten up* their own mother. Your daddy is the exception, not the rule. So don't ever put down black women, my sons--don't call us *"bitches 'n Ho's"* when we were <u>never</u> <u>protected</u> and never <u>offered love</u> in the first goddamned place--mainly because we were black.

And you know who your mother is. Your father has told you all your lives what a *"good woman"* I am and how he's been all over the world, but never found a woman who could compete with Naima. So you know what I'm telling you...is part of my love.

~~

But back to your father cheating. Because of my infibulation, I could not service your father the way I wanted to during pregnancy, and during all four of my pregnancies by him--I had co-wives for as long as they were needed, and it wasn't your father's suggestion or his fault. It was all my idea. So don't ever blame him.

We broke up in that moment, because like any other couple, our biggest struggle was to accept one another. And though we loved each other so very deeply--love is never enough.

October, 2006

The blessing for me is that Aquaman is so ever-present in your lives and so thoroughly devoted to your development as black males. He really is the one who raises you, despite what people think. And this is why I love him.

It's also why I continue to have a special relationship with him.

Your father comes to live with us every weekend--because more than anything in this world, we both love you and want to raise you to the best of our abilities.

We know how important it is for you to see us together and to see us being kind to one another. As your Grandpa Marvin says: *"Little boys grow up and do what they see their fathers do."* So this is why you see him bring me a flower every time he comes, and this is why he constantly compliments all black women in front of you, and this is why you have seen me treat him like a King. It was all for you--because we wanted you to believe in *our* world and to feel secure and to go forth in the world, to represent and protect what you come from.

He also comes just to eat your mother's cooking (smile)--because he can't get it anywhere else, exactly like he's used to it.

Everything that happens in your lives as children, your father knows about it and he phones me daily to help me make decisions about how you arc to be raised and to advise me on all manner of things from the direction of my career to whether or not it's O.K. for you boys to see a certain film or not.

You boys have been raised in a very afrocentric surrounding, because your father is a pure blooded Garifuna and your mother is a Sunni Egypto Gisi-Waaq Oromo. We are descendents of the true Black African people, and to give you an idea of our *"fears"* about having you born and raised in America, let me tell you a very brief incident I had with your father. *Ha ha*! He and I were shopping at the Mall in Los Angeles one afternoon (you can just imagine me, gliding through like a black Morticia Adams), and your father says to me, "Baby--I see now why the Black American men complain that they are being castrated. Look at the women these men are having babies with. They can't help but be castrated. These kids have black fathers and yet they look nothing at all like the black man or his people. In them, his image is killed. You look at some of them, and it's like he never existed. They have no African hair, no soulfulness, none of our people's features. What is the purpose of them? For hundreds of years, the white man has sought to destroy the black man, and now we do it to ourselves? I don't get the hype about all these mixed kids in L.A. They're just a symbol of the black man's castration."

And all your life, you saw your father and his uncles drink beer and dance to Burning Spear and proclaim: *"Ya Da Fe We Belize!"*

So you see, this is why you were raised so afrocentric. Your father was a true black man--a King. There was none of the African Pogo nigger or the Central American niggerstock in your father. He stood tall and uncommonly secure in his black flesh; his living black manhood, and it was always in his consciousness, throughout building his electrical company and all that he did--that his *seed* must continue, must be everlasting--that *"through our children we live forever"* and that he did not want to see his glory erased and his people conquered by the blood of the oppressors. This is the reason why, like me, Aquaman took enormous pride when people said that you boys look like a miniature Denzel Washington and Tupac Shakur. This is why he loved to stare and grin at *"the proof"* growing from your chocolate scalps. The symbol that he as a black man had not been defeated or castrated. That he was still in the world, still a King--still a Black man. And although we've broken up, we talk about it all the time--that perhaps I will someday have that daughter I've always dreamed about (by him, of course). A pretty little Lauryn Hill or Alek Wek or Jill Scott to trail me around the river and help me in the kitchen or keep me up to the fashion as a writer and womanist thinker.

Then again, after six pregnancies, with two of you born, three of you miscarried and one of you aborted--yet every one of you *"a boy"*-- I might not be up to it. Since I was Mommysweet's seventh child and her first daughter, I think I'm scared to get pregnant a seventh time. I have superstitions about a #7 baby, and although I'd love to have Lauryn Hill, Alek Wek or Jill Scott for daughters, I'm not so sure that I'd like to have a little Kola Boof. I am writing this young, but I feel much older than I am, and I am tired. I've had a very hard life. So, if you're reading this years from now, and you still don't have a baby sister-- that's what it was.

But anyway...just because your father and I raised you afrocentric--it isn't written in stone that you have to be *like us*. We would like that, but then again, you are your own people. The masters of your own fate. No matter what you do, I will always love you unconditionally, and whatever you feel is the best for you, I will accept that and honor it, even if I disagree, because that is what a mother does. She gives her children room to be themselves and to fuck up their lives as they see fit.

As I've told you from day one, *"The meaning of life...is that your deeds outlive you."*

~~

Each weekend, when your father comes to stay with us, he and I make love. It wasn't always that way. For the first year when we broke up, I refused to have sex with him. But as we started a second year apart, I decided that I didn't want to learn a new man and that it was just more convenient for me to get my needs met by a man who actually loves me. I tried dating other men, although you never knew it, because I wouldn't let them come to the ranch, but like I told you--I feel tired now in my life and my primary desire is to write my books, which takes up enormous energy and research and thinking; and to be honest, I don't feel pretty anymore and I'm constantly struggling to stay a size 8 now--so I just find it easier to occasionally sleep with your father, although I imagine that he'll someday begin a new relationship with another woman, and thereby force me to find a new man. Or just dry up alltogether. How it will end up, I have no idea.

But tonight, as I'm writing this, your father is here in my bedroom. He is asleep on the bed just a few feet away from me, lightly snoring, and it greatly reminds me of the time in London when I sat up staring at him as he slept on my little lumpy cot and I wrote this silly poem: "*stay away morning...fetch me not...O let there be a God who bid me stay.*"

Of all the men I've ever belonged to, your father was the only one that *I* picked (despite the lie you've often heard told, it's the *men* who usually do the picking in this world). Because women are mostly judged by their looks, they can't truly just *pick a man*. That's bull, the men do the picking. But with your father--*I* did the picking.

And when he wakes up tonight, knowing him--we will make love again, and after our bubble bath, we'll probably put on our song--"*Truly Adore You*" by Prince--and we'll hold each other close and dance around, cheek to cheek in a trance, and for the rest of our lives do what other young couples in America do...

...go for what we know.

SO MUCH THINGS TO SAY

"Because the nation had me down, look what I have found."

--India Arie

Strength, Courage and Wisdom.

● *November, 15th, 2006*

<u>My</u> doctors give me pills to ward off my chronic nightmares, but I never take them. I'm a control freak, which causes me to hate any kind of drug, because I can't stand to not be alert, not be listening, not be vigilant, not be...in control. And I have two small boys to protect. I can't afford to be *subdued* or incompetent. My babies need me.

But I sure will tell you. As I sit looking in the mirror, trying to fix myself up some days, I just feel so exhausted from the nightmares, and I keep contemplating plastic surgery (I know I'm a black woman and not yet 40, but shit--I need it). I do not look good for my age, and if it weren't for supermodel Iman's *Second To None Foundation* and her absolutely miracle-producing skin care products, people would see how unpretty I've become.

And I know it's true, because I've peaked in at AOL Black Voices.Com and read the young people in there commenting on how ugly am, how tired I look, how big my forehead is and how I remind them of the CryptKeeper. Of course, there's this one rather over-zealous poster, IsisNambi (aka Lydia Lovelace) who just praises me to high heaven and keeps every bit of news there is about me posted in heavy rotation--*thanks angel*--but I have to admit that I often find myself agreeing more with the haters than I do with Isis.

I've had an extraordinarily hard life and it shows.

•~~

The nightmares have been going on for about three years now, and they're excruciatingly real while I'm in them. Always, someone or some group of men are coming to kill me--and I can see them coming, but I can't seem to find a weapon; there's nowhere to hide. And then just as they run up on me or drive up pointing a gun out of a car window or kick in my bedroom door--I wake up gasping. Other times, I dream that I'm jogging and come upon a dead body in the bushes...and when I pull back the branches, the dead body is me. And once, I had a nightmare while I was *wide awake*! I was sitting on the edge of my bed as my bathwater was running, watching t.v., and then when I went into the bathroom to check my water--I saw myself in the tub, dead, with a bullet hole over my left eye and my gushing throat slashed. I started screaming and jumped awake--leaping out of the bed!

And so I can't sleep. I stay on the internet very late--either at my discussion board THE KOOL ROOM or at WOST.com (where I can watch vintage episodes of my favorite soap operas)...or I listen to CDs all night (I've become a major fan of the rock group *America*--their songs "Ventura Highway" and "Tin Man" blow me away) or I get up and go play my son's video games. I especially love "Gauntlet Legend" and "Mario Party" (I'm always Yoshi and I like to catch fish). Or I may start cooking a pot of greens or bake a cake.

Sometimes, I just sit on the porch and cry for hours and hours (which is really good for a human being, *it's good to cry!*), and then many other times--I write letters to people who are dead now. People I miss so much and even people I never knew--like <u>Susan Sontag</u>. The genius writer that I cherished and admired so much, and daydreamt so many times that I'd get to meet once I myself made it as a writer.

But she's gone now.

I tried to write a poem about her, but I felt as though my intellect wasn't worthy, and it wouldn't come to me. A poem is not true when it's only the heart. Like I tell people all the time. To love someone is not enough. You have to *understand* them for as deep as your understanding can go--but without emotion.

Emotion is like sugar burning in a skillet when you thought you were making caramel--but forgot that teaspoon of lemon juice to keep it from burning.

It's not enough--LOVE. It's never enough by itself.

Understanding born from intellect gives LOVE a good bouyant broth; a perfect caramel topping; a truthfulness. It makes it real--*or*--it allows you to let go and move on. To not be blind.

But, of course, I'm only saying all this...<u>because</u>...I'm an overly emotional lonely spirit. I have a broken heart that continues to beat. So at all times, my mind-drum is *off beat*, because of the pain.

But that's how I make such beautiful art. From hurting.

And I'm not smart enough *yet*, to write a poem about Susan Sontag. But, dear God, how I loved her.

~~

I'm not ready to die (if that's what the nightmares signify), but the older I get, the more I find myself on a cloud, sort of dreamily inhaling the scent of the freshest soil, Sudanese soil, and staring into the faces of my slain birth parents and listening for their blood as it seeps into the earth. Or I get intensely angry.

Recalling that day when they informed me that my Auntie Ramah had died back in Sudan. I still feel the bolt of shock as it pierces my heart all over again...and then I envision my Nana Glodine, and I hear her saying to me, *"chal, you is more then a notion."* Although Nana Glodine's dead too now--I see us separating colored clothes from the whites, I see us sucking our teeth at Jill Abbott on *"Young and the Restless"* (Nana say: "Dat 'ol trifling *Why-N-ch*!), I see us snapping green beans, shucking corn, canning the preserves we used to make, baking rhubarb cobbler, egg pie, rinsing collard greens (there was a fog in them one time!), I see us heating up the hot comb while I run and get the grease, slathering vaseline on our ashy legs, stringing popcorn for the christmas tree, walking up to the church with my little hand held firmly in Nana's--I see us in the third pew, Nana with her big easter bonnet on, nodding and saying affirmatively, *"Amen. Come on wit it, Preacha...Dess alright now. Aaaaa/MEN!"*

She holds her Bible down when it's time to read a scripture, so that I look at the pages and act like I'm reading, too.

I see me and Nana struggling as I help her to squeeze into her girdle. And I see her dark brown #4 wig plopped down on the styrofoam wig-head, shiny with a flip--and now all these years later, when I'm damned near 40 years old and wishing my Nana was here to play some Gin Rummy with--I miss that wig and wish to God I had that wig of Nana's. Not to wear it, but just to look at it--for inspiration.

I see my Auntie Ramah down on the banks of the Nile, barefoot, plump and thick-faced with glorious uncombed nappy hair--washing clothes on rocks. I see her holding me to her bosom and saying, *"You come from a people...you come from a place...you come from a nation.*

Naima!--the one who is victorious. The one--*who is praying.*"

I see the lion ready to pounce.

A big male one with the impressive mane.

Standing under the shade of a very tall tree, and I see Auntie Ramah standing across from him--her hands on her hips and her African hornet's eyes staring right straight deep as arrows back into that lion's evil stare. And she says to me--it seems *telepathically*, without moving her mouth--"Naima, you back up into the acacia, slowly."

And I'm too scared to move.

At any moment--I just know that lion's going to leap, jump running right at my Auntie Ramah's wide, plump perfect meal of a body--and plenty of the strongest men we knew have been ripped apart and eaten by lions, so I know a woman can't take a big lion like this. But Auntie Ramah gets tired of the staring contest with the lion.

She stomps her right foot like a horse would do and she shouts in a low, mannish voice, "رز خرزح سخذحش سخخس زر جخسدس (I'm tired bastard without a mother--come on!)."

The lion, very dourly, looks to his side--and just when he does that--*Auntie Ramah takes off!!!...peeeee-yune!!!!* Charging right at him as fast as I've ever seen any female run. Screaming high pitched as a pack of hawks..."*ailailailailailail!*", her whole body galloping with pure unholy murder, and that lion--I guess because he's caught off guard--haul tails and runs the other way for his life!

And in the split seconds that all that happens--I pee on myself.

But then when we get back to Omdurman, and Auntie Ramah is safe on the busy streets--she's pale as a ghost and can't bring herself to tell anybody what just happened. She falls on her knees and begins sobbing like a baby and praising Allah, "Allah, most merciful...most highest God, Allah...thank you for my life, Allah...thank you!"

And she's a wreck for two days straight. Crying, doing ablutions to ward off "*the jinns*" and praying.

I feel very powerful whenever I remember these two women, and just like I talk to the child I aborted and the ones I miscarried (calling them by the names I named them)--I talk to my Auntie Ramah and my Nana Glodine all the time. And I talk to my great leader John Garang and ask him for courage and better understanding, and I talk to Theo Van Gogh, and ask him to guard me and to send me signs so that I don't join him in a similar fashion, and I talk to Yvonne Vera, who I never knew, but whose writing I thought was nothing less than otherworldy and true.

I hear my Auntie Ramah telling me, "Don't fight, *win*! You're an African! When your father makes lion...eat lion. And whatsoever you eat, is what you are!"

● *November 21st, 2005*

Thanksgiving is coming--and so is my whole family!

Most people love Christmas (which I don't like) or they like Easter (which bores me so much) or New Year's Eve (Aquaman's favorite--but I hate noise and crowds)--for me it's thanksgiving. God, I love it so much. In fact, one of my most popular poems is called *"Thanksgiving Day"*. So not only am I feeling my usual excitement-- but my family is flying in all the way from the east coast and they're trusting me to make the entire dinner all by myself.

Although, I'm sort of the family cook--it's still an honor, because on thanksgiving, it's usually Nana Glodine (before she passed), Naima (me), my Mom and then my dad last, who do all the cooking, and almost every year, we all get together at someone's house--usually my parents, but one time we met at Tamala's house and then another year, we went to Aunt Beverly's, and we even met at Uncle Booey's house once.

As it's been many years since we all had to live in the same house for a w h o l e w eek together, it's especially th rilling , because I'm _**Kola Boof**_ now!--the underground novelist-poet nigeratti cult figure and black womanist activist, former mistress of Osama Bin Laden, hostess of The Kool Room internet discussion board and infamously hated by not only the mainstream media, but all kinds of establishment I've pissed off--and I know my good friend Alicia Banks is laughing.

I feel that for the first time in my life, my family's actually meeting the real me.

The kola nut at Naima's center.

 ## Family Drama

They love me no matter who I am, and as I begin to take comfort in that--the days become sweetly idyllic.

There is, of course, some drama. My sisters Spring and Tamala, who usually visit me separately, are with me at the same time, and therefore have to _share_ my attention, and to Tamala--it seems that I am fawning over Spring and catering to her. And it's true, I am--but what Tamala doesn't realize...is that as much as I love Spring, and as close as Spring and I have always been (and have gotten even closer in adulthood)--Spring doesn't believe that I love her.

And the reason she doesn't believe it, is because _she knows_ from our lives growing up together that I don't see her as "black". And no matter how I try to pretend that I see what an American sees, I'm not convincing and Spring knows me. Tamala and I are the two "dark skinned" girls, and Spring is very high yellow with green eyes and she knows that I pity her, because she doesn't have the _"proof"_ growing from her scalp. Please--don't get me wrong. Like any North African, I love long hair, it's just the _texture_ of her hair that I used to wish was more African like me and Tamala's hair, and even though I praise her hair now--she knows from childhood that I don't like her hair. Not in a mean way--I just pity it. Since the time we met as children, I felt bad for her. And you how mulatto Black Americans are--if you don't see them as _black_; then they don't believe that you love them.

But the fact is--I really do love Spring with all my heart, and that's what causes me to dote on her and do special things for her. I admit that I spoil her, but it's because I'm always trying to convince her that I truly love her as my sister--I'm always trying to make up for the hurt feelings she has surrounding the fact that she doesn't have God's hair like the rest of the family does. But to Tamala, it looks like I'm favoring her for the same reason that most people favored Spring all our lives--because she's not black.

So you can see my dilemna. And I tried to explain to Tamala that Spring needs that extra attention and love from us. And I truly believe that a lot of black people in America do this with mulattoes. We try very hard to make them feel accepted by constantly saying, "_Oh, you're so pretty_"..."_you have nice hair_".

I've seen a lot of people do that. Not just me.

My father, Marvin Johnson, is still a handsome 1960's styled black power oriented militant black man, and my mother Claudine is still a good christian black woman with pretty features and deep brown skin--the loving, comical, gardening and adopting other people's children type, and now that Nana Glodine is dead, she and I have finally become close like a real mother and daughter. The only thing is--they disagree vehemently about what the contents of my books should be about (my mother hates the public discussion of colorism, because she's <u>embarrassed</u> to admit that blacks themselves hate being black, but after being put up for adoption because of my dark complexion, I don't see how I could possibly be a writer and not honor what have become the central experiences of so many authentically black people), and as many of you already know--as my memoirs were being written and edited--I had to get a lawyer and fight my beloved publishers to keep my essay *"The Authentic Black Man"* from being thrown out of the book.

Now that we're gathered in the same house, in fact preparing lunch together in the kitchen, my parents (who've read the essay) begin to squabble their opinions out of their systems.

"You know I stand for your truth, Naima, and I understand your passion as a black woman, I'm a black woman, too--but this is why your career is not going good", my mother says in reference to the essay. "American people aren't used to this kind of blatant, raw, confrontational--embarrassing...*black eye*--and you're going to turn off a lot of African Americans who otherwise would have supported you. I mean, think about Marita Golden's book that you loved so much ("Don't Play In the Sun")...if you notice, she didn't have to give people a black eye to get her point across. And she included everybody's pain. You don't do that, Naima. And this whole thing about the word 'nigger', you need to drop it. You are such a gifted writer--*you could be richer than Terry McMillan by now*! But you keep bringing up the worst about Black Americans, and you're not one of us...and you talk about our famous black men like they're the lowest cretons--which I agree with you, some of them are--but my God, girl! And you just totally despise white women! How long you think you gone be able to call them '*white bitches*' and get away with it--ha? This is not a game, Kola Boof--this is your life and my grandbaby's lives, and you are not going to make it if you don't learn to set aside some of this anger and pain and activism and just mellow out. I mean you see how these white woman run these major publishing houses, and everytime some black editor gets excited about your work and wants to sign you up--you got all these evil things you said against white women coming back to haunt you. Them white heffas ain't gone let you get published talking about them like shit and acting crazy like you do on the internet. Just acting like you ain't got no home training. I swear."

Then it's my father's turn.

"Well, Claudine, that's why our people haven't gotten anywhere as it is--we always take a stand too late, and by the time we do, it's too little. Kola is doing just what she's supposed to be doing. She's not in this to be Terry McMillan--she's following in the footsteps of Malcolm X and Marcus Garvey." My eyes light up and my heart begins pounding as he says those two names. "I read that essay three times and I couldn't find a single thing in it that I didn't agree with. She told it like it is, and it's about time that somebody cared enough about black people-- I'm talking about the *real black people*, Claudine--the kind that you and me came from when black folks was worth a quarter....it's about time somebody cared enough to acknowledge that our whole community and our whole culture is dying, just falling in the gutter. I'm glad she wrote that essay! And as far as bashing black men--most of these motherfuckers need some serious bashing in they heads. Acting like a white woman is a goddess and our black woman ain't shit. Just like she said--what kind of real man refuses to give birth to his own image? Hell, these jive turkeys make me ashamed to be a brotha nowadays. I ain't never liked Sidney Poitier and Belafonte. That whole Jackson family ain't nothing but niggers who subconsciously miss slavery days. The only people who don't like Kola's books and who won't like that essay she wrote is the 'niggers' and the crackers, but the real true double-d-down brothas and sisters, those who love our ancestors and love being black--they gone love Kola Boof and fuck the rest. I done told you a hundred times, Claudine--our people need revolution, and don't nobody need revolution in this country more than the mother of our race--the dark skinned black female. Why is it that so many of yall black women is so scared of the truth, so scared of revolution when yall the ones ain't got shit to lose no way? Every damned thing my daughter said in that essay was nothing but the truth, and *Kola*--don't you change a goddamned word. I been a black man in this country over sixty years and if we hadda had women like you to begin with--we wouldn't be fucked up in the head now (That comment by my father angers me, because #1--it hurts my mother's feelings, and #2--black men are always pitting African women and Black American women against each other and blaming us on both sides of the Atlantic for *their* actions and how *they* turn out). You got-damned right I felt ashamed to be a black man reading that essay--knowing full well everything my baby wrote was the truth. Shit--fuck popularity, fuck money. Why the black man always gotta committ suicide, Claudine? You think I respect these motherfuckers, knowing full well that a whole got-damned race of people is being led down the wrong fucking road by a bunch of weak, self-hat'n stupid black dick-heads. It's 2005, and these motherfuckers *still* ain't shit!"

"Neh, see, Marvin--that's why she's like that now. You raised her on all that hate and Marcus Garvey, Malcolm X mess that belongs in the '60's! You know I believe in equality and you know I'm proud to be black just like you are--but you're going to get our daughter killed. You just keep on rewarding Kola for being big and bad. For being the son that none of the boys turned out to be."

Aquaman comes to live with us for the week that my family is with me, because he loves to fuck me with my parents in the house. It turns him on that my tall, rough military father is just down the hall while he's poking into me or reclining with his legs spread wide as I suck or pressing his muscles against my softness, dominating me, making love as Fantasia sings the hell out of *"Good Lov'n"*.

Our chocolate bodies melt into an ancient oneness.

And I get a whole week of waking up with the man I love and feeling the ache from him being inside me (having that gap walk for a few days) and kissing him so deep that all my pain and nightmares evaporate like they never were--so I love it, too, and I'm really happy this thanksgiving.

● *November 23rd, 2005*

The smell of cinnamon on baked apples and hardy nutmeg stirred into Senegalese whipped yams gently wafts through my house as the daybreak of Thanksgiving Eve crawls across Aquaman's horses and then the veranda and slowly inches past my kitchen window, casting the palm of God's warm hand across my pretty chocolate face.

I really do feel pretty now.

Aquaman and my sons have just completed a ritual that has become a tradition for the Kola men. They've gone to our wonderful Mexican neighbors down the road (a 50-something husband and wife) and picked out one of the huge, fat turkeys that the Mexicans grow on a sloped hill all year (the sloped hill makes the meat *much* juicier and the boys fuss until they agree on the turkey, which is what they look forward to every year) and waited while the Mexican wife slaughtered and semi-plucked the bird. Now, proudly, they drag it into the kitchen for me to finish plucking and cleaning it--and after that's done--I set it in a tub of brine (table salt and seawater) where it'll soak submerged until the next morning, as my turkey is always the very last thing I make (it goes in the oven at about 6 a.m.) before dinner, which Aquaman usually has me serve at 2 or 3 in the afternoon--because he's christian and takes our sons to the Belizean church (which takes hours to drive to), and then when they get back, they pig out all over again.

My mother and father come into the kitchen, squabbling over whether or not Condoleeza Rice will run for President. My dad, who *hates* Condoleeza Rice, is sure she will run against Hilary Clinton, whom he barely likes any better than Condoleeza--while my mother, (who's like me--totally against Condi's *politics*, but admires her accomplishments and her intellect and style) is saying that Condoleeza has already announced she's not running--but then my mother says that she bets Condi will run on the Republican ticket as Vice President, and she says that if the Republicans pair Condi with John McCain--then the Democrats don't stand a chance. Then she and my father ask me who I'm voting for and I say either Hilary Clinton or the Green Party, provided they have a better candidate.

My sister Tamala, however, bounces in to say that if Condoleeza runs in any capacity--she won't be able to help herself. She'll just have to vote a black woman into the white house.

And then my Uncle Booey comes flying in, yelling, *"You bet not vote for dat bitch!* Whut the hell is wrong wit 'chall new niggas!?"

"Mommysweet--is Condoleeza Rice your friend that was here for the cookout?" Because I'm an East Coast black, my sons say "cookout" instead of *"bar-b-q"* (which is West Coast). I tell my son, no, I don't know Condi Rice and she's never been here.

It's thanksgiving tomorrow (*yaaay!*), so Aquaman puts on Sarah Vaughn, because that's all I play on thanksgiving is Jazz music, my official song for the holiday being "What a Wonderful World" by Louis Armstrong--and then I also have to hear "Brown Baby/Save the Children" (1973) by Diana Ross, "Alabama" by John Coltrane and "Pigfoot and a Bottle of Beer" by Bessie Smith. But it's strictly jazz on thanksgiving eve and on dinner day at Kola's house.

For breakfast, I've made baked apples, Senegalese ginger yam pudding (because I'm Sudanese, I have to have a porridge with breakfast), bacon strips (the home made country biscuits are by the magic of my mother's brown hands), and I whip up a skillet of fluffy yellow cheese eggs and set a fresh pot of coffee on the table.

My dad squeezes us a pitcher of orange juice.

My sister Spring wanders in (talking on her cell phone to one of the many men who's chasing her), Tamala is yelling at her kids to sit down and stop running around (she and her husband divorced two years ago), and my big brother, Curtom, glides in with his second wife, Cherokee (a gorgeous deep dark skinned sister from Atlanta), and gives me a big kiss on the cheek and a smack on the booty, whining that I won't let him sample the cream cheese bottomed sweet potato pie that I make exclusively for him every year--then my brother Albert strolls in with his girlfriend, Shelley, who is white and very, very adorable, and knew *of me* from the internet before she met my brother and can't believe she's actually at Kola Boof's house for thanksgiving...and especially can't believe that I'm crazy about her.

My father says the grace and then everybody digs in, but as we're all eating, I can't stop my silent praying--thanking God for the blessing of having a family; people to belong to--and I have to keep my head down, because I begin to weep.

After breakfast, my brother Albert does the dishes and then we shoo away the men so that I can get back to cooking and have time with just my mother and sisters (and Cherokee and Shelley) as the warm California sun literally floods my kitchen with rainbows of pure magic November yellow, and from the livingroom, Billie Holiday's "What's New" turns into Anita Baker singing "You Bring Me Joy"...*you BRING meeeeEEEE joy!* I love Anita Baker! I scream, "Sing it Nita!"

My mother chops celery and onion for potato salad (this was supposed to be her year to *do nothing,* but she can't help herself), Tamala

337

tears collard greens, I slide a huge bed of macaroni and cheese (my speciality) in the oven and then turn up the heat on 30 pounds of chitlins that me, my mother nd Spring cleaned and washed last night--and then out of nowhere...big-mouth Tamala decides to amuse Shelley and Cherokee with my LIST (famous men with the biggest dicks, *see page 426*)--a list that I and 168 other women compiled now that I'm a member of the Alpharetta Secret Sister Society, a nationwide network of mostly snooty socialite and rich ghetto fabulous black women (many of whom are very famous--actresses, hip hop singers, models, news anchors, call girls--the $1,000 an hour type only--and college Deans, Presidents and Professors). Of course, because the list is the most accurate one of its kind ever compiled, I'm not embarrassed--but it's not something my literary mothers, Toni Morrison, Gayl Jones and Alice Walker would do, so I make a vow never to engage in such silliness again, and because I lose a bet with Albert that nobody in this valley sells marijuana--I'm forced to publish the list in this autobiography. *Drats*!

We ladies have a good laugh and then late that night, my mom (who is such a great sport) lets me style her hair with "blow pops" (the candy suckers) sticking out from her head just like me, Spring and Tamala used to do as teenagers. *She looks so cute*!

My dad just can't stop laughing about it, which the attention makes mom blush, and when Abbey Lincoln's hypnotic voice begins drifting through the house singing *"Afro Blue"*, he takes my mother in his arms and they slow dance on the front porch, nearly in darkness--a vintage 1960's black power couple who stayed together and raised eight children in the ghetto of S.E. D.C. We know what he's whispering; he always says to our mother, "Now and forever, Claudine."

~~

happy thanksgiving! Nov. 24th, 2006   Gobble/Gobble
Claudine: "Arnofo, pass Nana that bag of pecans."

I am crying this morning--because I'm so happy!

Spring, who is standing by the fireplace in her nightgown looking gorgeous, begins twirling around as Albert captures her on video mimicking an opera singer: "Happy *thanks...Giv-ing, Naima!*"

Tamala: "Jerrod, go put some vaseline on your ashy self!"

Another Johnson family tradition is that after football we watch four movies every thanksgiving: *"The Color Purple"*, *"The Prince of Egypt"*, *"Claudine"* (which I had mistakenly grown up thinking was about my mother--LOL) and *"Glory"* starring Denzel Washington, so my dad brings down the DVDs, commenting that he can smell the brine turkey and stuffing and can't wait to eat some cranberry sauce.

Wombe (who likes to trail his father all over the house): "Daddy you cain't say grace--grandpa gone say grace. They didn't give you nothing to do this year. *Sike!* You gotta fry bananas."

My Uncle Booey comes down and insists that everybody form a circle in the livingroom and join hands. He wants to say the Lord's Prayer--and whenever Uncle Booey wants to *"pray"* or *stomp*-dance to Bootsy Collins and the Parliament P-Funk, you Bet Not say no, so we make a circle and Uncle Booey begins breaking it down as only he can: *"Merciful Lawd who art in heaven...this is your son Booey 'n his family--hallowed be thy name, father...and I just want to say--give us this day...our daily bread..."*

Just like the Black Americans--I am <u>not an immigrant</u>. I did not choose to come to this country of my own free will, but was *forced* to come here after being driven from my birth land by my own Arab brethren and then out of my father's land by his evil yellow mother. And this is why I look at my family and all Black Americans as orphans as well. To me, they are magical people, because their hearts are broken.

I am not a victim and none of you should be sad for me--because these are my people now, the Black Americans, And we are *much* of the same muchness. سحخشزذخحصرر ،خحسسش حردس.

    There is no need for the spirits of Mahdi Pappuh or Mommysweet or Auntie Ramah to ever be in sorrow, because although I am nowhere near Africa and live in a strange land that hates nothing on this earth more than it hates the womb (son) and the crowning proof (daughter) of a black woman...miracle of miracles...I am <u>still</u> with family.

"THANKSGIVING DAY"
(*taken from the Kola Boof collection *"Nile River Woman"*)

I make no sound...but a heartbeat
I take no liberties with the devil
nor do I
smoke his dandruff
or cut his pathways
because
life is much too hard

and I love the slow pace of my God
and the cornered grins of my ghosts--I love the act of will
I savor the days of the earth/I love the height of the Sky

I cherish every Black man
with an unheard sorrow
because
our graves are just the same

and I live for the echo of my children;
listening for the bolt
            with the silent faith
            with the silent faith
that they have in me.
I make no sound...but a heart beat.

I am You
before
you was You

~~

INHERITANCE

•

WOMANIST PROSE, ESSAYS

Being and Becoming the
RED Dragon

Even before the SUN...the "Red Dragon" was the first God that mankind ever worshipped. It is still practiced today by scattered Aborigines in Australia and by the East African tribes that those blacks descended from. The "Red Dragon" is what we call a woman's menstration--her monthlies or as American women say *"her period"*. This was what my Mommysweet's ancestors and what most of the pre-Rah, pre-Baal, pre-Christian, pre-Islamic, ancient Nilotic and East Africans considered to be the most holy, mysterious and life-sustaining--the woman's monthlies--and because of its sacred status, they built temples and stone pillars to pray to it, to celebrate it and deify the female race just because of it. And the women who could miraculously *stop* bleeding (either through pregnancy or maturity) were considered "Prophets", "Angels" or "Witches". Kings, back in those days, considered a woman's body to be the most advanced technology on earth...and thus women were greatly valued and cherished. I suppose to you in America it would be called the "Goddess Era". The time of Isis and Kenya (daughter of God Kenyaku), Isis's real mother Marawi (Goddess of counting), the twins--Ala (Goddess of men's journeys) and Alu (Goddess of Trees, *"men"* being trees), Orisha, Nambi, Yemaya Olukun (Goddess of the Sea), Buk (Goddess of rivers and streams) and the first human being, Queen Asli Nalla (Eve)--the word *Asli* meaning "charcoal", and in the earth's first garden, the bare buttocks of the annun-Naturi (the twelve charcoal virgins) in what is called the time before time began...the twelve tribes of the seven sons...rising from The Goddess Flower (all African Women and *only* African women being the Goddess Flower, because there existed no other women on earth)...*black as all black put together*...the kiss of God's wife/Our Mother...Nya Goddess Aithiop, Nya Goddess Sudan, Nya Goddess Kamit. The womb of all humanity--Mother Afrika.

Our father, the Lord, decreeing:

(to the east) *And the birds are the birthmark of the world.*

(to the west) *And the birds are the birthmark of the world.*

Wives: *hoonta bon bon!* (God bless the happy chocolates)

●

This was in the days when African people loved women! (because the human race was so new and so in awe of the power of the female body). Only through her came life--and from her mighty black breasts came food! So she was God, our beautiful nurturing black mother. And now in 2006, people who know that I've created my own religion and called for the abolishment of all men's religions constantly make fun of me and ask--*"just what are your religious beliefs?"*

Well...my religion is called The Womb and like most people, I believe in God (the universe itself being God). I believe that God is not an individual (meaning that it takes the will of all beings to shape and direct the energy of love--love being God), and I believe that Love is for everyone. I also believe that <u>sensitivity</u> is the highest form of intelligence and that *"hate"*, like need, want and hunger, is a branch of "sensitivity" and therefore falls under the heading of LOVE, and that although hate can be self-destructive and can rot the soul like a cancer--if managed wisely, it can also be used to motivate and conduct energy, to spur revolution, and even though hatred is a White emotion and encompasses evil--it is also a good motivator for change, for rebellion and for protection, and like I said...hate is actually an annex of LOVE. So that our goal is to eradicate Hate and use it only for protection, but to *store* LOVE and use it as daily bread. *If you love me/ I love you.* If you murder my children/then I will murder you *and* your children. What we eat is what we brought with us *to share.*

One thing I never liked about Christianity in America--is that it doesn't allow the Black people to *hate* during those times when it's perfectly natural to hate, and because of that, they remain in bondage to their various oppressions. Christianity is a war tool that teaches you how to think like a slave. Just like Islam, it's a strategically man-made form of mind control placed on Africans and women. It uses the truth about God and the bible to make the believer passive and stationary. God, Mohammed, Jesus Christ, the Koran, the Bible--all of that is very good for you. But the part created *by men*--the religion--that is the part that's no good. You really waste your life in a mass hysteria when you should be out *free* experiencing life and demanding the good life *"right now!"*, not just in heaven--moving about the earth, constantly building your sensitivity and spreading the love of God.

I believe (a) that the meaning of life is that your deeds outlive you and...(b) that we exist primarily to love, to hurt and to learn how to be healed and heal others, through which we advance in gaining <u>sensitivity</u> and knowledge, and leave as a tiding--our offspring. I believe in making mistakes and living your life without the ridiculous stigma of "sin".

While I've been told by many of my Black American sisters and African sisters that I am backwards and will be going to hell if I don't accept Jesus Christ (YawWay, Prophet Ciisa) as my lord and personal savior--the fact is, *I do* believe in Jesus and Mohammed and the Holy Koran and the Holy Bible, I do love Allah, the God most high--but what I don't believe is that only men were disciples and conduits of the spirit of God, and what I don't accept is the image of Christ as a white blue eyed blond savior...not even the Greeks were white in the time that Jesus was alive, and we know that the Jews and Palestinians were much blacker back then than any of their bastard offspring would like to remember, so I don't accept this new world white supremacist imagery. I see Jesus as a dark, sexy philosopher, fully capable of lovemaking and dance. I see him as an African deity--meaning that he is capable, at any given moment, of turning into a man, a woman, a sky bird or my favorite animal, a dolphin. I see Jesus as a lover of Oromo coffee (which is the holy water drank at communion by my Mommysweet's people and is the color of African people; the richness of our flavors).

And as a Nilotic woman, I understand that both Jesus Christ and the Creator are much more honored when my breasts are *bare*--and that through the wisdom and nurturing of our mothers, our societies are more fair and honorable (as one of my father figures, Minister Louis Farrakhan says: *"a nation cannot rise above its woman"*). And I believe that men oppress and control women by convincing them that the sexuality of a woman is "dirty and sinful" and that women should be covered up and kept only for men's pleasure and procreation--while the men are allowed to roam free, to be gluttons of sex and exploitation, while we women are taught to stupidly idolize one man our whole lives and be a slave to men's respectability and men's insecurity--and that men *rape* to enforce this ideal of the woman's dirtiness and to enforce his rights in controlling her sexuality. In other words, he expects

346

to be loved, listened to, respected and given *his* mate's pussy exclusively--but then he also expects to be free of reciprocation. His penis and the fact that he can't get pregnant makes him free and she, the female, becomes an object, a symbol of both public saintliness and inate dirtiness. Whatever lust a man feels at any given moment is blamed on her and her inate powers of *"temptation"*, and in the Holy Bible, it says that women should be "shut away" during their monthlies--and in the Koran it says that woman is "impure" and suggests they be covered head to toe. But notice that these dirty putrid ass men who populate all these religions are not denied the full range of their humanity or covered up as though the sight of them displeases God. And notice that Christianity, Islam, the Jewish faith and all the men's religions openly espouse that God loves men more and that men are by nature morally sound, but that a woman must constantly be on guard against her inner-wickedness.

It's pure camelshit, and as women, we must not accept it.

This is why I tell women that we need to go back to our own religions--to the religions that our mothers had in the river.

I am You
before
you was You.

Just think of it. Women would congregate at some body of water together--a river, the ocean, a lake or a stream--topless as God intended (because our breasts are religious ornaments representing the circle of life), and we would give prayers of thanks for the Red Dragon that flows inside our fleshly universes, creating and sustaining the human race and the art of God. We would thank God for the children we bear, for the milk we produce, for the continuation and nurturing we represent. And in this way, men would automatically learn to respect, cherish and value the sanctity of both a woman's body and her worth. This would be a great improvement over the man-made religions that we're trapped in now, because women would be given their rightful place as divine equals of men. No longer could the Holy Bible instruct that a woman's menstral cycle makes her dirty (to be shut away), and never again could the Koran boast that woman is *impure*.

Our sons would no longer consider females to be (by nature) inferior--which is what Christian, Islamic and Jewish mothers accidentally teach their children by embracing and promoting the blatant sexism in men's religions--and please understand that "sexism" and "white supremacy" and "beauty evil" cannot exist in a society unless the vast majority of citizens are sexist and white supremacist and believe that beauty is more valuable than the soul. In America, most females are sexist by their belief in sexist ideologies, and pass these beliefs into their sons (*"You're going to be a heartbreaker when you grow up"..."boys will be boys"..."you're so lucky Kola--boys are so much easier to raise than girls"*)and most Blacks in America are <u>white supremacist</u> by their unshakeable belief that the white man's ice is colder--that the white man's truth is truer--and that anything white or *colored* by whiteness is superior to anything pure black--and in the realm of American "beauty evil", the entire society teaches us to be more impressed, seduced and protective of physical beauty...than we are of a person's soul--so that beauty (despite the fact that the human body begins to rot from the day it is born and is only beautiful for a short span of time) becomes a tool of *evil* as human beings place its value above the value of the soul, and as an example (and with John Singleton's horribly colorstruck film *"Rosewood"* in mind)--I can guarantee you that two strange elderly women looking like Toni Morrison and Rosa Parks would be welcomed into the homes of black Americans while two strange women looking like their brave ancestors Harriet Tubman and Sojourner Truth would not be welcome--and on site would be considered *"ugly"*, "trifling" and *"undesirable"*. The social construct of "beauty evil" erasing the worth and the souls of Harriet Tubman and Sojourner Truth.

And before anyone dare deny it--just notice the slim-faced Ethiopian women who are quick to receive greetings from Black Americans passing them on the streets of America, while in stark contrast, the negroid-faced immigrant West African women (the flesh and blood *motherseed* of the Black Americans) is avoided and looked past on the street--even to the point of lying on her (*"Africans have bad attitudes"..."think they're better than we are"*)...but then people who really do think they're better than Black Americans, such as Whites and Asians (Paul Beatty's people)--get nothing but warm greetings and acknowledgements from the Black American. The white woman, who for four hundred years sold (or watched be sold) infant black boys fresh out of their slave mother's wombs, so that she, the White woman could redecorate her parlor or go North to shop for velvet is *totally forgiven* (and forgotten) by Black Americans--but the West African woman, the one who was often burned alive *by black Kings* for voicing her opposition to the slave trade and who sang hymns to the ocean for four hundred years at the horror of her children being snatched away from her--is now *too ugly*, too Whoopi Goldberg-Alfre Woodard-Esther Rolle-India Arie (looking) to be greeted on the street by Black Americans as their mother. They'd rather pretend that Lena Horne and that bitch in New York Harbor is their real mother . And it's because--we all, as Americans--are collectively sexist, white supremacist and beacons of beauty evil (police will only search for *"beautiful"* bodies). These structures persist, because this is what we believe in.

So by instituting women's religions...our African and Arabic sons could no longer justify the mutilation of female genital organs; the Muslims would stop dishonoring women's humanity by covering woman's flesh (which is cleaner than men's flesh), and most radically, the power of women's sexuality would be unleashed and become recognized as owned by her, just as man's sexuality is respected, *expected* and owned by him--a woman could legislate her own sex and not be judged and condemned for it. If she wants to love one man and be a housewife and mother like Kola Boof--that's fine. And if, before or after marriage, she wants to sail the seven seas and fuck 100 men (occasionally doing two or three at the same time) like Kola Boof--then that's fine, too. The word "whore" could be changed to "*manlover*" or "Cassanovia" and mothers could proudly sit around the camp fire and tell their sons about their adventures--explaining which men they really loved and which ones they only bedded for survival--and that way, the sons could come to see their mothers the way they see their fathers, as humans who simply have a different genitalia than their fathers.

Many black women in America who cannot find mates (because America doesn't recognize the Black man's mother as a prized mate-- the babies come out "*black*", you see) and are not being offered "love" or "companionship" by men--are already living this way now.

And I say that there's nothing wrong with this, and that while certain black men who detest these women (for being too black, too ethnic) and enjoy looking down on these women--I say that these women should not be ashamed, should not listen to the words of a heartless vulture who hates the image of his own mother and has become spineless enough to suck his own dick, and should not deny their own pleasure....*although*, like anything else it's not what you do- -it's _how_ you do it, and the best way for a woman to retain control is to keep secrets, be <u>scientifically responsible</u> and be discreet.

So you see, I don't go to men's churches and I don't talk about God with people who hate and despise me. I hold church in the river with my sons, and I have never once went to the river and felt unwelcomed. And I don't need men to tell me shit about God--including Aquaman. He goes to his church, I go to mine.

I feel myself...mellowing out.
Mellowing, but not going quietly. I can't go quietly:

I am a woman, Yes
I have two mouths to speak with
my tongue is her tongue
her kiss is my evening/Night breeze woman

I am You
before
you was You

It pisses me off when I hear people claim that the societies of Africa are or were "matriarchal" (woman dominated) as opposed to patriarchal. What a joke. And the sad thing is that *western feminists* are the main ones espousing this lie--carelessly placing the word "matriarchal" in front of the word "matrilineal". African women don't run anything in Africa--if they did, then they'd do away with vaginal circumcision and polygamy and the whole endless onion of male supremacy and sexist double standards that cripple Africa.

Certainly, there have been extraordinarily powerful African women--individuals who rose up and left their mark on the landscape--but as a rule, Africa is ruled and ran by African _men_ and it always has been. The laws, the customs, the beliefs (even when those beliefs were Goddess religion based)--it was always and remains still a continent of patriarchal dominance and Queen Mothers who *affirm* the sexism of their sons. A black woman with a big enough mouth can be declared a "Witch" and bannished from her village at any given moment by any human with a penis and testicles. There is no matriarchy in Africa, that's western bullshit that stems from their portrayals of black women as "domineering" and "amazonian".

But the glaringly sad fact is that most African women are submissive and are not fully developed as human beings. Like the Black American woman, they are called "Strong Black Women", because they are the "back Bone" (what a pitiful compliment) of the villages, towns and cities--but they are not strong women at all. They are "<u>endurance</u> mules". Legendary for their long-suffering invisibility...carrying the weight of the world on top of their heads, carrying big ass children on their backs, making excuses for all manner of abuse that is committed against them, and then because they have proven for centuries that they...*don't want anything special for themselves* (other than to sacrifice and fight for the black man's redemption)...they get to be called *"strong"*. But black women, I've noticed both in Africa and in America, really aren't strong women. They're weak and you often see them left behind, bitter, withered down, fattened up and dried like relics against the poorest walls in town. All because they accept the station in life that others assign them, and a huge number of them believe they're *too ugly* to do anything with their lives (beauty evil can mute the soul), many of them waste their whole lives hiding behind the church or the extra fat they pack on their bodies as shields, and as a group, we have no man to protect us or fight for us (the black man only fights for himself or his master's woman, no one else, not even black children)...and because so many black women are cowards or have lost their voices due to their own sons not supporting them, the only person they're willing to challenge or fight is another black woman. And they do that all the time.

So there is your matriarchy. It doesn't exist.

Black women are the lowest on the food chain, because in general, no one has loved them, which is the way humans get permission to love themselves. And additionally, the whole world lies on them, scapegoats them and generally ignores their pain, because after all--

they're endurance mules. The one group of women on earth that can grow...unwatered. The one group of women who are repeatedly expected to *"be strong"* and take it like a man. And we're not talking about ultra-light looking biracials and mixed race women here.

We're talking about <u>Black Women</u>.

I believe that the time is now.

That in the 21st Century we will see, for the first time in over 500 years, the re-emergence of *the goddess flower*--the <u>authentic</u> black woman. The mother of Africa and bloodberry of the human race. Her perilous deep dark skin and hair like wool (*the proof*) redeeming and reawakening the truly ancestral part of us; the soul of us.

The black man's mother. Goodest of all good women.

And this is why I specifically asked that the African Blue Morpho butterfly be placed on the cover of this book. To represent her...and to begin dreaming her into being. Our real mother.

wing of the reasons...sweep up your children/Sweep up

Like sullen prayers you fly to me
I am a woman, Yes
I have two mouths to speak with
       There are men in my garden: my breasts are full
of mik and honey.
Grow inside me/Growing son
Wing of the reasons,
       I am YOU
       before
       you was YOU
Pretty blue Morpho/breezing inside
I am kissing your return, ma-Mah...Sweep up/sweep up

Come and see the wind move dirt
--behold the sistering, mothering weeping of God
I am like a prayer becoming chant.
I am like a chant becoming song.
I am a woman, Yes.

I have two mouths to speak with.
I am the river of blood...washing all stones.
I am LOVE
       loving Africa, loving Peace, loving the womb

I am the blue Morpho
       I am YOU before you was YOU
I am that mother dreaming you into being.
For surely I have not perished. For surely I am still alive.
For surely

I am the wing...of the reasons

"Blue Morpho (The Goddess Flower)" a poem by Kola Boof
© 2006

_____

The African Blue Morpho butterfly graces the cover of this book.

See What the Boys In the Back Room'll Have

"When you bring the people kola...you bring the people life."

--popular African saying

● *Late June, 2005*

After a month of carefully planning my book reading at Zahra's Books in Los Angeles, and after being interviewed on KJLH radio the night before to promote the public appearance--the local Police step in just two hours before the event and shut us down because of people in Anaheim claiming to be Palestinians and saying that they're coming to the event to kill me. Because of my nightmares, my face drops like a jowl and I feel the most debilitating weariness.

Deeply sighing, I apologize to the very kind black man who owns the popular black bookstore (Jim Rogers) and thank him for the invitation, promising that I'll come in and do a reading when people aren't so angry about the books I write and the things I have to say-- which Jim jokes may be never.

~~

Late that night, I have a small vodka (straight) and listen to Lizz

Wright's *"Salt"* cd as I attempt to get back into the world of my upcoming novel *"The Sexy Part of the Bible"*--which is not only a sensuous, neo-political look at cloning and skin bleaching in West Africa, but also the most difficult novel I've ever written, because along with the usual horniness I go through with a novel, I've also been beseiged with terrible bouts of weeping (just uncontrollable crying) and nose bleeds writing the book, and although I always become physically affected when I'm writing a whole novel or a short story (as opposed to a poem)--the physical changes usually don't happen until the middle of writing, but with *"Sexy Part of the Bible"*, I've been euphoric, haunted, depressed and drained like no book before it, and thus for me, as a writer, my main prayer when I fashion a novel (and that's really what I do--I *fashion* it) is for God to help me hurry up and be done with it. I hate writing (because, for me, it's so physical and mentally intense at the same time), but I can't live with the stories inside me, I have to get them out or I'd be back in the psychiatrist lobby, and so my advice to any student or novice contemplating the composure of literary work is simply this--*"You should always be getting to the good part."* That's my main rule.

You should always be getting to the good part.

And although you've heard me talk about writers whose works or politics inspired me the most (Morrison, Alice Walker, Sherwood Anderson, Sylvia Plath, Mari Evans, Gayl Jones, Richard Wright)--while my appreciation for <u>truth</u> usually comes from them, my actual writing style is *"fashioned"* and comes from filmmakers. And in particular, four filmmakers. First, I get my penchant for shading and infusing poetic devices from my very favorite silent filmmaker, Abel Gance, who made the breathtakingly intimate film *"J'Accuse"* (1919)...and for fellow silent movie buffs who are wondering what my favorite silent film of all time is, I would say *"The Ten Commandments"* (1923) by Cecil B. Demille--not for anything artistic, just because it so moves and entertains me...__and second,__ I get the templates for all my novels from the Austrian film genius, Josef Von Sternberg, who made Marlene Dietrich a superstar in such films as *"The Blue Angel"* and *"Morocco"* (both 1930), and who greatly influenced me by saying, basically...[no matter how realistic you tell the story, the canvas should be like a painted dream--the truth can never be served if the artist doesn't have a flair for presenting the truth with drama and beauty.]

And I cry now, because I so agree with Josef Von Sternberg.

When I was a teenager who couldn't speak English, but could escape through silent films, I always wanted to be Clara Bow, Greta Garbo, Lillian Gish, Louise Brooks, Joan Crawford or Marlene Dietrich (in fact, I loved it when *The New York Times* said I was "mysterious" and called me *"the African Garbo"*--I smiled for a week, because I'm actually quite boring, mannequin-like and silent in my home). And despite their glorious whiteness (Garbo, Crawford, Brooks), I recognized their larger than life *"types"* as being imitations of the magnificently sensuous dark black women who were queens, mothers, wives, priestesses, whores and sisters along the Nile river in Africa. I totally and completely related to Von Sternberg's films, because I recognized all his glass shots, erotic pathos and rituals as African. It's like reading the Holy Bible, it's all stolen and whitened, but you still recognize it. And through Von Sternberg, I saw the magic in dressing up a location so that it says something contradictory and the importance of photographing *"beauty"* to the point that it becomes "trapped" and defiled by the expectation of perfection, and I recognized the animalism, the gutteral instincts in men and women that makes them so instantly tragic. I learned to appreciate *camp* from Von Sternberg's movies. And so when my fans read *"Flesh and the Devil"* or *"Pure Nigger Evil"* or *"Sexy Part of the Bible"*, the canvas is a *painted* dream; whimsical and sensuous--but then also painfully realistic and always with a point of view. And this all comes from Von Sternberg.

The third filmmaker who influenced the way I fashion my books is of course the greatest black filmmaker of this century and the last--Senegal's Ousmane Sembene. And let me just say that as a child, they wanted me to love Mohammed, as a teen they wanted me to love Jesus Christ--but those men were greatly neglected because of my love for Ousmane Sembene. He, along with Malcolm X, Marcus Garvey and Alice Walker, is the hero of my life...because it was by watching his films that I came to truly love, appreciate, value and *believe in* the sacredness of what both my Mahdi Pappuh and Black American father had been raising me to see all along--the black perfection in black people--the importance of *that* flower, by itself.

I get my eye from Von Sternberg and my soul from Sembene.

And although I am quickly falling in love with the new Haitian filmmaker Raoul Peck (*"Lumumba"*, *"Sometime in April"*)...I cannot think of another artist, other than Toni Morrison, who so consistently presents the authentic faces, voices and the utter <u>wholeness</u> of black people with as much honesty, respect, love and all-powerfulness as Sembene does. Nowhere in his films are white supremacist ideologies allowed to seep through (unlike Spike Lee and John Singleton's works), and nowhere in his work does he fail to present the fact that the authentic black man and the authentic black woman are each other's and Africa's and black children's only salvation--and that you cannot truly value the black man without honoring the black womb from which it takes for him to exist (which is also unlike the works of Spike Lee and John Singleton). And so, because his masterpieces like "Guelwaar", "Moolade", "Xala" and "Ceddo" quite literally gave me a purpose, an identity and a soul--that is what I would like my work to do, as we are now in an age where we must not only combat the messages of the powerfully Eurocentric white media, but must also do battle against the mulatto-identified Nigger Media, the majority of which is created by self-hating dark skinned black men, both African and western, and not by mulattoes. As one African scholar calls it--"*The King Kong Follies*"--where a dark man and a yellow mixed woman are consistently shown rehearsing to be white people (invisible...which is what assimilation is about)--or shown trying to convince the audience that the yellow woman is the mother of his people and their people and their people before them ("Hotel Rwanda"); the black woman "disallowed" (it's the American *illusion* of inclusion that niggerstock so love)--because, of course, the womb of the black woman is what makes us authentic and makes us black in the first place--and so, as the dark skinned black man becomes "*King Kong*", he must disallow his natural mate's dark image and use the yellow mixed woman as a bridge out of his own reflection, out of Africa, so that he can eventually achieve mulatto status, which is just a jump off point for his ultimate goal--whiteness--which is attained by dumping off the yellow mixed woman and replacing her with an authentic white woman.

And that, of course, is the constant imagery we receive from Nigger Media (a good example being BET).

Notice how White People love to make films about Africa's very weakest rulers (Othello, Cleopatra, the Moors, who are now an extinct laughingstock)...but will never make films depicting the truly great black Kings and Queens who ruled by the hundreds, who fought against the transatlantic slave trade, and who...if depicted in films...would create screen couples who look more like "Taye Diggs and Lauryn Hill", "Danny Glover and Whoopi Goldberg", "Luol Deng and Alek Wek", and if we really want to talk ancestral black love--"Don Cheadle and Me'Shell N'degeOcello". But imagine how Americans, both black and white, must cringe at the very thought of sitting through love scenes between authentically African-featured black couples and depictions of heroism where blackness is shown as perfectly human by itself.

And notice how the racist Arab Egyptian scholars (who are not real Egyptians) rose up to protest when USA TODAY presented a scientific restoration of what Queen Nefertiti (using her own mummy) had actually looked like in real life--and it turned out that she looked like a dark brown black woman with Nilotic features (very much like my own)--and immediately, the world's white Egyptologists and the American journalists began screaming *"that can't be her--she looks like a man!"*, *"she wasn't black, she was biracial!"* (which is a lie, but even if Nefertiti were biracial in Egypt--so was Kola Boof biracial in Egypt, and I don't look any more mixed than the Black Arabs and Kushafs of Upper Egypt, all of whom are dark black and are also biracial--such as Anwar Sadat who was darker than Barack Obama). North African biracials do not look like U.S. biracials--our fathers are white but most of us look fully black.

Still, white historians who saw the photo in USA TODAY whined: *"That's one of her maids--that's not her!"*

And duly, a Black American man in Hollywood is now casting biracial all-American looking Halle Berry as Nefertiti, a role that would be more "realistic" with someone like Iman or Nona Gaye or Jamaica's queenly immaculate Nadine Willis playing the part. And another company is planning a film about Egypt's greatest female ruler, "Queen Hatshepsut"--a full figured bisexual woman who ruled as a man, built the world's greatest library and was a *"negroid type from Punt"* who looked more like Tichina Arnold, Oprah Winfrey, Missy Elliott, Angelique Kidjoe and Alfre Woodard than like any of the skinny _white_ actresses they are looking at to play her.

And so, it's Nigger Media that we African artists must diligently work against to create images that respect and honor blackness as wholeness--not an annex of white superiority--and because the filmmaker Julie Dash so brilliantly did that with her landmark film *"Daughters of the Dust"*, she was the fourth filmmaker to inspire and "set" what I do as an artist, and as I've often told friends and other artists--it's because I can't get financing to make the films I'd like to make that I write novels. But still, as I construct a book, I am seeing it scene by scene like a movie and I fashion a cinematic quality that gives a sense of right-nowness to my works, and then when the book ends, you are haunted (as my readers attest) by the images.

And because men are visual creatures and not so impressed by words as females are--this is how the white man rules the world (by the images he creates of each individual "*type*"), and it has been through these images that whites, mulattoes and self-hating blacks have been given reign to distort blackness, that blackness has been devalued and relegated to something that must be--evolved from. Which is how they try to cast Africa. As some cradle of humanity that is obsolete and without perfection in and of itself. And precisely because I do not take on the mantle of "*Mother Africa*" (supreme Mammy and earth mother of all mankind, having little time for her own children)...because I do not fit the archetypes that America has created for me to inhabit (who saw that French documentary that Walter Mosley narrated?)--and because I am still alive, and my black breasts are still bare and because I am saying loud and clear that *I am the future*--I am considered a threat and am not an image that either the White establishment or the Nigger HipHop Media cum Intellectual Colored Academics can embrace.

Many have dubbed me a "Uni-culturalist", an "Afrocentric", a "Queen", while frightened whites call me a "racist" and a "separatist", but the truth is--I'm an African mother. That is what I am period. I'm an African mother and my religion is The Womb.

And, unfortunately, this is the thing that made and makes the White women editors at the major publishing houses praise my skill and talent in one breath, but then do everything they can to silence my voice in the next, their white smiles radiant as they insist that I am (a) *Mother Africa* and (b) *that I have an obligation to transcend race.*

And as Toni Morrison so rightfully said, no one else in this world is asked to transcend race but the ones who are feared and not valued--the ones with black skin and nappy hair. Even the high yellow mulattoes and the biracials expect authentically black people to transcend race by remaining subordinate to the color rules--white on top, off-white on the balcony of white, yellow in the middle, brown on the lower bottom and literal black on the very bottom. And they call this "inclusion" and they call it "the human race" and they call it "one love".

All that bullshit.

And so here is the thing that I cannot get Americans to understand.

I have no obligation to any children but my own and the only children I claim are the black babies (visibly brown to yellow tanned), and just like any other race of women, I live and die to provide, to love and to nurture *my* children. I don't have time for yours, nor am I interested. My books have no obligation to white women, white children, mulattoes, Latinos, Asians, Arabs, American Indians. I love all those people, because they are human beings--but Mother Africa is not *their* mother, and the real truth is that they all hate Mother Africa.

Yes, they do!

<u>They hate Mother Africa.</u> Just like this two-faced white heretic Michael Jackson hates Mother Africa and would stand by and see all black people erased in the name of "one race", the *illusion* of inclusion and the lie that whiteness improves blackness rather than ruins it, they

hate my black womb (because it produces black men)--ask Walter Mosley about my black womb and what it produces. Coming from the father he did and the film he narrated, I'm sure he could go on all day about what a *black* womb produces and RE-produces--and they hate my black pussy, because a single egg from it can darken their pale Asian and Latino complexions; and they hate my nappy hair, because it's the mark of God, and they hate Africa and all the people in it, and as some black genius wrote in a book: *"They had to pity a thing before they could like it"*. And they try to pretend that *"pity"* is love.

They accept you--as long as you're willing to erase yourself.

And that's why <u>Mother Africa</u> hates their evil rotten two-faced "people of color" asses right back.

I wish they'd get a fucking clue.

You see these battalions of <u>good</u> White people coming to Sudan to *"rescue the lost boys of Sudan"*--but I ask any human with a brain--how do you claim to truly save a man without saving the womb from which he came?

Without that womb, there will be no more of him.

So what this *really is*...is a new form of colonization. You're taking these boys away to be "mentored" into <u>niggerdom</u> and to be trained to quote from your Bible--things a slave would say for 200.

Haha!

My work is no more racial than the works of my white idol, Sylvia Plath--no more shocking than her poem "Daddy", no more angry than her poem "Wintering", no more fabulist than her collected works all stacked on a table in Cambridge.

Just imagine me as Betty Crocker and there you have it.

There will be no assimilation of Kola Boof. You either love me as my complete self or fuck you. I don't assimilate.

Truly, God has made the human race a many splendored thing, and I love all human beings, I truly do, but I don't want to be white. I don't want my children white, mixed or in any way...lessened.

We are Africans, we are black and *the proof* is the crown that God gave us and only us. The cake is baked.

In the various African societies that I come from, there was always a principle used in storytelling, in fact it was a principle that tribal people employed in just about anything they did--be it choosing a mate, writing a book, building a boat, naming a child--and that principle was this..."*what will be the fruit of this 100 years from now*?" How much truer will it be after generations of men have passed it from one tongue to the next? And what do I want them to understand from it and how do I want this novel, this poem, this newborn child, this marriage to impact my people 100 years from now? What will the fruit of this be 100 years from now?

So in everything I do, I am much more concerned with influencing and shaping the future than I am with those who are living right now today. I happen to know that you can chant anything you want into being--and I am an African mother.

I don't give a fuck about nurturing the human race.

I *want* my black babies. And I want them forever.

THE AUTHENTIC BLACK MAN

"The blacker the berry...the deeper the roots."

--Tupac Shakur

*NOTE: For years, the publication of this book was held up by several things. One being Kola Boof's refusal to publish her memoirs without the inclusion of the following letter to her sons, as Russom Damba and later Cornel Chesney and Robert Wright felt that this letter might destroy the author's career in America and be misunderstood by American readers of all races, including blacks. Ms. Boof sought legal representation in having this "letter/essay" published and the content of this chapter in no way represents the views, beliefs or the sentiments of anyone at DOOR OF KUSH Publishing, however we respect Ms. Boof's right to tell her life story in the manner that is culturally and personally most important to her. <u>It has been edited</u>.

<u>My</u> dear great sons...you will be black men by the time you read this. The first generation of your father Aquaman's and my seed in this country. You will be *Americans*.

Of course, until you reach 18 (and neither of you is yet 10 at the writing of this book)...you are entering the years where your father is the one who raises and guides you the most now, because you are males, and as your mother at this stage of development, it's my duty to provide only two things other than love and mothering--(1) acculturation and point of legacy regarding your heritage (the bloodberry)--and (2) instruct you how to make generations ("*if my father dies, I will give birth to him again*"). What you will believe, what you will stand for and how you will behave as men in the world of men--is the realm of your father's teachings, not mine. For although I have built an oven on our grounds and have taught you how to cook, to build boats, ride horses and shoot guns--it's your father who gives me permission to do that and it's your father who teaches you how to be men, and once you are grown, you will testify that I never stood in the way of that and that I was greatly pleased by Aquaman's depth and skill in shaping you.

Your father is a great, *great* man...and I never expected to have a good man like your father--I expected nothing from men--but your father filled my womb with good men. The both of you are not only the best sons a mother could wish for, but you're the only dream your father ever had. Truly, there has been no disagreement whatsoever between Aquaman and I in how you were raised--but because he is the dominant force in your lives, there are many important things that I could not discuss with you...until now.

I do consider this letter to be the most important thing that I've ever written for you--it's a very long, long emotional letter, but in order for you to do your mother's bidding (as I know you will), you must read it all and get a thorough understanding of the matter at hand.

The beginning of what I have to say is the word "<u>nigger</u>"--and the fact that your father and I had one great fear in giving birth to black children in the United States, and that was the fear that our children might become "niggers". There is a gifted Scholar named Cornel West who believes it's imperative that black people must stop using this word (or "Pogo nigger" as it's used across Africa) and must erase it from the society--but because I see so much more strategically than him on this issue, I adamantly disagree.

And at the *heart* of my disagreement is the fact that I have never once heard the Black Americans accurately use the word "nigger" or convey that they fully understood what a nigger is.

Black Americans think of the word nigger as a racial slight--and in their minds it conjures up an ignorant black person, dark and poor. They immediately think of "ghetto behavior" and dark skinned single mothers on welfare and swarthy field hands and people eating pig's feet and greens. *But none of that*...is what a nigger is.

And my problem with erasing this word is that we have not yet *defined* the true meaning of it for our children (which is crucial). And as an African--when *I* hear the word nigger--I think of actual people like the singer Michael Jackson and the skin bleaching teenagers in Kenya and Nigeria; I think of much respected and beloved black men like Desmond Tutu, Montel Williams, Harry Belafonte, Ward Connerly, Kofi Annan--and all these people (*to me*) are niggers.

That's what *I* believe. That niggers are more than a word.

North Sudan and South Africa are *crawling* with niggers.

And we who are *black* need to identify what a nigger is and get rid of the niggers before we get rid of the word. You can't do it backwards, which is what happened with integration in the United States. The blacks were integrated with white people without any deconstruction whatsoever of their "plantation beliefs". In other words, they were expected to behave as *equals*--but after centuries of abuse and the assassination of their souls and their identities, they carried with them an abiding faith in the superiority of whiteness--no matter what they say. And I truly sense in this country that those blacks (worldwide) who *hate* the word "nigger"--hate it because they fear the truth in it. Because blacks are lazy and cowardly, they think outlawing the word will be enough. But it won't.

We Africans allowed ourselves...*allowed ourselves*...to be invaded, to be colonized and to be enslaved. 1,000 years in East Africa and 500 years in West Africa. And to this day--we are looking for some false "human race ideal", the illusion of inclusion, the lie that black people share some solidarity with Latinos, Asians, Indians and the White man's mother--denying our natural mates, our natural mother, our natural hair, our natural noses. Trying to make family out of everyone but each other, because we don't like ourselves, and worst of all--we don't like the sight of ourselves gathered together as just us. We feel it's a betrayal against the people who owned us.

Listen to your mother when I tell you two bitter truths: #1-White people hate blacks because they fear and *envy* color...and #2-People of Color hate blacks, because they're desperate to get away from the origin of their *color*. Everybody hates black--because God is *black*.

And the black scholar is right when he whines that race is a social construct. So is beauty. But <u>color</u> is not a social construct.

And nothing in this world matters more than color and "*the proof*" that grows from the scalps of God's children. The black man is conquered by having him continually kill the image of his own mother, thereby diluting his manhood an preventing his rebirth.

The Whitest womb is placed on top, even by the niggerstock-- and the Blackest womb is *buried* six feet under. Or to invert the opening sentence from Toni Morrison's novel "Paradise"--"*They shoot the* <u>*blackest*</u> *girl first*". All other wombs fall somewhere inbetween.

~~

I want you to understand my sons that no human being is *born* a nigger...they're <u>orientated</u> by being in an atmosphere with other niggers who *pass it down*--that being a nigger is normal. You remember the scene in "ROOTS" where Fiddler (a black man) beat Kunte Kente (a black boy) with a whip until he accepted his slave name Tobey?

You remember the Nigerian cab driver I told you about in Lagos? The one who was so desperate for everyone to know that his son was a biracial child that he blew up huge photos and rigged them to the outer roof of his cab so that while driving in the streets it appears as a billboard on the cab (both sides) announcing to his fellow deep black and chocolate fudge colored Nigerians that his child is no ordinary African--its mother is a fat white woman with a club foot that he met while she was prostituting outside the flat he was partying at in England and married (which is not me being cruel, *it's the truth*!).

Or...you remember my childhood Black American friend that I told you about--Brenda. She was fourteen like me, but much sweeter and less troubled than I was, and also a lot darker than I was, but not as intuitive or sensitive as I was. Brenda would come over and we'd watch an educational children's show we both loved--*The Big Blue Marble*-- and during one particular episode, we were literally swept away by the colorful images of people from foreign lands. They showed us the wintery wonderlands of Stockholm, Sweden (which I still find breathtaking), they showed bustling mobs of slanty-eyed humans crowding the streets and markets of Hong Kong, they showed us the running of the bull in Spain--purposeful bearded Rabbis praying in Jerusalem. They even showed brown mountain people in Russia.

Brenda and I had swooned with delight, vowing that we would grow up and visit these beautiful paradises.

But then they showed a major city in...the Congo. Swarming with chocolate fudge black Congolese. Before I could even finish forming my proudest grin, Brenda gasped and said to me, as if stumbling upon dead bodies, "Oh my God--why are they *sooo black*!? Now you know that's foul--all them black folks in one spot. Jess as ashy 'n nappyheaded, too! Girl, you couldn't pay me to go there!"

She had not even noticed the glaring, shared total whiteness of all the white people in Sweden. To her eyes--whites were just *people*.

It never occured to her that they shouldn't exist. Ditto for the Chinese, Spanish and Jews. But to this dark skinned black American girl, the endless ocean of Congolese humans was an (abnormality)--something to be feared and diluted. I saw _hate_ in her eyes. All my life, I've wondered what someone like Walter Mosley or John Edgar Wideman would have thought and felt about Brenda's reaction.

But my sons...before we can get to the bullet of what I'm telling you, you must understand that niggerism is not just people. It's a denomination of the religion of White Supremacy, which is what your white Egyptian grandfather taught me as a little girl...that the world's only true religion is white supremacy and that all others are just decoys. Millions of innocent black people around the world would deny it in a minute (many wish to kill me)--but they're still niggers.

A nigger is a non-owner of self. It doesn't matter how rich he is, in fact there are more rich and middle class niggers than ghetto ones.

A nigger lives _for_ his master and _through_ his master.

While he's busy painting his master's house--his own house is steadily falling into ruin. I think of Kofi Annan and the rap moguls who churn out music videos promoting and advertising the superiority of the womb of the white man's mother as I write that statement. But it goes literally for all of us. In some form or another, we neglect our own African _"pursuit of paradise"_--to build the white people's.

While the whole world of little black girls are rubbing bleaching cream into their skin and desperately framing their complexions with blond hair so they can look like what a nigger _likes_--the nigger himself can be found at the crosswalk telling the plainest white woman how "beautiful" she is and routinely upping the esteem of white women and girls while blaming the _lack of esteem_ in young black girls on the bad attitudes they've developed living in a world of absent father figures and black males who mostly want to exploit, put them down and abandon them--depending on how black they are.

By any means necessary, the White man creates a world of opportunity for white children and places the white womb of his natural mate as far into the heavens as he possibly can--but on the other end of the spectrum, the _nigger_ hates to set eyes on a black child--and presents to the world, when he can, a mixed child who more resembles his white master--and this child he holds up like a trophy, the pale legs of it loudly dangling against his dark black arms. A status symbol.

Please take a look at the beautiful little black slave babies that grace the back inside flap of this book (they're dressed in blue) and try to recall when was the last time that a black man outside of Africa proudly held up babies that black.

In America...you will notice that the black children get lighter and lighter with each new generation--while white babies remain white and they have a term for it. Ask John Edgar Wideman and Cornel West. It's called "_progress_ in race relations."

In order to eliminate "racism"--everybody is supposed to fuck everybody else (except the best whites, of course, which is practically all of them) until there's one big mulatto buffer race and no blacks. Getting rid of the black people, you see, is _the cure_ for racism. But look at Tiger Woods and Vin Diesel and Lenny Kravitz and Alicia Keys and Derek Jeter and notice how the white man..._gets whiter and whiter_.

White People

White people skim and rifle through my ideologies (and often my work), and because of that--they jump to the conclusion that I'm some type of militant extremist and they assume that I'm a "mad" black woman--a racist who hates them. None of which is true.

I love white people. I have enormous respect and admiration for their race, I don't think they're the only devils and a lot of my best times have been had with friends and lovers who happened to be white.

My publicist, Kate Wilson, is white...the woman who designs all my book covers, Marilyn Morse, is also white, and is a good friend. In my younger days, before I was rescued by your father, I had several white boyfriends, and although I'm not proud that the main two were married men, I do have mostly good memories of these white men. They were great buddies, wonderful lovers, they taught me a lot that helped me get ahead and they made me believe that I was beautiful. To this day--if I didn't have you boys and no black man wanted me or treated me good--I would be with a white man in a heartbeat.

But of course, Americans have very short attention spans (they speed read and they speed listen), so the biggest misconception about Kola Boof, publicly, is that I'm vehemently against interracial love and race mixing, which isn't true at all.

I believe that interracial love is a natural love that has always existed in the world, and I also know that in ancient times, on a level playing field where people came from equal ethnic status and parity of self-worth--it occured very infrequently and was considered a very unique relationship, because of the fact that so few people were willing to give up their own people, cultures and looks to merge with someone elses. But that's not what we have in America. What we have worldwide is an *epidemic of self-hate* (not love) among black people who, nowhere on earth, are from an equal ethnic status or parity of self-worth. And because I diligently point this out, it appears to those who know little about me that I'm *"opposed to interracial love"*. It's much more complicated than that--especially when massive numbers of Black American stock are being bred out and blacks in Africa are skin bleaching, wearing blond wigs and putting "light skinned" students at the front of the class, because they're learning from western culture that lighter people are *naturally* more intelligent than blacks. It becomes obvious that black people's interest in whites has nothing at all to do with <u>LOVE</u>--and everything to do with the desire for <u>erasure</u>.

Erasure makes them less colored and more acceptable and easier to assimilate, and because I love _my_ people (meaning most black people and half the mulattoes), I feel compelled to throw a cog in the nigger machine--to cause a malfunction, to save my own self by saving _my babies_. For as my idol, the great Arab Egyptian woman writer Nawal El Sadaawi so bravely said: _"The only thing diversity does is divides us from our own people."_ I'm sure that Nawal loved working in diverse atmospheres and didn't mean this statement to be taken as an "absolute"--but the cutting truth in it cannot be denied by any group of people in America. Diversity, in many ways weakens us, depresses us and only benefits the dominant culture (the whites).

The Light Skinned Yellow People

Black Americans, no matter what their station or class, have all been descended from (a) a majority slave kindred raised on plantations or (b) minority free blacks who internalized white supremacist belief systems and stood in solidarity with whites in supporting the institution of slavery and the belief that _authentic_ black people (the true bloodberry of Africa--which certainly _is_ the Dark Continent) are inately inferior to all European and non-blacks.

Just as in East Africa beginning in the year 700...so, too, in the Atlantic slave trade and middle passage--the black woman was raped en masse--but by Europeans. And, of course, being raped was nothing new to African slave women. We all know that when one tribe of Black men conquers another tribe of Black men--the first thing they do is rape the women of their enemy as a psychological tool to wipe out his future morale. _All men rape_ their enemy's woman, and since all men come from sexist societies where a woman and her vagina are considered "male property"--the raped woman is thereafter considered damaged goods (and through sexism, was never "human" to begin with, but was her husband's property).

During U.S. slavery, it literally excavated the pride of these proud African slave men to see their women raped and giving birth, left and right, to the pale mulatto children of their bloodthirsty white masters. Because these black men were powerless to protect their own women--they came to hate their women and to blame their women. And in turn, the abuse on one side from the white man and his spoiled yet oppressed selfish white woman and then the jealous hate on the other side from black men--*obliterated* the African slave woman's inner self. Most of the millions of those women that were brought here were "infibulated", so it's a lie that they were wanton sex creatures, craving sex. If anything, they feared and loathed sex and especially fainted (just as the stories go) in the clutches of Europeans, who to their African eyes, weren't even human beings. And already, back in Africa, these women had been submissive stock, not nearly as feisty as historians and black feminists like to pretend. So they were *obliterated* and transformed into a new "survivalist" stock of black women.

And in order to escape rape--a great many of them began to deliberately pack on as much extra body fat as they could carry. You've seen the photos of the head-ragged African plantation women nursing white babies--big fat "Mammys" the Americans call them. But these women deliberately did that (made themselves ugly) so as to escape their master's penis. But after 400 years of fattening their bodies as a defense mechanism during slavery--it became genetic--and when slavery ended...no one helped these women to heal or even acknowledged what they had been through. It was all about *"the black man"* and what he'd been through, and a giant part of their undoing, was the black man raising the mulatto woman above his natural African wife and dubbing her *"the black woman"*. And the authentic black woman, in the midst of her terrible self-hatred and self-blame...*told* her black sons to do this. To marry as light as possible. She saw her own black skin as the thing that had caused them to be hated and enslaved in the first place--*it must be cursed*! So she didn't want her children to bear her black negroid curse. She taught them to seek an easier life by coveting and seeking...the master's blood.

To the white man's credit--he came up with the most brilliant strategy in the history of White Supremacy. He decreed that *one drop* of African blood makes you black--which in turn forever sealed his "control" of Black Power by giving these abused, beat down black people <u>permission</u> to do away with their crown (*the Proof*) and their skin color--yet still *call themselves* "black", thus providing the illusion that even without their physical Temple...they still had their souls and were still standing on their own two feet.

Please sons...<u>go back</u> and read that last paragraph over again.

He was saying that the African race was such a disease that anything touched by it was contaminated, and in this way, <u>Whiteness</u> became the one purity--the only *cure*. And tragically, 400 years later, most Black Americans still accept and cling to our slave master's racist decree that anything that brushes against us...*is us* by default.

That we should think so little of ourselves that just *anybody* can be us.

And, of course, it only takes one lie to unravel the whole world--and the one drop rule is America's monumental lie.

But it worked at keeping Black Power safely under the control of the White race (not just the white man, but the white woman as well). The white woman played and *plays* an enormous role in helping him to rule and dominate and <u>undo</u> black people.

A Mulatto Elite was created ON PURPOSE, just as in Africa...to act as a Buffer group to keep the authentic Blacks invisible and to *"speak for them"*, compromise for them...and mainly...to identify with the White Power Structure and uphold its mandates, all in the name of speaking as "black folks". More than anyone else, the "root core" of the black human being was denied "representation"--the dark skinned black woman. (*And for many of those reading this on the continent of Africa, I am well aware that as far as you are concerned there's no such thing as "light skinned" black people...I understand that the dark skinned black is* THE *black person, but the majority of people who will read this book are our American brothers and sisters who live under a completely different system--given to them by their slave master*).

As I told you before, white domination requires that--"*they shoot the blackest girl first.*" So, alas, the Mulatto (yellow) woman was used by both the slave master and the black man just as she was used in Colonial Africa, as a "bridge out of blackness"--*a bridge out of blackness--*a <u>womb</u> that had the power to gradually breed out the African and lighten (compromise the blood of our progeny) generation to generation...until the people were so compromised and divided by physical difference--it was easier to convince them that their allegiance was not solely to themselves ("blackness") or in any way to their origins (Africa), but rather to the "dream" ("*we've always been mixed*") of the superior people through whom they were mixed with.

And since the White man rules the world through the white woman (as do all men rule through their women--as Farrakhan says, "*a nation cannot rise above its woman*"), the Black man was conditioned, trained and programmed to choose the lightest woman he could find-- thereby systematically rejecting his own personal power--which is the authentic black woman (the darkest)--and cancelling out his own chance at ruling his own domain. Instead, as a <u>nigger</u>--he rules alongside the white man's flank as a glorified mascot. Notice the black leader in America. He is usually influenced by the loving, ultra-supportive well meaning white or non-black wife--the White man's mother, or by the High Yellow wife (look at Spike Lee)--who, because the society doesn't recognize her true racial identity--is always either an imitation black woman or an imitation white woman. So you see, they control them both ways, and they keep the black man impotent by making it a "taboo" for him to stand in rulership with his natural mate, the authentic black woman at his side--no matter how many white men stand with their snowy white wives and snowy white families--the goal is to keep the two darkest blacks apart, so that the black man has no way of ruling and no way of being whole and complete.

Black Americans will constantly claim that it's a natural occurrence to have a buffer race of mixed, mulatto yellow people--that these are *"black"* folks and that we Africans come in a range of colors--but that's not really true. It's just something that Black Americans tell themselves to feel better about the fact that they are slowly breeding themselves out of the black race.

In Africa, we have been invaded, raped, enslaved, colonized and have whole nations of bastards in the North (Libya, Egypt, Morocco) and have light skinned tribes (or members) scattered around the continent from interracial sex between whites and blacks that has occurred for *a thousand years*...but we still are an overwhelmingly Black people possessing the crown that God put on our heads from the beginning of the earth. We have never been treated well by those small numbers of mulattoes and mixed race Africans who inhabit Africa--most of whom would kill you if you called them "black". It's nothing in Africa like the Black Americans claim, but they will bring film crews there and film the lightest people they can find--once again denying the true African representation of his own face--and especially, the black African woman is made invisible...by films like "Hotel Rwanda" and so called "African" singers like the biracial Rhian Benson of Ghana, a high yellow mulatto--and out of a nation of 15 million black women, many of whom can sing their asses off--they find the one high yellow girl (and Rhian Benson can barely sing on top of it) and they promote her as *"the African woman"*--but it doesn't matter that she can't sing. Her job is (a) to make black women invisible, (b) to claim to be representing them and (c) to keep the western world in control of the black man's chances at power by continuing the lie that the African woman is just naturally gold colored with silky hair and Euro-latin features...and remember, little black children are the main ones taught to embrace this lie, to <u>expect</u> black women to not be black.

Do you see now...how intricate the erasure is?

On the streets of Dakar in Senegal, the women are deep luscious purple-skinned gazelles, red chocolate beauties, ebony fudge delights, midnight plum goddesses and wet wood mahogany skinned pretty mothers...*but on the billboards above their heads*, much lighter skinned mulatto women are featured in every single ad...African, yes, but not women that we would see in the course of the week, and because of it--the self esteem of the authentic African beauties is destroyed as their men and boys are literally <u>programmed</u> through time and repetition to desire and seek out women who look nothing like their own mothers--nothing like a Senegalese. They are programmed to see this as "normal", to ignore and despise their own women. And in the midst of that Yellow Fever (as Fela Kuti called it)...the women become desperate to do anything (rape their hair, bleach their skin) to win the love and attention of their own men and children.

But imitating yellow looks only makes it worse. A circle of self-hate is embedded, and through the images of light skinned mixed race beauty--ambiguity reinforces <u>whiteness</u> as "normal". As superior.

The Authentic Black Man

I'm not telling you all this so that you can hate anyone--I'm telling you this so that as Black men in America, you can recgonize the careful planning of your own destruction. I don't want my sons to be niggers.

To build up whites and undermine Africa. And I know you're wondering--exactly what is an <u>Authentic</u> Black Man?

<u>Authentic</u>

All I can tell you is that there was a time back in Africa (for what seemed an eternity) when the black man was his own God just like the White man, the Arab man, the East Indian man and the Asian man is today. The black man had his own kingdoms, his own religions, his own languages, armies...mightier than thunder, his own black wife (the black womb that he held above life itself). Her reflection mirrored his exactly and spilled the landscape with his own dark children. A family created from his own loins--owned fully by his uniqueness. He was a whole and healthy human being in and of himself.

The tima (*the result of great fire*).

Africa was our heaven and earth--bittersweet, dangerous, wonderful and breathtaking--and God was a black man.

He was omnipotent, but not omniscient. He was a man, nothing more. But he was <u>*free*</u> and he ruled the world, the animals, the sky, the butterflies...and in that freedom he enjoyed the height of his maleness and spirit, his truth and will...and there was no whiteness touching him, holding him, limiting him, erasing him. *HE* was the Man--the only man that mattered--and his skin was blacker than nightwater, and so was his woman's, and their hair was like wool. *The Proof*. The one true hair. The Black Man. The true son of God.

The one that your white Egyptian grandfather ordered me to grow up and give birth to--because he himself so desperately wanted to be a black man. Those are the only words I can tell you to explain what he is--the authentic black man.

Although you're part Egyptian, because you're also black men, there are white people and mixed race people in America who will try to tell you that the ancient people of your grandfather's country were not black--but were white or mulattoes. That's camelshit!

And I want you to know that this whole science called Egyptology is a farce. There is no such thing as Sub-Saharan Africa. The whole concept is a creation of European revisionists spreading jealous lies through their rancid colonialism. There are more pyramids in the Sudan than in Egypt, but you see that the British had Lake Nuba built to cover up the connection between Egypt and its mother, Cush-Nubia.

The ancient traveler Herodotus wrote 2,500 years ago in his book "The Histories" that the Egyptians he saw were: *"black/with wooly hair"*. He did not use the word "melanchroes" (which means *dark*). He used the word "aethiopes"--which means <u>black</u>. No one from those times would use "black" to describe mulattoes. And although these stupid scholars used to fight with your grandfather, claiming that Nefertiti was Syrian-Palestinian (*my ass!*)...the fact is she was the daughter of an Egyptian government official and a Nubian princess.

Europeans and White Americans don't know shit about our history, so don't even listen.

Everything they do is to show Africa at its worst. To film and exhibit our poverty and our disease and our trespasses and to make Africa look as though it's a stinking hellhole--but they never show the *whole* picture. They want to submerge and suffocate Africa in their lies. To exploit, rape and steal everything from Africa and to portray our people as human trash. But I have traveled and lived all over this world, and there is no place...*no place*...more dear to God's eye than Africa. And there are no humans anywhere on earth with spirits so evergreen, possessing the greatness of beauty, the tenacity of survival and the riches of eternity as we Africans do. When you come from Africa, my sons--*you come from the best*! Don't you ever let these motherfuckers tell you a damned thing about being an African and being a black man. After God made the African, he fucked up all the other races and they've been jealous of us ever since.

Doing every ungodly thing they could think of--*against* us.

As your father told you: *"until the lions have their own historian...the tale of the hunt will always glorify the hunter."*

The Witch

More than anything, my sons--black women have a history of not being listened to and not being considered important.

●

500 years ago in West Africa...a small group of African Kings began to sell their own people into slavery. Over time, of course, it turned into one of the most lucrative business industries in the history of the world. European slave executives, with the permission of African Kings, vigorously took part in the capturing and selling of more than 60 million African men, women and children--and the tragic fact--is that many African women (and Queen Mothers) spoke against it and tried to convince the Kings that they were leading us, as a people, the wrong way. But unfortunately, these women were accused of *"male bashing"* and branded Fire Witches and considered disloyal to the African man and kicked out into the wilderness or sold or de-tongued or killed....and the black men rolled right along, doing what pleased them and not giving a damn about the tribe or the race.

The Secret about Hurting

In the United States, the one practice that Black men have that we're not ever supposed to talk about...is the fact that a good 60 to 70% of them are prejudiced against their own women (against *black* women) --and through some unspoken criteria--they enforce a rigid color caste system by which they judge the worth of black women by (a) how light skinned they are, (b) how Euro-slender their facial features look and (c) the texture of their hair (they don't like *the Proof* on a woman's head). You need only to visit a dinner party thrown by successful black men (or go to an NAACP function) and you will see that virtually all of these black men's mates are either Non-Black, biracial or high yellow mulatto women (and it's not by fate, but by design)--and then in the same evening, drop in at the local club (try a reggae club), and you will see that the non-black women and the lightest skinned black women are the ones that the black men approach to dance with--

--and then drop into the local prison or the welfare office, and you will see that the *majority* of the black women at the bottom are "the twins" of these dark men--deep chocolate skinned queens with nappy hair and full West African facial features. Many of them are beautiful, but *invisible*. These authentic black women are the ones most likely to be impregnated and abandoned (because they're *dark*, but the whole black community denies it), these women are the most likely to have *"fucked up"* lives--drug addiction, prostituting to survive and feed their kids. These are the women most likely to have been <u>fatherless</u> all their lives. And the reasons, my sons, all stem directly to the fact that they are *"too black"* to be accomplices in niggerism.

Naturally, the entire Black American community is ashamed of Colorist Pathology and a huge portion of them (especially men and yellow women) are in total denial about it--they're not only unapologetic about their claims of "preference", but they also conspire with their non-black and light skinned girlfriends in scapegoating and lying on the dark black women--stereotyping them as "bitches with attitudes", "golddiggers", "mad black women" (why shouldn't they be angry at the people who despise their color and race--especially when those people are their own fathers and brothers?)--and of course, to go along with this nationally accepted psychosis that afflicts the darkest woman is the betrayal by those imitations (the yellow women) who claim to be *"sisters"* representing them.

Instead of admitting that she benefits from a White Supremacist culture that places her yellow womb above a black one (because it's weaker)--the yellow woman is quick to cop out by claiming, *"Dark women are just jealous of me because I'm prettier!"*

And the whole society agrees with her, because in that moment she is representing <u>The White Gene</u> and the status quo.

Surely, this phenomenon has been spreading to Africa and to anywhere in the world where there are black populations, but of all the places I've ever been in my life, I've never seen it as bad as it is in the United States and Great Britain. Sociologists call it "Color Complex" and try to be politically correct by claiming that it "victimizes" the light skinned as well as the dark--but as an African woman, I just call it what it is--the epic betrayal of the Black woman by the Black man. In America, even when you walk into a room of all married black couples--the women are usually *yellow*--despite the fact that the vast majority of black women in this country are brown to black skinned, the black male almost always <u>seeks out</u> a woman lighter than he is.

Of course, for those of us who are African women, it's not the first time that the black man has sold himself out and sold out *black* children and sold out Africa (the woman). But, of course, it's shocking that someone with the same skin and hair as you--could hate you for yours. It's the clearest, most fine tuned, purest self hatred on earth, and after being put up for adoption by my own grandmother for being *"too black"*--I know it like I know the smell of cigarette smoke. It's been the lifelong movie that flickers before my brown eyes. The evil gravity that no black female can escape no matter where she goes.

Fuck the Devil

One of the greatest frustrations for me as an artist and as a black woman coming of age on the American continent, but with an African soul, has been my chronic ambilical love for black men, not just romantically or sexually, but inately--spiritually and naturally, as clearly as looking in the mirror at myself and as deeply as wishing to see myself and my people alive and well, always, and always with life, which is only possible through the kindred oneness that god gave to us when he/she created Africa and human beings from day one...and then having to be accused of *"hating"* black men whenever I endeavored to point out the evil color-based, hair-based separation in our stew, rather than having the society of "black identified" black people acknowledge the real truth--which is--that this is a society in which historically and right now today, our black men truly *hate* and despise black females (authentic ones to the core) and have historically sought to crush and erase them, and while doing so, have blamed the victims, and have done so with the encouragement and double-protection of the dominant white culture and with the *"looking the other way"* of generations of absent fathers and excuse-making yellow women (who, as the darker population diluted, were in turn demoted and hated as well)--and anyone who dared intervene (as anyone who truly loves black people would *have to* intervene) risked #1 (being accused of hating black men) and #2 (being made a pariah and outcast). But the fact is--the people that I most often saw destroying "the black man *and his community*" were black males, and the "good" black men were silent about it.

Silence equals consent, my sons.

Always know that even if you weren't the one committing a murder--the fact that you stood by and watched makes you just as bad. And also know (as I know you do) that your mother *loved* black men, and like most black women, wanted to do all she could for them as a group and as their twin reflection, but in America, black men wouldn't let us--because they didn't want us--and the reason they didn't want us, is because they didn't want themselves. The chronic prejudice that black men harbored against their own reflection (some of which they inherited from their self-hating black mothers) kept us in a constant funk of separation and miscommunication, hurt feelings--because "*black men*", as a group, <u>betrayed us</u> and consistently *lied* on us (as a group) to justify their transgressions and their abandonment--and for those reasons--the rupture became a virus. You hear everyone blaming the black woman, criticizing black women for their choices, but the fact is--*black women* had very little to choose from. It's women of other races who usually have the choices with black men. So our race dies.

Again, I'm talking about authentic black men and women here, and I don't know what Black Americans truly feel about our undoing, but for my African eyes, it's like watching the Slave Trade all over again, only this time, exactly what's for sale is far less tangible.

Perhaps our souls this time.

Gain the whole World

"Why talk about the black men who hung from trees...if we our black selves are not willing to give birth to those men again?"

--Kola Boof

When I was a little girl (14, 15, 16), reading the black power books of Amiri Baraka and the intellectual academic genius of John Edgar Wideman--I really thought these were some bad ass *baaad* black men--KINGS, and from the words they wrote in book after book, you would have thought, just like I did, that two men this conscious and aware of the virtual holocaust against black people would have been married to the most royal-blooded, satiny chocolate *proof*-headed ebony queens you could imagine...but, of course, that's the thing with insecure black men who speak from the penis...they can talk it for the masses, but in their personal lives, they're very rarely man enough to *affirm* it.

As a child, I idolized and loved John Edgar Wideman so deeply that I often fantasized three things about him...(1) that I was his daughter or niece...(2) that the reason I was learning to cook so good was because I was going to grow up and become his adoring wife (which I dreamt that about a lot of famous black men; I think all black girls did)...and (3) that he would someday become President of the United States and save us all from racism and injustice.

The shocker, for me, is that now that I'm in my 30's--I totally hate the man. I see him as the ultimate "nigger" and weak link. And not because he married a white woman--but because from the way he wrote so psychologically and so invasively about the dehumanization of black people, I know in my heart that he just has to be aware of the systematic destruction of little black girls (the womb of black men)...based on color and hair texture...*I know he has to know*...and yet, like every other black man in a position to speak up (and do so loudly) on behalf of little dark black girls--he never has.

And silence equals consent.

And this is the same man who wrote with such passion that there is no such thing as race, that all humans comprise a human race--and that the holocaust against black skinned people was wrong--and I mean, his works are relentless in trying to etch out the humanity of black people. But still, he not only chose to affirm the <u>white womb</u> and have children who look whiter than he already did (which to me, erases much of his argument about all people being one race, because in the end, he affirmed his slave master's people--not us), but he also wrote or gave interviews in which he encouraged other black men to abandon black women and to choose the white man's mother, because according to him, this was the surest way to improve "race relations".

What was to become of the masses of us little negro black girls?, I often wonder, when I think of John Edgar Wideman's plan.

Did he just assume that white boys would miraculously be there to marry and look after little negro-looking and African girls?

And after hundreds of years in this country, and the whole ugly history of black women (raped and defeminized)--what did he expect to happen to them, and how could he possibly run off to put yet another white womb on a pedestal while leaving behind and further dehumanizing millions of black wombs who had been raped, ripped out of their mental faculties and lynched by white media--and had *never* been protected by black sons like him.

Maybe it's because I loved John Edgar Wideman so deeply as a teen and expected so much from him--that I completely hate him and come to tears right now just trying to get off my chest the way I feel. Truly, there are no words to express what I feel about men like him (who have never been there for little black girls; never done a damned thing to affirm *US*; always looked the other way--or lied on us, like that fake catfish-faced sexist *asshole*, Ishmael Reed) and what I blame him for. I believe that I am right, and after all these years of carrying around such rage, that's all that matters to me. The whole world of esteemed white men, white bitches and Henry Louis Gates-*type* black people celebrate John Edgar Wideman, and yet all I believe about him is that he was a colorstruck, inferior black man who, like a pack rat, piled up untold academic achievements, talked smart, expressed his guilt at the history of black people--used his life's work to visit blackness *like a grave*--but in the end, affirmed not only white people and white supremacy (because, of course, the mixed buffer race that he and his wife creates is considered "superior" to authentic blacks, and he knows that)--but he sacrificed the little raven skinned nappyheaded girls. The people who utterly needed him (and men like him) the most.

387

I wrote this whole essay just because I've waited <u>all my life</u> to say to the whole world...that I hate John Edgar Wideman.

And I hate Sidney Poitier. Another man that the whole planet celebrates, but to me--is a nigger who affirmed the white man's mother and *her* humanity, but not mines and his own mother's, which in turn degraded his own. No wonder the whites celebrate men like him. And I'll never forget the time (I was about 15) I asked your grandfather, Marvin Johnson, why they never had Sidney Poitier star in a movie with Cicely Tyson (because they had been the two top black actors, prestige-wise and in fame), and your grandfather said: *"Because if they put Sidney Poitier in bed with Cicely Tyson--they'll give birth to the spitting image of Sidney Poitier all over again. Naw. Best he be paired with Diahann Carroll--or better yet--a real white woman."*

In the film "Guess Who's Coming to Dinner"--a smart man like Sidney Poitier allowed the message to go out that after his character's becoming a doctor and being nominated for the Nobel Prize, the only thing left that could *"validate"* him as a human being was marriage to the white man's mother. It was such a <u>N</u>iggerish movie.

And in America, this has been a constant fucked up message.

I read books from the 1920's where Black American men said, *"I don't haul no coal"*--which meant they wouldn't be involved with a dark skinned black woman, <u>because she was black</u>, and because her womb can do nothing but produce more blackness.

In other words--black humans are inferior.

I read about the famous actress-dancer Josephine Baker who fled from the United States to Paris right after a *black* stage producer informed her that she was very talented, but too dark skinned to play the leading lady in his latest stage production. Of course, the story has always been reported that she left America due to the white racism here--but the racism of black men against black women is never discussed, and also, I notice these black women who start out with black men or start out *wanting* black men--end up with white men. Iman, Josephine Baker, Naomi Campbell, Diana Ross, Whoopi Goldberg.

And I'm not discounting the fact that I believe that Diana Ross and Naomi Campbell are two supremely colorstruck sell out females-- I believe they are--but perhaps with acceptance from black men and the right leadership and guidance, they would have been different.

For black _boys_ it's different, because they come from a "hood" that consistently tells them that black women are inferior (not to be valued or protected unless they're mixed or yellow enough) and that only the black man is a human being. I've seen this with my own eyes all my life. Black women are called "Ho's", "chickenheads" and "golddiggers"--but the real golddigging *HO's* in the "hood" are white skanks like Kobe Bryant's women (the man admitted to being a cheater, was accused of rape and his wife got a $4 million ring and house for her mother--that's a golddigger...and of his white rape accuser--*how many men's sperm on her panties*?)--and other materialistic Ho's like Jennifer Lopez (who made a career pimping successful black men) and Michael Jordan's paid off mistress--but there's no song about them.

I've lived in America most of my life, and I've talked in depth with Black American women--and they don't want white men. The overwhelming majority of them love and desire black men--and they want them *black*. But to save face, to not end up alone and to not seem desperate (or become lesbians, as some of our straight sisters are able to do), they are forced to accept white and other men as their Kings. It's a tragedy only because it has nothing to do with "*love*"--it's all contrived; it's all political; reactionary, destructive, and in the end, it's the black race that loses. And loses big time. *Our race kills its own mother, to become "light".* Thus no one respects us.

This shit is just fucked up over here...and it's spreading to Africa and everywhere else. An epidemic of racial suicide.

You see men like Montel Williams claiming that he's some great eagle of a black man, rising from a mountain--claiming that white men *fear* him, because their white daughters want him so desperately--but what I see, is that the men like Montel are the ones surrounding themselves with white women (*successful* black men's hiring practices, something every black single mother in search of a job *to feed black children* knows about)--chasing down the white womb, and in the case of O.J. Simpson, Montel, Kobe Bryant and countless others--accepting the *base lowest stock* of the white man's mother for the highest position of marriage, obviously because these Non-black women are status symbols for niggers. I would like to ask Montel Williams--why should the white man fear somebody who refuses to give birth to his own image? Why fear black when it won't be black for long?

White men don't fear Montel Williams, Michael Jackson, Sidney Poitier, Bob Johnson (BET), Ishmael Reed, Stanley Crouch (aka vagina mouth) and underline especially not the rappers and rap moguls. The only people these men undermine and help destroy...are black people.

And I don't want you, my sons, to be *anything* like those men.

When I was a child, all of the black male leaders and all of the black men writers castigated the white man as "*the devil*"--the ultimate evil in this world--but in the daily lives of little nappyheaded chocolate skinned girls like me, it was Black Men and Black Boys that my black father, Marvin Johnson, had to confront about discriminating against me and my sisters. It was my own race of men who spit in my hair, called me "bitches and Hos" on the radio, gave little Puerto Rican girls free candy for having "*good hair*", and joked, quite seriously, that they would use me for sex but choose my light skinned sister for marriage (and eventually, they turned the same joke on Spring--placing a latina or white woman as the new prize). Black men, *not white devils*, did that to us. And while they were preaching about black men hanging from trees (the black women who hung were never mentioned), they refused to give birth to those men again. They didn't want black sons.

These black men could fight for the equality of black men and boys, but never did fight for the black *womb* that <u>produces</u> black men and boys (*They killed their own mother/and the white people watched*). Their real goal was inclusion in the body of the so called *"white devil"*. To become like him, to have access to the white womb, which like the mulatto womb, would now serve as yet another bridge *out* of his blackness. That pits me--the Black Man's Mother--as the thing to be destroyed, and yet I'm not supposed to say anything about my own destruction or my children's destruction. The black men of our communities, my father Marvin Johnson always said with embarrassment, were the ones who most considered our race "inferior". And by the time I arrived in America, the black community was crumbling, scattered and falling apart. The civil rights movement and your grandparent's Black Power movement had been replaced by the Hip Hop Holocaust.

<u>QUEEN</u>

My decree sons is this--*I want you to kill*. That's the reason I had you in this country. To bring about a better love. I want you to give birth to a new black man and <u>kill</u> the old one. But it's imperative that it be done expressly *the way*...that I tell you to do it.

<u>The Black Man is Wrong</u>

Right now, it's 2006, and worldwide--the black man is once again leading us (as a people) the wrong way.

Just as in the slave trade, those few black women who speak against his self-destructive pathology and his self-hatred are branded *"male bashers"* and are accused of hating black men rather than trying to give birth to and sustain them. The smartest men are in denial.

White Love

Let me tell you very briefly, a bedtime story, a true story, my sons, that <u>explains</u> white people:

•

Once upon a time in a little African village, there was an innocent black family with a father, a mother and five children. They had lots of love and hardly knew they were poor because the landscape was so beautiful and rich with natural wonders, and they had each other and had been through so much--fighting the elements, the animals and conquering their fears together. And they were nothing...nothing like the negative images of Africans that American media continuously shows on television and in movies. This family was like most African families--they were decent people, hardworking and perfectly beautiful to their own origins. They were a family.

One day...a white missionary and his white wife came to offer their religion to the poor African family, and when the whites saw that the African parents could not afford toys for their children--the whites decided to do something about it.

They went off and came back with huge bags full of toys and clothing and games for the children. Things that the African parents would have loved to have been able to give their children.

BUT...

...instead of giving these gifts to the African father and allowing <u>him</u> to present these wonders to his children himself (which would have made him appear larger in his children's eyes)--the white couple snuck out to where the children were playing in the jungle and surprised them with all these untold treasures. *Look what we brought you...look what we're able to do*! Hurting the African father's pride by doing for his children what he could only dream of doing himself.

Any decent human beings who truly wanted to help poor people would have given it to the parents to give out! But after they gave the children these gifts ...they then thought up ways to remove the father from the family altogether.

We have big jobs in another land that will make you rich...but you must be away from your wife and children for several years. And of course the wife is taught religion and the children sex and the husband beauty evil. The most worthless things in life are fixed as "civilization" markers, *reefs* to hang around the necks of the naive.

And so, the little African family...died.

The End.

•

Control

And this is a constant thing with the European people.

The white man and the white woman enter our communities, our villages, our black worlds...and they believe that if they show us images of their white hands saving us...then we will love them.

It never occurs to them...that what would really make us love them...is if they would show us images of <u>US</u> ...saving ourselves.

Remote Control

I want you to learn the <u>definition</u> of the word "assimilation":

Assimiliation: (Noun) The process whereby a minority group gradually adopts the customs and attitudes of the prevailing culture.

Do you see sons? *That's a nigger.*

It means a fucking nigger!

The state of being assimilated.

The process by which a sound is modified so that it becomes similar or identical to an adjacent or nearby sound.

The conversion of nutriments into living tissue; <u>constructive</u> metabolism.

People in America think I'm crazy.

They think I'm a dumb African and don't know how to read between the lines of what they say and write--they think I have no critical thinking skills. They think I'm nothing but a topless idiot who has no soul without them, no dream without them dreaming it for me first. They think I'm incompetent and that I would *want*...what a slave wants. They think I don't love my black babies.

They really believe I don't love my black babies.

And most of all--these motherfuckers *don't* think.

Great Lion

Boys, you know how much I love and fight with the Nigerian author Chinweizu.

He's of an age now that I imagine he'll be dead by the time you read this. But he wasn't just your mother's arguing buddy (and we mostly argued because he's such a blatant sexist--otherwise I might have gotten him to marry me after your father and I split up), but he was also one of Africa's greatest scholars--a man so brilliant that Toni Morrison edited his books at a time when her own writing career was surging to the very top (she edited his masterpiece, "*The West and the Rest of Us*")-- he is a controversial, very outspoken man of incredible vision, wisdom and courage. One of the few Africans of any era that the white people could not bribe, compromise or lessen. Not to mention flat out handsome as a movie star--I am proud when the literati circles in Africa call me the daughter of Chinweizu.

Before I talk about killing, I want to share just a little of our great lion, the scholar Chinweizu's writings on this matter:

But first of all, what is the nigger?

The Nigger is the African mangled by white power, a peculiar travesty produced by centuries of European imperialism and Arab hegemony. And alas! After more than a century of being completely in the dungeons of White Power, all of us Africans today have become Niggers.

The Nigger is the zombie into which White Power has deformed the African. The Nigger is a fake African--a person of African race, who has been stripped of African culture, and who is culturally Eurocentric or Arabocentric. The Nigger is a biological African who has internalized white supremacist superstitions, and become Afrophobic and even Eurochauvinist...the Nigger is a person with black skin, white mind and white spirit, an African salt that lost its savor, brown sugar that has turned sour. The nigger is a strange creature--the nominal African who despises his race, denies African culture, demonizes his ancestors, and yet expects, and even demands that people of the other self-respecting races of humanity should respect him and treat him as an equal member of humanity. The Nigger is possessed by the ideas and ideals of White Supremacy; the Afrocidal African who craves to be white, physically (eg. Wacko Jacko), or culturally (eg. the assortment of Black Europeans in the Homeland, Afro-Saxons in the Diaspora, and Omar Bashir with his criminal band of Arabizer-Jihadeer slavers and ethnic cleansers in the Sudan).

On Negrophobia: Psychoneurotic Obstacles to Black Autonomy

Negrophobia, the fear and dislike of blacks, is a great disease. It has killed more blacks in the last five hundred years than all other diseases combined; more than malaria, more than epidemics and plagues of all sorts. In the coming years, it could kill far more than AIDS. It is a psychological disease, a disease of the mind, which harvests dead black bodies every day. The blacks who died through slavery were killed by Negrophobia. The blacks who died all over the globe from white colonial aggression were killed by Negrophobia. The blacks who died in our liberation struggles--Bookman, Toussaint and Dessalines with all their soldiers in Haiti; the Mau Mau warriors in Kenya; the liberation fighters in Angola, Mozambique, Guinea-Bissau, Zimbabwe, Namibia, South Africa, Sudan and elsewhere--were all killed by Negrophobia. The blacks dying from the structures and policies of neocolonialism are dying from Negrophobia. The blacks killed by

AIDS, a disease manufactured by whites in the biological warfare labs of the USA and deliberately introduced into the heart of Africa and Haiti to kill off blacks, are dying of Negrophobia.

Ah, Negrophobia, I didn't know that hate could kill so many!

Negrophobia is a psychoneurosis, a mental disorder. So too is blancophilia, its twin. If someone hates everything black, including the black butterfly, including the most fertile soil, isn't he mentally disturbed? If someone loves everything white, including white trash, including white arsenic, isn't he mentally disturbed? Negrophobia and blancophilia form a syndrome, a characteristic set of psychoneurotic passions that occur together. The Negrophobia syndrome is characterized by melanotropism. A magnetic movement away from or toward different intensities of melanin, the skin pigment. Blancophilia induces a reflex movement towards things white, even toward white ugliness.

The stimulus object is white skin, any skin that is low in melanin. Negrophobia, for its part, induces a reflex movement away from things black, even from black beauty. The stimulus object is black skin, any skin blessed with melanin in a high dosage. Negrophobia and blancophilia, of course, are conditioned responses to White power and Black powerlessness.

Mommysweet skips a few pages to:

Negro Negrophobia makes blacks defer to whites. It makes bright black boys, the thinkers of the race, obey the IMF, the World Bank, GATT and the UN, even when they know that the orders from such outfits are aimed to destroy their own people. It makes black intellectuals swallow and spout any silly idea, provided it is put forth by some guru of the white world, like Marx, liek Jesus, like Mohammed. Negrophobia makes blacks accept leaders of thought and of action that are chosen for them by whites. It makes blacks revere any third class mind, any tinpot potenate, that whites annoint to confuse and mislead them. But for Negro Negrophobia, we would automatically reject any leader chosen for us by our historic enemies. But for Negro Negrophobia, we would throughly suspect the loyalty to the black race of any black Rhodes Scholar, of any black Nobel Laureate, of any black Faisal Laureate, of any black Lenin Laureate, of any black knight or peer of England, of any black elect of the French Academy. He would have to work extra hard to convince us that he is not an agent sent to help hasten our ruin. Believing the blancophile dogma that white is right, that white is quick-witted, that white is beauty and virtue and salvation; believing the negrophobe dogma that black is wrong, that black is is dumb, that black is ugliness and sin and damnation, the Negrophobic black does not feel comfortable in a blacks-only group. Blacks-only associations gives him claustrophobia; he must throw open the doors to let in some white skin to boss or spy on him; only then can he relax; only then can he feel that all is well with his world. Negro Negrophobia is, thus, a disease which drives blacks to crave racial integration and to espouse continentalist Pan-Africanism.

In multi-racial societies, it drives the black elites to flee to white suburbs. In the name of racial equality, they decapitate their own black communities, rob the ghetto of black leadership, and abandon it to confusion and predatory gangs-- in the name of black freedom they flee the black world. Similarly, in international relations, pulled by the call of the white, blacks are eager to join the British Commonwealth. They are desperate to join a French Community. They sell their sanity to join a Russian Collective. And an Arab empire? They disown their black inheritance to get into its latrine!

Listen sons:

They will pay any price, suffer any humiliation, to join any club formed by whites. But a Black community, a commonwealth or a league? They will not only *not* join, they will oppose it being formed at all!

The idea of blacks getting together, all by themselves, disorganizes their being. In their blancophilia they are self-made orphans desperately seeking white foster homes. For all their outcry on behalf of the black community, all they want is to disappear into the whiteness of the white world.

Our Fathers:

Senghor, Nkrumah, Du Bois, Cheikh Anta Diop and Mandela are proof that not even the best among us are immune from the Negrophobia syndrome. Of the great black redeemers of the 20th Century, only **Garvey** escaped the syndrome, principally because he was unequivocal and uncompromising on black solidarity.

All of these excerpts are reprinted by permission of **CHINWEIZU and are taken from various essays or his classic book, **"The West and the Rest of Us"**.

Kill or be killed

My dear sons--nowhere in the writings of Chinweizu or of your

mother is there hatred for any race of people. We both believe in the sanctity and beauty of human life, and our work reflects our respect and love for what God has created on earth in totality--yet we also believe that it's time for the <u>niggerism</u> of Africa (skin bleaching) and the <u>nigger</u> himself to be phased out.

The condition of the Black Race is always measured by the condition of the blackest woman--but black men are too stupid to realize that. Our whole race is trash right now, because we kill our own mother, but she is not inferior and we were not meant to live this way.

We are Africans. All black people are Africans and all Africans are lost...and we are meant to stand in the image of God; as it was in that image that we, the first humans on earth, were created. Your hair is the *proof*. Your wooly, nappy African hair. God's hair.

When I say...*I want you to kill*...it's not controversial. What I mean is that I want you to LOVE.

To remove white vision and LOVE the wholeness of blackness into being. To kill the nigger by choosing all that is his opposite. And to set this example for your children to make generations.

To truly love yourself, your flesh, your *Proof* and to seek out and devoutly love that Africaness when you see it in other black people all over the world. *I don't want you to be niggers*! I want your entire existence to be about the affirmation of and the fellowship with your own people and to be about the healing that they alone, as a group, must begin to enchant upon one another--to bring about the awakening of the authentic black man and the authentic black woman. *Together*. Not separated. But together--<u>*black* as all black put together</u>. Our complete utter perfect wholeness. Us. Only then can Africa rise.

I want you to give birth...to a new *breed* of black men.

God Is a Black Man

The light That I Blessed

Dear Eye
        (Open)
Our graves are just the same.

The light that I blessed is nearly dark as pure goodness.
He comes to me...he comes through me
He arises.
My everything.

Dear Eye
        (Opening)
Our graves are just the same.

Africa
Ageless with tomorrows.
Her grace so willing; her face of night.
Hand of our seed...time impregnating the dilemnas.
Oh great dilemna/not so great.

Opened Eye
        (see our lives/See our graves)
Swimming dance in the dream:

        Tree (man)
        Branch (penis)
        River (womb)
        Earth (woman)
        Laughter (children)

        The light that I blessed.
        The light that I blessed.

Eye of God.
The revolution will not be televised.
But will take place where it has always taken place.
In my womb of jungle stars and crimson nights.

In my songs to the white morning surf.
In my anger (smacking your taste buds like crab cakes).
In my brilliant petticoat of sorrow.

The light that I blessed:
sun full inside me
Penetrating water
            jellyfish lover/turning fossil to oil

Wave of my hand
hand of the stars
wand of my magic
sweet grave *0* matchbox...for my scars

Amaze me time and again.
Hand on my womb.
The light that I blessed.
The light that I blessed.

"The Light That I Blessed", a poem by Kola Boof © 2006

●

During colonial times, African women from every corner of Africa shared a popular saying that was usually spat in White men's faces. Our mothers, grandmothers and aunts would defiantly proclaim, *"...if my father dies, then I will give birth to him again!"* Many times, this was said into a White man's ear as he raped an African girl. This was her way, in all her powerless situations, to define herself as a woman who belonged to and was loved by a stronger, fairer being--an African man. We called our man, *The Conquering Lion*...because we always believed that he would someday rise up in this world and put us...up where we belong. Like the white man glorifies his white woman, we believed that our Conquering Lion would someday glorify us as well, and at last, make everyone bow down and respect us (for the whole world of men has degraded the black man's mother). Our mothers, aunts, sisters and grandmothers went to their graves singing and hoping for that day of the Conquering Lion.

I still believe in that day. I still love Black men. I still think of them as our Conquering Lion. But, of course, as a black woman writer, one who is smart enough to be a womanist, and one who is often accused of *hating* black men and bashing their reputation with every opportunity...there has been a great hostility towards me. This is a misconception about me that hurts terribly. My only comfort is that I am not nearly the first Black woman author (writing about the break down of our people) to be labeled a hater of black men. Long, long before Kola Boof, there was Flora Nwapa of Nigeria and Egypt's heroic and beautiful Nawal El Sadaawi, there was Alice Walker (whose entire brilliant career has been unfairly stigmatized by this accusation), there was my great love bell hooks, our Mother, Philosopher and Priestess Wordsmith Toni Morrison, who actually mints the humanity of Black men throughout all of her writings, but still, has uncovered a lot of situations that make them uncomfortable--there was Gloria Naylor, a truly loving, wise woman spirit, and Ghana's noble goddess flower, Ama Ata Aidoo. There was Nigeria's empress of wisdom, Buchi Emecheta and the genius from Senegal--Mariama Ba.

All of these women have either, through their writing or in public conversation, lamented the pain of having to tell one's own truth, one's own journey (as we women are obligated to do)...and then having to face public damnation and hostility from black men whose insecurity and guilt caused them to *misread* the manifold. They fail to see that it's our love for them, and often times our loss and disconnection from them, that brings about this need for healing, for venting and for public weeping. A black woman must always sign her signature, because she is a human being. It doesn't mean that she hates anyone.

In my case, I have named the men that I do hate. And I think it's clear that I hate the ones I perceive as trying to kill or undermine my people, and then again, I have to admit, deep inside--I don't even truly hate those men, as much as I'm just pissed off at them. And I don't have to be right! I'm human. I'm not a man's property or part of a school of fish. I can hate and judge as freely and with as much wrongheadedness as any man, because...my feelings count, too.

But still, it's loving others that really redeems us in life.

I am a womanist--but I am also a woman who was mostly shaped by great black men.

I don't see anything wrong with admitting that.

While one Arab white man who wanted to be black planted me in my mother and declared at my birth that I was: *"The one who is victorious, the one who is praying"* (and a *"bitch"*, don't forget)...another man, who really is black, Marvin Johnson--saved my life by adopting and rearing me, teaching me how to love myself, accept myself and how to make good on my birth father's edict. Truly, that's a lot more luck than most little black girls get in life, as I was blessed with two fathers on two continents, both of whom loved me.

And from there, it was like a watershed. Time and again, I was rescued by black men. When I was on the verge of a nervous breakdown as a teenager and needed psychiatric care, a Senegalese doctor, Dr. Diallo, saved me from the negligence of a self-absorbed white woman doctor. When I could barely speak English and had been given away for *looking African* by my evil light skinned Egyptian grandmother, it was the cinematic work of the greatest black filmmaker in history-- Ousmane Sembene--that resurrected, fulfilled and inspired me far more than any Bible or Holy Koran ever has. And because of Ousmane Sembene (*the hero of my life!* as an artist), I not only saw but <u>believed</u> in how sacred and undeniable the value of a black woman is, and Africa herself. As a child, sitting there in the dark, I received a kindred worthiness from Sembene, and I love him so deeply--to me he is a Saint and a Prophet. I consider him to be the purest, most truly African artist that ever lived. And he was yet another black man who affirmed and blessed my life.

The thing about lists is that they're part of arithmetic and we get them wrong--I'm atrocious at mathematics.

But my children's father, Aquaman, saved me from the dead end experience of being a lone activist woman and sexual athlete. He gave me children and showed me, through his sincerity and devotion, that I could be loved and that I deserved to be loved. And this is very rare for a black woman anywhere in the world to receive such a gift from a black man in her lifetime--because, although many of us have men, few of us are truly imbued and enriched by them in a spiritual, tangible sense. And though our ways have parted, I can honestly say that because of this strong black chocolate Garifuna warrior from Dangriga, Belize--I have been loved and given more than I had and been *changed*, in a good way, by a man's touch.

He caught me in his palm, held me down and healed me.

And I am forever grateful to Aquaman for that. It's because of him healing me that I truly, *truly* love men.

Novelist poet activist

My career was never planned. But every step of the way, black men were the ones who made it happen. Russom Damba, the Ethiopian, reading my script for *"Rain"* and insisting that I was meant to be a literary writer more than an actress, and starting a publishing company so that my scribbling in notebooks could begin to form a story, and lo and behold, it turned out that he was right.

The great restlessness that I felt from dead men that I idolized and wanted to be like--Malcolm X, Steven Biko, Marcus Garvey, Richard Wright and Langston Hughes--came out most powerfully for me in my writings, and with the sure wisdom of Sudanese compatriots like Deng Ajak, Riek Machar, and our great King of a father, John Garang, I developed courage and the will to be heard...*even at the risk of death.*

Speaks Truth to Men

In many ways...I began to think like a man and do things like men do them, because most of my adversaries and oppressors were men and there is a constant danger when a woman speaks truth to men.

The rappers Eric B. and Rakim and K.R.S. One lit me up inside and spiked my thoughts as an activist and writer. Along with the writer Paul Beatty (who, to me, is a rapper), these type of Modern Living black male artists made me realize that there was still the possibility of black males delving as deep as any female into the under-conscious of human thought, brevity and sincerity. These men gave me hope, because they were young and fantastically gifted and their anger, hunger and displacement reminded me so much of my own.

I had such a crush on Paul Beatty when I read "*White Boy Shuffle*" and recently felt so enraged when I read that he thinks he's ugly. But you see, that's what I'm talking about. Baroqueness.

I Love Black Men because

I love black men because they love me, and I realize that the black women who don't love black men--do not because those women have not been acknowledged, protected, healed or loved by black men. For if they had, then they would feel the way that I do.

I Love

Kalamu Ya Salaam, because of an essay he wrote on blues women. I thought it was one of the most truthful, loving things I've ever read a black man say about women--and when one considers all the many daring things that Kalamu Ya Salaam has written about and in the defense of women--you realize he's a gift to us. And on top of that, he made me see myself, because I feel very much like those jazz and blues age women. And I love Troy Johnson--the owner of African American Literary Club (www.aalbc.com), because of course, despite the fact that he really doesn't like me--it was him who launched my books in America (on his web site) and who gave me my own discussion board (THE KOOL ROOM) when I was living under protection with my children and couldn't go out of the house. And everybody knows that I love the writer and law Professor Derrick Bell (much of which has been discussed why)--but let me just say that beyond the personal inspiration and kindness he has shown me, I truly feel that his work is so unusually loving and nourishing towards all women and towards black women in particular. It's as though he determines to father and guide the ones that he can't see--the masses out there who have no fathers, no guidance and no love from black men. In the books of Derrick Bell, I feel so much fathering being done towards us all, and maybe that's because he was so old and I was so young as I read his works, but I just thank God so much for this kind of man, and I am very sad that the media and movies never portray the black men like Derrick Bell and Kalamu Ya Salaam...and another one, only I don't know him--Michael Eric Dyson. People claim that Michael Eric Dyson writes books *"kissing up"* to black women and to hip hop youth, but that's not true. What is true is that he's a protector of his people, and in the case of black women--he dares to know us. To contemplate and understand and comprehend us. He's one of the few men who isn't afraid of the snapping thunder a black pussy makes. He's a soul man and I find myself so enthralled with his ability to empathize and see the handle bars on hurt and how they can be ridden to a more sensible and fair conclusion. I just love what he does so much, and speaking for the angry young black girls in the ghetto that I came from in D.C., I don't think the writing establishment has a clue as to what Michael Eric Dyson means to those invisible, fatherless, uncared for princesses. He is literally saving lives just because he cares.

And Keith Boykin, the gay activist, bestselling author and my personal friend--is one of the strongest black men I know. And I get so much inspiration from his courage and *nerve.* I love people with nerve. And he's so handsome (like a movie star), but at the same time, he's a serious artist and a very brilliant thinker and he's been so gracious all these years--putting up with Miss Kola who's like a doting groupie kid sister that he can't shake. It's so funny getting his email saying: *"Kola, I have a life...I have my own drama!"* I'm just so proud of what he does for gay people and for our community in general--he's doing such important work that most other black men haven't the courage to risk, and I'm so glad that people reading this a hundred years from now will know that I knew him and that I loved him (*Oh, and I love the people who think I resemble him in drag in some photos.* Notice you've never seen us together and that we have the same initials KB.)

Of course, the never ending question that black women from Kenya to Ethiopia to South Africa and around the diaspora get asked is--why do African women love Denzel Washington so much? And of course, the answer is--his beautiful wife, Pauletta. It's so unusual, revolutionary and altogether refreshing that this Black American movie

King chose not only a black woman as his wife, but like him, one who looks West African, and in choosing her--he automatically chose and affirmed _all black_ _people_ everywhere. He gave the African diaspora an authentic looking African royal couple--an image of stability and integrity that we as black people could look up to and be proud of. And this is the secret reason why Denzel Washington is so beloved by the African people. He chose and *affirmed* the black family.

Yes, I hear the terrible rumors that Denzel and his wife are going to divorce--but I pray it's not true. I love him and consider him to be one of our greatest black men and in his film roles, a true symbol for my sons--of the authentic black man. People say he once cheated on his wife--*so what*! All men have flaws and weaknesses. There's never been a King that didn't fuck up somewhere in his life. Americans need to get real about life--the journey between a man and a woman must always be negotiated--*and some men are worth it*. But the thing about Denzel Washington is that he has self-respect, discretion, I've never once seen him humiliate or disrespect his wife and he's painfully aware of the adage: *little boys grow up and do what they saw their fathers do.* No matter what happens, Denzel Washington will always be a hero to me and one of our greatest black men.

And I love Spike Lee and KRS One, too. These are the kind of men I really respect, because they consistently use their work to stand up for us--our humanity--even when it could risk their success. And they are not as great as Denzel, but both are courageous men--I especially loved Spike Lee for being one of the few black men to publicly admit that he's "colorstruck" against dark skinned women and that he thought it was unnatural for a black man to be that way, but at least he admitted it and thereby let millions of dark women know that the problem wasn't with them. For that kind of bravery, I will always have a very special love for Spike Lee.

And I love this new politician Barack Obama so much! I think he could be the President one day. And my good friends, Kwaku Lynn Person, an educator, writer and activist whose roar is heard around the world, and Nathaniel Turner (*Chickenbones Journal!*), who like the Goddess Sijil, is a collector and keeper of everything our people do. I adore these men. Cornel Chesney and Robert Wright, the rich black men who started Door of Kush to publish my books.

And even black men I've spoken against--like the Honorable Minister Louis Farrakhan--it's not that I don't love him, and I do apologize for calling him a "white bastard", it's just that I was pissed off at his handling of the situation in my country, the Sudan. He was dead wrong about Sudan. But in many ways, he has influenced me and I have love for him. I think of him as a Conquering Lion.

I think of the great poet and publisher Haki Madhubuti, who I adore and admire so much, and especially because he brought Gwendolyn Brooks into her preeminence. He, to me, is a Conquering lion and a black man that I love. I think of voices out there--Stephen Malik Shelton, Randal Pinkett and Hadji Williams and the founder of Ligali in England, Toyin Agbetu, my good buddy Chris Hayden and the writer Chris Stevenson in Buffalo, and I see we have a future.

Time Capsule

My Auntie Ramah used to always say: *"God is a black man"*. And I don't know what she meant or how she meant that. But I think of the former Morehouse Professor and writer Mwalimu Bomani Baruti who sacrificed so much to own his own soul. I think of this writer named Gerald Early whose work I love so much. And of my idols Dr. Molefi Asante and Dr. Asa Hilliard and Cornel West and Walter Mosley--I really love who these men are--and Quincy Jones, who people expect me to despise, but no, I love his spirit and support. And yes, I can't wait for you all to read this 100 years from now.

This was my own womb. The light that I blessed.

I had outrageously wonderful sex with black men. I had great fun-filled friendships with black men. I got enormous guidance and wisdom from black men. I was sustained and supported in my career by black men. And my children's father, the only man I ever loved...was a wonderful, wonderful black man.

So it's not true that I hated black men. No.

I loved black men with all my heart...*and*...I was truly loved by black men in return.

CONQUER ME

African men have named me "Queen Kola".

My only hope now is that our magic will remember us.

This is a long book, because I might die.

It also rambles, because I might live.

But ultimately, I want to be *about* something. In the seed laid down by truly great men like Joe Madison and my christian Nuer brother Dr. Bern Yuot of Omaha, and my long lost and Oh-so-mysterious internet friend and inspiration...the man known as ABM. I want my sons and then their sons to make generations without selling their souls; without losing their black manhood. And I pray that more of us will seek out the mountain of wisdom that is written by the man I feel is our greatest Conquering Lion--Nigeria's very unsung Chinweizu. In classic books like *"Decolonising the African Mind"* and the landmark *"Voices from Twentieth Century Africa"* and his international hit *"The West and the Rest of Us"*...he masterfully behooves black artists and laymen alike to cherish the African soul. To live it and to wear it.

God bless you Great Lion, Chinweizu.

MOMMYSWEET

<u>Every</u> night, when I bathe and touch the scars on my vagina, I think of my birth mother--Mommysweet. I think of a particular time--one of the few--when she actually spoke to me. And I play it over and over, fishing for new meaning; what she said to me.

I have to admit that over the years, the sound of her voice has been replaced by my own, and it makes me cry because I've aged without her and I can't hold onto what she truly sounded like anymore, but still, I hold on to this memory of my mother speaking to me.

It was a night of mosquitoes and torch bugs, but the night air is sweet in Sudan--like breathing sweet rolls. She was tucking me into bed, but I couldn't see her face, because it was so black and the room was very dark; even her hands were like shadowy branches moving about my collar bone. But the thing about Mommysweet's beauty is that it was so real--it didn't need a face. You saw it in your mind, like a picture of pure royal velvet and only the white moon streamed through the window giving any light. And that light fell on me.

I remember that she kissed me gently on my forehead and over both my eyes and she whispered in my ear, "*Mystery...is a woman's chariot.*"

And then she left.

I Put A Spell On You

Anger comes from hurt and that is why nobody likes an angry woman, because she's hurting inside.

An angry woman is dismissed as *"bitter"*--which is just people's way of excusing themselves from having to heal that angry woman or to care about or understand her.

And whereas Roman Polansky can be known worldwide as a child molester and still manage to win an Academy Award in the year 2003, and whereas angry black men can rap and hip-hop their rage, uncut and completely raw, into the public consciousness and become celebrated, well respected millionaires from defiling their own mothers and poisoning their own communities..."*a woman*" being angry and exploring that anger...even in art...is still not acceptable, understandable or even pitiable by most of the people who order the society and think of themselves as fair judges of "rational behavior".

I used to be a very angry person, because in America, I felt that dead slaves were welcoming me--and no one believed me.

In my twenties, I slit both my wrists and traveled to different locations throughout the country putting my blood in the ground and envoking specific prayer rituals. I was putting a curse against the children of the ones who are erasing the black people. I went to Alabama, to Georgia, to Florida...I put my blood in the earth.

I took the greyhound bus.

I went to California, Texas, Tennessee, Pennsylvania, New Jersey, and both the Carolinas. I fucked a black college boy on the side of the road in Mississippi and another one in the back of his father's pick up truck in Tidewater. I put my blood in the ground. My scarlet fingers in their wet mouths.

I carved the faces of all the babies that the dead slave people sent to my heart into the trees of the forest.

411

I chanted silly chants and bared my breasts for night dogs and deer to see. Even raccoons came out in the moonlight to witness the beauty of my rage, and though it sounds insane--it was love.

I gave myself completely...to *the hurt*...that was sent to me.

It was God and the American slaves and the message to me--that *nothing ever dies*; and that what makes me special is that I am not really a part of the living, nor anything as wise as the dead.

I'm just...not afraid.

Then I had black babies, and a lot of my anger went away.

I imagine that I must be 40 by now. People are studying my books in colleges--and yet I never went to school. And just the other day, while listening to Mary J. Blige sing "*I Found My Everything*", a black intellectual friend of mines was looking at some of the topless photos on my books and thought he was complimenting me by saying that my image and work represents <u>*the past*</u> and that black people need that past in order to...blah, blah, blah. You see it's the academics and intellectuals who romanticize my image/work and see mysticism even where there is none. My friend was very wrong.

I am the future.

Kola Boof is the future.

In my yellow kitchen where friends often joke that I look like a Stepford wife baking cookies--I am the future; not the past.

And I am <u>*not*</u> a strong black woman.

And I hope that no one will ever think they are flattering me by making such a false claim. I am not strong.

I am a <u>*living*</u> woman. I live my life.

I have two mouths to speak with. The first one, is the mouth on my face--the second one is the mouth of my children; their image and deeds pouring forth from mines. Born out of me. I am _not_ a woman of color--that title doesn't do me justice. I am a Black woman.

I am the future.

I want to make films, to direct them, because to me--that's the most powerful medium in art, and that's always how I've approached and seen my work.

I am a political activist, yes (as much as I hate activism), but I would have preferred to do it with film.

It's just that I can't get financing, so I have to write novels.

But I believe what the eye can see.

I believe that the visual is the most powerful.

And that the attention spans of too many are becoming too short. They're more stupid than ever.

So we need the visual more and more, because the "hark" in words is too pure, too rich. It doesn't stay on the stomach.

I even use my body as part of my art. It's all a part.

I remember reading a piece that Zadie Smith wrote in _The New Yorker_ a while back--and how it hurt my feelings so deeply when she opened with some crass remark about her white boyfriend giving her a gift--a piece of art work or something; a mural that had black women and "nudity" in it--and how she, a supposed '_black woman writer_' didn't appreciate her white lover assuming that she was a part of those backwards, long ago bare fleshed black women--and in that moment of her pretentiousness, I gulped and then held up my head high and felt so incredibly proud to be African--and to be so authentic in contrast to artists like her and Betye Saar--women who claim to represent, explore and honor a continuum of black human womanness, that in reality, they aren't even equipped to understand, because the fact is--they're not black. Not for all their blinding <u>whiteness</u> and good intentions and academic documents stamped "head negress".

For the whole 26,000 years of us uneducated African women who lived in the highs of the clouds--naked, dirty and barefoot--I am grateful not to turn out like Zadie Smith and the other drones.

Wild honey is always better than the shelf kind.

So I am glad when Zadie Smith and the kente-cloth wearing imitations of life at SPELMAN College and so many other literary bon snots recoil in embarrassment at the sight of the Living Image, the bare black breasts, they so often claim to speak for.

I delight in the uncovering of their naked piss-faced ignorance, and at last/At Last--I get to speak *for my damned self*!

Everything in my life is about the beautiful babies I had.

My precious sons. My gifts.

I want to at least attempt to leave a better world behind for them and to empower other young Naimas out there. To make a mark that benefits black women (yes, more than any other daughters, my own), and I want to express what I have already described as the most important treasure to any artist--sincerity.

Sincerity.

I want my love to bloom and to wander and to be like sandpaper against the forces that have traditionally denied and impeded that love. I want my powers to be for the good and no matter what I do, good or bad, I want my people to know that everything I did was out of the

deepest, most weeping, most complete and utter love for my people--
and that I am standing until the bitter end for what Mahdi Pappuh and
Mommysweet stood for and expected me to stand for. As if speaking
as a first born son: *"though they died, I have not left them dead"*.

I am not a son, but dear ancestors, I have taken my father's spear
for as far as I could carry it, and I have exploded Mommysweet's silence
to the furthest extent that ink can print truth. I am mellower, wiser and
perhaps quite tired, but I still *see*...what I see. And my hope is that the
black women of the world will wake up from their delusions. And
that they will hear and understand me when I say that we can't possibly
go on this way for another few hundred years.

The hand that rocks the cradle is the hand that rules the
world...and we have _wombs_. The power to bring back the dead. And
in the beginning, before there was any White gene to produce White
people, it was those first humans--the charcoal colored Eves--who knew
that you could never really kill a man violently or with murder. They
knew that the only way to truly *kill*...was by giving birth. You don't
take life, you give life. And right now--we need a new son.

This tedious self-hatred; this taboo against our black mother and
men so spineless they could suck their own dicks is beneath us.

And we need to stop hiding behind the church getting on God's
nerves and _remember_ who we are. We need to remember that we are
Black women--the daughters of the earth's first garden and that the
oldest religion on this earth...*is our Black pussies.*

Every God that exists...became a God through us.

My sisters, it's time to kill.

SCRAP BOOK

Hidden Bonus Chapter

CONTENTS

The Africana Q&A: KOLA BOOF

Originally published: May 18th, 2004

Until recently no one has been able to pin Kola Boof down. To some she's a man-hating sex kitten looking to make a quick buck. To others, she is a heroine of the black girl womanist masses.

----

by Jennifer Williams

She's been called a liar, a whore, and an opportunist. She is an author, a mother, an activist and a poet. She poses with perky, coal black breasts bared on the back cover of each of her books. She is both the former mistress of Osama bin Laden and the daughter of a Somali princess. Call her what you will, but one thing you won't call her is afraid. Just who is this supa' bad, soul sistah? Her name is Kola Boof.

This tall, blue-black African goddess from Sudan has been kicking ass and taking names in the literary world for the past three years. Her publisher in Morocco was firebombed, her books are in and out of print, and the Islamic government of Sudan has placed a price on her head.

Until recently no one has been able to pin Kola Boof down. To some she's a man-hating sex kitten looking to make a quick buck. To others, she is a heroine of the black girl womanist masses. Her first book of poetry, *Nile River Woman* was just released and her erotic novel *Flesh and the Devil*, originally published in Arabic, is coming out soon. Boof's groundbreaking work *Long Train to the Redeeming Sin* is being reissued, and she has recently contributed to an anthology of short stories inspired by current events, *Politically Inspired*. Kola Boof's, born Naima Bint Harith, life story has been mired by either complete lies or bizarre half-truths and she wants to set the record straight.

•

You emerged seemingly from out of nowhere and you've been vague about the details of your life. What were you doing before you surfaced on the Internet a couple of years ago?

I was a writer and an activist living between North Africa and London, fighting against slavery in my homeland, the Sudan. I was heavily involved with gay rights in Morocco and with the Sudanese People's Liberation Army. I had been published already in eight countries and was struggling to find an American publisher for my books. Before that, I appeared in some really low budget Arabic films and had been a "paid party girl" for people like Moamar Khadafi and Egypt's President Mubarak. They used to pay non-Muslim actresses to attend their political balls. It wasn't prostitution, but I did secure some top dollar sugar daddies at those parties and eventually became the mistress of Sudan's Vice President [Hasan al Turabi]...and of course Hasan was the mentor of Bin Laden, who I didn't know at the time. By the year 2001, I had returned to America and given birth to both my sons by a wonderful black man in America.

The mainstream media hasn't been kind to you. Did you feel vindicated when the fatwa was verified by Fox News reporters?

It felt like a blessing because *The New York Times* published a completely distorted, slanderous article about me. The whole media laughed at me and demonized my image and there was nothing I could do to defend myself. *Essence* magazine didn't care that I was a black woman writer and *The New York Times* didn't care that I was an American citizen. It wasn't just hurtful, it nearly ruined my career. So today there is a fatwa on my life, my books have been forced out of print, and yet most people in America still do not know that I exist, but they know about Salman Rushdie and Taslima Nasreen. I have decided to boycott *Essence* and *Black Issues Book Review* for the rest of my life and I am eternally grateful to Fox News for honoring my struggle and for presenting me as myself. I am also grateful to Stephen Elliott for putting me to work and to *The New York Post* for keeping my name in the gossip columns, if not in the bookstores.

Why hasn't the black press embraced you?

Because black America hates the black woman in her authentic form. They want a woman who can reflect the whiteness they covet. They fear anyone who highlights or questions their self-hatred. They've always dreamt of some glorious Egyptian or Ethiopian queen...but I am a disappointment, you see, I am not at all what they imagined their Nile River goddess would be like. One journalist said that I'm a cross between Alice Walker, Madonna and Grace Jones. Just horrifying!

What was it like growing up in the Sudan?

In Sudan, because my father, Mahdi Pappuh, was Arab Egyptian, I was raised in a predominately Arab Muslim neighborhood that was very racist against my black African mother and against all black Africans. I only played with the Nubian kids on my block. Sudan and Egypt, in many ways, are the same nation — they have a terrible caste system based on color and religion. In both countries, North is for Arabs, South is for blacks. We were northerners. My father was an archeologist who desperately wanted black sons, but all he got was me. So he broke Islamic law and allowed me to eat meals with him and he taught me history, how to make boats and how to shoot guns. He took me with him on excavations and he always instilled in me that the world's only true religion is "white supremacy". He said that Islam and Christianity were just decoys to hide that fact.

African Americans took you in when you got here. How exactly did you get to America?

My parents were murdered, in my presence, at our home in Omdurman by the Murhaleen because Pappuh claimed publicly that he had witnessed slave raids. My Egyptian grandmother immediately received custody of me, but decided that because I was black, I would not be able to fit into my father's family. The Kolbookeks (our Turkish clan lineage) had spent decades trying to breed African blood out in the first place. So I was let for adoption and UNICEF arranged for me to eventually be placed with a black American family in Washington, D.C. In 1993, as an adult, I became an American citizen and in 1994, I returned to North Africa.

What do you think about the Nation of Islam's role in black America?

I think what they do for people in prison is astonishing and I greatly admire many of their social programs, but I do regard them as a political organization and I am very disappointed in how they mislead the black Americans on the issue of Arab Muslim-African relations. I assure you, the Arab man is not our brother. He is our rapist and our slave master for one thousand years in Africa. He is our devil bastard child, even worse than the white one. The Palestinians have been sterilizing black women since the 1950s. They also purchase African slaves just like all the other Arab nations do. I am disappointed that Farrakhan takes the side of Sudan's Arab Muslim slave trading government. Islam, like Christianity, is a foreign religion forced upon North Africans through enslavement. I experienced it to be a misogynist religion that catered to hatred and violence against women. Neither I, nor the sons of my womb shall stand for it, but since I am not God, I will respect and support other people's right to choose the Islamic and Christian religions.

Many African immigrants who come here as children find that they're forced to assimilate into black culture rather than mainstream American culture. What was your experience growing up in race-conscious America?

I found myself violently resisting both black American street culture and the mainstream Eurocentric culture. I noticed instantly that both were basically designed to destroy the black man and his family. My [American] Nana had a very distinct Southern culture that was seemed very West African to me. For instance, she would burn our hair out of the combs and brushes and she used the pot liquor leftover from cooking greens just as Mommy did back in Sudan. Nana sang spiritual songs without words, as Africans do. So her culture I clung to...and then later as a teen...I became immersed in hip hop and basically tried to recover the Nile river culture and the archeological Nilotic cultures that Mahdi Pappuh instilled in me. Of course, I also had prejudice against Americans, because I was raised in a nation that deeply hates America. So I had to get over my fear of Americans at first.

What was your childhood like?

I was under psychiatric care for most of my childhood. I had witnessed my parents' murdered in Sudan and then my grandmother gave me to UNICEF. I was deeply traumatized. My black American sister and I were molested together after I arrived. Then I found out, in a very traumatic way, that I had been vaginally circumcised at around three or four, an Arabic Oromo custom which separated me from my black American sisters. I was a very lonely, dreamy, misunderstood and alienated type of child. I think I wanted to die back then, maybe I still do.

When's the last time you went back to the Sudan?

I can never return to Sudan, the court in Khartoum has an order to behead me on sight. Two of my uncles in Sudan and one in Egypt, all Muslims, have been arrested and beaten up just for being related to me, so I tried in the beginning, to keep our family name vague. Of course my Egyptian grandmother, Najet, still lives north of Kom Ombo, pretending she's more Turkish than Arab and more Beja than black.

You were quite the Egyptian film starlet before shifting your focus to writing. How did you get into acting?

Films weren't my idea. Men kept telling me that I had such an incredible body and that I should be entertaining them with it. I wanted men's approval very desperately, especially black men. I was a very displaced, passionate and emotional young woman. I ended up sleeping with the men in North Africa, first to get lodging and food, then to get the parts in movies, and they were horrible parts! I played topless lesbian vampires and ancient Queens presiding over sinful Arabic orgies. I am very ashamed of that work, but I did it, so I must confess it.

I had always wanted to be a writer, but once Osama bin Laden slapped me across the mouth for saying that women could write books just as well as men. He wanted me to be Nefertiti and I wanted to be Alice Walker. Originally, I had wanted to make films so that the story of the authentic black woman could begin to be told. Most films about black women today are made by white men and black men. *Color Purple, Jackie Brown* and *Beloved* are three of the rare times that I saw authentic black women on the screen, but why must we always be set back in the old days? Black women are the future. We are alive still!

Do you absolutely insist on appearing topless on the back covers of your books? Could that be one reason you've had a hard time finding an American publisher?

Yes, I must be topless on the back of the books for religious reasons. But it's not the nudity that bothers publishers, trust me. They'd love it if I had flies coming out of my mouth and hanging tits and wrote the Aunt Jungle Book stories that white people love so much. But the greatest thing I can do in this modern, faux multicultural world is present the image of the authentic African woman. Non-Christian, non-Islamic. Purely African.

You don't think you'll ever be as good a writer as Alice Walker or Toni Morrison, two African American women authors you greatly admire.

I said that in an interview years ago, but the fact is...I was wrong. My biggest obstacle is that I can't afford to write. I have two children and no formal education whatsoever. I've never worked a nine to five job in my life, so there's nothing to write on a resume. My only sources of income have been men, movies and writing books. I can't afford to take four years to write a book — yet. I have to do it faster. But once I reach that level of financial security,

I know that my guts will drip across the American landscape like acid and good sex and sunshine. Like Aretha Franklin can sing, I too, am gifted.

What message should people take away from your work?

That God is NOT an individual. And that woman is half of God and that the world did not begin on the day that the Europeans were born. In fact, it very well may have ended.

Why did you come forward about your connection to Osama Bin Laden when you did?

I came forward when the British tabloids began asking me questions and threatening to expose me as an "accomplice" to Somi's terrorism. My former roommate was trying to sell nude pictures of me and Somi, which don't exist. I was very ashamed and I didn't want people to ever find out that I lived with Bin Laden, especially my American parents, but still, I couldn't risk being classified as a "possible terrorist" and getting deported. Once deported, I would be killed instantly. So I had to tell it...before my enemies did.

What is it like mothering while your life is in constant turmoil due to the fatwa?

I feel very guilty about the distress that my career causes my children, but then again, I had my career long before I had my sons. I spend all day, every day with my boys and I try to be competent, adventurous and honest, because the fact is, I don't know how to save them from Kola Boof's life. They were born into Kola just like I was born into Mahdi Pappuh. But boys are visual creatures; they aren't fascinated by words like girls are, so my lessons for them are usually silent and well thought out. They think their mother knows magic.

What's happening with your memoir *Diary of a Lost Girl*?

I still don't have a publisher for it, mainly because I won't allow Bin Laden's picture on the cover and because I don't want my vision compromised. *Diary* is not just my autobiography, it's also black womanist art, and it's one of the best things I've ever written. Several publishers want the book, but they're not brave enough to put it out as I wrote it or they aren't willing to pay me a decent advance. Hopefully, that will change.

What do you say to all those people out there who still don't believe you are who you say you are?

They should get on their knees and ask God if I give a damn. For if they do, they might not get back up.

• About the Author: Jennifer Williams is a freelance writer, activist and associate editor at <u>hipmama.com</u>. **Reprinted by permission of Africana.Com**

424

Umfitit

(Egyptian Chitlins)

• Very Delicious! (serve with thick wedges of corn bread)

In Egypt, the Black people eat their Chitlins over a bed of braised water lilies, both the tuber and flower of the plant. In America, I subsitute cantelope (sliced very thinly). This dish is also made very often with Sheep's Stomach, but I prefer it with the intestines. I don't usually like the seasoning called "Cumin"--but it's part of this dish. You should have thin slices of cantelope to make a serving bed, table Honey, 10 large tomatoes cubed, 4 Green Peppers sliced up, 3 large onions diced up--Cumin, Anise, Garlic--1 Habanero or Scotch Bonnet, Clam Juice, Virgin Olive Oil and Vinegar.

- Boil 10 or 20 pounds of Chitlins your normal way. <u>Cut them up</u>.
- Get a big deep Skillet (preferably stainless steel)
- REPEAT the following procedure as many times as it
  takes to prepare all your chitlins Egyptian style.

  ~~~

  • Heat up 1 cup of Clam juice with 1tbs. Olive Oil as Base.
  • Put in some of the sliced Green Peppers with it.
  • Be VERY CAREFUL adding a little slice of Habanero
    or Scotch Bonnet (this is a very HOT pepper).
  - Once boiling, Put in as much "Strained" Chitlins as you can get.
  - Pour 1/2 cup of Honey over the chitlins and mix in well.
  - Add your tomatoes--plus 1 Teaspoon each: Cumin,
    garlic, Anise and a palm of onions (I love onion--so
    this whole dish is really to your taste.)
  - Let this all simmer 30 minutes. Top with Vinegar.
  - Heap the Hot Sweet Chitlins over the Sliced Cantelope and serve
    with thick wedges of cornbread.

The 20 Biggest Dicks among Famous Men
(thick long penis and balls as a unit)
Compiled by The Alpharetta Secret Sisters Society

#1--Arscenio Hall

#2--actor John Amos (*"Good Times"*, *CBS*)

#3--actor James Woods

#4--actor John Ritter (deceased)

#5--(TIE) actor Vin Diesel and Rick Fox (L.A. Lakers)
#7--Michael Jordan (the Chicago Bulls)

#8--actor Jon Erik Hexum (deceased)

#9--comedian Jerry Seinfeld

#10--Kweisi Mfume

#11--Kareem Abdul Jabaar

#12--Thaoo Penghlis (Tony DiMera on *Days of Our Lives*)

#13--Ron O'Neal (played *Superfly*--deceased)

#14--singer Marc Anthony

#15--singer Keith Sweat

#16--John Salley (*who in the hell is he!*)

#17--rapper 50 Cent

#18--actor Mekhi Phifer

#19--Patrick Rafter (Australian tennis player)

#20--Rapphael Saddiq

UNITED NATIONS REPORT

U.N. Commission on Human Rights
Presented in Geneva, Switzerland
April 9th, 2003

Investigative Body Chair: Freedom House

Andrew Young
Malcolm Forbes, Jr.
P.J. O'Rourke
Zbigniew Brzezinkski
Jeane J. Kirkpatrick
Max M. Campelman
Presentation: Jennifer Windsor

**Taken from a 105 page Investigate U.N. Report entitled
"The World's Most Repressive Regimes of 2003"
From page 71:

In February, the editor of the English-language daily *Khartoum Monitor* was fined for publishing an article implicating the government in slavery. In July, security officials seized issues of the Arabic daily *Al-Horreya* (Freedom), preventing their publication. No explanation was given for the seizure. In September, authorities seized the issues of three papers and arrested one journalist for criticizing the government's withdrawal from peace talks in Kenya. **The same month, a Sudanese Sharia court found U.S.-based Sudanese author Kola Boof guilty of blasphemy. Boof was sentenced to death by beheading should she return to Sudan.** Boof wrote a book critical of Sudan's treatment of black women.

(taken from page 71 out 105)

427

THE METEOR That Is Kola Boof:
a white male journalist lends perspective

Originally published: Jan., 2006 Copyright © 2006 Mark Fogarty.

Mark Fogarty is a finance writer whose articles have appeared in The Chicago Tribune, Credit Union Journal. He is managing editor of N.Y.'s acclaimed National Mortage News and writes for Indian Country Today.

----

by Mark Fogarty

There are few books I've ever looked forward to more than Kola Boof's forthcoming *Diary of a Lost Girl.* I suspect much of the public attention when the book is published will focus on the controversial Sudanese author's story of her affair in the 1990s with Osama bin Laden. But I am much more interested in the story of how a shattered young girl, through intelligence and force of will, remade herself into a gifted and potent literary talent.

I first heard of Kola Boof through an extremely negative story about her in the *New York Times*, which denounced the Sudanese-born author as a liar and fraud, if memory serves, and made much of her literary "stunt" of appearing barebreasted on the back cover of her book of short stories, *Long Train to the Redeeming Sin.* (Kola claims she does this on all her back covers, to honor the ways of her Nilotic ancestors.)

I was curious about such a colorful personality, and why the *Times* would go to such lengths to pummel an unknown author so thoroughly and publicly. (I have since decided it was a hatchet job not worthy of "the newspaper of record"). So I visited her website (www.kolaboof.com), and e-mailed her to ask why.

Her website was not what you would expect. My first impression, from the many poems reproduced there, was that Kola Boof was a poet, and rather a sensitive one at that, not the deceptive fabulist of the article. Digging a little deeper, I found the first hints of controversy, the transcripts of several angry interviews, and some extremist opinions. (Media exposure and controversy seem to be synonyms for her.) Based on what she said, though, there was plenty to be angry about. The portrait of her native Sudan I gathered there from links and from several e-mails with Kola, was horrifying. I found references to slavery, starvation, genocide committed against her mother's African people, ritual infibulation inflicted on newborn girls.

Kola herself was also not what you'd expect. I found her to be an unfailingly polite and reasonable correspondent. When I engaged her on her racial views (she is a uniculturalist, and I am a multiculturalist) I found her respectful of my views even when they contradicted hers, which was often. (>>>Continued)

SCRAPBOOK: The Meteor That Is Kola Boof

I was intrigued, and I ordered *Long Train* from Amazon.com. A few weeks later, the Internet giant blandly informed me it was unable to fulfill the order. Kola's website had a more vivid description of the bottleneck. It said her African publisher had been firebombed in a (temporarily) successful effort to silence her criticisms of the Arab oppressors of the Sudan.

Add this incident to the growing legend of Kola Boof. It joins many other colorful stories, like the ones about her being Osama bin Laden's mistress, or a secret agent for the south Sudan liberation forces, or witnessing the murder of her parents by agents of the Arab-led Sudanese government, or having a Rushdie-like *fatwa* pronounced on her by Arab enemies, leading to a gunbattle with Muslim assassins on the streets of Los Angeles.

Unable to read her for myself, I didn't know what to make of Kola, so I turned the page and moved on. But over the next couple of years, the dreadful events transpiring in the Sudan began to intrude, even though at a glacial pace, on our American consciousness. When Secretary of State Colin Powell said (or almost said) that genocide was occurring there, I said to myself, that's what that writer said was happening. What was her name again?

Her name at birth was Naima bint Harith. She was born in Omdurman, Sudan, on the Nile River, either in the late 1960s or early 1970s. In full accord with her mysterious legend, she says she does not know the year of her birth, although she knows her birthday. (The official government record disagrees with the recollection of Kola's aunt on the year, but not the day.) She suffered the ritual infibulation mutilation commonly visited on girls in that region. Her father was an Arab archaeologist, and her beloved mother (she calls her "Mommysweet" in her writing) was a black African who has had a huge influence on her daughter's ideas and cultural identity. After the horrifying murder of her parents, she was adopted out to America, and grew up in the tough Anacostia section of Washington, DC. A troubled youth there was followed by her return to Africa, where she became an actress in the African soft-core film industry and met bin Laden, among other adventures. How she became womanist author Kola Boof, writing in an English she did not master until her teen years, will be at the heart of her new book. I don't give a damn about Osama bin Laden. But Kola Boof, the lost girl who transformed herself against long odds into an original literary voice and lightning rod of controversy—this is a story I am fascinated by.

Although her writerly focus is on her native Africa, Kola's literary vocation takes its cues and traditions from the American writers she read as a girl, like Toni Morrison and Alice Walker. Returning to the United States (she has become a United States citizen), she is now a writer, mother (a role she gives great importance to) and outspoken advocate of south Sudanese independence from the Arab-dominated government in Khartoum. When I reacquainted myself this year with Kola through e-mail (we have never met), I found she was back in print (Door of Kush Publications) and I was able to order two of her books: the harrowing *Long Train to the Redeeming Sin: Stories of African Women*, and her proud poetic statement of identity, *Nile River Woman*.

Let's get the boobs thing out of the way first. On her website, Kola says she poses that way to honor the ways of her Nilotic ancestors, the women of the Nile she passionately identifies with. The other possibilities are vanity (the woman can take a picture), or publicity stunting.

After some thought I myself believe the pictures come from a grand romantic imagination, one that is true to its own principles, no matter how quixotic. And as for the rest of her legend, I believe about Kola Boof what Huck Finn says of his creator, Mark Twain: that the stories he tells are mostly true.

I was not expecting *Long Train* to be as good as it is. Based on the media fracas around her (bomb threats often disrupt her book signings) and her controversial way of tackling arguments in public (taking no prisoners) I was expecting these stories to be blunt and pointed, parables easily read for evidence of their author's intent. I did not expect them to move me to laughter, outrage or tears as they did. This is the realm of serious literary art, and in this book Kola Boof proves to be a serious literary artist, compelling, heartbreaking, surprisingly subtle at times, even funny.

Not many ideologues are very funny, but try Kola's "Black America Diva Girl." I was chuckling from the get-go, over a couple of African women and their American friend back in Africa plotting ceaselessly to be able to go to an Angela Bassett movie. What isn't funny is the submission to males that makes all the machinations necessary. I'll pay this story the highest compliment I know: I didn't want it to end. I wanted to know which Angela Bassett movie it was, and what these women thought of it and whether it was worth the high price they had to pay to see it. (I'm guessing "What's Love Got to Do With It" might bear on the themes raised in the story, but subtle Kola never says which film it is.)

Then there's "Boy Magic (a love story)," the story of a young woman ravaged by AIDs. Raped by a prominent landowner, (rape is a frequent visitor to Kola's work) the girl travels to the capital city for justice, only to be thrown into jail for false accusation. If not for the intervention of a white social worker, she would have died there of AIDs. Someone looking to beat you over the head with a point would have made the rapist give the young girl AIDs, but instead she has acquired it from her consensual lover, who she celebrates sweetly in flashbacks. The story of this dignified dying girl, whose death song remembers to savor the few moments of happiness in her tragic life, made me reach for the Kleenex.

Then there is the powerful "Day of Vow," which tells about a young African girl whose short life is outlined by three tremendous images of fire: a burning classroom in which her schoolmates die, the glassblowing forges where she develops a wondrous artistry her white bosses blithely co-opt, and a blazing meteor that ends the book with the apocalyptic sentiment: The black woman is the meteor that is coming to this earth. The Grand Guignol at the end may be a touch overdone, but this powerful story will stick in your mind. Kola's stories are often bloody, but unlike, say, Quentin Tarantino, who seems to regard violence as an aesthetic ingredient, Kola's heroines live in a bloody world and are quite likely to be caught up in it.

It's impossible not to think of this story as a parable of Kola's own life: her early devastation, the development of her wordsmithing ability, and the death threats that apparently stalk her now. Her blazing meteor not only announces Kola Boof to the world, but in its fiery self-destruction warns of potential bad endings.

I believe I know another trait of Kola's not immediately apparent in her bomb-threatened store and radio appearances: heartbreak. By the evidence of this book, the lives of African women are short, fatalistic and violence-prone. Like Sisyphus walking back down the hill, they have the occasional joy or respite, (like Nuntandi's boy magic) and they are an essential guide to the generations by child rearing and passing the traditions down the ages. By telling their stories straight and (usually) avoiding the bombast that sometimes creeps into her public appearances, Kola underlines the pathos and tragedy as any great literary artist would. She is humble, and lets her stories be great.

Her book of poems contains truly important work like "There Is Slavery in the Sudan," which tells it as straight as the title. Everyone in the world should read this poem. It also contains one of the most beautiful poems I have ever read, "Christmas on the Nile," about Kola's birth mother. (The true deep secret about Kola Boof may be her understated gentleness.) In marked contrast, *Nile River Woman* also contains one of the most obscene poems I have ever read, which describes in both Dutch and English (languages of African oppression!) a film director's crude proposition of an actress. Kola does not say the director is white and the actress is black, but her dual-language translation suggests it strongly. She continually surprises and challenges you.

Kola's poems insist on her identity as a black woman and a storyteller, two things which may even be genetically connected through her repetitions of the assertion "I am a woman, yes./ I have two mouths to speak with." Although self-identity is prominent, (confident lines like "I am tall enough to nurse the moon," or "My loyalty is to my womb" and poems like "I Am My Own Daughter") she takes time also to look at "Black Men's daughters/ tired, hungry and wet" and to ponder "the secret of the mothers at the bus stops." The manifestation of a potentially great literary talent in these two books is what makes me so anticipate *Diary of a Lost Girl* (a title taken from one of the silent films Kola loves, and a rather humble book title for someone sometimes referred to as Queen Kola). I want to know how Naima, the half Arab, half black daughter of the Nile (bint il Nil) was adopted out of Africa to America to eventually become Kola, the talented and battling woman literary warrior she now is. I suspect that "Kola" is her attempt to re-create a powerful identity out of the blasted life shards of the lost girl, Naima. How she did it is a wonder; I suspect it took the strength of the Nile.

The public Kola can certainly be something of a loose cannon, given to excesses of rhetoric, and her ideas on race, born out of experiences of genocidal hatred, are harsh and unattractive. We have had to agree to disagree on multiculturalism. (I continue to hope that this scion of Arab, black African and African-American lineages will come to see the value of many cultures living together in peace, our American ideal if not reality.)

Kola has a talent for pissing people off, and lines like "I am tired of Jesus and Mohammed" and "But your Koran covers me in shit" can offend literally billions of people at once. The excessive Kola who can rant at Arab or white "bitches" sometimes creeps into her writing, and in at least one poem she threatens to kill some white ones. This isn't good poetry or good anything else. I suspect, though, that when push comes to shove, the reality will not be bloodshed but will be more like the serio-comic episode described in one of her interviews, when white women came to protest in front of her home and she turns the garden hose on them. And while she has never favored the American-brokered peace deal in the Sudan, after the recent death of southern Sudan leader John Garang she publicly called for that peace to be kept.

SCRAPBOOK: The Meteor That Is Kola Boof

I prefer the writer to the public personality. I believe the marks of literary greatness can be discerned in Kola Boof. Coming from the womanist tradition of such American writers as Alice Walker and Toni Morrison, she adds and blends an African experience into that tradition. Her pen name, cobbled together from the kola nuts African children eat as sweets and the heartpounding "boof" sound of African drums, underlines her African identity as well as her American experience, with its near-matches to "Cola" and cartoon sex kitten Betty Boop.

Her love of her African forbears is deep and touching, and you can readily see the source of her great strength in their vast Nile River. It is a testament to her astonishing literary potential that she can make readers like me, whose ancestors left Africa many thousands of years ago, feel a racial memory of the strength and beauty of that fabulous river. Kola Boof also is an American writer, whose work touches on a deep American theme of migration, the heartfelt (and heartbreaking) nostalgia for the old traditions that can co-exist with the desire for assimilation in new traditions. Daughter of Africa, she is also daughter of the African diaspora. She is both black American diva girl and *bint il Nil*, daughter of the Nile.

● **Mark Fogarty is a finance writer whose articles have appeared in The Chicago Tribune, Credit Union Journal, New Mexico Business. He is the editor of National Mortage News and writes for Indian Country Today.**

Kuir Garang, an SPLA military commander and member of the ruling family wrote the following poem in <u>honor of Kola Boof,</u> <u>addressing the poem to</u> *"My dearest Queen Kola"*.

"Against jejune fidelity"
(a poem by Kuir e Garang--**Translation to English**: Kuir e Garang)

Damned a spook, spurned   Stripped of significance

And image Caricatured by all, Least, Not to mention

The providence *treasure,* That is weighed to serve 'em

The least and draw 'em the weak, But the iron heart builds

The fancy of their might, Like lion tamed to harm,

No tourists, and there   Has his nature enjoyed,

When stripped of pride-strength. Their existence with Equity, to be seen and see,

That which Strikes naivety, Breeds the essence,

Of their cosmic Indispensability, with paradox,

Their indispensability when they ink To convey, the hardest they did-thought!

But the truest path that withers the Mired hate and thought extermination,

When touching the untouchable, And pen-speak the unspeakable,

To stamp the soul of *needability*, Of that dark voice, to lay scrap

Dogmas and expose vapid piety, Now they want to see you down,

But, you will speak and exist not exit!

© 2005 Kuir e Garang

KOLA BOOF'S SPEECH IN ISRAEL

●

Sudanese American author Kola Boof gave the following speech on Israeli radio in Tel Aviv, Sunday March 28th (2004). Ms. Boof's powerful message resulted in over $600 million worth of guns, ammunition, food and medicine being sent to Sudan's South Rebel army. The speech is reprinted this week in several Jewish American and Jewish European newspapers.

 <u>KOLA BOOF said</u>:

My dearest ones in Israel, the devil has been very busy. For no matter who risks life and limb to tell the truth about the evil injustices carried out by the Arab Muslim governments of North Africa and by the mullahs that advise these governments, the media in America has responded with a hideous prejudice against Jews, against black African Sudanese, and against any fair-thinking person who dares despise the Arab imperialism that is not only destroying the Middle East, but now threatens to destroy authentic African culture of the Nile River more than it already has. It does not matter that I speak as the daughter of an Arab Egyptian father, a woman born Islamic in Omdurman, Sudan, or that I am an accomplished African woman writer, obviously of some intelligence. It does not matter that my parents were murdered in my presence, because my Arab Muslim father spoke out against the building of Lake Nuba and the enslavement of Dinka children by Arab Northerners in Sudan. It does not matter that I have witnessed Muslim women rolled up in carpets and set on fire, because they failed to produce male children. It does not matter that I speak, most regrettably, as the former mistress of two of the Arab world's most powerful men, Hasan al Turabi and Osama Bin Laden, or that I have been a paid hostess at the parties of President Hosni Mubarak and Moamar Khadafi, or that I provided proof of this before I was profiled by Fox News, and therefore, have knowledge of their true faces. Anyone who speaks the truth in America about the evils of the Arab world is ignored, shunned and accused of supporting the so-called Jewish desecration of the Arab birthright. (Continued..)

434

Of course, we all remember that the Black Plague was blamed on Jewish people, even in nations where there were no Jews living, and this today, is the similar anti-semitic blame game, but for being a black African woman who has said so in America, I have been written off as "crazy", "emotional", "a whore" and "a hoax". I don't deny that I'm a controversial, provocative public figure. I reject all man-made religions, be it Christianity, Islam, the Jewish faith, Buddhism or any worship that was created by men. I am a womanist and an African mother. I bare my breasts in the river once a month and I believe in the womb. *Yet still*, I have not lied about the atrocities of the Arab world. I have not lied about the cruel evils of Islam against African people and those who refuse to join it. **I have told these truths, not because I hate any race or religion of man**, but because I believe that it's wrong for human beings to take part in any cult of hate, any orgasm of violence against other humans. According to my Sudanese Zarpunni (the women's neighborhood) and all the black women before me, the Palestinians have sterilized black women since the 1950's. It is well known by African women that our wombs are loathed in Arab nations, because it is our wombs that produce the authentic black man. Our tongue bequeaths him his heritage and identity. Who on this planet will deny me this truth.

In America, I have been greatly criticized by my black American brothers and sisters for supporting Israel instead of Palestine, but as a black woman and a mother of black children, how can I support the colorstruck machinations of the Palestinians? Unfortunately, the Americans have truly mistaken me for a witch, because the Arabs have money to get their message out and I have only my books and no money, *and even then* the media portrays me as an extremist and a supporter of Bush and the conservative republican which is an unmitigated lie. I am as liberal and Democratic as any American black, but I also know the truth about Arab Muslim societies and about the culture that creates terrorism. The Black Americans have no knowledge of the true history that has existed more than a thousand years between the Arab Muslim invaders and the authentic African people. The powerful light skinned Black American even looks more like the dark skinned Arab than like the authentic charcoal African, so they are often weak to the propaganda of false Islamic organizations in America. Organizations that spread the lie that Islam is an African religion and that the Arab man is our brother, the Israeli our enemy because of whiteness. They feel no bond with Israel.

But for the sake of my own nation, the Sudan, I am committed to changing that. I feel very strongly that Israel and New Sudan should form an alliance against the Arab world. Obviously, I am in disagreement with my beloved hero, Dr. John Garang, but I truly believe that the peace talks in Machakos *will produce nothing* but dust, riches for the sellouts, and eventually, more Arab Muslim racism, more exploitation of blacks by the Oil companies, more black slaves for the kitchens of Jordan, Palestine, Egypt, Iraq, Libya and Saudi Arabia. Because I am a woman and because the men love money more than they love justice, I am given a kiss on the hand and not taken seriously. I am even denied my place of honor in the organization's struggle to free Sudan. My black brothers of Sudan are very sexist and have called me Queen, but then expected the Queen to lay on her back and be a mere follower. In time, of course, they will regret this, because I am a very intelligent, impassioned person. I say now to anyone that will listen...(continued)

-and I don't say it for tired old men, I say it for future generations - that the Arab Muslim government in Sudan must be overthrown. There is no other way. It is impossible to have true peace and solidarity with the people who have called you "abeed" for a thousand years, stolen and sold your children into slavery, raped your mothers and killed your fathers, over taxed you, stolen your land from you and subjected you to racial profiling. It is not in the hearts of the blacks to go on being ruled and humiliated by the Arabs. And because my people have named me "Queen Kola", and because I have not yet lived up to that title, I feel that I must denounce the money offered in the Kenya peace talks and instead uphold the wishes of the people's hearts:

that we be liberated at last from racial, religious and economic dehumanization and oppression by not just Arab Sudan--but by the Arab world.

It's no secret that the freedom fighters of Southern Sudan have received guns and ammunition from Israel. Truly, your loyalty to the Goddess Sudan has been flawless, and I submit, sincerely, that I love you for loving my people. I stand by Israel, not only because Israel has stood by me, but because the Palestinians have defiled me.

I truly pray that someday, there will be peace, love and brotherhood between all mankind. The Arab, the African, the European, the Jew, the Asian and all others, I pray, will someday stand as one, but at this moment in time I am very sad to report that the Arab world is not our friend, and that we must recognize this or perish. I submit that both Israel and New Sudan must stop at nothing to prevail against the evil forces that choke them with malice and threaten their very existence. For if the Arabs were to lay down their weapons today, there would be no more violence. But if we of Israel and Sudan were to lay down our weapons today, we would be dead, and the whole world would be witness to yet another genocide.

War is hell, my beloveds. But so is love. And sometimes, kicking a man's ass is the only love he will accept.

Let us stand against the Arab world, as David slew Goliath. This is not what we wanted, it's what they wanted. And our children deserve our protection.

In the words of the ancient Nubians--"So let it be written, so let it be done."

Tima usrah! (through fire comes the family)

THE FUNERAL of JOHN GARANG
an interview by Jane Musoke Nteyafas
*Originally appeared in Bahiyah Woman Magazine 8/6/05

Following the funeral of John Garang, I had the opportunity to interview Kola Boof, a controversial Sudanese American novelist who has also been a long time champion for the cause of the Southern Sudanese people, through her writings and her outspokenness. Kola Boof first met John Garang in 1978, when at the age of five years old, her Arab Egyptian father, the late archeologist Harith Bin Farouk, took her to Garang's home where the two men discussed the formation of what would much later become the SPLA. Boof was adopted in 1980 by African-Americans in Washington, D.C. following the murder of her Sudanese parents after they complained of witnessing slave raids in Sudan. Often referred to as "Queen Kola" by the South Sudanese who love and adore her and now living in the United States, I found Boof to be quite eloquent even while grief stricken over Garang's death. Here's what she had to say.

Jane: You are known in the international scene as a very dangerously controversial writer. Please tell us in your own words exactly who the mysterious Kola Boof really is.

Kola: Well, I'm an African mother of two sons and I'm an artist. I use the written word as my vehicle for art, but someday, I hope to make films about Black women's lives. But for now, I'm a novelist, I'm a poet and I'm sometimes involved in the politics of North Africa.

You had the opportunity of having met John Garang when you were a little girl, can you please tell us what kind of man he was like? What was your relationship with him?

I had no relationship with Garang as a child other than playing on his floor and repeatedly asking for cups of water or peaking in and out of the rooms. I remember that he was a very humorous, lovable figure with a keen seriousness. My father would bring him information as Garang was contemplating leaving the Arabic government in Khartoum and starting up a rebellion, which he did years later. I remember him being appalled when my father reported to him that there were actually Arab people conducting slave raids and selling Dinka and Nuer children like cattle.

John Garang is being mourned by many African states and even very many North Americans. Can you please explain why his death is a loss to Africa and to the Sudan?

His death is a loss, because he brought the North and the South together in Sudan. He was a brilliant politician, a provocative thinker and a great speaker. He was able to capture and inspire the minds of the South Sudanese people as well as demand respect from the Northerners. I don't believe that the peace agreement would have been possible without Garang's commitment to peace and to justice. He was sent to us by God.

There are many people that do not know the atrocities that are happening in the Sudan, can you please elaborate on that?

We have a peace agreement right now, so in the interest of making it work, it's best not to dwell on the evil that completely possesses Sudan. I look forward to Salva Kiir Mayardit's leadership, and I pray that he can find a new experience for the South Sudan.

You were part of the SPLA. Can you tell us what the SPLA is? What was your contribution to this group?

The Sudanese People's Liberation Army is a world wide network of mostly Southern Sudanese, committed to the liberation of the Black African indigenous Cushitic people of Sudan. It's well known by now that I was a secret agent for the SPLA. A novelist and former paid party girl who used my way with words to persuade others to help my people. Over the years, I've acquired a lot of guns and ammunition for the South Rebel Army and instigated attention to their plight. As a woman, I determined to bring justice to the South Sudanese people...by any means necessary.

Earlier this summer, you debuted a poem in honor of your friend, slain Dutch filmmaker Theo Van Gogh, which you said was the most painful thing you had ever written. How painful was writing the poem for John Garang and what were your emotions as you wrote it?

I cried terribly while I was writing Garang's poem, mainly because I knew that no one in America would care. You know—I am so isolated in America where people don't understand what it's like to be me in this society, and especially, where the American press is often nasty towards to me and assign demonic motives to my work and my feelings, mainly because they don't give a damn about Sudan or what it's like to be a black Sudanese woman, all alone, in a huge, Eurocentric nation like America. So it was very painful, and it was rushed, because many people around the world were pressuring me to get out a poem for Garang's funeral.

What does the _expression "Choll Apieth" mean? What does the poem about John Garang mean?

It means "black is beautiful" in the Dinka language. The poem is about the fact that although we do not have Garang's flesh anymore, we can always summon his spirit within ourselves. He will live forever through us.

What do you think about the terrorist bombings in London and Egypt? Do you think America is next?

Oh definitely - and it's very sad, because in America, the people don't take the government's warnings seriously and they really should, because terrorism is the new frontier in world warfare. Chemicals and things are eventually going to be used, and because I was raised in a culture that taught me that I should strap on a bomb and blow up innocent people'in the name of Arab imperialist progression and religious superiority - I know better than most Americans that terrorism is real. Americans are very spoiled people and they don't want to hear about it.

I recall a few years ago, there were British reporters making fun of your name and claiming that you didn't even exist. Arab media reported that you were a cannibal who hate human flesh.

Well, I still hurt very badly over that treatment and the fact that the New York Times wrote an article basically making fun of me as well. I really was an obscure womanist writer and activist at that time - they had never heard of me - and to them, my name and my story sounded fantastic and outlandish. I had been Bin Laden's mistress, my parents murdered in front of me and just... larger than life realities that they thought I was making up. But I'm not the first black woman whose life experiences are dismissed and not believed, simply because she's not the package that the media wants. I was very happy, however, when FOX NEWS spent several weeks fact-checking my story and proved that I had lived with Bin Laden in Morocco, and I was especially thrilled, because their intention had been to discredit me.

Your fans want to know. When can we expect your latest novel?

My next novel is called "The Sexy Part of the Bible", and it's really, truly powerful. It has a lot to do with cloning in Africa. I finally have a major literary agent in America, so it should be published in the United States by January 2007. Before that, in December 2005, will be the release of my autobiography "Diary of a Lost Girl". I also have a new poetry collection coming in 2006.

What's next in Kola Boof's personal life?

Hopefully time... raising my sons and exploring my art. I would like to move away from politics and controversy.

About Jane Musoke Nteyafas

●

Jane Musoke-Nteyafas, poet/author/artist and playwright, was born in Moscow, Russia and currently resides in Toronto, Canada. She is the daughter of retired diplomats. By the time she was 19, she spoke French, English, Spanish, Danish, Luganda, some Russian and had lived in Russia, Uganda, France, Denmark, Cuba and Canada. She won the Miss Africanada beauty pageant 2000 in Toronto where she was also named 'one of the new voices of Africa' after reciting one of her poems. in 2004 she was published in T-Dot Griots-An Anthology of Toronto's Black storytellers and in February 2005 her art piece Namyenya was featured as the poster piece for the Human Rights through Art-Black History Month Exhibit. She is the recipient of numerous awards for her poetry, art and playwriting and is becoming a household name in Toronto circles.

Kola Boof's poem *"Chol Apieth"* was written expessly in memorium of the great Sudanese leader, John Marbior Garang, and <u>was read by members of the SPLA during his state funeral.</u>

"Chol Apieth"
(*black is beautiful*)

In the river crossing and coming through us
The egg has not drowned/Our mother's long war
—hand of Nhialic, The blood
In the river crossing

and coming through us

Behold today/ that cattle have no tongues
And that the earth is cold where Macardit tangles
in the raid of horses/ charging in our wake.

—we have lost our best son
—we, who bring the morning her spears
—we who are like birds/tired of the Crashing
And have seen the Sky
itself
fall against our dreams

Chol Apeith, warriors!
In all my conversations:
the ones who are victorious...the ones
who are praying

Knowing that Papa Garang shall rise again
In the eye of our fists—the chant of our shouting
The Yoke of New Site/golden as sun and birth
This victory of the everborn's heartbeat...steadily rising
Be it on one foot—Garang
(be it on one foot)
Our hero of the landscape
In the river crossing and coming through us.

In all my conversations—

(continued)

Come through here...river
Bloody Cross and our father rising from it
to deliver this Everborn;
bring us your cattle and your courage—
bloody womb; our mother, the Goddess Sudan.
Enchant us this victory.

His place with God/And no more flesh.
Everborn the victory...and no more flesh.
Garang...Garang
our best son!
And no more flesh.
Bird of the Sky—black as all black put together.
And no more flesh.

We who give birth to you again—and no more flesh.